D1378568

www.wadsworth.com

wadsworth.com is the World Wide Web site for
Wadsworth and is your direct source to dozens of online
resources.

At *wadsworth.com* you can find out about supplements,
demonstration software, and student resources. You can
also send email to many of our authors and preview new
publications and exciting new technologies.

wadsworth.com
Changing the way the world learns®

FROM THE WADSWORTH SERIES IN SPEECH COMMUNICATION

Communicating with Credibility and Confidence

Diverse People, Diverse Settings
Second Edition

Gay Lumsden
California State Polytechnic University, San Luis Obispo

Donald Lumsden
California State Polytechnic University, San Luis Obispo

THOMSON

WADSWORTH

Australia • Canada • Mexico • Singapore • Spain
United Kingdom • United States

THOMSON

™

WADSWORTH

Executive Editor: Deirdre Anderson
Publisher: Holly J. Allen
Development Editor: Greer Lleuad
Assistant Editor: Nicole George
Editorial Assistant: Mele Alusa
Technology Project Manager: Jeanette Wiseman
Marketing Manager: Kimberly Russell
Marketing Assistant: Neena Chandra
Advertising Project Manager: Shemika Britt
Project Manager, Editorial Production: Mary Noel
Print/Media Buyer: Tandra Jorgensen
Permissions Editor: Stephanie Keough-Hedges
Production Service: Ruth Cottrell
Text Designer: Carolyn Deacy; adapted by Andrew Ogus Book
  Design

Photo Researcher: Terri Wright
Copy Editor: Pam Suwinsky
Illustrator: Seventeenth Street Studios; adapted by Judith Ogus
Cover Designer: Qin-Zhong Yu, QYA Design Studio
Cover Images: Background (from top left to bottom
  right): Students in the Library/Jeff Maloney; Couple Walking
  in the Jardin des Tuileries/Mel Curtis; College Classroom/
  Scott T. Baxter; Students Listening/Doug Menuez.
  Color image in foreground: Students On Campus/
  Doug Menuez.
Compositor: Better Graphics, Inc.
Printer: Phoenix Color BTP

Printed in the United States of America
1 2 3 4 5 6 7 06 05 04 03 02

For more information about our products, contact us at:
Thomson Learning Academic Resource Center
1-800-423-0563
For permission to use material from this text, contact us by:
Phone: 1-800-730-2214   **Fax:** 1-800-730-2215
Web: http://www.thomsonrights.com

Library of Congress Control Number: 2002106307

ISBN 0-534-50944-4

Wadsworth/Thomson Learning
10 Davis Drive
Belmont, CA 94002-3098
USA

Asia
Thomson Learning
5 Shenton Way #01-01
UIC Building
Singapore 068808

Australia
Nelson Thomson Learning
102 Dodds Street
South Melbourne, Victoria 3205
Australia

Canada
Nelson Thomson Learning
1120 Birchmount Road
Toronto, Ontario M1K 5G4
Canada

Europe/Middle East/Africa
Thomson Learning
High Holborn House
50/51 Bedford Row
London WC1R 4LR
United Kingdom

Latin America
Thomson Learning
Seneca, 53
Colonia Polanco
11560 Mexico D.F.
Mexico

Spain
Paraninfo Thomson Learning
Calle/Magallanes, 25
28015 Madrid, Spain

Brief Contents

Detailed Contents

Part I   Understanding Communication Processes

Part II   Creating Dialogue

Part III Building Interpersonal Relationships

Part IV Communicating in Groups and Teams

Part V Speaking to Public Audiences

Preface

We believe that communicating should be challenging, effective, and fun. Yes, fun. Of course, communication can be deadly serious. Words can start or end wars; they can manipulate and abuse humanity—or raise human relationships to great heights of understanding and compassion. Communication also is simply making a friend, or selling an idea, or playing, or sharing emotional highs and lows, or exchanging tender words of romance. Your everyday communication—conversing, working with a team, even giving a speech—should be stimulating and interesting and gratifying. In fact, the people who communicate in the rarified atmosphere of international negotiation would tell you that they even—no, especially—love the challenge of working out critical communication exchanges. Communication *can* be fun, even when it's serious.

The good news is, you have a start. You already communicate constantly with yourself and with others. Sometimes you feel comfortable and successful in your communication; sometimes you may feel awkward or ill at ease. That's natural, because effective communication is so important to you. Communication is the vehicle for making your life what you want it to be, both in your personal relationships and in your career goals.

We've written this book to help you make that vehicle work for you. Everything we hope you will learn—theories, facts, feelings, approaches, and abilities—all add up to two critical attributes that we want you to *own* by the end of this course:

- *Credibility*. Other people will want to listen to you because they trust you and believe in you. Your credibility is critical in all forms of communication, whether you're talking to one person or a thousand. This book develops credibility as an overriding theme so you can, first, recognize the credibility you now have and, then, start working to develop your credibility further.

- *Confidence*. You will learn how to manage nervousness, turn it to your advantage, and be able to speak confidently to others—one on one, in groups, or to large audiences. Confidence is based on knowing you've been successful in the past and anticipating success in new experiences. Whatever your confidence level is now, you can build it by practicing the strategies presented in this book, including relaxation and visualization techniques, to reduce your stress and improve your performance.

Fortunately, confidence and credibility are attributes that you can develop right along with increasing your competence in a range of communication situations. This book is designed to help you do that. It is based on several assumptions—first, about students and patterns of learning and, second, about the common threads that weave through all types of communication.

About the Second Edition

The philosophy and the substance of the first edition remain, but we have made the following changes:

Tightening and shortening.   We have abbreviated the text somewhat, on the advice of our reviewers, in part by eliminating the original Chapter 4, "Creative and Critical Thinking: Processing Ideas." We have incorporated much of the substance of that chapter into the rest of the book as well as into Chapter 3, now titled, "Perception and Thought: Making Sense."

Clarifying language.   For the many English-as-a-second-language students who use the book, we have simplified some of the language, again on the advice of reviewers. That change includes eliminating most colloquialisms and slang, although we have left in common language devices that clearly have roots in identifiable metaphors. Our own experience has been that students can track metaphors and find this useful in developing their English usage.

Updating.   In addition to updating resources and research, we have provided more information on using technology effectively for both research and presentation. Some of this content is included in the text, and some appears in new boxes, instructions, and exercises.

About Students and Learning

Our experience has shown us that many students share certain characteristics in learning to communicate more effectively. Even those who are best-prepared have to cope with:

- *Overcoming nervousness.* Students often are nervous about speech communication classes. Almost everyone gets anxious about communicating at one time or another, and almost everyone believes she or he is the only one who feels this way. So this book starts with where you may be right now—shaking in your boots. We have found that students frequently have a low opinion of their own competence and credibility. They often say they know nothing worth listening to (that is, they are not credible) and think they can't make people want to listen to them (that is, they are not confident). These are lonely feelings, and we want you to change those perceptions.

- *Acquiring knowledge and skills.* Students become good communicators when they acquire knowledge, develop positive feelings, and practice specific skills. Having knowledge helps you explain, with theory and facts, how people communicate. Positive feelings about yourself and communication situations enable you to approach communication confidently and wisely. Finally, both your knowledge and your feelings provide the foundation for practicing and implementing specific communication skills. To help you develop all three strands of learning, each chapter begins with a list of objectives categorized according to "knowledge," "feelings and approaches," and "abilities."

About Common Threads Throughout Communication Experiences

If you can talk to a friend, you can talk to an audience. That statement may seem extreme, but we believe it's true. Certain basic skills are common to every type of oral communication: with yourself, with another person, with a group, with an audience. In fact, all types of communication are more alike than they are different. This is true across cultures and across experiences. Often students believe their foreign accent, their American dialect, or their particular voice or physical characteristics will block their communication. Students even worry about their gestures because they reflect a particular culture. Not one of these individual characteristics means the student has a communication problem. It's only a matter of developing the skill to turn what seems to be a disadvantage into an advantage, and you already have the foundation for doing that.

This book develops common skills first, step by step, so you can adapt them later to each type of interaction. Presentational speaking is discussed at the very end of the book, but when you get there you will have already developed communication strength in other contexts—and that strength will provide the foundation for speaking to an audience. As your confidence grows in using these approaches with one person or a few, you will find it easier to communicate with more people. Some important common threads among all communication situations include ethics, adaptation, and creative and critical thinking.

Ethics. Any time you communicate, you make ethical choices about what to say, how to say it, and how to act. Those choices reflect how you regard yourself, your listeners, and your subject; they have consequences that affect you and the people with whom you communicate. In this book, we explain why we believe that dialogical ethics provides the best approach to communication by helping you to build relationships, to work cooperatively in groups and teams, to involve audiences deeply in your public presentations, and to establish a sound base for your credibility and confidence.

Adaptation. Communication in today's world requires understanding and adapting to diverse individuals. Both personally and professionally, you will communicate with people who vary widely in background, ethnicity, culture, abilities, gender, and sexual orientation. Diversity can enrich communication with the multiple perspectives it makes available; when you understand how to communicate with people different from yourself, you can transcend potential barriers to communication. That's why the book integrates issues and information about diversity—especially in culture and gender.

Creative and critical thinking. Communicating effectively, both as a giver and receiver of ideas, integrates both artistic and analytical approaches. Creative and critical thinking are essential to all communication because they involve analyzing, understanding, creating, organizing, phrasing, and supporting ideas. Whether you are talking to yourself about a problem you must solve, working out an idea with a friend, brainstorming an idea with a team, presenting a persuasive speech, or simply listening intently, you're using both creative and critical thinking. This book will help you develop these skills in every context of communication.

Features

We've tried to make this book user-friendly for you. *Communicating with Credibility and Confidence* has some special features to help integrate and apply the concepts. These include:

- *Terms* boldfaced and defined in the text and included in a glossary at the end of the book.

- *Competencies* listed at the beginning of each chapter so you can see what you're trying to accomplish.

- *Boxes* to stimulate discussion by presenting brief excerpts from contemporary publications on technology, culture, communication in business, interpersonal relationships, and so on.

- *Short quotations* as marginal inserts to stimulate thought and discussion.

- *Exercises and activities* that systematically develop competency through individual, dyadic, and group work and presentations. The exercises are designed to achieve two goals: to introduce a wider range of communication genre and to build skills incrementally.

- Integrated technology activities, called *Cyberpoints*, that direct you to interesting and relevant World Wide Web sites relating to concepts discussed in the text, to the student resources at the *Communicating with Credibility and Confidence* Web site, and to InfoTrac College Edition to research communication issues and find speeches to read and critique.

- *Web site* that provides self-assessment and observation forms, resources, and examples for students to use as supplementary information.

- *Workbook* containing self-paced exercises and experiences for students.

- *Instructor's manual* that develops the course so your instructor can choose a traditional approach to the class or a collaborative learning approach, together with syllabi, schedules, assignments, new activities and experiential exercises, examinations, and resources.
- *Art* that includes photo case studies, cartoons, models, diagrams, tables, and illustrations of concepts.

Overview of the Book

The book will lead you to achieve three major goals: develop your credibility to yourself and to others; develop your confidence in your own communication; and develop skills that enable you to achieve your goals through communication. That starts with the experience and abilities you already have, so Part I focuses on what communication is, how it functions, and how it influences your present and future life. We use this foundation for examining the nature of credibility and confidence. From there, we explore the essential roles of perception, critical thinking, and creative thinking in your communication.

Part II discusses creating dialogue with others. Here you will strengthen your listening and questioning abilities as well as your nonverbal and verbal communication skills—a background that applies to all communication situations.

Part III examines your communication in interpersonal relationships, including situations that help communication with another individual grow and develop, personal relationships with friends and family, and relationships in college and in your professional life.

Part IV develops your abilities to work in groups and teams. Group communication involves all the knowledge and skills covered in the previous chapters and applies them to achieving common goals through teamwork. Your communication helps you build effective teams, provide leadership, analyze problems, and develop solutions in group settings.

Part V prepares you to make speeches. Public presentations involve speaking to inform an audience about a topic and persuading an audience to change its attitudes, beliefs, or behaviors. Everything you have learned to this point serves as the foundation for the extensive preparation and effective practice that develop your skills as a credible, confident public speaker.

Acknowledgments

Many kind, patient, and insightful people have helped us develop this book. Our students—past and present—have provided the "proving ground" for much of the material, and they have contributed excellent ideas and enormous inspiration and encouragement. We especially thank the students who gave their time and thoughtfulness to reading and evaluating early drafts. The text reflects their suggestions for material and revisions to make it better and more student-friendly.

We also appreciate our department colleagues at Kean University and at California Polytechnic State University, San Luis Obispo. We feel we have worked with the finest faculty—personally and professionally—anywhere. Not only have they always been open and willing to share their great ideas, but they have been extremely patient as we have grappled with this project. Specifically, our colleagues at Kean University, Bailey Baker, Cathy Londino, Chris Lynch, Kristine Mirrer, Freda Remmers, and Ernest Wiggins have given us helpful feedback based on their extensive experiences using this text in their classes.

Faculty members across the country made excellent contributions to this text through their thoughtful reviews of multiple drafts. Our thanks go to Blanton Croft, Northern Virginia Community College–Woodbridge Campus; Rita M. Miller, Keene State College; Victoria Orrego, University of Miami; Ingrid L. Peternel, College of DuPage; and Carole Shaffer-Koros, Kean University. The work by these reviewers built on that provided by those who worked with the text's first edition. We also thank them for their contributions: Martha Ann Atkins, Iowa State University; Ruth Aurelius, Des Moines Area Community College; Melissa L. Beall, University of Northern Iowa; Marco Benassi, College of DuPage; Mary Bozik, University of Northern Iowa; Barbara Breaden, Lane Community College; Diane Casagrande, West Chester University; E. Neal Claussen, Bradley University; Michael Eaves, Valdosta State University; Robert Edmunds, Marshall University; Michael Elkins, Southern Illinois University; Stephen A. March, Pima Community College; Robert W. Martin, Ithaca College; Lee McGaan, Monmouth College; Sheila Merritt, Mesa Community College; Diane L. Rehling, St. Cloud State University; and Deborah Shelley, University of Houston–Downtown.

Wadsworth has supported us with an outstanding cast. We are grateful to Deirdre Anderson, executive editor; Greer Lleuad, development editor; Jeanette Wiseman, technology project manager; Nicole George, assistant editor; Mele Alusa, editorial assistant; and Mary Noel, project manager. Pam Suwinsky served as an exceptional, sensitive copy editor, and Ruth Cottrell effectively and patiently brought everyone's work together to make a real book.

Finally, we want to thank our family and close friends for their love, support, and tolerance. Although we are always with them in spirit, we'd rather be together in person—and we hope we can compensate for some of the time we have sacrificed in the process of developing this text. It's to our kids and grandkids (who have both grown and multiplied during this second edition)—Ed, Tom, Diana, Carolyn, Bill, Maria, Zoe, Savannah, Rita, Rita D., and Anna Maria—that we dedicate this work.

Communicating with Credibility and Confidence

Chapter 1

Communication Dynamics: Exploring Concepts and Principles

Objectives for This Chapter

Knowledge

- Know how communication affects success in relationships and careers
- Understand the concepts of communication processes
- Explain the components of a model of human communication
- Know the qualities of effective communication

Feelings and Approaches

- Appreciate the challenge and potential satisfaction of communicating effectively
- Want to create transactional communication with others
- Approach communication as an ethical process

Communication Abilities

- Involve yourself in communication transactions
- Begin monitoring and adapting your communication to people and situations
- Consider the receiver when planning to send messages

Key Terms

intrapersonal communication
interpersonal communication
dyadic communication
group and team communication
presentational communication
mediated communication
communication
process
verbal cues

nonverbal cues
transactional process
sender
encode
transmit
channel
noise
receiver
decode

feedback
communication dilemma
effective communication
ethics
dialogical ethic
credibility
ethos

You spend most of your waking hours communicating. Most people find it positive and enjoyable in some situations—and scary in others. If you're an enthusiastic communicator, great. You've got a fine starting point for this course. If you're one of the many individuals who find communication less inviting, don't worry. You can become an excellent communicator. In fact, we intend that, by the end of this term, you will have a good start toward:

- Knowing you are credible both to yourself and to others
- Feeling confident of your ability to communicate in different situations
- Being skillful in achieving your goals through communication

Reaching these goals is a gradual process. You'll add knowledge about communication at every step; you'll learn how to harness your feelings and approaches to communication situations; and you'll practice communication in different contexts to develop both skill and confidence. To help you keep focus, each chapter in this book begins with a list of objectives categorized according to these three types of learning—knowledge, feelings and approaches, and abilities.

To begin, we look at how communication influences your life. Then we take a detailed look at what the communication process is and how communication works, why it frequently doesn't, and what qualities make communication more effective.

Why Communication Affects You

Your communication affects most aspects of your life. Look, for example, at one of Tanisha's days:

At 8:30 a.m., Tanisha opens one reluctant eye and looks at the clock. "Oh, no!" she yelps. "My paper was due at eight o'clock!"

As she tears out the door, her roommate smiles and hands her a cup of coffee to go. "Thanks—you're awesome!" Tanisha responds gratefully as she heads for her car. Listening to the traffic report on her car radio, she avoids a traffic tangle by taking an alternate route. At 8:50, she wheels into the parking lot and motors toward the first space she sees, but another car noses in just ahead of her. She yells at the driver, who yells back. Tanisha decides not to waste time arguing and, after cruising around, finally finds a parking place. She reaches Dr. Saunders' office at 9:10, apologizes, and persuades her to accept the paper.

Then Tanisha goes to her communication class and gives an oral report. She gets a high grade, so she feels pretty good. In her history class, she listens carefully, takes notes, and asks questions to clear up the foggy points. Then, in sociology, she works with a group of students to plan a term project. Between classes, she checks her e-mail and then has a quick conference with members of her service club.

When classes are over, Tanisha goes to her job as a waitress. At 6:00 p.m., she takes a break and calls home to tell her roommate when to expect her and to thank her again for being so quick with the rescue coffee. At work, her charm and skill earn her a healthy set of tips and a customer's report to her manager that she's an excellent employee. At 10:00 p.m., she arrives home, exhausted but pleased by the day's successes. She spends a few minutes on the Internet to examine some reports for a paper assignment that's due next week. Finally, she turns on the television to get a quick update on the news and to relax by watching her favorite comedian before turning in.

At no point in this day did Tanisha stop communicating—she talked, she listened, she responded. She achieved her goals by communicating effectively in a range of contexts and for a variety of purposes.

Communicating in Contexts

Notice the variety of contexts in which Tanisha communicated: with herself, one-to-one both in person and on the telephone, in a group setting, with an audience, and through media. Each context has distinct characteristics, but in all of them communication uses closely related knowledge, feelings and approaches, and abilities.

■ **Intrapersonal communication** is within yourself, as you respond to stimuli from the environment, from others, and from yourself. Tanisha talked herself into getting up and going to school; she stopped herself from arguing with another driver; she deliberated about how to approach Dr. Saunders. During the day, she had many conversations with herself—about everything from "It's time to eat" to "Now, be calm; you'll do fine on this report." You communicate with yourself constantly, even while you are also communicating with others.

Intrapersonal communication Communication to yourself in response to your environment, other people, or yourself

■ **Interpersonal communication** is a dynamic process between or among people that touches people emotionally and psychologically (Miller & Steinberg, 1975). Tanisha's interpersonal communication included expressing appreciation to her roommate, persuading Dr. Saunders, and talking with friends and customers. Interpersonal communication is sometimes called **dyadic communication** because most often two people, or a dyad, are involved, although interpersonal communication may occur among more participants. More important, whereas dyadic communication may be as superficial as, "Hey, lady, where's the nearest phone?" interpersonal communication generally involves personal sharing of issues ranging from discussing your career aspirations with a friend to agonizing with your mate about where your relationship is going (Miller & Steinberg, 1975).

Interpersonal communication Dynamic process among two or more people

Dyadic communication Interactions between two people

- **Group and team communication** involves socializing and/or working with a small number of other people. In the class project group, Tanisha communicated with several people to achieve a specific goal; she also had a quick meeting with her service club between classes. In group and team communication, you do all the same things as in intrapersonal and interpersonal communication. However, you can't interact as intimately with several people at once as with one, and interactions may be more complex.

- **Presentational communication** occurs when a person addresses a small group, a class of 20 students, or an auditorium full of people. In her communication class, Tanisha presented information to her classmates using the same essential skills as if she'd been communicating interpersonally or in a group. *The skills of communicating interpersonally and in groups carried through into her skills of presenting to an audience.* As a speaker, Tanisha adapted those skills and brought in some others, too; she had to make her message clear to a larger group of people, and that required her to organize, plan, and rehearse her communication differently. In Tanisha's history class, her role in presentational communication was as an audience member who listened, questioned, and took notes on the speaker's information. Both as speaker and listener, she applied her abilities in intrapersonal and interpersonal communication in the context of her classroom group setting. Like Tanisha, you will learn to adapt your interpersonal skills to public situations as this course proceeds.

- **Mediated communication** is channeled through a written or electronic medium such as newspapers, magazines, telephone, computer, radio, or television. Tanisha listened to the radio so she could adjust her route to school; she checked her e-mail, used the Internet, and watched television for news and entertainment when she got home. She probably saw an infinite number of billboards, glanced at or read newspapers and magazines, listened to commercials, entertainment, and news on the car radio, and perhaps read flyers left on her car windshield.

  As you listen to and watch media, you are a single member of an enormous public audience. You then communicate about messages you receive through media with yourself (intrapersonally), with others (interpersonally), or in groups. You refer to mediated information in your research for presentations. When you are a member of an audience, the speaker gives you information, much of which was gathered from media sources. Media messages strongly influence what you think about, what you talk about, and how you think and talk about it. Finally, you may use media to reach others with your information or ideas.

These various communication contexts are distinguished mainly by numbers of participants, individual roles, the medium, and the settings or environments in which they occur. Figure 1.1 shows these types of communication as a continuum of communication experiences. At each stage, the communication enlarges and changes according to the situation.

The preceding discussion suggests some basic principles of communication contexts:

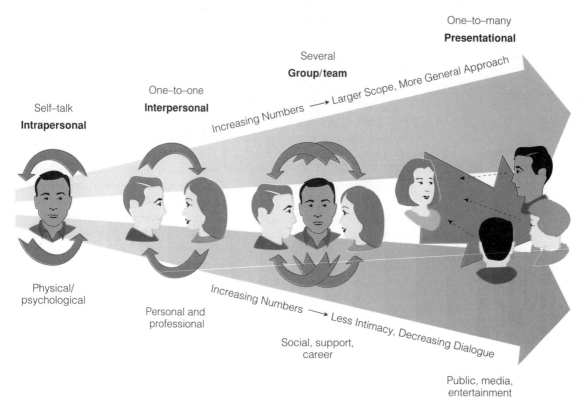

Figure 1.1 *Continuum of communication types*

- Intrapersonal communication is ongoing and interacts with all other types and contexts of communication at all times.

- Communication abilities are closely related in each type of communication event, yet each context requires its own special skills and adaptations.

- In any communication context, the characteristics, needs, and goals of the other person(s) should influence a communicator's choices and adaptation of messages.

- As the number of people increases, the degree of intimacy and face-to-face interaction with each person tends to decrease, yet the sense of contact and feeling of relationship can be maintained.

For now, it is important for you to observe how these principles operate in your own communication and to be aware that *the knowledge and skills you develop for contexts covered early in this book provide a foundation for each type of communication you will develop later.*

Communicating and Your Success

If you were asked what you want most in life, what would you say? A happy relationship? Family? Spiritual development? Education? A successful career? Financial security? How do you achieve any of these? John Stewart (1999) states, "There's a direct link between the quality of your communication and the quality of your life" (p. 6). Your communication can help to develop and nurture your relationships—personal and professional—or it can weaken them. In fact, your communication experiences actually can affect your emotional *and* physical well-being. At work or at home, positive intra- and interpersonal communication can strengthen your health, self-esteem, and self-confidence, but negative communication is directly correlated to stress-related diseases (Lynch, 1990).

In the workplace, your career can depend on your communication. Employers say that the twenty-first-century workforce must be able to speak, listen, know how to learn, think creatively, solve problems and make decisions, negotiate with others, work in teams, provide leadership, and choose ethical and honest courses of action (NY Department of Labor, 1996). All these skills reflect one's ability to communicate with oneself as well as with others in interpersonal and organizational settings.

Both in personal and professional relationships, effective communication is becoming more important every day. Why? Because society changes.

Changing relationships and families. Expectations and roles for men and women are changing rapidly, and so are family structures and ways of living. Children may have one parent or several; they may have no siblings or a variety of full, step-, and half-brothers or -sisters. Both parents may work away from home, one may work while the other stays home, or one or both may work based in the home and stay connected with the office electronically. Families may be spread across the continent or the world.

Organizational demands. Whether you work in a corporate, nonprofit, or academic environment, your organization will expect you to take on more responsibility and involvement, to communicate at all levels and in many ways. More and more organizations are using teams to make and implement decisions. People who used to compete against each other now must cooperate, and that requires a whole new set of leadership and teamwork communication skills (Lumsden & Lumsden, 2000, pp. 9–12).

Diversity at work and in the community. You live and work with people of every color, religion, and sexual orientation, which requires that you bridge many differences. The Bureau of Census projects astonishing demographic changes in the United States in the next 50 years, with the white majority changing from 74% in 1995 to 53% in 2050, while some other groups will more than double their proportion of the population during that time period. People of Hispanic origin will increase from 10% of the total population to 25%, Asian and Pacific Islanders from 3% to 8%, and blacks from 12% to 14% (U.S.

Department of Labor, 1999). So communicating successfully takes more work than it once did. Understanding people whose backgrounds differ from yours requires thinking more deeply about how they see things, how they express their ideas, how they listen and respond.

How Communication Works

If you're going to use communication to enhance the quality of your life, your relationships, and your career, you need to know just what communication is and how it functions. Let's examine this in three ways: first, by looking at definitions and models of communication processes; second, by seeing why communication involves more than simply transferring an idea from one person to another; and third, by identifying specific characteristics of communication.

Communicating Is a Process

Communication Using verbal and nonverbal cues to transact meanings

Communication is the process of using verbal and nonverbal cues to transact mutually understood meanings between two or more people within a particular context and environment. Let's look more closely at the elements of this definition.

Process An ongoing, constantly developing and changing operation

Process. As a **process,** communication constantly develops and changes. For example, suppose someone says something you think is amusing; you laugh. The other person is hurt; it wasn't meant to be funny. You apologize and clarify why it amused you. The other person has to be persuaded. You try again to achieve an understanding. Eventually, you manage to work it out. That's a complex process that moves, doubles back, and moves again in a widening spiral, as more and more ideas, feelings, and information go into the transaction between or among people (Dance, 1967).

Verbal cues Words used to convey and interpret ideas

Verbal and nonverbal cues. **Verbal cues** use words and structure, listening and questioning, to convey and interpret ideas. For example, you might say to your professor, "Could you explain what this means?" The specific words and the way they are ordered convey your request. **Nonverbal cues** rely on vocal characteristics, speech patterns, body postures, facial expressions, space, time, touch, and other personal behaviors or objects to communicate. Along with your request for clarification, you may lean toward the professor and point to confusing material in the book; you may underscore your puzzlement by wrinkling your brow, tilting your head, and raising your voice at the end of the question. The professor would interpret your verbal and nonverbal cues according to many factors, including his or her needs, interests, culture, and experience.

Nonverbal cues Body postures, facial expressions, and other personal behaviors or objects that communicate

Transactional process
Interaction in which each person gives and takes to achieve understanding

Transaction. As a **transactional process,** communication entails each person giving and taking bits of meaning. Think about a shopping transaction. When you leave a store, you have less money and an item you didn't possess before. The store is down one item in its inventory and up some in income. The exchange involves intangibles, too. If you are satisfied, you will recommend the store to someone else. If you and the clerk both feel good about the transaction, that may affect how you interact with someone else in the next few moments.

A transaction, therefore, is more than a simple trade, and all contexts of oral communication reflect transactional elements. This may be easy to recognize when you're working out an understanding with a friend—you each explain what you mean and then you each adapt to the other's remarks. Even in public speaking, you notice listeners' nonverbal cues—perhaps they look puzzled or disapproving—and you adapt your messages to ensure their understanding and acceptance. When they give you verbal cues through questions and comments, you further adapt to help them comprehend your message. Communication transactions actually alter each person, maybe only in mood or only for a moment, but sometimes in something as deep or long-lasting as a belief or value.

Mutually understood meanings. Words don't have meanings—people do. You use words and nonverbal cues to represent what you mean, but your listeners' backgrounds and experiences with the language shape how they understand your meaning. As a communication transaction proceeds, you and the others together take bits of meaning from one another to create a new mutual understanding.

Sometimes, people think that everyone in the transaction agrees on exactly what the meanings are, but each individual actually has a very different understanding about the message. Haney (1973) calls this "bypassing." For example, your friend asks, "How was the wedding?" and you respond, "Beautiful!" What neither of you realizes is that your friend was referring to the wedding you attended three weeks ago, which was a disaster, but you're thinking of the one you attended last night, which was wonderful. You've bypassed, but you each leave confident that you have a clear understanding.

Context. Often, *context* refers to whether an interaction is intrapersonal, interpersonal, group, public, or mediated communication, but context also is affected by the purpose or goals, the occasion, and the communicators. These all interact to create different expectations for message content and communication behavior. A job interview and a marriage proposal, for example, are both interpersonal and have many communication factors in common, but the participants' specific goals and role expectations affect how the transactions proceed.

Environment. The physical conditions within which the communication occurs set up a social and emotional environment that affects people's interactions. Think how different the interaction is, for example, in a classroom with chairs arranged in strict rows rather than one with the chairs in a circle.

Here's an example of how your message might be affected by the environment, the context, and your friend's understanding when the two of you engage in a process of transacting a meaning. You enter a restaurant to have lunch with your friend. You greet her with, "How's it going?" as a casual way of saying "Hello." She, however, interprets your question in terms of what's on her mind—a problem with her new boyfriend. "Terrible," she answers. You, of course, have no idea what's "terrible" in her life, so you're surprised. "What's the problem?" you ask, and she tells you she's upset. You ask, "Why?" At the beginning, there was a wide gap between your idea of the context and your friend's understanding, but now the gap begins to narrow. As she explains her problem, you listen, question, and finally comprehend what's bothering her. You have negotiated an understanding of her message.

The process and your messages would have been different in another context or environment. If you'd been meeting with a work group to plan a project, for instance, your friend might not have responded, "Terrible," preferring to discuss her problem later. Or you might have simply clucked sympathetically without asking what the problem was, because it was neither the time nor the place to pursue the issue.

A Transactional Model   Sometimes, a model or diagram helps to clarify how a process works. Figure 1.2 uses a model to show the processes whereby Raj and Melody transact meaning. Either person could start the communication process, or they might start talking at the same time. Simply to clarify the interactions, we show the process beginning with Raj (on the left). Both people have their individual expectations and understanding of the context of the event, and both start with their own backgrounds, including such elements as their gender, culture, experiences, and values. These may be similar—but they may be very different. Raj's background, expectations, and context perceptions influence how he puts together a message. Melody's background, expectations, and context, in turn, influence what she understands Raj to mean. As Melody creates meaning from Raj's cues, she responds with verbal and nonverbal cues based on her own background, expectations, and so on. With each exchange, Raj and Melody both adapt and refine their interpretations of the other's meaning. If the process is working well, the two understandings come closer together until the participants believe they understand each other adequately to meet their personal goals for the exchange.

A Step-by-Step Model   Let's take one small interaction segment of the process and break it down into still smaller components to focus on some factors that affect a transaction's success. Such a brief segment may take no more than a nanosecond, and the interaction we show is only one of many that could occur simultaneously as the two people transact their meanings.

We jump into the transaction at the point where one person responds to stimuli and gets an idea. The cartoonist's use of a light bulb is not a bad way to represent an idea—after all, thoughts *are* a system of chemical-electrical impulses within our brains. The brain creates a specific impulse pattern when

Figure 1.2 *A transactional model of communication*

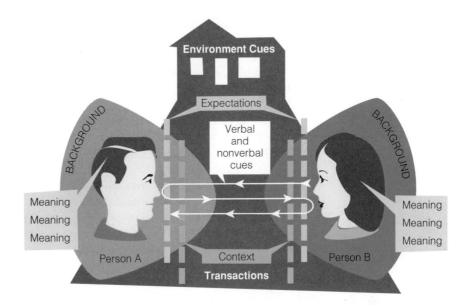

Sender's idea

Sender Person who transmits a message

Encode

Encode Represent an idea with a symbol

some cells fire and others do not. To communicate an idea, one person must stimulate a pattern of chemical-electrical impulses in the other person's brain so that the listener generates a similar thought. You could liken the thinking process to that of computers, of course, but linked computers can communicate with perfect clarity. Human brains are more complex than computers and cannot be linked directly, so people must rely on a complex, roundabout route to make a connection.

With that in mind, let's take a "frame-by-frame" look at how one person tries to get an idea into another person's mind.

Sender's idea. The message **sender** has an idea to express. If the idea is not clear in the sender's mind, it is difficult for the sender to communicate it. People frequently speak or act before being fully aware of their own thoughts, putting their mouths in action before their minds are in gear. The participants can work together to clarify ideas, but it's easier when the sender knows what his or her thoughts are before starting to talk.

Encoding. To share the idea, the sender must **encode** it—that is, represent the idea with a symbol for the other person to interpret. Both words and nonverbal behaviors represent codes that humans use to convey what they mean. The sender searches mentally for symbols that best represent his or her thoughts. It's not easy, however, to select just the right words or behaviors to represent an abstract brain activity. Language is imprecise. Many words have multiple meanings, and a variety of words might represent any one idea. Nonverbal cues are often even less precise. A large working vocabulary and

Transmit

Transmit Speak or act so that symbols are available to the other person

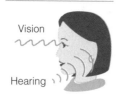

Channel

Channel Means by which cues are carried from sender to receiver

Noise Stimuli that compete with a message in a channel

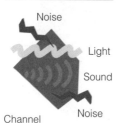

Receive

Receiver Person who picks up cues using the senses

Decode

Decode Translate symbols and cues into meaning

awareness of nonverbal cues improve one's chances of selecting the most appropriate symbols.

Transmitting. Selecting a symbol to represent an idea, however, doesn't get the message outside the sender's head. The code is **transmitted** through speaking and/or acting so those symbols can be available to the other person. Oral transmission depends on the sender's abilities to speak with sufficient volume, vocal clarity, and emphasis. Nonverbal cues require expression and movement skills to illustrate and represent ideas and feelings.

Channel. Speaking or acting puts symbols into the communication **channel,** the means by which cues are carried. In face-to-face communication, message symbols travel from sender to receiver as sounds through air waves and as visual cues carried by light waves. In mediated communication, cues travel via electronic codes or broadcast frequencies.

　　Once in the channel, symbols encounter **noise,** which means more than loud sound. Noise includes all other stimuli present in the channel—visual, aural, olfactory—that can disrupt, distort, or totally block a message. The sender's message must have enough attention-getting properties to compete with all these distractions and reach and win the ears and eyes of the receiver.

Receiving. If the cues are transmitted with enough intensity to overcome competing noise, they reach a **receiver,** who picks up the verbal and nonverbal cues through sensory organs. The receiver may or may not attend, depending on her or his abilities, habits, and motivations. A person's psychological state may create another kind of noise that distorts the sender's cues, or a person may be hearing- or sight-impaired or simply be distracted by other stimuli or noise in the channel. The cues, as perceived by the receiver, travel to the brain as nerve impulses.

Decoding. Now the receiver translates the nerve impulses back to symbols and **decodes** these cues in terms of his or her background and experiences (as we demonstrated with Figure 1.2). In the decoding stage, the receiver gives the symbols meanings, which can differ considerably from the sender's intended meanings. Speaking the same language does not ensure that any word means the same thing to different people. Sometimes, too, people see and hear what they anticipate, which could differ from the actual symbols the sender transmitted. People often misunderstand others' messages to the extent that George Bernard Shaw once described the United States and England as "two countries separated by a common language."

Receiver's ideas. The ways a receiver decodes symbols create brain patterns that stimulate specific ideas. Communication is successful if the ideas the receiver creates are substantially similar to the sender's original thoughts. Even the clearest idea, transmitted skillfully with the most appropriate symbols, relies

Receiver's idea

---

on the receiver's mind for successful communication. Receivers' backgrounds and experiences shape the interpretations, the value judgments, and the feelings with which they react to the message.

Feedback. The only way to ensure that the receiver's understanding matches the sender's is for the receiver to provide **feedback**—possibly questions, a look of puzzlement or a nod of understanding, or a restatement of the idea—to let the sender know how the symbols were received and interpreted. Then the original sender becomes the receiver, and the whole process continues as each strives to understand the other and to be understood. Good feedback requires careful listening, thinking, encoding, decoding, and *checking* for accuracy. Feedback may fail because people don't want it (it takes time and effort) or because they assume the understanding is clear and bypass one another's meaning.

In any communication transaction, will the ideas in each person's mind be precisely the same? As you can see in the preceding "filmstrip," the answer generally is no. Here, each individual has a different symbolic system associated with the words "go out Saturday." Fortunately, human communication doesn't usually demand exact re-creations of ideas. Some people believe it is nothing more than a "happy accident" when any two communicators create messages that are exactly the same. With thoughtful encoding and sending, with feedback, and with cooperative transactions, however, mutual meanings are not accidental. They are achieved because people work at them.

Communicating Is Not Transferring Ideas

The oft-repeated phrase "But I *told* you . . ." reflects some mistaken assumptions people make about communicating. To avoid falling into this trap, keep in mind the following truisms.

Sending does not guarantee receiving. People often conclude erroneously that if they've said it or written it, they've communicated. Sending a message only means it was transmitted; it ensures nothing about what happens after that. Your message must reach a receiver, who in turn must perceive and interpret it correctly, for communication to have occurred.

Ideas cannot be "given" to another person. Even when the receiver receives and processes your cues, you can't say you transferred something from yourself to another as if handing over a piece of cake. When you serve the cake, you no longer have it, and the other person does. In communication, receivers create their own version of ideas from the symbols as they perceive them. The sender provides stimuli for receivers to create the thoughts but does not actually deposit his or her own ideas in their heads. Communication is like the educational process: Teachers provide stimuli, but learning happens only in the mind of the student. Teachers don't make learning happen—they just provide opportunities.

Communication cues are not always intentional. Sometimes, you might send *unconscious* cues via facial expressions, posture, clothing, or even the tune you're whistling. When others observe those behaviors, they may assign meanings to them—and those meanings may be wrong. Such situations are *not* interpersonal communication, because there's no sharing and feedback. Those interpreting your cues are communicating *intra*personally, however, reacting internally to messages as they interpret them, and possibly assuming the cues were sent intentionally.

Communicating Can Be a Dilemma

To communicate or not to communicate, that is the question. If you do communicate about something, how to communicate? What might you win? What might you lose? Everyone faces a dilemma sometimes—the choice between satisfying their needs and meeting their goals versus taking risks with their communication.

People communicate because they *need* to; consciously or unconsciously, you communicate to fill some need or reach some goal. Your goal may be simple—perhaps to get directions to someone's house. Or it could be more complex—to satisfy a psychological need, to give or get crucial information, to give or receive help, to influence others, or even to entertain others.

You might have multiple goals in one transaction, although some could be more important than others. For example, when Ron, a student of ours, worked on a team project, his primary goal was to get an A. In his teamwork, Ron communicated to give and to get information, to give and receive help with his teammates, and to influence the team's choice of project presentation. Because

On March 14, 2000, Ray Kurzweil was honored at the White House as the recipient of the National Medal of Technology, the nation's highest technology award. Mr. Kurzweil makes some interesting projections about how we may experience human communication just a few years from now.

Consider these ideas for 2019:
- Computers are largely invisible and are embedded everywhere—in walls, tables, chairs, desks, clothing, jewelry, and bodies.
- Three-dimensional virtual reality displays, embedded in glasses and contact lenses, as well as auditory "lenses," are used routinely as primary interfaces for communication with other persons, computers, the Web, and virtual reality. . . .
- People are beginning to have relationships with automated personalities and use them as companions, teachers, caretakers, and lovers.

Projections for 2029:
- Permanent or removable implants (similar to contact lenses) for the eyes as well as cochlear implants are now used to provide input and output between the human user and the worldwide computing network.
- Direct neural pathways have been perfected for high-bandwidth connection to the human brain. A range of neural implants is becoming available to enhance visual and auditory perception and interpretation, memory, and reasoning. . . .
- A majority of communication does not involve a human. The majority of communication involving a human is between a human and a machine.

From Ray Kurzweil (2000). *The age of spiritual machines*: when computers exceed human intelligence. New York: Penguin.

Ron was also testing his skills as a comedian in local comedy clubs, he had the additional goal of entertaining his classmates.

Ron was successful in reaching all of his goals, but what if his efforts to be funny had fallen flat? He took a risk in incorporating comedy into a serious group report.

Often, you have to weigh the risk in communicating. You want to be sure your choice is right for a given situation or at a given time. Taking risks in communication is part of growing, developing, reaching goals, and meeting your needs. Sometimes, however, the need and the risk are both so strong that individuals face a **communication dilemma,** a conflict between the need to communicate and the desire to avoid the risk involved. A parent, for example, may need to advise a child but dread a confrontation. Or, you may want to take on a challenging assignment at work but fear you might fail. Everyone has faced similar communication risks at some time.

Communication dilemma Conflict between need to communicate and desire to avoid risk

Rejection. The approval and acceptance of others is a great motivator for communication. "Hey, I got an A on my paper!" you announce at home, expecting congratulations. But what if they shrug and turn away or say, "It's about time"?

Obligation. Sometimes, communication requires something from you. When you urge your friend to join a walk-a-thon for charity, you'll be expected to walk, too. When you listen and learn how to perform a task, you may be expected to do it well. Frequently, people are more motivated *not* to comprehend a message than to get it correctly. For example, people used to think little about drinking and driving until media campaigns made them aware of the potentially lethal consequences and, therefore, that "friends don't let friends drive drunk." Now, people who have paid attention to the message know they should take the keys away from a friend under the influence. Having understood the message, their responsibility is to make sure that the friend gets home safely.

Change. People tend to avoid change. They feel more comfortable keeping their attitudes and beliefs than modifying them. Suppose, for example, you're thinking of changing your major. You could talk with a career counselor to help you figure it out, and the conversation could lead to a change. Or, the prospect might make you apprehensive; you might fear the different coursework, your family's response, or your ability in the new subject. Sometimes, it's easier to avoid communication that might influence you to change.

Irreversibility. It's scary to realize that you can't take back what you said. A judge may instruct the jury to disregard a witness's statement, but that doesn't erase the experience. A friend may demand, "You take that back!" but the words have been spoken. You can say, "I'm sorry" or "Forgive me." You can add more layers of communication—talking about the talk—in hopes of giving the words a different slant or of burying them deep enough to reduce their impact. Still, scar tissue may remain.

Failure. Fearing failure may involve all of the preceding and more. If you fail to get or give information effectively, for example, you might then be rejected, or obligated to try again, or simply frustrated. Sometimes, people even fear success—because it can lead to change, obligation, or others' higher expectations, which, in turn, raise the stakes even higher. Fears of failure or success can be enormous stumbling blocks for people in all aspects of life, especially in their willingness to communicate.

Being aware that communication involves a dilemma between need and risk is enormously helpful in two ways. First, it helps you to identify choices you must make yourself. Second, it helps you to understand when others may be reticent, unclear, or defensive in their communication; they, too, must weigh their needs and their risks. Effective communication often demands that you take this risk but that you minimize it with careful preparation. The cliche "Nothing ventured, nothing gained" is good advice to keep in mind when you face most risks.

A wonderful way to understand communication is through stories. The process people use to tell stories exemplifies the ways people connect with others in other formats as well. Storytelling illustrates the process as it involves explaining human experience with detail and images; it is rich in ideas and simple in its direct contact of person to person. "Storytelling is connecting— teller to tale, then teller to audience, and finally audience to story" (Cooper & Collins, 1992, p. 26).

In fact, in today's corporate world, the phrase "Tell your story" is used to guide employees who must write reports or make oral presentations. Storytelling has become a technique to involve employees in problem solving and to teach new techniques of management and teamwork. It's an approach for finding the best ways to create, understand, and share ideas. That's the heart of the communication process.

Telling a story is a good place to start thinking about how to get the images and feelings and experiences out of one person's head so another person can start to imagine them. Stories provide the human experience of person-to-person understanding. The following story illustrates the importance of the personal connections when "telling your story."

I was working in central Africa as a Peace Corps volunteer when the trucks rolled into our village. On the side of the trucks were the words "RURAL ELECTRIFICATION." Many of the elders spoke out against the changes this new electricity would bring, but Nkundi, the wise old storyteller of the village, pointed out that change need not always be feared. Soon there was light even in the middle of the night. Electricity had not been in the village long before a television set arrived. It was quickly installed in a gathering place for all to see. When I went to the storytelling circle, I saw the television on top of Nkundi's stool, surrounded by listeners agape with curiosity. Nkundi stood alone away from the circle.

I wasn't able to return to the circle for a couple of weeks, but when I did, things had changed again. The television set had been moved to the side; it was covered with a cloth. Nkundi had resumed his place on the storytelling stool and again was surrounded by listeners. No longer were their faces filled with curiosity; now they were alive with wonder. Nkundi paused as the children laughed, and I asked a small boy, "Is the television set broken?" "No," he said and went back to listening. Again I tapped him. "What," he said, clearly annoyed at the prospect of missing any of the story, which I knew he had heard before. I asked, "The television set . . . doesn't the television set know more stories than Nkundi?" The boy thought for a moment. "Yes, the television knows more stories. But my storyteller," he smiled a gap-toothed grin, "my storyteller knows me." And again the child left me for the world of the story.

From Cooper, P. M., & Collins, R. (1992). *Look what happened to frog: Storytelling in education*. Scottsdale, AZ: Gorsuch Scarisbrick, pp. 26–27.

What Makes Communication Effective

We've explored definitions and models to understand what communication is and is not. But what makes communication *effective*? We use this term in a very specific way. For us, **effective communication** achieves its objective, enriches the people involved, and provides a foundation for future communication. Three qualities in particular influence your communication effectiveness: responsibility, ethicality, and credibility.

Effective communication Communication that achieves its objectives, enriches people involved, and provides foundation for future communication

Responsibility

To create a transactional process, all participants must cooperate and share responsibility for making it work. Remember the old saying that marriage is a 50–50 proposition? Communication (and marriage, too) is a 100–100 proposition: Each person has to give 100%. For communication to work, each participant must be deeply invested in the success of a transaction and be willing to go as far as needed to achieve understanding. Each must take responsibility for both the process and the results of the communication. If you're talking to someone who isn't listening, you need to find a way to get that person's attention. If you're listening and don't understand someone, you need to work at the interaction until you do.

Process Responsibility   To make a transactional process work, you have to be deeply involved. In fact, the amount and quality of your involvement are major components of your communication competency. Your involvement shows through three characteristics:

1   *Attentiveness*: Focusing on important cues from others in the environment

2   *Perceptiveness*: Being aware of and assessing accurately the meanings of others' cues and responses

3   *Responsiveness*: Evaluating a social situation and adapting to it appropriately "by knowing what to say and when to say it" (Cegala, et al., 1982, p. 233)

Your involvement shows that you're highly absorbed, you care, and you're a partner in the transaction. It enables you to communicate appropriately in different situations and contexts. You can develop successful qualities in your interactions by practicing three special skills:

1   *Understanding others*: Learning to perceive others' needs, wants, and beliefs—their emotional and intellectual states—correctly. Your accuracy in understanding demands that you listen carefully, watch how others respond, seek feedback, and check your perceptions (see Wackman, 1973).

2   *Self-monitoring*: Being aware of how your own behavior may affect others (Anderson, 1990). As another person responds to you, ask yourself, "What am I

doing that gets this reaction? Is it what I want? Should I change my approach to help the other person receive my ideas more positively or understand them better?"

3   *Adaptability*: Being flexible in responding to the other person. As a self-monitor, you can develop a wide repertoire of possible behaviors to adapt as necessary to make communication work (Duran, 1992).

Here is an example of positive involvement. At work, your coworker seems cranky, while you're tired and worried about tomorrow's exam. You snap at her over a minor problem. She becomes even more annoying, and you want to snap at her again. Instead, you think, "If I go off the handle, I'm not going to find out what's going on here. I'm going to drive a wedge between us. Is that what I want?" So you take a deep breath, put your own weariness on hold, and say, "Hey, I'm sorry I was so abrupt. Can we talk about it?"

In so doing, you are intensely involved in the interaction; you understand accurately (your coworker's unhappy about something); you self-monitor (check your own behavior); and you adapt (modify your response). In sum, you help to develop your relationship.

It's true that if you adapt your communication simply to manipulate or deceive others, you're being hypocritical and unethical. In contrast, however, when you self-monitor and adapt to make it easier for others to share ideas and feelings and to enlarge understanding, you act according to an ethical code that respects the interests and rights of others. In this context, your ability to understand others, to self-monitor, and to adapt behavior can contribute to your communication confidence and effectiveness.

Outcome Responsibility   Does the following exchange sound familiar?

"If *you* would just listen, you'd understand me."

"If *you* would say it clearly, I would understand."

Who is at fault? Who knows? Sometimes, people won't take responsibility for the outcome of communication and seek to blame someone else when it fails. They tend to feel vindicated if they can account for having sent the message, even though, as we pointed out earlier in this chapter, sending a message does not ensure anyone's receiving it. Disclaimers of responsibility come with phrases such as:

"It was in the memo I sent last week."

"It's in the college catalog."

"We covered that at our last meeting."

"It was on the bulletin board."

"Didn't you read the instructions?"

Such statements imply that "It's not my fault. I'm covered." Communication's goal, however, should not be just to protect yourself, but to have the other person understand your ideas. The "I told you" syndrome reflects a refusal to take responsibility for the results—to work through communication until a message has been understood. You can't guarantee another's agreement or compliance or even full understanding, but outcome responsibility means that a communicator works hard to ensure that the idea is comprehended.

There was a tragic example of poor communication and blame assignment—of a lack of outcome responsibility—in early 1993. Several children in the state of Washington died of food poisoning from undercooked hamburgers served by a quick-service restaurant chain. Investigators concluded that the meat wasn't cooked as required by new government standards. The chain's management initially responded that it had not received the new guidelines. Then it stated that it had indeed received them but had misplaced them, and consequently had not communicated them to the restaurants' cooks. The government had "sent" the guidelines, but in this case, "telling" failed to ensure communication. Communication had failed between the government and restaurant management and between management and workers.

Ethicality

To a great extent, talking about communication means talking about ethics. **Ethics** are codes or beliefs that your upbringing, religion, culture, and experience have given you for making moral judgments and committing acceptable acts. Like everyone else, you have ideas "about what is right or wrong, fair or unfair, caring or uncaring, good or bad, responsible or irresponsible, and the like" (Jaksa & Pritchard, 1994, p. 3).

In communicating, you make ethical choices about what you say or don't say and how you treat your communication partners. You face conscious or unconscious responses to ethical questions about both the process and the content of your communication.

Conscience: A small, still voice that makes minority reports.

Franklin P. Adams

Ethics of Process   An *ethic of process* refers simply to how participants treat one another as they communicate. Are they open and sharing and honest? Or are they manipulative and deceptive and closed? We, your authors, believe that a **dialogical ethic** is your best approach to communication. A dialogical approach creates a climate in which people are able to be authentic about who they are. Communicators include and confirm the worth of others; they are "present" (accessible and attentive); and they share a spirit of mutual equality (Johannesen, 1996, pp. 66–68). In a dialogical ethic, each person's right to be heard—and to be different—is respected and protected, and you recognize the inherent tension between "letting the other happen to me while holding my own ground" (Stewart & Zediker, 2000, p. 232).

Dialogical ethic Process based on the value of sharing ideas and feelings with another

Communication ethicists Jaksa and Pritchard (1994) point out that you can know what *you* believe is right and wrong, good or bad—and still be tolerant, still see shades of gray in issues, and still have respect for others' beliefs and ways; in other words, you can create dialogue and learn from one another without compromising what you believe (p. 17).

Think of dialogue in contrast to monologue. *Monologue* is one-way, self-centered communication; it is not concerned with the listener. Monologue is akin to giving a speech to a mirror or into a tape recorder. *Dialogue* involves mutual commitment, give-and-take, listening, negotiating new meanings, and shaping ideas together. Dialogical communication is more evident in interpersonal and small group communication, but its spirit also infuses public speaking when you talk *with* rather than *at* your audience, when you are sensitive to their feedback, and when you adapt to their needs.

Ethics of Message Content   *Ethics of content* determine what you will say, how much you reveal, how honest you are. Democratic societies rely on an ethic of content that gives people the best and most complete information possible in order to make reasonable personal and civic decisions. Even though you all too often see these expectations violated, an ethical communicator should provide messages that respect listeners' need for:

- *Truth*: Before speaking, weigh alternative statements for their accuracy, so you can make the most honest statement possible. Be authentic; keep from "projecting a false image, or 'seeming' to be something [you're] not" (Johannesen, 2000, p. 153).

- *Individual freedom*: Phrase ideas so that your listeners can see what choices are available. Avoid manipulating others in ways that subvert their rights to decide for themselves.

- *Fairness*: Present messages so that they show more than one perspective and acknowledge the value of ideas other than your own.

- *Respect*: Consider how messages might reflect on your character and on that of others. If words might make anyone feel diminished or inferior, replace or modify your message to respect others' feelings.

Credibility

Credibility How your message and your character are perceived

Credibility is a matter of how one person perceives another and his or her message. In all communication situations, your credibility depends on the listener's judgment of your character and the listener's willingness to attend to and believe in you and your message. Obviously, credibility is closely tied to a communicator's ethics, but the two are not the same. Ethics are in the communicator's thoughts and behavior, credibility in the receiver's perception. Unfortunately, ethical messages are not always believable, and credible messages are not always ethical. Because credibility for both speakers and messages lies in the minds of listeners, different receivers may perceive the same speakers and messages very differently.

People perceive a person's credibility based on their prior knowledge about the individual as well as that person's statements and actions when actually sending a message. More than 2,000 years ago, Aristotle explored what made speakers credible to their audiences. He identified "**ethos**," the way an audience perceived a speaker's believability, as involving good character, good sense, and goodwill (Roberts, 1954, p. 91).

Because your credibility is tied so closely to your effectiveness, it is a theme that recurs throughout this book. Specifically, the next chapter examines the concept in much greater detail and explores ways you can enhance your personal credibility as a communicator in all contexts.

Ethos A speaker's believability: "good character, good sense, and goodwill"

Summary

Success in your life and in your career relates to effective verbal and nonverbal communication in intrapersonal, interpersonal, group and team, and presentational situations. Understanding communication provides the foundation for developing attitudes and abilities that will increase your personal effectiveness.

Communication is the process of using verbal and nonverbal cues to transact mutually acceptable meanings between two or more people within a particular context and environment. The communication process involves senders who encode ideas with words and actions and transmit them through a channel that includes distorting and competing noise. Receivers pick up and decode the cues in the context of their backgrounds, expectations, and experiences and create meanings from them, sending feedback to develop successful transactions.

Communication helps people meet needs and goals, yet communication involves taking risks. People's need to interact but their desire to avoid the discomfort that interactions might produce can create communication dilemmas.

The challenge that this course and this book present is to learn and implement qualities that make your communication effective. These include taking responsibility for the process and the results of your transactions, applying ethical principles to guide the processes and the content of your communication, and developing your personal credibility and the believability of your messages.

Exercises

1   Meet with two other people and get to know one another. Find out about your majors, interests, goals, likes, and dislikes. In addition, find out the answers to these questions:

   ■ How would you describe communication in your family (open, limited, loud, quiet, funny, serious)?

- Where do you think your family communication habits come from (your culture or other background traits, experiences, and so on)?
- How do you think your family communication has influenced your own communication habits and feelings?

After you've gotten to know one another, each of you can introduce one other person to the class. Make your introduction fairly short but interesting. Make sure the class learns the *name* of the person and something by which to *remember* him or her.

2   In a group, share some of your funniest or most ridiculous communication experiences. These can be anything from misunderstandings to conflicts to embarrassing situations. Then do the following:
   a   Choose one or more of these situations to share with the class.
   b   Create a short skit that portrays the situation. Be sure every member of the group is in the skit.
   c   Perform the skit for the class.

3   In a small group, examine the frame-by-frame communication model in this chapter. In what ways would the model change if people were sending and receiving in languages other than their native language? Assume, for this exercise, that these people still think only with their first languages. Draw the new model.

4   Choose an experience you have had or one you would like to have. Prepare to "tell your story" to the class in a short presentation. Think about the images you have in your mind, and consider the most appropriate verbal and nonverbal messages to express them so the listeners can create the meanings in their minds. What background will the listeners need? What sequence will help you keep the ideas clear? What details will help them "get the picture"? Practice telling your story out loud until you are comfortable with the material. Then, share the experience with the class.

The icons for the exercises throughout this book identify the types of communication activities each involves:

   Intrapersonal—individual work; planning and analysis activities

   Interpersonal—dyadic; one-to-one experiences

   Small group—working with a few classmates

   Presentational—sharing information with your class or other group

5 Observe a televised public speech. For a period of 10 minutes, analyze the following:

- To what extent does the speaker exemplify dialogical ethics or content ethics as these are developed in this chapter?
- In what ways does the medium of television affect the speaker's application of these ethical concepts?

Be sure you identify the specific aspects of the speech that lead you to your conclusions. Write a brief report of your findings, and prepare to discuss them in class.

Cyberpoints

CCC

WEB SITE

1 Communication can be a frustrating experience. Go to the *Communicating with Credibility and Confidence* Web site at http://communication. wadsworth.com/lumsden and click on Chapter 1. Then click on *knots*, by R. D. Laing. Consider the questions posed at the beginning of the poem.

2 Go to the *Communicating with Credibility and Confidence* Web site at http://communication.wadsworth.com/lumsden and click on Chapter 1. Then click on "If a tree falls in the forest." Examine the similarities and differences between that question and issues of communication.

3 Use *InfoTrac College Edition* to locate and examine articles on ethics. Using the material from your search and from the text, prepare a decalogue (i.e., 10 do's or don'ts) that an ethical communicator should follow.

maseiffert

Chapter 2

Your Communication: Developing Credibility and Confidence

Objectives for This Chapter

Knowledge

- Understand the factors of communication credibility
- Know ways to enhance your credibility
- Understand what influences communication confidence
- Know ways you can increase your confidence

Feelings and Approaches

- Want others to perceive you as a credible communicator
- Feel greater confidence as a credible communicator

Communication Abilities

- Set and work toward personal communication goals
- Visualize and develop personal attributes of credibility
- Visualize and develop confidence in communication

Key Terms

credibility	coorientation	visualization
competence	dynamism	self-talk
objectivity	communication apprehension	affirmation
trustworthiness	relaxation techniques	

On the last day of the semester, our student Miriam walked to the front of the room, looked around, smiled, and confidently proceeded to give an outstanding speech. She was in command of the room, of herself, and of her topic. Her classmates listened eagerly, believing in her and in what she had to say.

Miriam, who was an immigrant from Colombia, had started out the term nervous about making speeches in English. She mumbled, she couldn't look at her audience, she forgot what she planned to say. Her classmates were kind and supportive—but unimpressed. What happened? Miriam developed confidence in herself and became aware that she was a credible person with something valuable to communicate.

How would you feel in Miriam's shoes? To what extent do you think others believe in you and what you say? How deeply do you believe in yourself and your message? The purpose of this chapter is to help you answer those questions both with credibility and with confidence in your ability to communicate your ideas. It introduces you first to elements of credibility and to ways you can develop it in your communication. Then the chapter helps you to examine what your present level of confidence is, how it has developed, and how you can improve it in communication situations.

Communicating with Credibility

The way people respond to you depends partly on their previous knowledge about you and partly on what you say and do at that moment. Are you credible to them? That depends on several factors and influences. Let's examine them.

Credibility Factors

Credibility How your message and character are perceived

In the previous chapter, we noted Aristotle's observation that people see your *ethos,* or **credibility,** in terms of your goodwill, good sense, and good character. Contemporary research similarly finds that credibility is how people judge a person's competence, objectivity, trustworthiness, coorientation, and dynamism (Whitehead, 1969; Tuppen, 1974). Figure 2.1 illustrates how one person might see another and evaluate both the individual and the message using these criteria.

What do you think when you see a picture of a woman pastor in her pulpit? How do you think people might assess her credibility? Would she have to work harder than a male pastor to establish her credibility? To what extent would all members of a given place of worship agree on her credibility? To what extent do you think members of various religious groups might agree?

Competence Perception of a person's expertise, authoritativeness, and skill

---

Competence **Competence** is the degree of expertise and qualification, authoritativeness, and skill a person demonstrates. Your competence is reflected in your preparation, information, ability to adapt to and work with others, and ability to think creatively and critically.

You develop and demonstrate competence in these ways:

- Recognize what you know and do well. This involves specific content information, but also your ability to work with people. For example, you already have *content competence* in some areas. You may be excellent in math but mediocre in literature, or weak in music but strong in sports history. Your competencies reflect your interest in and knowledge of these topics.

- Identify your *process competence*, which may vary according to the context. For example, you might already be excellent in face-to-face communication but terrified and bumbling in a presentation, or good at explaining but less effective at persuading.

- Develop both content and process competence by finding areas in which you're effective and practicing those behaviors—keep doing whatever you're doing well.

- Build new strengths. Work on content through preparation and study; work on process through considering, analyzing, and practicing the communication abilities that help you work with others.

Objectivity Perception of a person's ability to look at different points of view and suspend personal biases

---

Objectivity **Objectivity,** like Aristotle's concept of "good sense," is looking at various points of an issue, suspending personal biases; being reasonable and dispassionate; showing respect for others' opinions; and examining evidence, rea-

Figure 2.1 *How a receiver perceives another person's credibility*

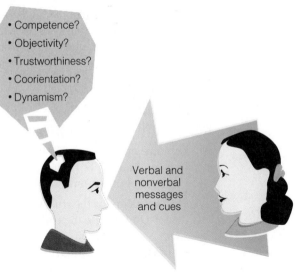

soning, and values before taking sides. In democratic societies, where discussion and debate are the means by which issues are decided, the ability to be an objective judge of ideas is particularly crucial.

Developing objectivity is a matter of disciplining your thinking and phrasing your thoughts in your everyday life. As you read, study, research, and write for classes or for pleasure; as you listen to lecturers, radio, and television; and as you interact with others, practice the following habits:

■ Try to look at every issue from more than one side. Even when you feel strongly about something, anticipate how someone who feels differently might argue or justify another position.

■ Look for reasons and evidence to support various points of view on any issue.

■ Read and listen to viewpoints other than your own, and evaluate them honestly and fairly. Often, even when you disagree with someone's position, you can agree with some of the underlying values, evidence, or reasoning. This may not change your own opinion, but it will help you maintain your objectivity about others.

■ When you interact with others, be receptive to what they have to say, and phrase your own responses to acknowledge their points of view before you argue for your own. Withhold judgment until you've heard all sides of an issue.

Trustworthiness **Trustworthiness** is the result of consistent and honest behavior, or "good character." People trust those who show sincerity and ethical behavior, even under pressure. An individual's approach to communication, as well as what he or she says, is shaped by ethical beliefs and choices.

Liars when they speak the truth are not believed.

Aristotle, fourth century B.C. philosopher, teacher

Trustworthiness Perception of a person's consistent and honest behavior

Trust is a fragile attribute, and communication cannot get very far without it. In personal relationships, the violation of trust can be the beginning of the end. In public life, loss of trust can destroy careers. In 1988, for example, a U.S. senator who had presidential ambitions was revealed to have plagiarized speeches. That news removed him from consideration as a candidate; the public could not have trusted him as president. If he lied about his speeches, they thought, what else would he lie about? As a communicator, therefore, you must guard your character and reputation closely. Ask yourself:

- Do I live up to what I say? Can I be trusted to follow through on a promise or commitment? To protect another person's confidentiality? If I hear a rumor, do I pass it on or stop it?

- Do I speak up for the trustworthy, ethical action when choices are to be made? Do I choose the truth when a lie would be easier?

Coorientation Perception of a person's similarities to and concern for listeners

Coorientation **Coorientation** is the ability to communicate similarities to listeners and concern for their well-being, similar to Aristotle's concept of "goodwill." It's easier for people to identify with someone who shows coorientation with them because they see common interests, values, objectives, and needs. Credible communicators connect with listeners because they care about how their actions might affect others, not only about their personal objectives.

Your coorientation with someone starts with seeing common interests that bring you together. People need to sense that you care about them and that, in some way, you and they are part of the same picture. Here are some ways to develop coorientation:

- Look for ways in which you and others *are* similar—backgrounds, attitudes, values, beliefs, or, perhaps, goals.

- Find ways to express that coorientation with others. But don't assume others are "just like you." Rather, value and seek to understand the differences among people of other cultures and backgrounds and value the insights of people with different experiences, building your opinions and ideas on that foundation.

- Listen carefully to others and express your support, if not your agreement.

- Show verbally and nonverbally the kind of openness, friendliness, and supportiveness that says, "We're working this communication out together."

Dynamism Energy with which a person compels the interest of others

Dynamism **Dynamism** is the energy, vigor, intensity with which an individual compels the interest of others. While dynamism can be vital to influencing others, it is a tricky element of credibility, because people's reactions vary widely with individuals, cultures, and contexts. If someone is too loud or intense, those from quieter cultures may find their dynamism offensive, or if a leader conveys negative messages too intensely, group members may achieve less consensus and satisfaction (Lumsden, 1972, p. 78). You may be dynamic with a strong voice, grand gestures, and colorful language; or you may be dynamic with a softer voice expressing passionate feelings and strong convictions. Do you remember Mother Teresa? Her communication reached around the world, yet she was as soft-spoken as a breeze. Her incredible intensity, her commitment, made her dynamic. She had that magical quality called "charisma"—drawing others to her and making them want to follow her lead.

You can adapt dynamism by using these guidelines:

- Believe in what you communicate, and talk about it with an enthusiasm that reflects your beliefs and feelings.

- Connect with others by using eye contact and body position.

- Be sensitive to others' feedback. Take a hint from the way they act. If they seem overwhelmed or offended, something's wrong. If they light up and seem to key in to you, you're probably doing fine. If you're speaking in a loud, intense voice, for example, a North American might find it authoritative and dynamic, but a Thai might draw back, thinking that you're aggressive, perhaps even angry (Dodd, 1991, p. 221).

- Adapt to the situation. If you need to listen sympathetically to a distressed friend, keep your energy under control. If, however, a business meeting is sagging, vitalize it with humor, gestures, and an expressive voice.

If you think you're generally a little too low-key, work on using your eyes, face, body, and voice to communicate energy and enthusiasm. If you're naturally dynamic, that's great—but be careful. Watch for responses; don't bowl people over, don't dominate, don't keep the emotional pitch at a constant high. The idea is to let dynamism energize your messages, not to let it overwhelm other people.

All of these credibility factors can come together at once. Suppose, for example, you are trying to persuade someone to vote for your candidate. In your explanation, you might truthfully acknowledge the opposing candidate's strong points, demonstrating your trustworthiness and objectivity. Then you could explain why your candidate's attributes serve values and beliefs that you and your listener share, showing both your competence and coorientation as you present a logical, reasoned argument, demonstrating your competence and objectivity. If you also speak with passion and sincerity, using dynamism to underscore your appeal, and respond with sensitivity to feedback—you've got it all. Each credibility factor portrays the quality of your message and supports your listener's perception of you as a credible person.

Credibility Influences

It's important to realize that individuals also weigh credibility according to the situation and their individual constructs. For example, a comedian who keeps you in hysterics may be morally corrupt, but maybe you don't really care too much—you're just interested in being entertained. Possibly your friend Jeff is flaky and incompetent, but he's a good guy and your coorientation with him is more important to you than his reliability. Or Professor Sullivan might be objective, competent, and trustworthy, but she shows neither coorientation nor

You know who they are. They're the people in the office who seem to have legions of fans from every department. For instance, it may be the person who can stop by the office of his boss—or any other senior manager for that matter—for an informal chat on a whim, while everyone else on staff seems to have to set up a meeting at least a week in advance. "What is it he has that I don't?" you may wonder. What he has, in a word, is charisma.

A recent University of Pennsylvania study shows that charismatic leaders get better performance from their employees and have more influence within an organization. But you don't have to be born with charisma. You can develop it. . . .

From Phaedra Brotherton's article (2000, April) in *Black Enterprise*, 30 (9) 152.

dynamism as a teacher. You might not go to the comedian for advice, nor ask Jeff for help on an exam, nor care to socialize with the professor. Perhaps you overlook some deficiencies because the other characteristics are more important to what you want in each situation.

You might also have an individual standard of credibility that excludes some criteria and includes others. A gang member may find a tough, chain-swinging, domineering leader credible, but perhaps you would find that same person *in*credible.

A person's view of credibility is influenced by many things, including cultural values and norms. A young western Apache, for example, listens to the "wise words" of elders who are credible because of their "reputation for balanced thinking, critical acumen, and extensive cultural knowledge" (Basso, 1990, p. 59). Many Anglo North Americans, however, grant little credibility to older people because they believe that aging is associated with the loss of intelligence and memory (Carmichael, 1991, p. 130).

Communicating with Confidence

Communicating is easier and more fun when you are confident, although it's perfectly normal to have some apprehension about communicating. Even in the United States—where people are great talkers and value communication highly—virtually 100% of the population are anxious about communication in

Roger Fluet, a volunteer at Covenant House in New York City, wrote the following poem about the anxiety he felt as he completed his training and was about to take his first call on the "Nineline" (1-800-999-9999), a hotline that runaway kids and teens are encouraged to call from the United States, Canada, and Mexico.

This is horrible.
I'm thinking like a child again.
This is all new to me.
This training is too overwhelming.
Am I supposed to remember all of this?
I'm not sure if I understand.
Is anybody else getting all of this?
Is *everybody* getting all of this?
These feelings are really scary.

How can I be expected to be able to help a kid in crisis?
What if the caller is smarter than me?
What if they realize that I'm unsure of what I'm doing?
Maybe I will know what I'm doing.
Am I ready?
I am definitely not ready. Well, maybe.
Am I supposed to know?
God, I wish I knew.

I'll never be able to answer those phones.
What am I supposed to say?
What do they expect of me?
What if I say the wrong thing?
I don't want to screw up.
What if I get a drug call?
Or a pregnancy call?
Oh, my God, a suicide call.
I can't handle this.
"RING . . . RING . . . "
"Covenant House Nineline . . . "
Stick to the model.
The supervisor is only a touch-of-a-button away.
Hey, this isn't so bad.
I think I'm really helping this kid.
Wow, thank goodness for the model.
Maybe I am ready
This is all new to me.
I'm thinking like a child again.
This is great.

How do you think Roger's credibility and confidence were developing as he took his training? What do you think happened as he took that first call?

Reprinted by permission of Roger Fluet

some context (Richmond & McCroskey, 1995, p. 48). Many businesses are so concerned about managers' confidence that they provide training to develop their self-assurance in their ability to be open, candid, and courageous; to take risks; to explain their ideas and decisions; to trust themselves and to trust and empower others; to involve themselves in issues; and to provide leadership (Ireland, Hitt, & Williams, 1992, pp. 36–37).

The best help is to examine what has influenced your own feelings about communication and to understand how communication apprehension works.

Influences on Confidence

You already have some personal starting points for your confidence that come from several influences in your past and present life. Some of those influences are from your culture and people around you, and some are ideas that you develop from observing yourself.

Influences of Culture, Gender, and Other People   Experiences with family, culture, and other people impact on how free you feel to communicate, with whom, in what contexts, about what topics, and when.

Culture.   Every culture and identity group communicates according to group norms that reflect the group's worldview, religious and political structure, and fundamental values, all of which may influence how willing a person is to communicate under what circumstances. Overall, for instance, people in Hong Kong and Micronesia are very reticent, although they are more willing to communicate in groups than face to face—as opposed to the United States or Australia, where people are most comfortable in dyads (Asker, 1998, p. 168). Even how *much* people talk may be culturally influenced. In the United States, for example, talkativeness is considered a virtue. In Sweden, people are expected to be more judicious in their conversation (Richmond & McCroskey, 1995, p. 34). In the United States, therefore, a quiet person might be thought to be shy, whereas in Sweden, the same person might be thought to be appropriately restrained.

Gender or social status.   Your gender and class ranking within the larger society may affect, to a large extent, your communication opportunities and confidence. In each society there is a "power elite . . . those who *dominate* culture, those who historically or traditionally have had the most persistent and far-reaching impact" (Folb, 1991, p. 122). The elite maintain power over others who hold less political, economic, and social influence—frequently, women and various ethnic groups. One way the dominant culture maintains power and prestige is through downplaying the communication of subordinated groups. When subordinate members realize that dominant members won't listen to them, they may see themselves as inferior. That perception undercuts their confidence, which weakens their communication, creating a vicious circle. That may explain why women public speakers experience more apprehension than do men (Behnke & Sawyer, 2000, pp. 187–195).

Family norms.   Every family, too, has its own ways—noisy or quiet, open or closed, supportive or defensive—and anything in between. Family rules teach children the expectations of themselves that they carry into adulthood. Compare two kids, Erin and Tyler. Erin's family expects each member, including the children, to share in decision making. At family meetings, all are encouraged to speak out and are listened to respectfully. In Tyler's family, one adult makes all the decisions, and no one—especially not the children—can discuss or question them. Later in life, these family experiences may influence Erin's joy and confidence in leadership and Tyler's apprehension and followership.

Models. From babyhood on, people copy the examples of parents, family, friends, and other models. Adolescents often imitate their peers as well as television characters whom they perceive as peers. In fact, media heavily influence self-image and interpersonal communication. If the models are credible, confident, and competent communicators who interact ethically and humanely, that's positive. Media, however, are known for perpetuating racial and gender stereotypes, both in fiction and nonfiction programming (Smitherman-Donaldson & van Dijk, 1988), and people sometimes model their communication after stereotypes they see. Then their behavior may reinforce others' stereotypes of who they are, diminishing their credibility and weakening their confidence in interacting with diverse people. Fortunately, with the increase in the numbers of women and people of color in politics and business, media are forced to increase coverage of these positive models of effective communicators in a variety of hues and gender.

Special people. Certain individuals often exert great influences on a person's life. You might be influenced by your brother or sister, your mother or father, your teacher, your pastor, or perhaps a family friend. One management consultant and corporate trainer calls these important people "wizards" (Tice, 1983, pp. 1B 1–8). Wizards are people whose authority you believe much more than you believe others or yourself. With that power, your wizards' words and responses to you can shape your perceptions of yourself and your communication.

One way other people have affected your communication style and comfort is through *reinforcement*, strengthening or weakening your responses through rewards or punishments. These may be physical, of course, but they also may be emotional and psychological. As a child, your family and primary groups reinforced your behavior. In adolescence, your most important reinforcement may have come from your peers (Smith & Fowler, 1984). As an adult, your behavior is reinforced by many people and events, but especially by your personal wizards and your own self-talk.

A person is likely to repeat the rewarded behaviors and avoid the punished behaviors, but sometimes reinforcement has the effect of convincing people that they "just are that way," even if "that way" is a detrimental way. Such thinking can lead to *self-fulfilling prophecies*, whereby individuals predicted to behave in a certain way then fulfill those expectations. That behavior, in turn, further reinforces their expectations and actions to the point that it becomes a vicious circle.

Here's an example: Rosa once gave a poor report in class because she had insufficient information. She was embarrassed and told herself she just wasn't a good speaker. Her father, a very special wizard in her life, now wants to help. So he keeps reminding her, "Don't make a fool of yourself."

When Rosa gets a new assignment, she does excellent research and prepares thoroughly. When she gives her speech, her teacher and classmates praise her research, her reasoning, and her overall presentation. Does Rosa believe them? She wants to—but she doesn't. Why? Because *she* knows her presentation wasn't perfect. She was nervous and forgot some things. Her listeners don't know that, but she does. So she believes the speech was not as good as they think it was. Besides, her wizard's voice in her mind says she is an imposter who made a fool of herself again. Rosa tells herself the teacher and class are wrong, that they're just trying to cheer her up.

They are *not* wrong. Rosa doesn't realize that forgetting something does not necessarily ruin the research or the speech. More important, she can't see what she did well because her well-meaning wizard's warnings are drowning out her successes. All she can see is the negative.

If you've ever had such an experience, however, be of good cheer. First, not all wizards are negative. Sometimes, like the Wizard of Oz, they can show you that you have a heart, or brains, or courage and then send you out to use them. Second, you can stop listening to the negative influences and become your own wizard, find your strengths, and build on them.

Influences from You What words do you use to describe yourself? "I am a good communicator"? "I'm a lousy speaker"? "I'm a good listener"? Your own experiences combine with influences from others to create your self-concept—the mental picture you have of who you are. As you communicate—at home, at school, at work, in the community—others respond in ways that reinforce your behavior.

Your *self-concept*, consisting of the attitudes and beliefs you've developed about yourself over your lifetime, affects not just your credibility and your confidence but also your actions and your perceptions of others. Research has found, for example, that success in school is greater for young African American and Mexican people whose self-concept includes a wide variety of possibilities than for those who see themselves in stereotypical terms (Coover & Murphy, 2000).

One theory suggests each person has three "selves" (Wilmot, 1987, pp. 52–58):

1   Your *looking-glass self* is based on the views of you reflected in the eyes of people who are important to you—your wizards. Seeing that reflection, a person may create a self-fulfilling prophecy and make it come true, for better or for worse.

2   Your *self by social comparison* is how worthwhile you think you are by comparison to others around you. "I'm just stupid," one child thinks, seeing that classmates solve math problems more quickly, or, "I'm a good artist!" as she observes that her pictures are better than others'.

3   Your *self in social roles* is your perception of how you respond to what you believe society expects of you. As society evolves and expectations change, it's increasingly difficult to know how to fulfill them. It can be frustrating to juggle roles that require spending "quality time" with the kids, being attentive to a spouse, and meeting the demands of a high-level career.

Martin Luther King, Jr. (1964) created an image of a child forming self-perceptions when he wrote, "You seek to explain to your six-year-old daughter . . . that Funtown is closed to colored children, and see the ominous clouds of inferiority beginning to form in her little mental sky" (p. 81). King sensed how his daughter must have seen herself, not by any truthful measure, but according to the stereotypes and negative comparisons and expectations of a prejudiced world. Society was showing her a clouded looking-glass self, and her parents' task was to let her see her real worth, to provide her with a looking glass of clarity and beauty.

It's also true that you may perceive your own communication on the basis of other factors, including self-attributions, language, and skills.

Self-attributions.   People often see something they have done and then attribute characteristics to themselves as part of their self-concept and the reason for their behavior (Harvey, Orbuch, & Weber, 1992). "I speak well, so I must have a self-confident personality," they might reason, or, "I can't communicate with my family without fighting because I am basically a high-strung person." The attribution may be false, but it can become a "reality" in the person's self-image.

Language.   The more fluent you are in your language, the easier it is to get a point across and the more confident you become. Often, people who are confident in one language are uncertain about expressing ideas in a new one. Constantly trying to translate thoughts can be exhausting and frustrating, and often listeners are impatient. Sometimes foreign speakers just give up. Even in their own language, however, people sometimes feel they have an inadequate vocabulary and, therefore, lack confidence in their ability to express themselves. Lacking confidence, they are silent. What a pity; frequently, their vocabularies often are better than they think. Besides, vocabulary can be developed.

Skills.   Often, people look back at their communication experiences and see only their faults—or only their virtues. A realistic assessment can determine how effectively you improve your skills and build your confidence. Many students, for example, worry that they "talk with their hands too much." This belief undercuts their confidence when they make a speech. Yet, rarely is excessive gesturing a problem for one of these students. In fact, their tendency to move and gesture is a great basis for developing dynamic communication. Recognizing that fact can help them to build their skills *and* their confidence.

Communication Apprehension

Sometimes, for some folks, in some situations, communication just seems far too difficult. The communication discipline has many terms for this problem. *Reticence*, for example, suggests that an individual is a bit anxious about communicating and tends to hold back, and therefore may feel like and even be perceived as an incompetent communicator (Keaten & Kelly, 2000, pp. 166–167).

Research often measures the degree to which people want to participate in a range of communication situations as a *willingness to communicate*, finding that people who like to communicate are perceived by others as more credible, sociable, composed, competent, extroverted, and attractive (Richmond & Roach, 1992, p. 101). It's worth the effort to acquire a taste for interaction.

To get a quick picture of your own feelings about communicating, fill out Form 2.1 at the end of this chapter. The results can indicate your starting point for confidence, pleasure, and effectiveness in communicating.

Sometimes, people are really anxious about communicating; they say, "I'm so shy" or "I'm just too nervous" or "I have such butterflies, such stage fright." These responses all reflect **communication apprehension,** "an individual's level of fear or anxiety associated with either real or anticipated communication with another person or persons" (Richmond & McCroskey, 1995, p. 41). Almost everyone suffers from communication apprehension under some circumstances, but if it is extreme it can contribute to poor communication and to loneliness (Zakahi & Duran, 1985, pp. 50–60), or sometimes to students' lower grades and even to the probability they will drop out of school (Ericson & Gardner, 1992). Most communication apprehension is a temporary problem, some is deeper. There are four basic types of communication apprehension (Richmond & Mc-Croskey, 1995, pp. 42–48):

Communication appre-hension Level of fear or anxiety associated with communication

1   *Context communication apprehension. Context* refers to whether you are speaking one on one, in a group, or in a public presentation. Many people are perfectly comfortable talking in class, for example, but anxious when they must make a speech. In fact, most people—at least 70%—experience moderate to very high anxiety about public speaking. The good news is, observers do not see speakers who are anxious as any less competent than those who are not (Carrell & Willmington, 1998, pp. 87–95).

2   *Audience communication apprehension.* You might feel perfectly comfort-able when asking your friends for a donation to your favorite cause but be very nervous about asking a faculty group for the same thing. Almost 95% of the population "reports being scared about communicating with a person or group at some point in their lives" (Richmond & McCroskey, 1995, p. 46). A recent poll found that men are more comfortable expressing an opinion, telling a joke, and giving directions, whereas women feel better talking about relationships, complimenting another, or negotiating social events (*Spectra*, 2000). These are stereotypical, but apparently true, differences—however, men and women are equally comfortable in workplace communication.

3   *Situational communication apprehension.* Even a person who is breezily confident in just about any situation can suddenly choke up on wedding vows, for example. Situational apprehension is just a transitory response to one partic-ular situation, whereas context apprehension is a repeated framework for com-munication such as public speaking or interviewing.

4   *Traitlike communication apprehension.* This is like a personality trait—a gnawing, constant anxiety about communicating in almost any context. Fortu-nately for the 20% of North Americans who suffer from traitlike apprehension, it can be alleviated with professional help.

As you can see, communication apprehension ranges among individuals from an occasional emotional spasm to a seriously problematic condition. Some students enroll in a required speech class—and then drop it because of apprehension—every semester up to their senior year. That kind of apprehension is demoralizing, but there are ways to get it under control. Many colleges have learning centers and/or counseling centers that can help with this problem. In most instances, however, no matter how awful communication apprehension *feels* at the moment, it can be alleviated. Phillips (1991) concluded that people often are apprehensive because they do not feel they have the necessary communication skills. As this book progresses, you'll learn ways to manage your stress and develop confidence in your communication abilities.

Realistic Confidence

As we have seen, it's possible to be too timid, too quiet, and/or too anxious. It's also possible to be too confident, too brazen, too sure of oneself. People need to assess their skills and to develop the confidence to pursue their opportunities. In the United States, for example, women may be at a disadvantage because, while they tend to be better at identifying their own limitations than men are, they more often underestimate what they *can* do (Clement, 1987). As a consequence, they often lack the confidence to pursue challenging careers for which they would have been well suited.

A *little* anxiety is a good thing. Some apprehension probably reveals that you understand the situation and your responsibilities. Before giving a speech, you may think, "If I quote this statistic incorrectly, I'll give all 25 people in my audience the wrong idea." Or, before giving your best friend some difficult advice, you may say to yourself, "If I say this in the wrong way, our relationship may be damaged." Your logical concern over possible consequences may make you nervous; at the same time, you may prepare your message more carefully, think through your ideas more thoroughly, and consider your listeners' needs with greater sensitivity.

Sometimes, students' confidence actually slips a bit as they begin to learn more about communication. The more they know, the more they realize communication isn't a simple matter of "just talking." As they develop skill, however, they learn how to prepare better and their confidence becomes better founded, stronger, and more convincing to others.

Developing Communication Confidence

We're going to offer you some proven strategies to help you develop confidence and communicate more effectively. We have seen these approaches work over and over again. By learning to relax, visualizing how you want to be in your communication, setting goals, and practicing your skills, you can be confident and effective.

Relax Away Your Stress

Some situations are stressful. You might postpone a difficult phone call for days or have nightmares about asking for a raise. Some folks dread meeting new people. Many speakers get fluttery stomachs, shaky knees, sweaty palms, and dry mouths as they approach the podium. These symptoms are normal, but confident communicators know how to *interpret* their symptoms, manage them, and make them useful.

Communication stress is a circular set of relationships between psychological factors and physical symptoms that lead back to psychological responses. Figure 2.2 shows what happens.

Hao is about to go to an interview. He feels unprepared and anxious. His body receives this message about his feelings from his mind and interprets it as a threat. When people are threatened, their instinct is either to flee or to fight. Hao's sympathetic nervous system, which doesn't know the difference between the emotional threat of communicating and the physical threat from a gun, prepares for "fight or flight." His adrenaline surges and his heart beats faster; the increased adrenaline makes him a little nauseous and shaky in the knees and stomach; his head feels fuzzy and his mouth goes dry (Lefton & Valvatne, 1988, p. 123). Hao becomes aware of these symptoms and thinks, "I'm scared—I can't do this—I'm going to be sick." As his mind wrestles with his anxiety, it sends another SOS to his body, which reacts by pumping yet more adrenaline.

The problem is, Hao's mind and body are interpreting every response negatively, and his anxiety is increasing rapidly. "I'm just too nervous," he tells himself. He doesn't realize that confident communicators *also* feel anxiety and that they also get a good shot of adrenaline from their systems, but that they interpret it positively. It gives them the vitality and dynamism to do a good job; it makes the situation exciting and challenging. The stress isn't the problem, it's the interpretation. You can learn to accept normal stress and use it to your advantage.

Relaxation techniques
Methods used consciously to help you reduce anxiety

The first step is to relax. "Impossible!" You say? Not so; it's possible and essential. Research has shown that **relaxation techniques,** when used *before* you actually get into specific situations, help you develop confidence and effectiveness in your communication (Hopf & Ayres, 1992). Relaxing slows breathing, lowers pulse rate and blood pressure, eases muscle tension, and focuses your attention. By consciously relaxing, you can help clear your mind for studying, reduce stress before an exam, counteract exhaustion during the course of a long day, and prepare for a difficult talk with another person or a presentation to a group.

There are a number of approaches to relaxation. Here is one called "deep-muscle relaxation":

1   Get comfortable, close your eyes, and concentrate on relaxing your muscles.

2   Breathe slowly and deeply. Imagine the oxygen flowing through your bloodstream, reaching all parts of your body.

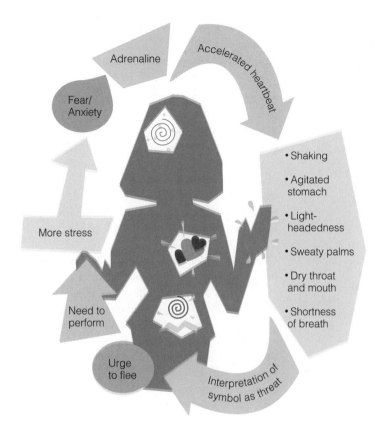

Figure 2.2 *How psychological stress and physiological symptoms are interpreted negatively to increase apprehension or stage fright*

Adrenaline

Accelerated heartbeat

Fear/
Anxiety

- Shaking

- Agitated
  stomach

- Light-
  headedness

- Sweaty palms

- Dry throat
  and mouth

- Shortness
  of breath

More stress

Need to
perform

Urge
to flee

Interpretation of
symbol as threat

3   Now begin relaxing your body, starting with your toes. Envision them relaxing. Think of the blood as circulating freely around your toes, making them relaxed, warm, and comfortable.

4   Continue this process up into your feet, ankles, and legs. Work slowly, thinking of each muscle relaxing, all the way through your body.

5   Concentrate on areas where you have the greatest tension—perhaps your back, shoulders, or neck. Tell yourself you feel them relaxing, feel the blood circulating, feel the tension flowing out of them.

6   When your entire body and mind feel relaxed, allow yourself a few moments of floating in that easy, comfortable state.

7   Now, tell yourself that the muscle relaxation will continue and that you will feel comfortable, at ease, and energized for your communication. Picture energy flowing back into your body.

8   Open your eyes, and you're ready to communicate with confidence.

As you work through your relaxation exercise, actual physiological changes take place. Your adrenal glands are calmed, so they pump out less stimulation to your nervous system. As you feel the reduced physiological stress, your comfort level increases. *With practice, you can reach a point at which you can relax yourself in a matter of seconds, even as you walk down a flight of stairs or across campus.* We can tell you from personal experience that this technique works, especially when you combine it with visualization and affirmation techniques.

Visualize Your Success

The human mind is incredibly powerful. We can't emphasize this enough: *What you see in your mind and how you talk to yourself can determine your success or your failure.* It really is up to you. For some people, the "seeing" is the most effective; for others, the talking is (Ayres, Heuett, & Sonandre, 1998); a person whose fear is very powerful may need to see a professional who can help identify which method is best for that individual (Dwyer, 2000, pp. 72–81). For most folks, we recommend doing both visualization and verbal affirmation.

Creating Successful Images   In **visualization,** you create a specific mental image of your successful performance to use as a kind of mental practice for the event ahead of you. Athletes have been using the technique for some time. Dick Fosbury, Olympic gold medalist in the high jump, says, "I developed a thought process in order to repeat a successful jump: I would 'psyche' myself up; create a picture; 'feel' a successful jump—the perfect jump; and develop a positive attitude to make the jump. My success came from the visualization and imaging process" (Ungerleider, 1992, p. 48). What he did in his mind, he did with his body. Fosbury revolutionized the way athletes approach the high jump and broke through previously imagined limits of possibility. When you watch the Olympics today, you see every high jumper using both visualization and the "Fosbury Flop."

When an individual goes through a *mental* rehearsal for a physical action, the muscles prepare to perform that action. In a sense, they practice silently what they are to do. In the same way, your mind can rehearse the image of what you want to do as a communicator. To create visualizations for your communication, follow these steps:

1   See yourself in a specific communication setting, such as an interview, a speech, or a conversation. Picture yourself as confident and in charge.

2   Picture clearly what you would be doing in a perfect performance. See and hear yourself as you communicate in the situation. Create a complete mental picture of the entire event, as if you're watching yourself on a videotape replay.

3   Imagine your emotional response to the experience. Sense how you would feel in the context of the transaction. Suppose you're preparing to confront a friend about her drinking problem. You'd feel confident that you're doing the right thing—concerned, caring, serious, determined, focused on her and her problem. If you're preparing to make a speech, however, you might feel confident and well prepared, excited about your information, involved, eager to inform your audience, physically coordinated, and dynamic.

Visualization Creation of mental image of a successful performance

Self-talk Messages to yourself to improve your approach or performance

Affirming Successful Interactions   What we're talking about here is **self-talk.** Far from meaning you're crazy, talking to yourself to improve your approach or your performance is smart. "As a learning strategy it promotes the learner's selective attention to appropriate features of a skill" (Anderson, 1997, p. 31). Some people call this process "managing your mind" or "inner leadership" (Neck & Barnard, 1996, p. 24).

Human behavior—including communication—involves thinking, feeling, and doing, and people seek to maintain an equilibrium among the three. This may be why your mental image of your communication is stronger when you also use words to describe it; the words affirm in your thinking the things you've visualized yourself doing and feeling.

As you change your actions you also can change the way you think about yourself. For example, improving your grades improves your self-esteem. But the opposite is also true—changing the way you think about yourself can change the way you do things. Seeing yourself as a better student can affect your performance—and your grades. Using self-talk and visualization, then, allows you literally to practice and train mentally to reach your goals.

Affirmation Positive, present-tense description of a desired achievement

You can guide your self-talk by writing out an **affirmation,** a statement that is a personal, positive, present-tense description of achievement using words depicting actions and feelings (Tice, 1983, pp. 12–3, 12–4). Let's consider each element:

- *Personal.* Affirm what *you* visualize yourself as doing, describing the act precisely as it is to your senses: "I am walking confidently in to my interview appointment. I'm excited about the interview. I'm smiling and holding out my hand. I shake hands firmly and wait to be invited to sit down."

- *Positive.* Keep the affirmation positive. If you talk to yourself about what you want to avoid, you only highlight the wrong behavior. For example, instead of saying, "I'm not using a lot of 'uhs,' or 'you knows,'" say, "My words are flowing fluently, I know exactly what to say, I'm expressing my ideas clearly."

- *Present-tense achievement:* Use terms to describe your actions as if they are happening now instead of future tense. For example, say, "I *am* confident and at ease," not, "I will be . . ." The present tense makes the action firm: it's *now*.

- *Action words.* Include specific sensory details; words describing movement and responses are easy to visualize—for example, "I am keeping direct eye contact with my audience" or "My gestures are strong. They emphasize my important points."

- *Feeling words.* Use words that describe your emotional reactions to involve the feeling dimension of your thinking-feeling-doing relationships. You might say, "I am energized and eager to tell my listeners . . ."

An affirmation statement for a public speech might go: "I am well prepared, speaking fluently and energetically, moving comfortably, gesturing dynamically. My audience is attentive and supportive. I care about my listeners, and I enjoy watching and listening to them to make sure they understand my ideas. This is enjoyable, and I do it well."

Practice Your Skills

You might have to overcome old habits to improve your communication abilities and develop your confidence. Nothing substitutes for good, hard practice. Keep in mind, however, that practice does *not* necessarily make perfect; repetition of any behavior simply makes it habitual. Only *perfect practice makes perfect.*

"I absolutely will *not* mispronounce 'cinnamon' this time," the television cooking show host promises himself. And he mispronounces it again. "Okay," he says to himself, "cimmanon, cimmanon, cimmanon. I've got it." No, the speaker has ci*mm*anon, not cinnamon. Or, "I *will* use eye contact when I speak," the political candidate declares. So she practices her speech looking at chairs, gets up to deliver the speech, and looks straight at the listeners' chests, not their eyes. How embarrassing! These people practiced, but they practiced the wrong things.

The experience of many people, and a lot of research, suggests that training, knowing what you're talking about, and good practice reduces apprehension and improves the quality of your communication (Ayres, Schliesman, & Sonandre, 1998, pp. 171–179; Roach, 1998, p. 138). You build confidence by knowing what you want to achieve, visualizing it, affirming it, and practicing it correctly. Correct practice involves setting realistic goals and then reinforcing your positive behaviors to achieve the goals.

Setting Goals Before setting specific goals, envision what you'd be thinking, feeling, and doing when you're a credible, confident communicator. Think about the processes, principles, and qualities we've discussed so far; review the characteristics that make communicators effective in your own eyes. See yourself as communicating in the way you want to see yourself and be seen by others. Then analyze that vision to select a few attainable goals for yourself.

Selectivity. You will achieve more success if you select two or three goals to work on at a time rather than a lot all at once. Begin with those that will provide you with the greatest progress in your development.

Attainability. Break down complex objectives into realistic smaller steps. Think of these as practice goals. If you were a weight lifter, you'd set practice goals to lift a certain amount in each session. You'd make those goals challenging but attainable, and you'd work to reach them in your practice sessions. The principle applies to communication, too. Perhaps you're comfortable talking one to one, but uncomfortable in a group. Then a first goal might be to speak up more at your project group meeting. After some success, you would set a new goal, perhaps to ask questions or to express an opposing opinion.

Achieving Goals   When you've isolated a goal, you can use visualization and affirmation to help you practice mentally. Then you practice physically. Here are some steps:

1   Prepare for your actual practice (that could mean researching information, planning a statement, memorizing a quotation, and so on).

2   Practice your behavior in the situation you've selected. As you experience some success, go back over the *successful* behaviors; practice them in your mind.

3   Don't dwell on the unsuccessful behaviors. Identify what you want to do better and rehearse the *right* way to do it.

4   Set new, slightly more difficult practice goals.

5   Repeat the process with the new challenge.

Suppose you want to speak out in class more confidently. Your first goal could be "to ask a question in class." Visualize yourself doing that, fulfilling an affirmation statement something like this: "I am listening carefully and when I don't understand something or I'm curious about a related idea, I want to know the answer. I raise my hand and the teacher acknowledges me. I speak up clearly and organize my question so the professor and the class understand me. The exchange makes the class more interesting and I enjoy learning as I listen and question."

You could have practice sessions with a friend, working to make your questions clear, direct, and confident. Then choose a class in which the teacher encourages participation so you *can* ask questions. Do your homework so you're prepared. Then go to that class, listen, review your affirmation statement in your mind, and ask a question, as clearly and confidently as you can. This, too, is practice. Pretty soon it becomes easier, and you actually *do* enjoy the transactions with the professor and your classmates. You're involved, and you like it. You're achieving a communication goal. You're on the way.

If your performance doesn't conform to your visualized practice, use it as a learning experience. "Trial-and-error learning" cannot occur if you never have errors. When you make a mistake, focus on it only as a means for identifying what will work better next time. Then forget the mistake and start to visualize yourself using the new, improved behavior in your next opportunity. Write and rehearse your affirmation and, at the first chance, practice it perfectly.

Summary

Your credibility and your confidence influence the success of your personal life and your career. Credibility is how others perceive your competence, objectivity, trustworthiness, coorientation, and dynamism; credibility is also affected by the situation and by individual constructions of what a credible person is. To become a credible communicator, you need to make each of these attributes part of your life and practice communicating them to others in your interactions. When you know that others find you credible because of qualities you genuinely have, then you can feel more confident in yourself and your message.

Confidence results when you feel you can meet the challenge in a communication situation. Your culture, gender, status, family, and other background experiences have contributed to your feelings about yourself as a communicator. Some people are more willing than others to communicate, and some suffer from more apprehension than others. Everyone feels some anxiety about communicating in one context or another; the key is how you manage it. If you react to your physiological symptoms negatively, your fears will increase the symptoms, and you will feel even less confident. If you interpret them positively, you can use them to "fuel" an energetic and dynamic delivery—and thus increase your confidence.

Assess your skills and build on them as a foundation for developing greater confidence. Your confidence will grow as you learn to use relaxation techniques and to visualize and affirm your performance. With appropriate practice, you can attain your goals as a credible, confident communicator.

Exercises

1 Complete Form 2.1 at the end of this chapter. Instructions for scoring are included. What do you think this self-assessment reveals about your willingness to communicate with others? When do you feel perfectly comfortable? When do you begin to get a little anxious about a situation? What factors have influenced your feelings? Think about your background experiences, family, culture, role models, and so on. How have they affected you? How can you now change any of your behaviors that may have weakened your confidence in the past?

2 Think back over your experiences, and identify an occasion when you felt you communicated very well. Did you, perhaps, create new understanding out of an argument with a friend? Persuade someone to listen to your point of view? Teach someone how to do something?

Now write a brief description of the situation and identify as precisely as possible the following:

- What factors of credibility do you think you brought to the situation? How do you think the other participant(s) saw your credibility? How did that affect your interaction?

- How did you communicate your credibility? What did you say and do that made the other person(s) feel you were credible?

- How confident did you feel in that situation? Why? If you were apprehensive, what was it like? How did you manage it? How did your confidence level affect the way you communicated?

3 Make a list of communication goals you would like to achieve. Make them as precise as you can, and identify a situation in which you could practice some skill toward achieving that goal. Now, visualize yourself communicating exactly the way you want to in that situation. Write an affirmation statement for the goal. Remember to phrase it in the present tense and to make it descriptive of your specific behaviors, your positive feelings, and the positive responses you get from others.

4 With a small group, share your goal and affirmation statement. Make sure each person's goal is in present tense, positive in tone, and descriptive of specific behaviors and others' responses. Now, do the following:

  a With your group, design a short practice situation for each person's affirmation. Make it something you can do with members of the group role-playing the person or group in which you want to develop your skill. Make notes for your practice situation.

  b Close your eyes and relax. Have a group member read your affirmation aloud to you while you visualize the situation clearly.

  c With the group helping you, practice your goal behavior.

  d Have your group give you feedback. Start with what you did well, and talk about how you can make it even better. You might consider rewriting your affirmation to make it stronger.

  e Repeat this process so every member of the group can practice his or her affirmation.

5 Listen carefully to a speaker, either on television or in a public performance (this could be a politician, a preacher, a lecturer, and so on). As you listen, analyze the speaker's credibility. Consider the factors of objectivity, competence, trustworthiness, coorientation, and dynamism. Also consider the situation and your own construct—what you think is important for the speaker to be credible to you.

Now prepare a 2-minute report on the speaker's credibility. Explain briefly who you heard, where, on what topic, and in what context. Then describe how much (or little) credibility you saw in the speaker. Be as specific as possible in describing the speaker's behaviors and quoting statements that demonstrate your point. Present the report to the class.

Cyberpoints

1 Are you interested in women's body images and how they affect self-confidence? Use *InfoTrac College Edition* to locate the article "Body Feelings Sink Women's Self-Image," from *USA Today*, v 128, i 2656 (Jan 2000), p 7.

2   Want to know more about how people use visualization to improve their performances? Use *InfoTrac College Edition* to search on the keywords *visualization*, *imagery*, and *self-talk*. You'll find several articles there.

3   If you're interested in what makes folks credible, use *InfoTrac College Edition* to search on the keywords *credibility* and *charisma*.

CCC

WEB SITE

4   For an example of a speech analyzed for the credibility it conveys, go to the *Communicating with Credibility and Confidence* Web site at http://communication.wadsworth.com/lumsden and click on Chapter 2.

5   Go to the *Communicating with Credibility and Confidence* Web site at http://communication.wadsworth.com/lumsden and click on Willingness to Communicate and Communication Apprehension Surveys to find out how different people (cultures, genders) respond.

6   For a wonderful insight into self-concept and self-confidence, go to the *Communicating with Credibility and Confidence* Web site at http://communication.wadsworth.com/lumsden and click on the Maya Angelou autobiography *I Know Why the Caged Bird Sings*.

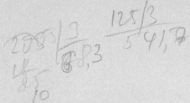

Form 2.1

Self-Assessment of Willingness to Communicate

Following are 20 situations in which a person might choose to communicate or not to communicate. Assume you have *completely free choice*. Indicate in the space at the left what percentage of the time you would choose to communicate (0 = never, 100 = always).

_____5_____ 1. Talk with a service station attendant

_____100_____ 2. Talk with a physician

_____5_____ 3. Present a talk to a group of strangers

_____100_____ 4. Talk with an acquaintance while standing in line

_____40_____ 5. Talk with a salesperson in a store

_____100_____ 6. Talk in a large meeting of friends

_____50_____ 7. Talk with a police officer

_____20_____ 8. Talk in a small group of strangers

_____100_____ 9. Talk with a friend while standing in line

_____20_____ 10. Talk with a server in a restaurant

_____50_____ 11. Talk in a large meeting of acquaintances

_____5_____ 12. Talk with a stranger while standing in line

_____100_____ 13. Talk with a secretary

_____100_____ 14. Present a talk to a group of friends

_____100_____ 15. Talk in a small group of acquaintances

_____5_____ 16. Talk with a garbage collector

_____5_____ 17. Talk in a large meeting of strangers

_____100_____ 18. Talk with a spouse (or girl/boyfriend)

_____100_____ 19. Talk in a small group of friends

_____20_____ 20. Present a talk to a group of acquaintances

Summarize your scores on the Scoring Form on the following page.

Scoring for Form 2.1, Self-Assessment of Willingness to Communicate

Subscores:

Group Discussion
Add scores for items 8, 15, and 19; divide by 3 _____

Meetings
Add scores for items 6, 11, and 17; divide by 3 _____

Interpersonal conversations
Add scores for items 4, 9, and 12; divide by 3 _____

Public speaking
Add scores for items 3, 14, and 20; divide by 3 _____

Stranger
Add scores for items 3, 8, 12, and 17; divide by 4 _____

Acquaintance
Add scores for items 4, 11, 15, and 20; divide by 4 _____

Friend
Add scores for items 6, 9, 14, and 19; divide by 4 _____

Total Willingness to Communicate Score

Total subscores for stranger, acquaintance, and friend;
Divide by 3 _____

From: McCroskey, J. C. (1992). Reliability and validity of the willingness to communicate scale. *Communication Quarterly*, 40, 16–25.

Chapter 3

Perception and Thought: Making Sense

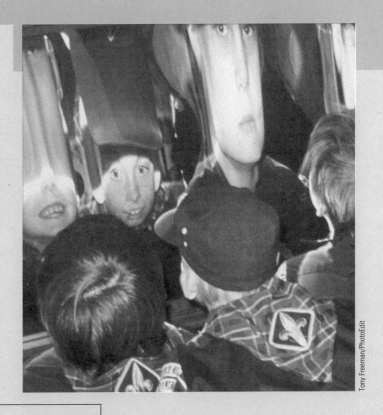

Objectives for This Chapter

Knowledge

- Understand how people perceive and interpret stimuli
- Know what factors affect the process of perception
- Understand how critical thinking works
- Understand how to analyze an argument for its validity and truth

Feelings and Approaches

- Be aware of how factors of perception affect your own and others' messages and interpretation
- Be confident in using critical thinking to receive and plan communication
- Enjoy examining factors of perception and reasoning in messages

Communication Abilities

- Use critical analysis to understand perception and messages
- Develop valid arguments through critical thinking
- Develop messages that aid others' perception and understanding
- Attend to others' messages perceptively and analytically

Key Terms

intrapersonal communication	culture	critical thinking
perception	gender	inductive reasoning
sensory fatigue	hierarchy of needs	deductive reasoning
selective attention	social exchange theory	cause-and-effect reasoning
shaping	consistency needs	

A few years ago, we were watching a production of the musical *Cats* when a bomb scare halted the show. The audience was quickly ushered outside, where the actors proceeded to continue their performance. When a van carrying the bomb squad drove up, one of the actors waved it through the crowd with a gallant bow. After the officials checked the theater and pronounced it clear, most of the audience trooped back in for the finish of a marvelous performance. We enjoyed the whole incident enormously and have told and retold the tale. When Don tells it, the van is white. When Gay tells it, the van is black. We both saw the same van—we both even remember the "cat" actor who directed it through the crowd. And we're equally sure of its color. Who is right? We'll never know. Each of us has a different reality about that van.

That's okay, because we know that *each person creates his or her own reality*. No matter what "really" happens, the reality you *believe* in is the one you *perceive*. That's the event you think about and, sometimes, discuss with others. Communication is about bringing human realities closer together. Sometimes, the gap between what two people perceive or think is so enormous that each must use great energy and discipline to understand the other.

Fortunately, knowing something about how people perceive and think can help you to improve communication in three ways: First, you can more accurately and confidently perceive messages from others and from your environment. Second, you can think more accurately about what these mean; and third, you can communicate your thoughts more effectively and credibly so your receivers respond to them the way you intend.

With all that in mind, this chapter will examine how people perceive their "reality" and how to use critical thinking to understand and respond to that reality more effectively.

The Process of Perception

Intrapersonal communication Internal monologue in which perceived information is processed

Perception is a fascinating part of communication, because it is the unseen foundation for creating and responding to ideas within yourself and between you and others. All at one time, you listen to others, notice things, and talk to yourself (usually silently) about the messages you receive and the ones you intend to send. That self-talk is **intrapersonal communication,** an ongoing internal monologue during which you process information that you perceive.

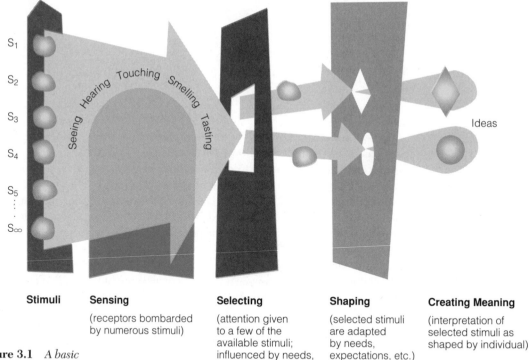

Stimuli	Sensing	Selecting	Shaping	Creating Meaning
	(receptors bombarded by numerous stimuli)	(attention given to a few of the available stimuli; influenced by needs, expectations, etc.)	(selected stimuli are adapted by needs, expectations, etc.)	(interpretation of selected stimuli as shaped by individual)

Figure 3.1 *A basic perception model*

Perception Process of becoming aware of and interpreting stimuli

Take a look at Figure 3.1 for a glimpse of the process. **Perception** is the process of becoming aware of and interpreting stimuli. First you *sense* (see, smell, taste, touch, . . .) those stimuli. Then you unconsciously *select* one of those stimuli to attend to (for example, there are millions of light rays that bend to allow for numberless shades of colors, but what do you see? That bright red shirt over yonder). Having unconsciously acknowledged a stimulus, your mind starts to *shape* it into something you can understand and, finally, to see some *meaning* in your perception.

Let's examine each step separately and identify ways you can verify the accuracy of your perceptions as a communicator.

Sensing

Sensory fatigue State in which senses become tired while processing stimuli

Humans experience the external world through their five senses: hearing, seeing, smelling, touching, and tasting. The senses are essential to communication because they serve as the receptors for cues available within the environment. Yet people often miss important cues (such as a chunk of the professor's fascinating lecture!). Why? The senses tend to tire quickly from too many or too much repetition of stimuli, experiencing **sensory fatigue.** When they do, attention declines. Figure 3.2 demonstrates how this works.

Figure 3.2 *A demonstration of sensory fatigue*

Stare directly at the heart's center for 20 seconds. Then look at a plain white background until an image appears. What do you see? Has the heart appeared on the plain white field? What color is it?

After staring for just 20 seconds at the heart against its white background, your sight receptors have fatigued. When you shift your gaze to the plain white background, you see the heart's color has changed. You perceive the new shade because your sensitivity has been dulled to the original color. Because white reflects all colors, you now only see what is left after the original heart's color is removed.

The same fatigue happens to the other senses. Have you ever walked into a room that had a strong odor but found, to your relief, that the smell disappeared quickly? The odor did not diminish; rather, your sensitivity to it decreased.

Why does a communicator need to know that? Because in communication, too, a repetitive stimulus such as monotone speaking or a speaker standing motionless dulls the receivers' attention. Message senders, then, need to find ways to keep listeners' senses acute; listeners need to find ways to offset their sensory fatigue.

Selecting

At any given time, your senses are bombarded with an infinite number of external stimuli. You cannot respond to every stimulus that reaches your sensory receptors—you would be so overloaded you might go berserk. What you do, therefore, is pay **selective attention,** focusing on "one detail so much you do not notice other events . . . " (Plotnik, 1999, p. 565).

Selective attention
Process of focusing on one detail and not noticing others

Look at Figure 3.3. Do you see a dog? Bird? Rabbit? Bell? They're all there. Knowing that, can you see them all now? Can you see them all at once? Really, your eyes shift quickly back and forth, focusing on one and then on the other, excluding the others for that moment. Selecting a stimulus is like tuning a radio; when you set it for one station, you don't receive what's being transmitted on all the others. To be confident of your perceptions, you need to "tune in" or select essential message cues.

Figure 3.3 *What do you see?*

Shaping

Once you focus on a specific stimulus, you may shape the cue to suit yourself. That is, an incoming stimulus goes through personal filters or screens that you have developed from your individual experiences. With personal **shaping,** you may perceive a stimulus very differently than it actually is.

Shaping Perceiving a stimulus through personal filters or screens

Remember Play-doh, the claylike substance for kids? You can put it into the Play-doh Factory, a small device on which you place a template in the shape of a crescent, a star, and so on. Then you press the Play-doh through, so the material comes out in the template's form. That's a simplified form of what you do when you process message stimuli. You receive verbal and nonverbal cues; then you reshape them through the "templates" that you have created from your background and experience.

Look at Figure 3.4 and read the message aloud. Look at it again. Most people see only one *the* when they look at this for the first time, but it really says *the* twice: "Faces in the *the* Crowd." That's because people expect to see only one *the*—rarely does English include two *the*'s in a row. In perception, people may shape stimuli to conform to what they expect, need, or want to perceive.

Creating Meaning

After you select and shape stimuli, your knowledge and experiences affect how you decode the message and what it means to you. Unconsciously, you sort through your memories to find how they relate to the present stimulus. What you find could lead you to understand something close to what the sender intended, or to believe the message means something you can't identify, or even to have a meaning almost opposite to the speaker's intent.

Figure 3.4 *What do you read?*

Someone says to you, for instance, "That's a great new haircut!" Depending on your past experience with that person, his or her nonverbal cues, and how you happen to feel about your appearance at the moment, you might think that's a nice compliment—or an implication that anything's better than your last haircut, which looked like a haystack.

Look at the *Peanuts* cartoon on p. 58. The meanings Linus decodes from the clouds differ significantly from Charlie Brown's. Linus could not perceive Thomas Eakins or the stoning of Stephen, however, if he had never learned about them. One reason colleges usually require a range of introductory courses is to provide students with broad frames of reference from which to interpret their worlds.

The meaning you draw from any stimulus, then, is directed by your experiences. Consider the points of view of three different baseball umpires. Miguel says, "Some are balls and some are strikes, and I call 'em the way they are." He believes his perception and reality are one and the same. Yoshi says, "Some are balls and some are strikes, and I call 'em the way I see 'em." He knows that perception and reality are not always the same. But the legendary umpire Bill Clem showed the best understanding of perception when he said, "Some are balls and some are strikes, but they ain't nothin' 'til I call 'em."

Nobody sees a flower—really—it is so small we haven't time—and to see takes time like to have a friend takes time.

Georgia O'Keeffe, 20th-century U.S. artist

Factors Affecting Perception

You see somebody as friendly; your friend Peggy perceives her as hostile. You both think you're right because each of you is influenced by a wide range of personal characteristics. How you "see" something may be the result of your physical and psychological states; your beliefs, attitudes, and values; your culture and gender; your motivations; and/or your goals and expectations.

Physical and Psychological States

Have you ever felt your senses were dulled temporarily, perhaps by exhaustion from studying for an exam all night or from a severe cold? What happens then? You may have trouble separating and recognizing concepts or perceiving stimuli accurately. Or, a person's perception may be blocked by a physical

Reprinted by permission of UFS, Inc.

condition such as hearing or vision loss. Sometimes that leads to *using* other senses more efficiently. A person with hearing impairment may read lips, interpret nonverbal cues, and communicate in sign language, or someone who is vision impaired may listen intently for nuances of meaning.

Psychological factors also can get in the way of perception. A person who is very anxious may be unable to listen and comprehend (Fitch-Hauser, Barker, & Hughes, 1990), fearing, perhaps, that the new information will be too difficult to understand. In fact, people who are apprehensive about listening often perceive themselves as incompetent and the message as too complicated and difficult. This leads them to process poorly what they hear (Preiss & Wheeless, 1989).

Beliefs, Attitudes, and Values

Your beliefs, attitudes, and values—which are closely related, but quite distinct—form screens that shape your perceptions and influence interpretations:

- A *belief* is something we think is true because of our experience or learning (Baum, Fisher, & Singer, 1985, p. 54). Beliefs may be about any object (Asia is the world's largest continent), past event (World War II ended in 1945), and/or future occurrence (the Red Sox will never win the World Series). Right or wrong, your belief does influence new perceptions.

- An *attitude* is a way you evaluate and act toward something, favorably or unfavorably (Eagly & Chaiken, 1993, p. 1). These positive or negative responses affect your interpretations of new objects and ideas.

- A *value* is part of a cluster of related attitudes and beliefs, providing priorities for your choices on the basis of what you think is good or bad, right or wrong, worse or better (Johannesen, 1996, p.1). Values dwell in a person's deepest self, a core of important concepts that deeply influence his or her perceptions and judgments.

Beliefs, attitudes, and values may all be closely related, but they may also be different. A student may value education very highly, but believe herself to be incompetent, a belief that would make her perceive classes as too difficult. That might be reflected in a negative attitude toward attending class. Her professors might interpret that behavior as meaning she doesn't value her education. But, if her belief about herself changes through some good experiences, her perception of (and attitude toward) her classes might also change, so that belief, attitude, and value would converge to make her perceive her educational experience favorably.

Culture and Gender

Culture Systems of beliefs, values, customs, behaviors, and artifacts shared within a society

Gender How one sees oneself in relation to society, sex, and roles

What is a culture, anyway? Samovar, Porter, and Stefani (1998) remark that there are hundreds of definitions, but they boil **culture** down to "a system of shared beliefs, values, customs, behaviors and artifacts that the members of a society use to cope with their world and with one another . . ." (p. 36). Essentially, your culture structures how you see things.

So does your gender; but gender doesn't just mean whether you are male or female. Wood (2001) says **gender** is a "social, symbolic creation" (p. 22), one acquired through experience, time, and cultural development. Gender, therefore, is the way you see yourself and others in relation to society, sex, and roles.

Tannen (1990) even suggests that gender is a culture in itself: "If adults learn their ways of speaking as children growing up in separate social worlds of peers, then conversation between women and men is cross-cultural communication. Although each style is valid on its own terms, misunderstandings arise because the styles are different" (p. 47).

We know that deeply held values often come from cultural and gender experiences. Hall (1976) tells us, "One of the functions of culture is to provide a highly selective screen . . . [that] designates what we pay attention to and what we ignore" (p. 74). The greater the diversity of those involved in the communication, the more complex are the transactions among their screens and memories as they shape stimuli and create meanings.

Language

If you know a word for an idea or object, you might perceive it. If you don't have a word for it, you might not. If the word you have for an object is slanted or loaded in some way, you might perceive the object in a distorted or prejudiced manner. Just think of the implications of that statement. If you grew up in a household where members of another race were referred to with a nasty term, you might perceive every member of that race negatively—only because of the attitude conveyed through that language.

It's also interesting, we think, that the words available in a person's language may affect his or her ability to perceive distinctions among items. There have long been theories that within a culture people develop words to make fine distinctions among concepts that are important to them (Whorf, 1964).

Time is a good example of the relationship between language and perception. Many tribal languages depict time differently from English, reflecting a difference in how people actually respond to the passage of time. (The Sioux, for example, do not have words for expressing past and future tense (Dodd, 1991, p. 125), while the Hopi view time as a psychological concept, not as an external period of hours or days (Whorf, 1964).

One of our students from Uganda tried to explain to us that in his tribal culture, which had no concept of hours, friends might agree to meet at a path into the village "the next day," with no set time appointment. Both individuals would get there, and neither would be late or early. How could that be? He finally got us time-obsessive North Americans to see that without a set hour, the friends had no basis to *perceive* "early" or "late." The one who got there first simply waited until the other arrived.

Motivation

"I'm just not motivated," your little sister says as she stares blankly at the textbook, unable to perceive anything she needs to learn for her exam. You shake your head and keep on studying, knowing you would be humiliated if you flunked the test in your class. Why are you motivated and she is not?

Perhaps you have drives or needs that are different from your sister's, so your responses are different, too. A *motive* is a reason, a drive, perhaps a need, that spurs individuals to move in some direction, so motives also influence an individual's perceptions and actions. To communicate successfully means to appeal to others' motives as well as to understand your own.

There are a multitude of theories about what motivates people. Some useful ones for understanding perception in communication are:

Hierarchy of needs
Ascending levels of need, each of which must be fulfilled before next level can be achieved

- A *hierarchy of needs.* Maslow's **hierarchy of needs** theory is old (1970), but very useful. In Figure 3.5, you'll see ascending levels suggesting that people must fulfill each level of need comfortably before they can be concerned with the next level. The first rung is, of course, physiological needs. The second rung is needs for safety and security, preceding a third need for

Figure 3.5
Maslow's hierarchy of needs

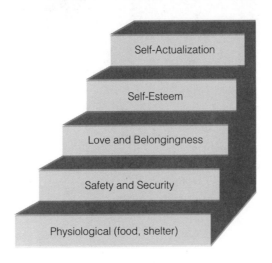

Self-Actualization

Self-Esteem

Love and Belongingness

Safety and Security

Physiological (food, shelter)

social fulfillment or love and belongingness. Once an individual feels a sense of being fulfilled here, she or he can move ahead to feeling a need for self-esteem; once self-esteem is adequate, then a person can climb toward what Maslow called "self-actualization," seeking fulfillment in personal intellectual, artistic, or spiritual growth. Understanding that people's awareness of their needs may ascend level by level provides insight into how best to communicate with them. For example, you might think that simply offering to tutor your younger sister in math will appeal to her—after all, you can help her improve her grades. Ah, but if she is at that all-consuming teen-aged level of social needs, math success might not be nearly as motivating as social success. You might assume she'll perceive your offer as a good one when, in fact, she might perceive it as offering to interfere in time with her friends. Your offer might appeal more if you present tutoring as a way to free her for more social time in the future.

Social exchange theory
Choosing an action based on the weighing of rewards and costs

■ *Social exchange needs.* Kelley and Thibaut's (1978) **social exchange theory** explains how people perceive communication as an opportunity to reap rewards or to avoid costs or punishment. The theory suggests that when people weigh their options, they predict the results of a choice. They consider if the rewards will outweigh the costs, how that result will compare to what they minimally will accept, and how the result would compare to other possible choices. Think of it this way: Little sister might compare spending evenings with you improving her math grades to spending the evening with friends and finds tutoring unattractive. But if she then weighs this decision against the probability she won't be allowed to go out at all if she doesn't improve her grades—well, then, her motivation still is social, but the cost-benefit analysis begins to make your tutoring offer look pretty good.

Consistency needs
Striving to maintain balance among attitudes, beliefs, values, behaviors that motivates people to choose among conflicting information

■ *Consistency needs.* Festinger's (1957) cognitive dissonance theory notes **consistency needs,** and suggests that people need to feel consistency

Someone asks:

Would you like to do so-and-so? A picture forms in my mind and as I look at it, it is either appealing or unappealing and I say yes I would or no I wouldn't. But this picture is not precognitive, it is a composite of past experiences that will be more or less unlike the coming event.

Hugh Prather, 20th-century pilosopher, in *Notes to myself* (1990), New York: Bantam.

among their attitudes, beliefs, values, and/or behaviors. If people are conscious of inconsistencies, they feel a dissonance—a kind of tension—between the two cognitions. When the tension becomes great, they are motivated to reduce it in some way. For example, your friend's grandfather is in a nursing home, and Grandpa's lonely. His grandkids love him (Cognition 1), but they don't visit him often (Cognition 2). These two cognitions are dissonant, and that dissonance makes the grandchildren feel uncomfortable, perhaps guilty. According to the theory, they will be motivated to choose among these options: Change Cognition 1 and stop loving Grandpa—not likely; Change Cognition 2 and go see Grandpa more often. If they actually do it, fine. If they don't, their choices are to avoid negative information or seek positive information—perhaps by avoiding anything that reminds them of lonely old folks in nursing homes and/or eagerly listening for reports that other people are giving Grandpa plenty of company. These are unconscious ways of rationalizing or manipulating one's own perceptions to relieve that feeling of dissonance that comes from knowing your actions are in conflict with your values.

Ways to Check Perceptions

Like everyone else, you only "see in part," so it's necessary to check your perceptions and interpretations. A way to do this is by using the following techniques to acquire more information and to build a wider field of view:

- *Ask other people.* Compare your observations and interpretations with others. Look for similarities and differences. Rely on multiple senses. Does what you see support what you hear? Are there contradictions? You may see a sweater that looks soft, for example, only to touch it and find it's scratchy.

- *Observe again.* When possible, repeat the observations. Review the scene, watch a video replay, or observe the situation from a different angle. Good science tries to reproduce research results to ensure accurate conclusions; this is a good habit for everyday life, too.

- *Consider possible misinterpretations.* How might your perceptions have led you astray? Did something in your background or expectations influence your interpretations?

- *Consider possible changes.* Just because something was true once doesn't mean it will be again. Perceptions can be made more accurate by "dating" events; if you say, for example, "When we went to Grant Park in spring of 1993, it was great," your statement doesn't set up a perception that it's still great today. Maybe it is, maybe it isn't.

- *Examine generalizations.* Watch your perceptions for generalizations, and mentally "index" thoughts with characteristics relevant to the situation. Consider this statement: "*As a teacher*, John is outstanding." John may be a dolt as an auto mechanic, so indexing acknowledges that John the teacher may differ from John the mechanic (or the cook or the writer or . . .).

- *Assume there's more.* Consider your perceptions and your statements about them to be incomplete. Mentally or verbally add, "etc." to acknowledge the probable existence of other unnoticed or unstated attributes.

The Process of Critical Thinking

There is enormous personal power in the ability to think clearly and analytically. Can you do it? Of course you can, if you are disposed to do so and if you develop the skills. When you do, you will be more confident in yourself and more credible to others. In fact, these abilities are so important that the National Education Goals Panel (1991) declared the prime objective for colleges is *to increase the proportion of graduates "who demonstrate an advanced ability to think critically, communicate effectively, and solve problems"* (p. 237).

When you think critically, you are thinking about thinking; you are analyzing the processes by which you or someone else arrived at a conclusion. **Critical thinking** is a lot like perception, but it is deliberate analysis rather than unconscious response. You perceive—then you analyze the data, the reasoning, and the validity of conclusions. That is, in thinking critically you're analyzing complex ideas and to what extent their connections to data and to one another are valid. Such thinking involves more judgment, analysis, and synthesis than the memorized or mechanical approach you might use for a simple task (Halpern, 1994, p. 29). For example, you can remember and repeat a joke without much thought, but if you analyze it to see if it might offend a specific audience, or if you give it a new twist to amuse yet another audience, you're using the higher-order skills of critical thinking.

Unfortunately, people often make mistakes just because they are not disposed to think critically. Good thinking depends on more than ability; it

Critical thinking
Deliberate analysis of data, reasoning, and conclusions

requires the disposition—the inclination, willingness, or motivation—to do it. For example, even though a basic skill in good thinking is being able to see more than one side of an argument, researchers have found that most people who have this ability don't use it unless specifically asked to do so (Perkins, Jay, & Tishman, 1994, p. 68).

The point is, you need both the disposition and the ability to use your higher-order skills—first to want to think and then to think well. Good thinking includes:

> *Thinking in a broad and adventurous way; Sustaining intellectual curiosity; Thinking across multiple contexts and perspectives; Building knowledge and understandings; Being intellectually careful and clear; Seeking truth and evidence; Being analytical and strategic.* (Perkins, Jay, & Tishman, 1994, p. 73)

We've paraphrased some descriptions of specific types of critical thinking from Perkins et al. (1994; 1992) to show how you can apply these abilities to build your confidence and enhance your credibility as a communicator.

In *problem solving* you think of strategies to plan approaches, achieve communication goals, and monitor your progress and your communication.

In *decision making* you think of alternative approaches, review them objectively, and wisely choose the way you phrase and support messages for specific audiences and situations.

In *justification* you think of multiple viewpoints, distinguish between different frames of reference, and use good evidence and arguments to present and analyze ideas objectively and competently.

In *explanation* you think of interpretations and ideas, use supporting evidence, build and adapt explanations, and logically connect reasons to conclusions.

In *design* you think of ways to structure messages that adapt to goals, organize the parts strategically in relation to one another, and consider alternative approaches.

Idea Logic

We—Don and Gay—have always enjoyed critical thinking because it's like playing with ideas or doing a puzzle, examining what goes into ideas, what makes them good, what makes them bad. Critical thinking involves looking at the data, the reasoning, and the validity of drawing a conclusion. When you learn to use these analytical tools, you become more astute both as a listener and as a communicator whose messages are logical, credible, ethical, and appropriate to your goals. Let's examine the tools of critical thinking one at a time.

Starting with Data   A professor of ours once explained his exams (they were fiendishly specific) this way: "You all think you can think—but you can't think without *facts*. So I want you to tell me facts." He had it exactly right. Thinking starts with data.

If your information is inadequate, so will be your conclusions—no matter how well you think. So the first step is to evaluate the source of information by asking:

- *Is the source primary or secondary?* A primary source is the newspaper, book, article, speech, or person that originally presented the statement. Getting information directly from the original source doesn't guarantee truthfulness or accuracy of the data, but it does tell you the information is precisely as it was originally stated. In a secondary source, someone has summarized, paraphrased, or quoted material from other sources. Thus, secondary source information may be interpreted differently than the original source intended.

- *Is the source qualified?* Does the individual have expertise on the subject? Are his or her academic degrees, experience, and training sufficient? Are the qualifications relevant to the specific issue in question?

- *Is the source reputable?* Is the person acknowledged and respected by other experts in the field? Do other experts refer to or quote the source?

- *Is the source ethical?* Is she or he honest, known to be objective and fair-minded? Does the source have the best interests of the audience in mind?

If sources don't live up to these standards, you should be skeptical of their credibility. As a source yourself, applying these criteria to your *own* habits will tell you how credibly and ethically you are handling the information you give to others.

Understanding Reasoning   We've noted that when you perceive something you make an inference about it. The expression "leaping to conclusions" is apt, because an inference is a mental leap. Critical thinking helps you determine if your "leaps" will land you on solid ground.

To test your reasoning, you have to examine each part of the process. We have diagrammed this process in Figure 3.6 (Toulmin, 1958). As the figure shows, reasoning starts with *data*. Data may be anything that stimulates an inference—a personal observation, a statistic, a quotation. Often, data are the evidence with which you prove your point to a receiver. From that data, you make an *inference*. The broken line linking the data to the claim/conclusion indicates that the inference may be unconscious, so critically analyzing an inference may mean finding an unstated connection of which a person may be unaware. The inference leads to a *claim*, a conclusion that might involve a judgment of some kind. Consciously or unconsciously, you have a *warrant*—a rationale for connecting your data to your conclusion. For example, Sarita says that ice cream is good for people (data), so you decide to have ice cream for lunch. Your rationale (probably unconscious) is that the ice cream will be good for you—or maybe you just want ice cream and Sarita has given you an excuse. Is Sarita credible? Is she correct? And if that wonderful food is good for people

Figure 3.6 *Diagram of an argument from data through reason/inference to conclusion*

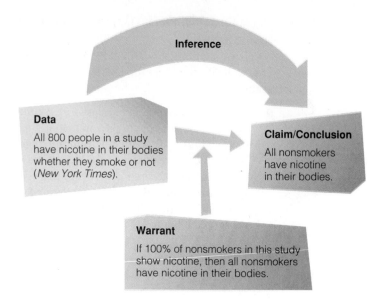

Inference

Data

All 800 people in a study have nicotine in their bodies whether they smoke or not (*New York Times*).

Claim/Conclusion

All nonsmokers have nicotine in their bodies.

Warrant

If 100% of nonsmokers in this study show nicotine, then all nonsmokers have nicotine in their bodies.

in general, is it good for you in particular? And if it is, are there other issues in making this decision that you haven't considered?

When you draw a conclusion based on reasoning from data or evidence, you've created an argument for your conclusion. But is it a good argument? Competent and credible communicators use critical thinking to analyze and evaluate relationships among the data, the warrant, and the conclusion to determine an argument's quality. *Good* arguments are building blocks for effective messages, whereas *bad* arguments are a jumble of invalid, untruthful, or unacceptable ideas.

Logicians have made it easier to evaluate an argument with their analyses of types of reasoning. We'll look at inductive, deductive, and cause–effect reasoning, as well as combinations of these types. To better understand these approaches to thinking, we'll examine how each might be used to reason from these data reported in the *New York Times* (1993):

> The first 800 people in a Federal study of exposure to tobacco smoke had signs of nicotine in their bodies whether they smoked or not. (p. A10L)

Inductive reasoning
Drawing a general conclusion from specific cases

Inductive reasoning. You're using **inductive reasoning** when you draw a general conclusion from specific cases. In this instance, from the 800 specific cases of people who showed signs of nicotine you *might* draw the general conclusion that all people must have signs of nicotine in their bodies. Would that conclusion be valid? To find out, you can ask:

- *Are there enough cases in the sample to justify a conclusion?* Are 800 cases sufficient to generalize to all people?

- *Do the cases represent the same population as that to which the generalization will apply?* Or, did all 800 come from one region? Were they in a similar group in terms of age, sex, race, socioeconomic status, and so on? If so, they were not representative of "all people."
- *Are there exceptions to the general conclusion?* Have any people been found without nicotine traces? In this case, earlier studies did show some people without nicotine traces.
- *Can the exceptions be accounted for without weakening the conclusion?* Perhaps the earlier studies were done so long ago that conditions may have changed.

Analyzing these questions may lead you to reject the generalized conclusion as improbable or to limit it as "possibly" true for people in the region of the study or for people similar to them rather than for "all" people.

You've often heard advocates on each side of a controversial issue use statistics to support contradicting generalizations. As a critical thinker, you would look carefully at their sources for their statistics, whether they actually support the speakers' generalizations, and whether they outweigh the evidence on the other side.

Deductive reasoning. What if you start with a generalization and move to a conclusion about a specific instance? That's **deductive reasoning.** For example:

Deductive reasoning
Drawing a conclusion about a specific case from a generalization

All 800 people in the study have nicotine in their systems.

Paul was examined in that study.

Therefore, Paul has nicotine in his system.

Questions you can ask to test deductive reasoning include:

- *Is the generalization accurate?* Yes, because it limits the generalization to those who were examined.
- *Is this specific case the same as the ones encompassed by the generalization?* Yes, Paul was one of the 800.
- *Is this specific case different in some way that makes it unlikely to fit the generalization?* No, Paul was part of the tested group.

That reasoning is okay. But what if the generalization is changed?
Most people living in the northeastern United States have nicotine in their bodies.

Paul lives in the United States.

Therefore, Paul has nicotine in his body.

Now apply the questions for examining deductive reasoning. Do you have good evidence that *most* people have nicotine traces? Does Paul live in the Northeast? Even if you can answer yes to both these questions, do you know whether Paul falls into the "most people" category, or is he one of the minority who does not have nicotine traces?

Deductive reasoning can be invalid, and, because people often blindly accept the general statement as true, it can be tricky. Much advertising counts on automatic acceptance of questionable generalizations that may not even be stated. For example, a commercial tells you that Tantalizing Toothpaste will make your smile brighter and shows a sad-faced loner transformed into the life of the party after brushing. There are two unspoken generalizations: that the product will make any user's smile brighter and that all people with bright smiles have exciting social lives. Both generalizations are untrue, so the reasoning is both invalid and untrue.

Combined reasoning. Usually, the reasoning people use combines deductive and inductive reasoning, often incorporating other types of reasoning as well. One of the most common is cause-and-effect reasoning, in which people believe one event caused another because one event occurred after the other one.

Look at the combination of reasoning methods you might use to conclude that you will take a communication class. A friend tells you her communication class helped her make better grades in other classes. She's using **cause-and-effect** reasoning. Other friends tell you the communication class was interesting. You generalize from those cases that communication is always a good class. That's *inductive* reasoning. Because you believe communication is a good class, you conclude that you, specifically, will like the class, too. That's *deductive* reasoning.

Is your combined reasoning valid? To find out, you can ask:

- *Do you have sufficient examples?* Your friend is just one example.
- *Has the "effect" been preceded by the same suggested "cause" every time, or are there exceptions?* Did other students like the class? Every single one?
- *Did the suggested "cause" happen concurrently with other events that could be alternative "causes"?* Could your friend just like the teacher a lot?
- *Do other "causes" or multiple causes seem more probable?* Did she like the teacher, like the subject, win prizes at speech competitions, admire good speakers?

Qualifying Conclusions Very few conclusions are absolutely certain, so you try to determine just how *probable* the claim is. This may be difficult to figure out if a communicator has left parts of the argument unstated or exaggerated the conclusions. You may have to guess what is not stated as well as to analyze what is said.

As you examine the argument, you may doubt some of the data, rationale, or claim. If you're the speaker, you are ethically obliged to qualify any areas of which you are unsure, perhaps by explaining or supporting the source, data, or rationale, and by using terms such as *perhaps, possibly, probably,* or *almost certainly* to indicate how probable the conclusion is. As you see, each qualifier

Cause-and-effect reasoning Drawing the conclusion that one event is responsible for the occurrence of another

I f truth, rather than defense of one's erroneous beliefs, is made the ideal, then being shown you're wrong is a joy. It is a thrill to realize that now you're in possession of the facts, whereas previously you were mistaken in what you thought was the case.

Gloria J. Leitner, poet and writer, in A legacy from parent to child, *The Humanist*, March–April, 1997, p. 43.

implies a different degree of certainty. If there is a lot of credible evidence and the reasoning is strong, you may be justified in saying the claim is "almost certainly" or "very probably" true. If evidence is slight or the reasoning is shaky, your claim just might be "possibly" true.

The Process of Planning Messages

It may seem to be a lot of work to develop accurate perception and critical thinking habits, but it is well worth it. These skills will make you more confident as well as more credible to others. It's a matter of planning messages that attend to your listeners' perceptions and their sense of logic.

Consider Audience Perceptions

Earlier in this chapter we talked about how people perceive and think. Getting others to understand and accept what you say is all about engaging their personal perceptions by adapting to them, stimulating their attention, choosing language, and organizing ideas in ways that help them understand and accept what you say.

Adapt to Receivers　A message misses the mark if it isn't adapted to the listeners, so you need to know everything you can about them. First, what do they know about the topic? How much background detail do you need to provide? If listeners are highly informed, you can enter the dialogue at a different point than if they have little or no information.

Besides knowledge, however, you need to examine what goes into your listeners' perceptions; the motivations, attitudes, values, beliefs, needs that drive them; the ways that their culture and gender affect them. That is, everything we talked about as part of perception will affect the way your audience hears and responds to your message. Given these insights into your audience, you can make intelligent choices in planning what you say and how you say it.

Choose Appropriate Language   A long time ago, Aristotle observed that language choices should fit the speaker, the situation, and the listener. That means:

- *Use understandable language.* Don't talk down, don't talk up—just talk *with* people. Consider their age, education, and experience as well as their personal values, beliefs, attitudes. Usually, it's best to avoid words that might be unclear to the listeners, but some topics involve specialized terms or jargon. When you introduce new words, be sure to define them.

- *Avoid sexist terms.* Sexist language excludes people, so gender-specific language should be used only when the distinction is important to the message. For example, using only masculine pronouns (*he, him, his*) implies the subject is male, even if that's not your intention. Similarly, words you use may imply a sexist judgment of a person. Even though most of our students tells us there is little difference between the words *lady* and *woman*, when we ask who is most likely to become the manager of a major corporation, a "lady" or a "woman," the same students express a strong preference for a "woman." These responses are based on unconscious stereotypes, so it's best to avoid even seemingly innocuous sexism.

- *Create word pictures.* Words can create a mental picture that intensifies the receiver's perception. You can rouse sensations of seeing, feeling, hearing, smelling, or tasting by describing vividly what an object or an experience is or how it functions. "The child looked sad" is not as vivid as "The child's huge, dark eyes welled with tears, and one ran slowly down her cheek."

- *Tell stories.* Stories can be marvelously personal and real to listeners. You can draw a story from anywhere—from your own or someone else's experience, from literature, or from your imagination. To craft a story into a tool for enhancing your messages, use this advice from a professional storyteller (Egan, 1986, p. 41): First, identify what's most important about your topic. Then find internal conflicts that create drama (good versus evil, poor versus rich, strong versus weak, ideal versus real). Now organize the content to develop with a feeling of drama. Select a conclusion that resolves conflict and punches home the point. Finally, find a way to get feedback that shows you if listeners understood. The most indifferent audience will suddenly become entranced!

Organize Ideas Clearly   Perception being what it is, it's easier for listeners to follow well-organized messages than random thoughts or long lists. In his classic study, Miller (1956) found that people can process only five to nine ideas at a time, with seven being the "magic number."

To illustrate, read the following line; then cover it up and repeat it out loud:

dog, red, four, two, blue, one, cat, horse, yellow, bird, green, three

Could you remember it all after one reading? The list has more than seven items, so most people would not recall all of them on the first try. Now look at them this way:

dog, cat, bird, horse

red, blue, yellow, green

one, two, three, four

It's easier to remember when similar items are grouped together. Miller (1956) calls this process "chunking" information. In the example, you have only three major chunks to remember; within each chunk, you have only four related items. Even though the list totals 12 items, it's easier to remember the chunks.

Your message will be easier to understand if you organize it this way:

1   Chunk your ideas in groups of related items.

2   Create no more than five major chunks in each message.

3   Include no more than five subgroupings or items in each major chunk.

4   Maintain a clear, identifiable, and logical relationship *among* all major chunks.

5   Maintain a clear, identifiable, and logical relationship among all items *within* any major chunk.

Provide a Framework   Just letting your listeners know where you're going and where you've been is amazingly helpful. All this takes is three simple steps: (1) *Preview* what you are going to talk about and maybe even what you are not going to talk about. (2) Use *transitions*; connect each aspect of the message to other parts with a word bridge (for example, "But not only do we need to do this for others; we also need to do it for ourselves"). And (3) *summarize* what you have said. A quick review of the key aspects of a message helps ensure a clear understanding.

For example, you might say to a salesperson, "I have two major concerns about a new car—price and safety [preview]. I absolutely cannot pay more than $17,500, but the safety features are just as important [transition]; I want air bags, antilock brakes, childproof locks, and a security alarm. So, let's see what you have available for less than $17,500, with those safety features [summary]."

Keep Attention   A very old joke has it that a farmer explained to a visitor that you have to train a mule with tender, loving care—but then he hit the mule with a stick. When the visitor looked puzzled at this contradiction, the farmer explained, "You have to get his attention first." As a communicator, you can't hit your audience with a stick, so you have to find more subtle ways to get and keep attention. Here are some important factors:

- *Movement, change, and contrast.* Audiences snap to attention when ideas, language, voice, body, and visual images juxtapose in contrasting ways. It may be in words and ideas, such as with John F. Kennedy's oft-quoted call, "Ask not what your country can do for you, but what you can do for your country." But contrast also is essential in varying voice, tone, pace, and inflection, and physical movement.

- *Intensity.* Intensity may be emotional, conveyed by a moving story or other information that touches receivers' passions. Intensity may also be in the loudness, brightness, or sometimes the repetitive impact of a message. In his stirring 1963 speech, Martin Luther King, Jr.'s reiteration of the phrase "I have a dream" created a repetitive vocal intensity that combined with the emotional intensity of each dream he expressed.

- *Familiarity.* Listeners attend to examples related to their experiences; for example, news broadcast viewers are likely to be drawn in by coverage of their school, town, or immediate neighborhood. Many speakers, entertainers, and politicians arrive at communities in advance, or send people ahead, to capture local tidbits to include in their presentations.

- *Humor.* Humor—when appropriate to you, to your listeners, and to your point—helps keep listeners focused on your message. Your humor should show your credibility as an outgoing, friendly, enthusiastic, positive, and open person who is sensitive to others' feelings (Booth-Butterfield & Booth-Butterfield, 1991, p. 206). You might use humorous short stories, exaggeration, facial expressions and body movements, quick responses to the unexpected, absurdity or irony, generalizations with obvious humorous intent, wordplay and puns—all these can be effective. It's absolutely essential, however, that your humor focus on what you want to accomplish in your message—irrelevant jokes can destroy your credibility and undermine your other objectives.

These concepts for getting attention apply in all communication contexts—even in one-to-one communication, sensory receptors begin to fade fast. The person who sits like a lump and drones on soon is left alone. Someone who is energetic and enthusiastic draws others' attention by making the conversation a lively, vivid experience.

Consider Audience Reasoning

"I'm no rocket scientist," someone may say, "but I know when something makes sense." People do have a sense of logic, and they like to have their intellect respected. It makes sense to make sense with logical messages.

Think of it this way. Imagine a map that shows a town in the northeast corner and another town in the middle of the map, but indicates no roads between them. How do you get from one town to the other? Ideas are like that—they need "roads" to connect them. Receivers may miss a speaker's reasoning because the message doesn't connect ideas. When that happens, the receiver may be confused and fill in the gaps with incorrect assumptions.

For example, suppose you are interviewing for a job as an accountant. You want to communicate your competence to the interviewer, so you say, "I have excellent qualifications for this position." That's a conclusion. You sound confident, which is good, but you need to provide data as evidence for your excellent qualifications.

You explain your data—accounting courses, relevant extracurricular activities, and previous job experience. Now the message becomes more complete, logical connections develop, and your credibility begins to emerge.

To be sure your interviewer sees exactly why your qualifications are good, you add the third element, the rationale, to explain why and how the data relate to the conclusion: "My courses, my activities, and my previous work experience [your data] have made me a very competent accountant. The position I'm applying for demands the kind of skills I have [your warrant], and I believe this makes me an ideal candidate for the job [your conclusion]." Hearing the three parts of your reasoning connected makes it easier for the interviewer to understand and accept your ideas.

Whatever the situation, imagine yourself as the uninformed or skeptical receiver of your message. What does that receiver need in order to form a reasoned, accurate judgment? Then plan the message that will give him or her that rationale.

Creating messages in this way ensures that you are logical, thorough, and ethical in your approach to your receivers and that they have a chance to truly understand—and accept—your ideas. This increases your confidence in your communication because you know you have a clear plan. Finally, it increases the listener's sense that you are credible, because you have demonstrated your competence, objectivity, and trustworthiness in creating a message that is complete and comprehensible.

Summary

When you receive or give a message, you start from an intrapersonal process of perception that unconsciously selects one stimulus from multitudes of available stimuli in your environment. You then attend to that stimulus and shape it into something you can recognize. From this mentally shaped stimulus, you create some meaning. The process is influenced by your physical and psychological states; beliefs, attitudes, and values; culture and gender; language; and motivations, including needs, beliefs, attitudes, and values. With all of these influences, your perception may be incomplete or inaccurate, so it's important to check perceptions carefully.

Just as people can be shaky in their perceptions, so they can be shaky in their logic. It is vital for a communicator to be a good critical thinker, evaluating the source and the data from which an argument is drawn, analyzing the rationale for a conclusion by looking at the type of reasoning (deductive, inductive, or cause-effect) that is used, and examining connections among these parts and to the claim that is drawn from them. Often arguments are incomplete, leaving out the rationale or the connections, and you must hypothesize what connections might be, analyzing their potential validity or invalidity for the claim. Because most arguments are based on the probability, not the absolute certainty, of a claim, analysis should recognize and state the degree of probability for a claim, using terms such as *possibly*, or *probably*, or *certainly* to indicate that probability.

Awareness of perceptual factors and skill in understanding and creating logical arguments are part of planning effective messages. You consider first the audience's perceptions, including the degree of knowledge they have about the topic, and then finds ways to adapt to those receivers, choosing appropriate language, organizing ideas into a limited number of clearly related chunks of five or fewer ideas, using variety and stimulation to gain and keep attention, and developing arguments that use good data, clear rationales, and reasonable qualifiers to draw valid and ethical claims.

Exercises

1 Observe a situation for a brief period of time (perhaps in a train station or the student center or at home). Then write three paragraphs about your observation. In the first paragraph, write only statements of observable fact. In the second paragraph, write only inferences that *could be* concluded from the fact. In the third paragraph, write only judgmental statements that *could be* made about what you observed and the inferences.

2 In a small group, create an optical illusion (such as the one in Figure 3.3). Your illusion can be two-dimensional or three-dimensional. You can use paper and pencil, or objects, or people. Be creative. Present your illusion to the class and explain what steps in the perception process are involved that make it difficult to perceive the illusion accurately.

3 Recall an occasion that resulted in two people misperceiving each other's messages. With a classmate, do the following:

   a   Analyze the factors—personal and/or message—that caused the misperceptions.

   b   Make notes about your analysis so you can refer back to them.

   c   Quickly work out a brief skit in which you demonstrate that misunderstanding.

d   Present the skit to the class.

e   Ask the class to identify what factors might have caused the misperceptions in your experience.

Relate the other students' analyses to your own. Explain what you and your partner thought were the perception issues; did the class see the same thing? Or were the other students' perceptions also influenced by factors that caused yet another set of perceptions? If so, what were they?

4   Select an abstract idea or concept from recent work in any class you are taking (such as democracy, socialism, existentialism, romanticism, probability, truth, and so on). Work out a way of defining and explaining that concept to the class, using the suggestions in this chapter for organizing and facilitating message perception with context, attention-getting approaches, and adaptation to your receivers. Time your definition to be no longer than 2 minutes, practice it, and present it to the class.

5   Select an advertisement or an editorial from a magazine or newspaper. Analyze the argument, examining the source and the data that are used, the rationale and the type of reasoning it involves, the qualifiers that are (or ought to be) used, and the claim that is made. Identify areas where a part of the argument is not stated, and hypothesize what it seems to be on the basis of the appeal that is made to audience perceptions. In what ways do you think the argument is valid? In what ways do you think it is invalid?

Now, rewrite the argument so it would be valid. Do you have to add qualifiers? Suggest more data? Write or rewrite the rationale? Rewrite the claim?

Cyberpoints

CCC

WEB SITE

1   Do you wonder how your brain works to do all these wonderful things? Go to the *Communicating with Credibility and Confidence* Web site at http://communication.wadsworth.com/lumsden and click on *Brainworks*. You might be fascinated with what goes on up there and how you can improve your use of your brain.

2   There's a whole other area of thinking that you can use: Creative thinking. Go to the *Communicating with Credibility and Confidence* Web site at http://communication.wadsworth.com/lumsden and click on *Creativity* for ways to understand and improve your creativity.

3   Do you want to improve your creative and critical thinking? Go to the *Communicating with Credibility and Confidence* Web site at

http://communication.wadsworth.com/lumsden and click on *Teasers* to stir up your brain.

 4 For more information, use *InfoTrac College Edition* to locate and examine periodical articles. For example, under the keyword *perception* you might take a look at:

Bower, B. (1998) Self-motion perception heads for home. *Science News, 154,* 324.

Gregory, R. (1998, Dec. 19) Snapshots from the decade of the brain: Brainy mind. *Clinical Review, 317,* 693–696.

Tomkiewicz, J., Brenner, O. C., and Adeyemi-Bello, T. (1998, February). The impact of perceptions and stereotypes on the managerial mobility of African Americans. *The Journal of Social Psychology, 138,* 88–93.

Chapter 4

Listening and Questioning: Negotiating Meanings

Jose Luis-Pelaez, Inc./CORBIS

Objectives for This Chapter

Knowledge

- Understand why and how listening and questioning are important to communication
- Identify barriers to good listening and questioning
- Recognize the qualities of good questions for various situations
- Understand goals and approaches for different types of listening and questioning

Feelings and Approaches

- Have confidence in using listening and questioning skills in various communication contexts
- Sense another's satisfaction in being listened to
- Value opportunities to be an empathic listener
- Feel credible in listening and questioning roles

Communication Abilities

- Convey credibility as a listener and questioner in interactions
- Overcome barriers to listening
- Listen actively in one-way communication situations
- Use listening and questioning interactively
- Use empathic listening and questioning in appropriate situations
- Listen and question collaboratively in dialogue

Key Terms

Have you ever heard a conversation like this one?

"Are you *listening to me*?"

"Of course I am . . ."

"What did I say, then?"

"Uh . . . you said . . . uh . . ."

"You see? You *weren't* listening!"

"Well, I've heard it all before."

Is this relationship in trouble?

Here's another conversation you may have heard—or had:

"I covered that," says the professor, "on Wednesday."

"Well," says the student, "I was here Wednesday."

"Then you must have heard my 40-minute lecture on that subject," says the professor.

"Yeah, but I didn't get it," says the student.

Is this student in trouble?

In the first conversation, two people may be torpedoing their relationship by failing to listen to each other. In the second, the professor assumes that "covering" the lecture material meant it was "heard." That isn't necessarily so. Researchers learned long ago that most people forget 50% of a speaker's information immediately, and half of the remaining information within 8 hours. Therefore, by Wednesday evening, this student—even with average listening—would have been lucky to remember 25% of what the lecturer said that morning (Nichols & Stevens, 1957). Twenty-five percent wouldn't be enough to pass the exam. Furthermore, our hapless student not only lost information needed for the test but also suffered damaged credibility with the professor—all due to inadequate listening and questioning skills.

In this chapter, we will examine how listening and questioning affect success in all aspects of your life, from your career to your personal relationships. We'll identify barriers that block effective dialogue, examine different types of listening and questioning, and explore ways that you can increase your effectiveness in dialogue.

Listening and Questioning for Your Future

Your success in life depends largely on your ability to communicate, which in turn relies greatly on your ability to listen and to ask the right questions effectively. Let's look first at why listening and questioning are important and at how these skills can enhance your professional and personal life.

Reasons for Listening and Questioning

There are many reasons for taking your time and energy to listen carefully to and ask questions of someone, such as:

- *Expanding or deepening knowledge.* You may want to get information, to increase your understanding of a concept or a person, or perhaps to assess a situation by listening and questioning to identify and analyze specific content.

- *Strengthening your confidence.* Often, you ask questions, listen intently, and confirm what you've heard to build confidence in your own knowledge or your ability to meet some goal.

- *Analyzing and evaluating information.* Listening and questioning perceptively allow you to analyze the assumptions, reasoning, and logical validity of what you hear.

- *Building your credibility.* When you listen carefully and ask perceptive questions, perhaps in an interview, at work, or in a group project, you show your coorientation with others and can indicate that you are trustworthy, objective, and competent.

- *Helping and supporting another.* You may put your own interests on hold and listen purely for the purpose of filling another person's need to be heard.

- *Building a relationship.* When you engage in dialogue with someone important to you, you have the opportunity to deepen your understandings of each other and strengthen bonds of trust and understanding between you.

Importance to Your Academic and Career Success

What do you do to succeed in classes? You read, of course, and do assignments—but from 55–70% of your classroom time is spent in listening (Floyd, 1985, pp. 2–15). You listen to the professor and ask questions; you work with other students in groups, listening and asking one another questions; you make presentations, listen to questions, and answer them; and you listen to others' presentations and ask questions. It's no surprise that students who listen well are more successful academically than those who do not, often even exceeding the level their standardized intelligence quotients would predict (Legge, 1971).

In the workplace, your dialogue skills are equally crucial. Most North American employees spend about 60% of their time listening to others (Brown, 1982), and the higher they rise the more they listen. Excellence in corporations is "built upon a bedrock of listening, trust and respect for the dignity *and* the creative potential of each person in the organization" (Austin & Peters, 1985, p. 5).

Effective managers are distinguished by their ability to empathize, to respond to others' concerns, to create an open atmosphere for speaking out, and to solicit ideas from subordinates (Redding, 1984); in fact, "effective leaders prove they are more than managers by willingly honing their listening skills" (Lucia, 1997). Eighty percent of executives responding to one survey rated listening as the most important skill in the workforce (Salopek, 1999), and more than 50% of Fortune 500 corporations who responded to another survey consider listening so crucial that they provide special training in it for their employees (Wolvin & Coakley, 1991).

Whatever your career, your listening skills may be critical to success. John, a former student of ours, is a graphic artist. John works at a computer, with the client watching over his shoulder and describing what she wants. John must listen attentively and ask precisely the right questions to transform the client's thoughts into graphic form. John's listening is the conduit through which a client's ideas and his own creativity can flow together; his questions direct and alter the process to achieve the results they both want. Because he is good at this process, John's credibility is so strong—both with his company and with his clients—that the most difficult and important accounts often are assigned to him.

Importance to Your Relationships

Of course, you don't need *everyone* to understand you deeply; many minor transactions need minimal interaction. Even in relatively impersonal relationships, however, listening counts. Who wants a dentist to drill a tooth before listening and confirming which one hurts and how much? In more personal relationships, dialogue is that much more important. People can make or break their relationships with the way they listen and question each other. Sometimes they don't even realize how important the following interactions can be:

- *Confirming one another's worth*. In building a relationship, you may offer an idea or a feeling tentatively, waiting to see how your partner reacts. **Confirming** occurs when the other person listens and asks questions that value you and your message—and this allows you to offer more of your thoughts or emotions in the dialogue.

- *Reducing risks*. When a person listens to you attentively and asks appropriate questions that help you to make yourself understood, you tend to trust that person, and that trust reduces your risk in communicating openly.

- *Building mutual support*. As you and another person listen carefully to each

Everything has been said before, but since nobody listens, we have to keep going back and beginning all over again.

Andre Gide. French Nobel Prize Winner for Literature

Confirming In dialogue, one person listens and asks questions that value the speaker and the message

Barbara Bocci, one of our students, shared this experience with us:

When my oldest son was just a toddler, he scolded me because I was busy making dinner while he was telling me about an incident at school. I assured him I *was* listening to him, but he argued, "You're not listening with your eyes."

A three-year-old taught me that each person wants to feel that he or she has our undivided attention. I began to set aside a few minutes before bedtime to spend personal one-on-one time with each child. Twenty years later they still remember our special sharing times.

other and exchange understanding, you weave a web of mutual support that encourages both of you to share more of your thoughts and feelings.

- *Developing shared meanings.* Through the process of dialogue and mutual support, you and another person are able to explore new and uncharted realms, learning more from each other and negotiating new meanings in your relationship.

Sadly, we have all seen relationships in which this kind of dialogue never happens. Sometimes, even people who have been married for years seem not to listen to or to know very little about each other. Their relationship is built on a shallow foundation and bounded tightly by windowless walls.

Listening Barriers

To err is human, they say. Unfortunately, even if forgivable, to err in listening is counterproductive and expensive. Workers who were surveyed about their supervisors, for example, rated the supervisors who had not received listening training as the worst listeners (Brownell, 1990). As for expense, Steil (1981) estimates that "with more than 100 million workers in this country, a simple $10 mistake by each of them as a result of poor listening adds up to a cost of more than a billion dollars," and he adds that most of us "make more than one listening mistake every day" (p. 2). Why? Although there can be many problems with the message, with transmission, or with a receiver's hearing loss, more often listening fails because of inadequate skill and/or mental blocks to listening.

Inadequate Skills

You may hear the stimulus but not listen to the message; listening and hearing are not the same thing. To *hear* is to receive a stimulus; to *listen* is to process information. Sometimes, people don't listen well because they have not learned how—or they have learned the wrong way.

Elgin (1989) notes that some people have had "nonlistening habits for so long that they are almost *incapable* of listening—if they had a listening gland, it would be atrophied from disuse" (p. 90). If you ask your friends, you'll find that few, if any, have had any formal training in listening. Although listening is the most used communication skill, it ranks last, after writing, reading, and speaking, in the amount of time spent on it in formal schooling. It's assumed that people "just know" how to listen. Not so.

Even worse, people often were trained as children to *turn off* their listening in order to avoid difficult situations. Consider statements that families make, such as, "We don't listen to those things in our family," or, "Don't pay any attention to him," or, "Pretend you don't notice" (Bolton, 1979, p. 176). Many adults already have established nonlistening habits that protect against risks from challenges, threats, or responsibilities. It's as if they believe that covering up their ears and humming will make the bad things go away, but instead the bad things just remain and grow.

True, everyone listens poorly sometimes. You've probably had moments when it was virtually impossible to concentrate on what a speaker was saying or when something blocked your ability to perceive clearly. The causes of those problems may rest in an inability to focus, in inadequate responses to the message content, or in emotional barriers. Let's look at some of these.

Focusing Problems   Often, students tell us that concentration is their biggest problem in listening. Concentration can be a problem for anyone for any number of reasons:

- *Disinterest in the topic.* If you're using self-talk such as "This is boring or uninteresting or irrelevant," or "I couldn't care less," it's sure to keep you from finding something to be interested in, and you probably will not hear a word the speaker says.

- *Distractions.* Cues from inside your own head or from external sources may keep you from listening. If you're thinking about your biology test next period or the attractive person who just walked by the door, you'll miss what the speaker said—and if you listen to someone else's gossip with one ear you will not hear the speaker with the other. People really can't hear two things at once.

- *Fake listening.* This approach is popular with the "wide-asleep listener," who nods brightly, looks directly at the speaker, and dreams on into oblivion. Unfortunately, the speaker may be fooled into believing the message is

As we look at the picture, we get the feeling that something special is happening. What kind of listening seems to be going on? How do you think the father and daughter feel? What about the picture shows you that feeling?

Elizabeth Crews/The Image Works

clear and fail to ask for feedback needed to ensure that everyone understands the ideas.

Content Responses   Sometimes people react to what they hear in ways that block their concentration and understanding. These reactions can take several forms.

- *Listening only to details.* You may miss the major concepts by focusing on small details. Some details might be important, but you need to get main points—the "broad brush strokes"—first. Think of details as the way the speaker supports or explains ideas. Otherwise, you may derail a conversation (or your lecture notes) on to a minor issue when there was a much more important point to discuss.

- *Assuming interpretations or details.* You may want to "fill in" what the person didn't say or what you didn't hear, but your fillers may be wrong. This is another reason questioning is such an important part of listening.

- *Zeroing in on one idea.* Once you focus on one specific point that you want to refute or support, everything else the speaker says is lost. You are mentally running circles around the idea, poking at it, obsessed with it.

- *Rehearsing responses.* If you're zeroing in on one point and mentally phrasing what you'll say in rebuttal, imagining yourself scoring points with your brilliance, you'll not hear another word. Moreover, by the time you have an opportunity to state your rebuttal, it often is obsolete.

- *Taking copious notes.* If the context is, say, an interview or a lecture, beware of writing down every preposition and article. Excessive notes can obscure the key ideas of a speaker's statement. If you're tempted to ask, "What did you say just after you said, 'and the'?" you'll know you aren't focused on the central ideas. Take notes on important information and fill in the supporting details later, if necessary.

Emotional Blocks   Listening is hard when the material challenges long-established beliefs or prejudices. That's why sometimes people erect any or all of the following barriers to listening.

Stereotyping or labeling. Sometimes people think they know what the speaker thinks or will say, because they have preconceived ideas about that person or his or her group. The individual may be different from those expectations, but how can you know if you've already decided what you'll hear?

Judging the messenger rather than the message.   Perhaps the speaker does something that distracts your attention from the message—but if you react emotionally to the speaker's manner, appearance, dialect, posture (or any number of other things), you are likely to miss the point.

Reacting to loaded words.   Everyone reacts to some personal "god" words or "devil" terms that can instantly divert their attention. Certain words may have positive or negative connotations that offend you or that trigger dreams and fantasies. In the 1980s, for example, some groups were attacking others by calling them "secular humanists," implying that they were for humans instead of for God. One day, Gay was talking about "being human" in her interpersonal communication class, and a student reacted angrily. After careful questioning and dialogue, she found that he had reacted to the word *human* as if it were synonymous with *secular humanist.* Deciding that Gay's politics were all wrong, he stopped listening too soon to hear the full statement. He had pushed the pause button when he heard one of his loaded words and hadn't heard the rest of the message.

Overload and anxiety.   Listening is difficult when you're overwhelmed by external and/or internal stimuli. Communication often occurs in groups or in environments that bombard individuals with concurrent messages. The more individuals are talking at once, the more messages you must attend to and process concurrently. One result can be **information overload,** in which you have more data than you can process and remember.

Even one-to-one communication can be difficult when there's too much to think about at once. "I've got too much on my mind" isn't just an excuse. Information overload is a genuine problem. When listeners are overloaded with information and uncertain about their listening skill, they often become apprehensive about how well they will understand or remember, and this anxiety interferes with their ability to listen to and comprehend new material (Beatty, 1981).

Listening and Questioning Approaches

It's easier to avoid the problems we've just discussed once you're aware of them, but an effective listener and questioner also adapts to different contexts and purposes. At times you'll want to listen actively, or interactively, or empathically, or collaboratively.

The beginning listener needs to learn the value of silence in freeing the speaker to think, feel, and express himself.

Robert Bolton, author and president of a communication consulting firm

Information overload
State in which listener has received more data than can be processed and remembered

Listening Actively

To some lectures or sermons you may listen without asking questions or commenting aloud, or you may listen to a friend without commenting or listen quietly to others in a group. In each case, you are silent—but listening actively. **Active listening** is a mental as well as a physical process in which you are "tuned in," engaged with the speaker, involved in shaping your understanding of the speaker's meaning. To listen actively, you need to commit yourself to a number of specific behaviors.

Active listening
Process in which listener focuses on and silently questions speaker's ideas to shape and understand the speaker's meaning

1   *Get set physically for listening.* Place yourself where you can see and respond to the speaker; use nonverbal cues such as leaning forward, maintaining eye contact, and nodding at appropriate times. This helps support the speaker, and it also helps you to concentrate.

2   *Screen out distractions.* Hang a mental sign that says, "Person at work. Do not disturb." If your mind does wander, pull it back quickly. If the distracting thought is compelling, make a quick mental note to remind yourself to follow it up later. This will free you to get back to full listening.

3   *Set aside stereotypes and assumptions.* Listening with an open mind won't necessarily change or undermine your beliefs, but it may give you new ideas and interpretations. Putting biases aside, at least temporarily, will permit you to listen and assess information objectively.

4   *Focus on main points, concepts, and evidence.* Don't be stopped by small details. If a detail worries you, make a quick mental note to clarify it later; then listen to what comes next.

Thought speed Time between the rate of human speech and the rate of listener's ability to process information

5   *Use thought speed for processing material.* **Thought speed** refers to the open time between the rate of human speech (125–175 words per minute) and the rate of listeners' ability to *process* information effectively (500–600 words per minute). You can use that open thought time to daydream or, far preferable, to process and analyze what you're hearing.

6   *Organize and key the information while you're listening.* Listeners may recall 70–90% of specific verbal and nonverbal cues when they receive well-organized messages, but when the speaker is disorganized, listeners lose a lot of data (Benoit & Benoit, 1991). Unfortunately, because speakers often do not organize their ideas, you may have to do it for them as you listen. Mentally connect ideas and "chunk" points into clear groups so the relationships make sense to you. Create analogies and metaphors, or connect ideas with familiar examples, to help you understand and remember.

7   *Analyze and respond to the information mentally.* This does not mean arguing silently with the speaker, but rather thinking of questions about the material, noting discrepancies for future analysis, noting the speaker's evidence and reasoning, and making connections that help clarify your understanding.

Listening and Questioning Interactively

Interactive listening and questioning Dialogue in which listener analyzes speaker's ideas and asks and answers questions

You'll note that active listening requires an involved mind and a physically attentive body, but no direct verbal interaction with the speaker. In most situations, however, you listen actively and, in addition, you interact. **Interactive listening and questioning** involves developing dialogue, cooperatively analyzing ideas, and asking and answering questions. As you listen, you identify questions, phrase them mentally, and select the right moment to ask them. Often, you follow up with another question to confirm your understanding of the speaker's answer. Generally, questions in interactive processes serve these four purposes:

1   *Clarify information.* You might ask, "Can we go over that point again, please? It's not clear to me," or, "Could you provide an example of how that would work?" or, "How would you define that concept?"

2   *Develop incomplete information.* Perhaps you'd ask, "How often does that happen?" or, "What is the effect of that?" or even, "Can you tell me more about that?"

3   *Foster critical thinking about information or ideas.* For example, you might inquire, "How should that information be interpreted?" or, "How does this information square with other data on the same subject?" or, "What is the rationale for this?" or, "Is this ethically defensible?"

4   *Examine the communication processes.* Especially in a group, you often need to ask, "Does anybody else have anything to say?" "How can we manage this conflict?" "Is this fair to everyone?"

Asking questions that will get clear answers isn't always easy. In fact, it's really an art, but you can do it with these guidelines and a genuine commitment to making communication a two-way dialogue:

■   *Know what you want to ask.* Be clear about what you're looking for. If you're not sure, say so; describe briefly what you're uncertain about and ask for clarification.

■   *Be as specific as possible.* Ask just what you need to know. If you must precede the question with an example, observation, or hypothesis, keep it clear, objective, and concise.

■   *Don't make speeches that pretend to be questions.* If you have a point to make, say so: "I don't have a question, but I do have something to say. . . ." Then say it.

■   *Ask one question at a time.* If you have a two-part question, preview it: "I have a two-part question. Part one is . . . part two is . . ." This helps the speaker to answer, and it keeps issues clear so you know if and how your question has been answered.

- *Confirm information with feedback questions.* If you think you understand but want to be sure, state briefly what you believe the speaker said and ask if it's correct. Confirming is an essential step before acting on messages that would result in investment of energy, time, or money.

- *Ask in ways that help the speaker answer.* "Could you please clarify that?" is too vague; the speaker may have to grope around to answer it. Good ways to help a speaker clarify a point include asking for examples or definitions, paraphrasing what you think the idea was, and giving your own examples or analogies and asking if they represent what the speaker said.

- *Listen to questions others ask.* Often, several people want to follow up on the same idea, so someone else may ask your questions. Don't repeat a question that has already been answered satisfactorily but, if you have a question that follows up, state the connection so the speaker understands what you want to know.

- *Probe for further information.* Ask (tactfully) for supporting evidence for a statement; probe for assumptions of facts or values that the speaker may have made; ask about ethical issues or dilemmas. This can be done with minimal defensiveness if you ask in a supportive, investigative spirit rather than an argumentative, competitive spirit.

- *Ask analytical questions.* As you listen, phrase questions that get to the logic of a statement, the rationale, the evidence. Examine the relationships among the data, warrant, and claim, and weigh the degree of probability that a speaker's conclusion is valid. Listen critically, and when it's appropriate to raise the questions aloud, focus them so the issues can be discussed and the speaker doesn't feel defensive.

- *Ask hard questions tactfully.* Don't turn the questioning process into a personal attack. Ask about underlying assumptions and values, about ethical issues, about credibility—but ask them in relation to information and issues, not to the speaker as a person.

- *Ask questions ethically.* Ask to learn the truth, to understand, and to clarify. Ask questions that support the communication process, rather than using questions to manipulate others, to distort information, or to score points.

Following these guidelines will help you get the information and insights you need from an interaction. Furthermore, your questions will support your own credibility by showing clearly your goodwill toward the persons involved and their ideas.

We regret to note that sometimes communicators use questions manipulatively, to lead the receiver to say or do something against the person's better judgment or wishes. Twenty-five hundred years ago, the Greeks distinguished between two kinds of questioning. One was "dialectic," designed to lead the participants to the truth through questioning, listening to, and answering one another. The second was "eristic," using questions to win a point by leading the receiver to reveal a weakness or concede a dispute.

To be an ally to a homeless person is very simple: Approach him with an open mind and listen to his story. Don't listen with the idea that he's a typical Terry the Tramp—listen to him as a person. And don't go to a bureaucrat for answers, ask a homeless person what he needs, and what he can do with your help.

Doug Castle

Doug Castle, a homeless man in Seattle, gets at the heart of Steven VanderStaay's *Street Lives: An Oral History of Homeless Americans.* Van-

derStaay . . . reminds us that it is the listener as well as the teller who causes the "story" to exist. His active listening and dialogue with a large and diverse cross-section of homeless Americans has allowed him (as listener/interviewer) and the homeless people (as tellers/interviewees) to mutually rewrite history.

From a review by Tom Montgomery-Fate of Steven VanderStaay (1992), *Street Lives: An Oral History of Homeless Americans*, New Society Publishers. In *Sojourners*, October 1992, pp. 43-44. Reprinted by permission of the publisher.

You often see eristic questioning used to put people on the defensive or to win a point. There's the television image of the attorney, for example, badgering and haranguing a witness in order to trick the individual into the appearance of guilt or to diminish the credibility of the testimony. This questioning approach does not lead to understanding, clarity, or truth; rather, it subverts the process. An ethical questioner listens carefully and asks questions in such a way as to arrive at the truth and to develop genuine dialogue.

Listening and Questioning Empathically

Empathic listening
Listening that focuses on the speaker's feelings

Empathy
Understanding the ideas and feelings of another person

Whereas active and interactive listening center on a speaker's information, **empathic listening** centers on the speaker's feelings. **Empathy** is understanding the ideas and feelings of another. It's different from sympathy, or feeling *for* a person; empathy is feeling *with* a person. The purpose of empathic listening is not to express your feelings, but to help others to express theirs. An empathic listener hears and reflects the feelings and ideas that seem to be behind the speaker's words. In that way, you hold a mirror up for the speaker, helping him or her to identify feelings and thoughts more clearly, to find personal insights from your reflection of what you hear and see. You merely provide the support and the empathy.

Lest you think listening with empathy is only what counselors do, you might be interested to know that in management, "actively listening to and empathizing with what other people have to say are two of the important qualities of leaders. . . . Leaders who possess these qualities have the potential to promote positive work relations, inspire trust and bolster their companies' bottom line" (Lucia, 1997, p. 1). Sometimes you listen empathically to a friend's troubles, but other times you listen empathically in situations such as working with a team, in discussing plans with your family, even in listening to a lecture to help you understand the speaker or to enable you to give appropriate, helpful feedback.

Suppose you want to listen with empathy to a person. Here are some ways to open the door (Bolton, 1979):

- A *description* of the other's nonverbal cues: For example, "You look bright and happy today!"

- An *invitation* to talk or to continue talking: For example, "Please go on," or, "Care to talk about it?"

- *Attentive silence:* Giving the other person time to consider whether and how she or he wants to talk.

- *Close attending:* Eye contact and posture demonstrating your interest. (p. 185)

As a person speaks, you need to develop your understanding *and* to communicate your empathy. Here are some ways to listen empathically and interactively at the same time:

1   *Tune in to the speaker.* Watch for nonverbal and verbal cues. Be aware of body posture, facial expressions, gestures, and voice as they convey emotion. Be sensitive to the ways the individual phrases ideas and to cues that indicate defensiveness or some other emotional response to your dialogue.

2   *Be tentative with your empathy.* One person can never know precisely what another is experiencing, so be careful about using phrases like "I know just how you feel." Let your caring, empathy, sensitivity, and intelligence make you aware that the speaker is feeling something. That gives you a basis for trying to understand and, possibly, an ability to share some part of that feeling.

3   *Be careful in communicating your empathy.* Emotional responses are complex, personal, and private. Even when you empathize intensely with others, their privacy deserves respect. Communicate togetherness with your eye contact, body posture, face, and voice, but don't push; be sensitive to the other's preferences. Some people can open up easily; others want your support but don't want to say too much. Showing that you are listening intently is the most important element.

4   *Question carefully to develop empathy.* With open, supportive questions, you can develop a shared base for mutual empathy. Ask tactful questions, and allow the other person to maintain a "comfort zone" from which to answer. Perhaps, for example, your friend reports angrily that the boss gave a raise to a much less competent worker. You might be assuming too much or allowing your friend too little room to answer if you say, "I'll bet you chewed him up in little pieces! You must have been so mad. . . . Were you furious?" A more

empathic and less pushy response might be, "Wow—tough situation. Do you want to talk about it?" Or, if you're sure he or she wants to talk about it, you might simply ask, "How do you feel?"

5   *Paraphrase.* In your own words, restate what you think the other person is saying and feeling. General statements such as, "You sound like that made you pretty angry," or "That must make you feel pretty good" work best. Be careful not to project your interpretations beyond the speaker's own statements, or detract from attention to his or her story by telling your own.

6   *Ask for feedback.* This will enable you to confirm or correct your impression. You also can ask for examples or explanations of the other person's feelings or ideas. In the proper context, you can share your own experiences to help bring together a shared empathy, but always keep the focus on the other's experience rather than your own.

7   *Be sensitive to "ism" issues.* These include sexism, racism, classism, and handicapism. No one should have to endure racist jokes, sexist statements, cultural or ethnic slurs, power plays, or comments that reflect negatively on an identity group, style, affiliation, or disability. People may not even recognize that such comments are offensive until they themselves are on the receiving end—until some comment touches a nerve. An empathic listener will be alert to others' responses to unintentional or intentional insults. That means more than just avoiding making insensitive remarks yourself. It may mean giving an empathic response that helps another deal with someone else's offensive comment or letting a speaker know that such messages aren't acceptable.

Listening and Questioning Collaboratively

At its best, communication is a collaborative process—**collaborative listening and questioning** proceed when the speaker and the listener work as a team to develop a shared understanding. Such an effort draws on all your skills of active, interactive, and empathic listening—and more.

Stewart and Thomas (1990) talk about a similar concept as dialogic listening, a process of building new meanings and insights through dialogue. The concepts of dialogue, dialogic ethics, and dialogic listening all rest on the belief that humans can communicate with respect for one another and for themselves, with the objective of mutually seeking truth and justice.

Here's the difference between the types of listening and questioning: In active and interactive listening and questioning you are focused on gaining information; in empathic listening and questioning, you are focused on the other person's feelings; collaborative listening and questioning is an intensive dialogue in which participants work to shape their ideas, as if two or more people had an uncut piece of marble and, together, they chipped and shaped away at it until they created a three-dimensional "sculpture of meaning." Stewart and Thomas (1990) identify four distinct features of this kind of collaborative dialogue:

When somebody really listens to me, without judging or evaluating me, it feels damned good. . . . *When I am prized, I blossom and expand, I am an interesting individual. In a hostile or unappreciative group, I am just not capable of much of anything.*

Carl Rogers, Ph.D., psychologist and author

Collaborative listening and questioning
Dialogue in which speaker and listener work as a team to develop shared understanding

1   *Mutuality*. The entire process focuses not on individual interests but on *all* participants' interests.

2   *Open-ended playfulness*. This allows the participants to develop their thoughts creatively, opening paths to new ideas and insights.

3   *Presentness*. The process is centered in *now* more than the past or the future.

4   *Issue-oriented*. The focus is on ideas and issues that are *in front of* the participants, not on the motivations for responses. It is not, in other words, psychotherapy.

Listening and questioning together in this way can be a playful process, but it also is focused and intense; it is genuine teamwork in developing ideas. Admittedly, the process takes time and effort—but the result is worth it. Stewart and Thomas (1990) identify four techniques that can help people build a dialogical listening process.

1   *"Say more."* This phrase encourages the other person to develop thoughts and suggestions, think more deeply, and identify more possibilities. You might repeat "Say more" several times in a dialogue to keep your partner talking to clarify and expand ideas.

2   *"Run with the metaphor."* This phrase suggests that when one person creates a metaphor, the participants should carry it further, play with it, and use it for deeper analysis. A couple is discussing their relationship, for example. It might go like this:

> "Our relationship is just a dance on ice."
>
> "What kind of a dance?"
>
> "Ballroom—dipping and gliding . . ."
>
> "That's nice . . . kind of sweet."
>
> "Yes, and I like it sometimes, but it seems as if it's all on the surface— maybe more like skating without knowing what's underneath the ice. . . ."

Here, the couple changes the metaphor and, if they run with it, they may find out what's really at issue in their lives.

3   *"Paraphrase plus."* This phrase describes the give-and-take of reflecting and adding information. You put another person's statement in your own words and *then* develop the ideas further. Next, your partner paraphrases what *you* have said before, adding a response. As you do this together, you begin to discover new ideas or sculpt a deeper meaning. Let's continue with our couple as they use paraphrase plus:

> "I think you're suggesting that we might have some problems we haven't recognized [paraphrase]. That may be true—like maybe we don't listen to each other enough, or we don't deal with the problems with our parents [plus]."
>
> "You're saying that lack of listening is undermining our relationship and so are our parents? Maybe so—in fact, maybe if we really listened to each

other we could deal with the parent problem more effectively. Like, for example, I feel that you don't really listen when I tell you what your mother does. . . ."

Working together this way, these two people can truly create some understanding and improve their relationship together.

4 *"Context-building."* This phrase refers to the need to explain your frame of reference for your statements and encourage your dialogue partner to explain his or her context. Questioning can help. In our example, the dialogue might continue with context-building like this:

"When do you feel that way? Is it all the time, or are there particular circumstances?"

"Well, it seems as if you ignore me especially when I'm upset about how she handles the kids. . . ."

Now, they are beginning to build a context that will help to reveal important issues they need to resolve.

In our example, the couple is listening interactively for information, empathically for feelings, and dialogically to build new meanings. Dialogic listening gives them the tools of "say more," "run with the metaphor," "paraphrase plus," and "context-building" to reach new levels of understanding. Don't think, however, that a collaborative dialogue is only for solving personal problems. Do you need to develop a special team project? Do you need to better understand a philosophical view in one of your courses? Collaborating with someone through dialogue, listening, and questioning can help you create a new idea or better understand an old one.

As we've said, these approaches to "sculpting" meaning take time and commitment. Furthermore, people must learn to do them together because each technique is cooperative. "Say more" can get tiresome if you don't understand that your partner is deliberately pushing you to think more deeply. Suggesting that you "run with the metaphor" will sound silly if you don't know that it means to continue developing the metaphor until you have a new insight from it. This type of listening and questioning is a skill that people learn, develop, and use together because they are motivated to search for more complete, more mutual interpretations and because they want to build effective interpersonal or work relationships.

As Figure 4.1 shows, each type of listening serves a different purpose, but they often work together. You might listen actively, taking notes, as a fellow student tells you about a class you missed; you might move into interactive listening and questioning, asking questions to clarify, confirm, or expand your understandings. Then you and your friend might start discussing how you feel about the class or the professor or your future. At this point, your listening and questioning may develop empathically—to provide support and reflection for the other's feelings—and you might begin to collaborate in a dialogue that takes your understandings about the course material or about your personal feelings deeper and further than they've been before.

Figure 4.1
Relationships among active, interactive, empathic, and dialogic listening

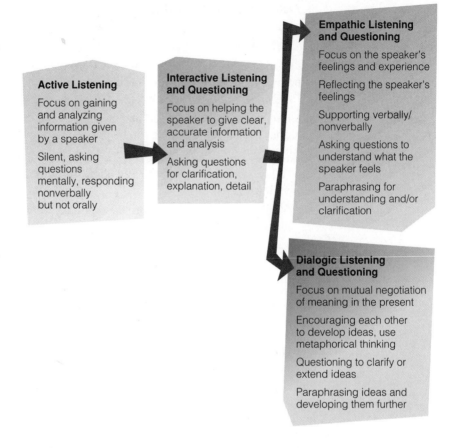

Active Listening

Focus on gaining and analyzing information given by a speaker

Silent, asking questions mentally, responding nonverbally but not orally

Interactive Listening and Questioning

Focus on helping the speaker to give clear, accurate information and analysis

Asking questions for clarification, explanation, detail

Empathic Listening and Questioning

Focus on the speaker's feelings and experience

Reflecting the speaker's feelings

Supporting verbally/ nonverbally

Asking questions to understand what the speaker feels

Paraphrasing for understanding and/or clarification

Dialogic Listening and Questioning

Focus on mutual negotiation of meaning in the present

Encouraging each other to develop ideas, use metaphorical thinking

Questioning to clarify or extend ideas

Paraphrasing ideas and developing them further

Listening and Questioning Skill Development

Although most people do not listen and question as well as they should, it is possible to develop these abilities. Effective listening and questioning contributes to your credibility with others and your confidence in yourself. To be good at listening and questioning, you need to commit yourself to the effort, prepare to develop your skills, and practice the tips we've given for active, interactive, empathic, and dialogic listening and questioning.

Commitment

Listening and questioning are hard work. They take intense concentration and strong self-control. Although a long day of really listening to others takes little obvious physical effort, it can leave you feeling as if you'd moved a truckload of furniture. Commitment to listening means a willingness to work hard, to put everything else aside, and to concentrate on the other person and the ideas.

Preparation

The first step is to develop your listening skills. Carefully examine how you listen and how you question, and then select specific areas in which you'd like to improve. Visualize yourself listening or questioning in ways that perfectly fulfill that image, then write an affirmation statement (see the guidelines on page 43: an affirmation should be phrased positively, in the present tense, and should describe your feelings and behaviors as well as the speaker's response to you).

The second preparation step takes place when you are in a situation that requires careful listening. Try doing the following:

1   *Relax.* One simple way to relax so you can focus on listening is to breathe deeply. Take several slow, deep breaths; feel the oxygen circulating through your body and brain. As you breathe, think of being calm and centered on the other person. Then, as you listen, if your mind begins to wander or you begin to feel stress, repeat the deep breathing.

2   *Set your mind for listening.* Make a mental commitment to intense listening; block out distractions and focus your eyes and your mind on the speaker.

3   *Identify your goals in listening.* Know why you're listening to this person: to get information, to deepen or expand your knowledge, to establish your credibility, to support or help, to develop a relationship. Identifying your goals will help you center your attention on the person and the message.

Practice

In listening, as in other skills, the key is to set some small practice goals—very specific, very clear skills you want to develop. Review your affirmations as you visualize your successful behavior. Then practice your listening and questioning in the context you've selected—a classroom, a dialogue with a friend or family member, or an interaction at work. After you've practiced, assess your success. When you feel you've listened well or asked questions effectively, review what you did. Keep rehearsing and practicing what works well. Then look for opportunities to practice again. Soon, your confidence will grow as you become comfortable with these skills and as you enjoy your experiences more. Furthermore, the feedback from others will show you that they find you credible and appreciate your ability to listen and to ask intelligent, useful questions.

Summary

The abilities to listen and to question well are essential to get information, to build your own credibility and confidence, to support or help another person, and to build relationships. These skills are also essential to success in your school, career, and personal life. Unfortunately, hearing impairments and environmental conditions can hinder good listening, as can inadequate skills, focusing problems, poor content responses, emotional blocks, information overload, and anxiety.

Active listening involves silently processing and interpreting information; interactive questioning and listening involves asking questions to clarify, confirm, or develop information. In empathic listening and questioning, the listener focuses entirely on understanding and reflecting back the feelings of the speaker, using questions and paraphrasing to help the speaker understand his or her own feelings. Collaborative listening and questioning uses dialogue to focus on a mutual process of "sculpting" new or deeper meanings together by centering on the present, helping each other build context for ideas, and developing understanding through "paraphrasing plus," "running with the metaphor," and "saying more."

Developing skill in listening and questioning demands commitment to hard work and preparation through relaxation, visualization, and focus on the moment of listening. This requires centering your attention on the speaker and the objectives for listening and questioning. Finally, you can develop your abilities by setting goals and by practicing each type of speaking in appropriate contexts and situations.

Exercises

1 How good are your listening and questioning skills? Use Form 4.1 to find out. First, complete the assessment on your own. Then ask a friend and your boss or your teacher each to complete the form based on how she or he would rate your abilities. Now compare the three ratings. Where are the ratings the same? Different? Why? In what ways do you think you listen well? In what ways do you think you need to improve as a listener?

2 With a small group, observe a televised, taped, or live dialogue between two people. Identify what barriers blocked the participants' dialogue and what listening and questioning skills they used to arrive at understanding. What would you suggest to the participants to improve their listening and questioning? Then develop a group report on the observations.

3 Think of a time when you have experienced or observed either very good or very bad listening and questioning. This could be something that happened to you, a friend, or a family member; it could be something you saw in a public place; it could be something you saw on television or in a play. Analyze what you observed in terms of the following questions:

What were the circumstances or context of the interaction?

Who were the participants?

What were the participants' individual purposes in the dialogue?

What types of listening and questioning did you observe?

What barriers did you observe?

What worked effectively in the transaction?

Now, briefly describe the experience and your analysis of it to the class.

4 After each member of the class has given his or her report for Exercise 3, meet in small groups and do the following:

a   Identify what most experiences/observations had in common. What general principles can you derive?

b   Identify what seemed unique among the observations. How can you account for the differences?

c   Create a list of 10–15 rules for good listening and questioning, based on what you've read and what the reports have revealed.

d   Share your list with the class.

Cyberpoints

1 Want to see what trainers are doing to help folks in the workplace to listen better? Use *InfoTrac College Edition* to locate *listening.* Under that, find Article 20, Richard M. Harris, Turn listening into a powerful presence, from the journal *Training and Development,* 51 (7), 9.

2 Have you noticed that people of different cultures seem to have different styles of listening? You can find out more about that using *InfoTrac College Edition* to locate *listening,* and check out Article 18, Cultural differences in listening style preferences: A comparison of young adults in Germany, Israel, and the United States by Christian Kiewitz, James B. Weaver III, Hans-Bernd Brosius, and Gabriel Weimann, *International Journal of Public Opinion Research*, Fall, 1997, 9 (3), 233.

CCC

WEB SITE

3 Are you curious about how the physical process of hearing works? Go to the *Communicating with Credibility and Confidence* Web site at http://communication.wadsworth.com/lumsden and click on *listening*.

Assessment of Listening and Questioning Skills

For each of the following statements, check the response that best describes the listening/questioning skill.

	Usually	Sometimes	Rarely
I/You:			
1. Am/are motivated to listen and question well.	___	___	___
2. Am/are interested when others speak.	___	___	___
3. Manage distractions well.	___	___	___
4. Pay attention well.	___	___	___
5. Get major ideas.	___	___	___
6. Take only necessary notes.	___	___	___
7. Don't jump ahead and make premature judgments.	___	___	___
8. Don't stereotype the speaker.	___	___	___
9. Don't jump on an idea and focus only on it.	___	___	___
10. Don't think only about what I/you want to say.	___	___	___
11. Control emotional reactions to loaded words.	___	___	___
12. Give positive nonverbal support to the speaker.	___	___	___
13. Keep mental attention on the speaker's ideas.	___	___	___
14. Approach dialogue as a mutual process of sharing ideas.	___	___	___
15. Encourage the speaker to extend ideas.	___	___	___
16. Paraphrase others' ideas to confirm or extend meanings.	___	___	___
17. Show empathy for the speaker appropriately.	___	___	___
18. Ask questions to clarify information.	___	___	___
19. Ask questions to help develop and analyze information.	___	___	___
20. Know what I/you want to ask.	___	___	___
21. Ask specific questions.	___	___	___
22. Ask questions clearly.	___	___	___
23. Ask for information with examples, definitions, and analogies.	___	___	___
24. Use open-ended questions to allow the speaker to elaborate.	___	___	___
25. Use probing questions to get at specific information.	___	___	___
26. Build on questions others ask.	___	___	___
27. Ask questions ethically.	___	___	___
28. Do not use questions to manipulate the speaker.	___	___	___

Chapter 5

Nonverbal Communication: More Than Words Can Say

Objectives for This Chapter

Knowledge

- Understand the types and functions of nonverbal cues
- Know how culture, gender, and individual variables affect nonverbal communication
- Identify ways in which nonverbal cues contribute to developing credibility
- Know how nonverbal interactions affect confidence

Feelings and Approaches

- Be sensitive to others' uses and interpretations of nonverbal cues
- Approach nonverbal communication as a way of enhancing verbal messages
- Feel confident in using nonverbal communication effectively and credibly

Communication Abilities

- Decode others' nonverbal cues accurately
- Use nonverbal communication confidently
- Use eyes, face, and body to convey messages clearly
- Use voice and speech dynamically, clearly, appropriately, credibly
- Adapt nonverbal communication to individuals and settings appropriately

Key Terms

nonverbal communication

vocalics

detractors

communication accommodation

kinesic

synchronous messages

proxemics

territory

personal space

haptics

artifacts

monochronic culture

polychronic culture

"**Y**our actions speak so loudly I can't hear a word you say." This old saying rings true; your message and your credibility rely not only on your words but also on the impact of your nonverbal communication. Andersen (1999) goes so far as to say that "nonverbal behavior, in particular, determines the persuasive impact of a message . . . " (p. 247).

Nonverbal communication is communication that accompanies, replaces, or carries verbal messages, such as your vocal or facial expressions, your posture, your movements, or even the ring you wear on your finger to symbolize your commitment to another person.

Nonverbal cues affect your credibility, and they also reflect and reinforce your confidence or lack of it. At the intrapersonal level, you monitor and respond to your own cues. If you are anxious, for example, your hands might shake and your mouth might feel dry. Your confidence level may drop, and you might hesitate and talk too slowly or too quickly, causing your listener to think you're unsure, unprepared, or even untruthful. In contrast, being in control of your nonverbal cues helps you feel more confident, and your listeners get a better impression of your message and your credibility.

That's the intention of this chapter—to help you develop your credibility and confidence through understanding how nonverbal communication functions and sharpening your ability to encode and decode nonverbal messages effectively.

Nonverbal communication Communication that accompanies, replaces, or carries verbal messages

People trust their ears less than their eyes.

Herodotus, 5th-century B.C. Greek historian

Communication: More Than Words

What you say and how you act go together, interrelating to confirm or to contradict your verbal message, and listeners react to that interrelationship. Early research (Ekman & Friesen, 1969; Knapp, 1978) found that nonverbal cues interact with words to repeat, to emphasize, to complement, to substitute, or to contradict the words, as well as to regulate the entire process of conversation. For example:

- *To repeat:* You confirm the words "I'm very pleased" with a smile and a warm facial expression.

- *To emphasize:* You might say, "I'm very pleased," with a raised or lowered voice or with tears of joy or gratitude.

- *To complement:* You could accompany "I'm very pleased" with a hug and kiss that add an unspoken "and I love you very much."

- *To substitute for words:* Eye contact and a warm smile can communicate "I'm very pleased" without a word being said.

- *To contradict the verbal message:* Your "I'm very pleased" delivered with a sarcastic tone and a frown may be heard as "I am not at all pleased."

- *To regulate conversation:* Nonverbal cues affect who can talk, when, to whom, and for how long. If, for instance, you say, "I'm very pleased," and the other person smiles silently and waits, you may feel the need to say more, or if she or he smiles and then looks at someone else, you probably will be silent.

Nonverbal Cues Shape Transactions

For better or for worse, nonverbal cues shape your transactions with others. For example, people adapt their communication to another person's based partly on how the other person communicates nonverbally. When a person seems pleasant and involved in the communication, others respond with more smiling, nodding, and pleasantness in return (Le Poire & Yoshimura, 1999). You can see this effect even on the job; supervisors or subordinates who use nonverbal immediacy—that is, they physically show involvement in the person and the moment—"generate reciprocity and accommodation leading to a more positive work environment and more desirable outcomes" (Richmond & McCroskey, 2000, p. 85).

You may, in fact, perceive 60–70% of a person's meaning from nonverbal rather than verbal cues (Andersen, 1999, p. 25). Adults especially use nonverbal cues more for judging a speaker's emotions and attitudes than for recalling and analyzing information (Burgoon, Buller, & Woodall, 1989, p. 155), although young children may believe words more than nonverbal cues (Woolfolk & Woolfolk, 1974). Maybe this is why adults are confused when children take a teasing comment as a serious rebuke; the adults mean to signal "just kidding" nonverbally, but the children don't recognize or focus on those signals.

Why are nonverbal cues more believable? Perhaps because, first, *nonverbal cues are harder to control.* When the muscles in your jaw clench with anger, for example, you may have trouble relaxing them enough to sound believable when saying, "No, really, it's fine." Second, *nonverbal cues come from many sources at one time,* so they may outweigh the words. Our friend Mike cannot hide his irrepressible humor. He may make a serious comment, but if he sees an underlying joke, his eyes twinkle, his voice rises, the corners of his mouth turn up—and we know there's something funny in the back of his mind. Third, *nonverbal cues are more unconscious than verbal statements.* You may be unaware of looking at your watch, twitching your foot, folding your arms, and tapping your fingers—but an observer might interpret those behaviors to mean that you're rushed or nervous.

Nonverbal Cues Are Hard to Decode

Most folks don't decode nonverbal cues very well. Take lying, for example. Feeley and Young (1998) conclude that, "over twenty-five years of research in behavioral lie detection has yielded one consistent finding: humans are not very skilled at detecting when deception is present" (p. 109). Even so-called experts in lie detection have trouble. In one study, out of 509 experts in detecting deception (psychiatrists, court judges, police detectives, polygraphers, and Secret Service officers), only the Secret Service officers did better than chance at detecting lies from nonverbal cues (Goleman, 1991).

Personal Influences   Some individuals do seem to decode nonverbal cues more accurately than do others. Women appear to be better at interpreting others' expressions of emotion (Swenson & Casmir, 1998), and middle-aged people seem more perceptive about nonverbal cues than young or old observers, although contextual and situational cues, as well as knowing the individual, make decoding easier for anyone (Leathers, 1992, p. 49).

Cultural Influences   It's also critically important to understand that an individual's culture may determine his or her nonverbal communication and not to assume that others' nonverbal behaviors will mean the same as yours. You cannot know everything about another's culture, but you can keep one principle in mind: Nonverbal communication is a deeply rooted, often unconscious, reflection of a group's understandings about one another and how life should be. In a recent trip to Bali, for example, we (your authors) were struck by two things: People spoke very softly, and they invariably responded to a smile with a brilliant, warm, open smile of their own. We found ourselves speaking more softly than we do in the United States and enjoying the feeling of openness and peace that emerged from this smiling culture.

A good communicator is aware of how unconscious and culturally shaped nonverbal cues can be, and is careful both in giving and interpreting nonverbal cues. This awareness can help you to be a more sensitive nonverbal communicator in any context.

Voice and Speech: Instruments of Communication

"It's not *what* you say but *how* you say it." In this class, your voice and speech are the instruments you use to make people understand you for every oral assignment, and in your life, they carry your meaning every time you speak to someone.

Using Voice and Speech

Vocalics How the sound of your voice and the way you speak affect how you are perceived

The sound of your voice and the way you speak are powerful influences on how a listener perceives you and your message. The technical term usually used for voice and speech communication is **vocalics,** which include such nonverbal cues as pitch, tone, volume, range, and quality of voice, and even detractors such as "um" and "you know." These vocalic characteristics make you want to listen (or not), they help you understand the message (or not), and they affect how you much you like the speaker (or not).

You need an open vocal quality and vocal variety to keep your listeners' attention and emphasize your meaning. That means you can vary your *inflection*—variety in pitch, volume, and rate—to give meaning to your words:

- *Pitch* is the high or low tone of a sound. Everyone has an individual natural pitch, with a possible range of low to high pitches. Varying your pitch emphasizes meaning and keeps listeners interested—and increases your credibility as well (Ray, 1986).

- *Volume* is the softness and loudness of speech. You can increase or drop volume to intensify or dramatize meanings and to increase your impact. Speaking louder may increase your credibility, for example, while speaking softly at an intimate level may make the audience see you as warmer and friendlier (Ray, 1986).

- *Rate* is the tempo or speed of speech. People may be most favorably impressed when your rate is close to or slightly faster than their own (Street, Brady, & Putnam, 1983) and consider you competent, intelligent, and objective if you use a quick tempo (Buller & Aune, 1988; Giles & Street, 1985)—although a slower tempo may make a speaker seem more thoughtful and trustworthy (Woodall & Burgoon, 1983).

To illustrate the relationship between inflection and meaning, say these seven words: *Yvonne said Karriem gave a great speech.* Try varying your pitch, volume, and rate the way each of these speakers would make the statement:

- Someone expressing surprise that Yvonne would have made that statement
- Someone expressing surprise that Karriem could have done so well
- Karriem talking about Yvonne's speech
- Yvonne implying that she really thinks Karriem's speech wasn't that effective

With each change in inflection, you change what those seven words mean. The changes may be subtle, but they provide entirely different interpretations.

You can also affect a listener's response to you and your message through your articulation and fluency. This involves:

- *Articulation* is pronouncing words clearly and correctly. When you speak articulately, your listeners feel you are confident and composed. If people need to listen too hard to understand you, they may become impatient or dismiss you with some stereotype.

- *Fluency* is speaking smoothly, without detractors. **Detractors** are sounds and words interjected instead of pauses between words and sentences, as speakers often do when they are nervous. Two types of detractors are most common: *vocalized pauses,* which are sound utterances such as "um" and

Detractors Sounds and words interjected between words and sentences

"er," and *verbalized pauses,* which are filler words such as "you know," "like," "and," and "and so forth." (Like, um, y'know what we mean?) Speakers frequently are unaware of using detractors, and such utterances become habitual. Everyone uses detractors occasionally, but habitual use diminishes your effectiveness.

Adapting Voice and Speech

As with all communication, self-monitoring and adapting are important to good use of your voice and speech. Stereotypes and negative judgments are not fair, but they exist. Saying "goin'" instead of "going" or "dem" instead of "them," or even speaking with a regional dialect can cause listeners to jump to conclusions about the speaker's education, class, status, personality, character, mood, race, age, gender orientation, and even body type (Giles & Coupland, 1991, p. 32).

This may pose a dilemma to people who speak in a dialect or with an accent. Even if standard speech gives you more credibility in a given context, trying to change your speech may feel like you're abandoning who you are. Sometimes family and friends ridicule an individual who goes back to the neighborhood with a new way of speaking. Fortunately, it's not necessary to replace one set of speech patterns with another; it's possible to learn how to accommodate to different groups and situations.

Communication accommodation Methods used by people to adapt to others' communication behaviors

By using **communication accommodation,** "individuals adapt to each other's communicative behaviors" (Giles & Coupland, 1991, p. 63). In other words, they learn to switch codes for their listeners. Some U.S. senators, for example, seek training in "how to drop their regional accents when they are in Washington, and how to pick them up again on the campaign trail" ("Where to Drop," 1993, p. B4 L).

It makes sense to know how to communicate most clearly for whatever situation you are in. If you were in France, it would be an advantage if you spoke French; yet when you returned to North America, you would return to using English. Similarly, if you and your family and friends speak an informal dialect, why give it up? The point is to be able to switch when you meet with others who are not part of your in-group.

If you'd like to improve your use of voice and/or your speech, take a look at the *Communicating with Confidence and Credibility* Web site—there are some good ideas there.

Body Movements Large and Small

Kinesic Movements of the eyes, face, and body that people perceive as meaningful

Your body, mind, and the environment communicate constantly. As the brain processes information from internal and external signals, the body responds with **kinesic** communication—movements of the eyes, face, and body that people interpret as meaningful messages.

Comedienne Marsha Warfield, in a "Comic Relief" tribute to Michael Jordan, showed the ability to switch her language in the following segment of her monologue:

It's great to be black. We have our own language. We don't like the sound "th," so we don't use it. We just use "f." We don't say "teeth," we say "teef."

Her articulation was perfect in both codes.

Eyes and Face

The face is the mirror of the mind, and eyes without speaking confess the secrets of the heart.

Jerome, 4th-century A.D. Christian saint

Usually, people get their first impression from your eyes and face. How can you use them well?

First, it's still good advice to *use eye contact when you speak*. For most North Americans, eye contact increases your credibility; you are more dynamic, and listeners find you more believable, likable, and persuasive (Beebe, 1980; Burgoon, Coker, & Coker, 1986; Kleinke, 1986; Hornik, 1987). If you're in an interview, sustaining eye contact with the interviewer makes you more likely to be hired than a person who looks away or down (Burgoon, Manusov, Mineo, & Hale, 1985).

Appropriate use of eye contact, however, varies widely from culture to culture. You might hear an American parent say, "Look at me when I'm talking to you, young lady!" and an African parent demand, "Don't you dare look me in the eyes when I'm talking to you!"

However it is interpreted, eye communication in interpersonal, group, and public communication settings accomplishes two important functions. First, eye contact *signals attention and/or intimacy*. For example, it is in your favor when eye contact shows your professor you're paying attention—and when some couples gaze at each other steadily, they increase intimacy and feel more liking and passion for each other (Kellerman, Lewis, & Laird, 1989). Second, eye contact helps *establish and maintain power and control*. In Western cultures, people who maintain eye contact while *talking* seem dominant (Dovidio & Ellyson, 1982), and people who maintain eye contact while *listening* to a person of higher status appear subordinate, perhaps explaining why women (who historically have been subordinate) tend to value and use eye contact more than men do (Pearson, Turner, & Todd-Mancillas, 1991, pp. 134–135). In Africa, people listen without eye contact to people whose position is higher than theirs (Byers & Byers, 1972). Imagine the cultural misunderstanding when a Western

This woman who has just won an Olympic Gold Medal and this Bosnian woman who just learned that her husband has been killed in Sarajevo have very different emotions. Some of their nonverbal cues show these differences, yet some aspects of their behavior are much alike. What is it that shows you the emotions they are really feeling? Look at their supporters— what is different and yet the same with them?

employer talks to an African employee who, being polite, avoids eye contact— and the supervisor interprets this as insolence or indifference.

Though the eyes make the contact, the face speaks first and loudest. Early on, Ekman and Friesen (1967) found that people interpret *how* others feel mainly from their facial expressions and the *intensity* of their feelings from their body cues. From the face, people judge a person's attractiveness (Alicke, Smith, & Klotz, 1987), dominance (Berry, 1990), and kindness and warmth (Berry & MacArthur, 1985). They even watch when and how people smile to judge their credibility (Ekman, Davidson, & Friesen, 1990). A smile that is genuine and appropriate to the situation powerfully communicates your trustworthiness and your confidence (Bugental, 1986).

Fortunately for communication across cultures, people across the world seem to express basic emotions with the same facial movements. In various studies, Japanese, Americans, English, Spanish, French, German, Swiss, Greek, and South Pacific Islanders recognized happiness, surprise, fear, anger, sadness, disgust, contempt, interest, bewilderment, and determination in the photographed faces of people from other cultures (Ekman, Friesen, & Ellsworth, 1972; Forsyth, Kushner, & Forsyth, 1981; Leathers, 1992).

More finely tuned expressions, however, may be controlled by your cultural background, your gender, or your social status. In Japan, for example, disgust traditionally is not shown in public (Ekman et al., 1987), so this feeling may be covered with an opposite expression, such as smiling. How confusing to a Westerner!

Posture and Gestures

The intensity of your feelings, your personal power, and the very meaning of your message carry through your body. The way you stand or sit, gesture, or even move your shoulders or your head, reinforces or weakens your communication.

Posture   Parents and teachers preach, "Stand up straight!" and, "Don't sprawl!" That's because it's long been known that *good* posture—straight but relaxed—increases others' perceptions of an individual's competence and confidence (Burgoon & Saine, 1978). Your body posture conveys information about how you see yourself in relationship to another person, how you feel about yourself, and how you feel about a topic.

Your posture indicates three aspects of your relationship to someone else: immediacy and involvement, rapport, and dominance and control.

Immediacy and involvement.   Effective communicators talk at a close conversational distance, face each other directly, lean forward, and maintain an open body position; they don't move around randomly, but they do gesture frequently. These cues show interest, indicate that you are responsive to others, and encourage conversation (Burgoon, et al., 1989, p. 315).

Rapport.   Rapport develops because people feel some mutual empathy, coorientation, trust, and concern. Immediacy and involvement behaviors help to build these feelings, which are essential to cooperation and intimacy in a relationship. So does *mirroring*, with which one person reflects another's body posture, facial expressions, and voice with the same behavior. Mirroring may be unconscious behavior, stemming from a person's empathy for another, but it is most effective in connecting with someone you're close to or someone who is discussing a problem with you as a friend or counselor. In more casual conversation, mirroring can strain communication (LaFrance & Ickes, 1981); perhaps the mirrorer seems to be trying too hard or even to be mocking the other person.

Dominance and control.   Control postures are ubiquitous in social life, but they vary by culture, situation, and gender. High-status Japanese bow to be polite—but low-status Japanese bow lower to show deference. North Americans are seen as powerful when they sit or stand in an erect, but relaxed and open, posture—and North American men often show dominance by leaning or tipping their chairs back, whereas women often avoid dominance by adapting their

"Ignore him. He just walks that way to bug his parents."

positions to their conversational partners. This may make women's partners more comfortable than men's, because women's behavior appears more accommodating and interested (Pearson et al., 1991, p. 140).

You strengthen and reinforce your words when you use **synchronous messages**—that is, hand, body, and head movements that coordinate with your words. Synchronous messages also increase people's view of you as competent, composed, trustworthy, extroverted, and sociable (Woodall & Burgoon, 1981).

Gestures Some gestures are clearly understood within a culture, but most are unconscious expressions of a feeling or an idea. Ekman and Friesen's (1969) classic research identified these four specific types of gestures:

1 *Emblems* have well-defined meanings within a culture or an identity group. Observe the emblems used by umpires, coaches, pitchers, and catchers at a baseball game or those used by lovers across a crowded room who want to be somewhere else, or the emblems used in American Sign Language. But be careful with emblems. Take a gesture into another culture, and it may convey a radically different meaning. In the United States, your hand held up with the palm outward means "Stop!" In Greece, the same gesture is an insult. In the United States, your raised hand with the palm inward and fingers wagging means "Come here." In Italy, it means "Good-bye."

2 *Illustrators* "show" what your words mean, adding clarity, dynamism, and emphasis. An emblem and an illustrator can be the same: You might shout, "Stop right there!" and raise your hand, palm out, as if to block action. Often, however, an illustrator emerges for a specific point. You might say, "Teamwork is interdependent, interwoven, cooperative," for instance, and weave your fingers together to illustrate what you mean.

Synchronous messages
Hand, body, and head movements that coordinate with spoken words

3   *Regulators* control turn-taking in conversations. Gestures will encourage people to talk—such as nodding to acknowledge a speaker's point or giving a thumbs-up sign—or to switch speakers, with signs such as rapid head nodding ("Yeah, yeah, it's my turn"), looking at watches, fiddling with objects, moving into closed-off body positions, or, perhaps, moving as if to leave.

4   *Adaptors* are habitual actions that in some way help to manage a person's needs, emotions, or relationships. They are unconscious shorthand moves directed toward the self (head-scratching, neck-rubbing, ear-pulling) or toward someone else (pointing, shrugging, nodding). An object, such as a pencil, can be used as an adaptor, too. Listeners often interpret adaptors negatively (Manusov, 1990). For example, you may fuss at your hair because you hate your new haircut, but others may think this adaptor means you're nervous. Or you may innocently point to an object with your left hand and deeply offend a person from Thailand, where that's an obscene gesture. In general, it's better to avoid adaptors except for those that serve a practical purpose—such as using a pointer to show a spot on the map.

Students often worry that "I talk with my hands too much!" But usually they err on the side of too little movement rather than too much. Just keep in mind two issues: First, keep gestures synchronous and consistent with your verbal message, using illustrators and emblems to make your messages clear, dynamic, and moving. Second, keep your body movements in proportion to the number of people you're speaking to and the amount of available space. In an intimate conversation, keep gestures close to you. In a speech, use gestures big enough that everyone can see them, and strong enough that people believe that *you* believe what you're saying.

Space and Touch

You can make someone very comfortable or very uncomfortable by how close you position yourself to them or how you touch. Both the use of space, called *proxemics*, and touching, called *haptics* in the language of communication study, strongly influence not only the way people express relationships but how they perceive issues of power and control.

Space   When you choose a seat, back off because someone's "in your face," or stand up to give your report, you're using and reacting to proxemics. Burgoon et al. (1989) define **proxemics** as "perception, use, and structuring of space as communication" (p. 74).

You've no doubt seen people passionately defend their "territory" or "personal space." A **territory** is a specific place that you feel you own in some way, whereas your **personal space** is your invisible, "adjustable bubble of space surrounding an individual that is actively maintained to protect the person from physical and emotional threats" (Burgoon, et al., 1989, p. 81).

You cannot have a proud and chivalrous spirit if your conduct is mean and paltry; for whatever a man's actions are, must be his spirit.

Demosthenes, 4th-century B.C., Athenian statesman and orator

Proxemics The perception, use, and restructuring of space as communication

Territory A specific place that you feel is yours

Personal space Space surrounding an individual actively maintained to protect against threats

Consciously or unconsciously, people often use space to get what they want. Sometimes the goal is positive, as when an individual moves closer or farther away to accommodate someone else's comfort zone. Although a leader may sit at the head of the table because Western expectations typically are that the person of highest status take that position, today's leaders often deliberately sit elsewhere to open discussion and empower others.

More negatively, people sometimes use space to control or manipulate others' responses by crowding them, standing threateningly over them, or keeping them at an extreme distance. Some executives sit behind enormous desks at the far end of a large room, with a visitor's chair placed some distance away. This manipulates the visitor into feeling powerless and keeps control in the hands of the executive.

What happens when someone invades your personal space or territory? You probably show increased physiological stress (Epstein, Woolfolk, & Lehrer, 1981) and signs of anxiety and defensiveness. People mark their territories with fences and graffiti; they glare when someone approaches their typewriters; they get to class early so they can claim "their" seat.

How much space does a person need? In early research—with middle-class, white males from the northeastern United States—Hall (1969) identified four boundaries that seemed to define acceptable distances: intimate, personal, social, and public. Although specific distances vary according to culture and gender, these categories seem generally to indicate comfort zones for individuals:

1   *Intimate distance* (to about 18 inches): This zone is for comforting, loving, maintaining intimacy, and playing contact sports.

2   *Personal distance* (18 inches to 4 feet): This is a comfortable conversational distance for most North Americans. If you get closer, you're "inside the bubble" and you make the other person uncomfortable; if you move farther away, the other person may feel an urge to close the gap.

3   *Social distance* (4 to 12 feet): This is about right for interacting with strangers, business contacts, store clerks, and so on. Often, the space is set by a desk, a counter, or some other barrier that implies, "This close, no closer."

4   *Public distance* (12 to about 25 feet): This is average for addressing groups or getting someone's attention from a distance. It's too far away for confidentiality but far enough away to spread a message to a number of people (pp. 117–125).

Cultural influences.   Culture exerts a powerful influence on just how much a person needs under what circumstances, and that need swells or shrinks with the type of activity and the participants' ages, relationship, and racial or cultural homogeneity or heterogeneity (Dolphin, 1988, p. 322). How close you want to be to someone whose background and culture are the same may be quite different from how close you want to be to someone different. Even the language you're using may affect distance choices. Sussman and Rosenfeld (1982) found, for example, that when speaking in their own languages, Japanese stayed the greatest distance away from each other, North Americans were closer, and Venezuelans were closer still. When all spoke in English, however, both Japanese and Venezuelans conversed in about the same space range as North Americans did.

Gender influences. Similarly, gender roles affect nonverbal behavior and interpretations within any culture. A number of research studies, for example, indicate that "women are perceived to be more social, more affiliative, and of lower status; as a result, space surrounding women is considered more public and accessible than space surrounding men" (Stewart, et al., 1990, p. 90). In practice, that means that people would be more likely to crowd into a space taken by a woman than by a man. It also means that if a woman actually takes more space, others may be uncomfortable with her violation of their expectations.

Touch Touching and being touched is a deep biological and psychological need, technically called **haptics,** the communication of touching. Historical health records of infants who were deprived of touch—in orphanages and hospital incubators—indicate that lack of tactile stimulation related to higher infant mortality and to later health problems. What does touching communicate? Experts suggest the following:

■ *Support.* Touch can convey warmth, reassurance, or comfort (Marx, Werner, & Cohen-Mansfield, 1989), with a hand on a friend's shoulder or a hug just when it's needed. Sometimes, touch helps to heal the body and the mind. Leathers (1992) comments that "given the therapeutic power of touch, it is a sad fact that many individuals who most need touch are the least likely to receive it" (p. 133). The ill, the lonely, the old—they are most likely to be untouched and to feel unloved.

■ *Power.* Unfortunately, touch can also be used to exert power over another person. In Western cultures, the individual who has highest status and greatest power is allowed to touch those of lower status and power, and he or she is most likely to be the one who touches (Major, 1980; Scroggs, 1980). If you have higher status or dominance in a situation, you need to be wary of touching others in intimidating ways. One consultant describes an incident in which a manager who patted his subordinates on the arm or back to motivate them offended his Asian employees, some of whom asked for transfers (Copeland, 1988).

■ *Affiliation.* Touching is a clear clue to people's liking and affection for each other (Collier, 1985). It also signals the development of interpersonal relationships according to cultural norms for what kind of touching is acceptable at which stage.

■ *Ritual.* Rituals define the large and small beginnings, transitions, and endings in people's lives, and touching helps to mark those moments, as in handshakes or kisses for greetings and farewells, or in major events, such as a wedding, when guests kiss the bride. In a sense, these touches remind us that transitions are a part of life and add security and importance to such moments.

Cultural and gender influences. It's imperative to realize how extensively culture and gender influence the way people use and perceive touching. Because it's difficult to make broad generalizations about these influences, you just have to be observant and sensitive to possible differences. For example, research has found that in casual conversation Italians and Greeks touched more than the English, French, or Dutch (Remland, Jones, & Brinkman, 1992) and that African American men touched each other more than white men did; African American women touched each other more often than white women did; and both sexes were more likely to touch others of their own race than people of another race (Smith, Willis, & Gier, 1980).

Men and women within specific cultures also may touch differently. Some studies have found that while Western women distinguish between affiliative touching (for warmth and affection) and sexual touching, Western men don't see the differences (Pearson, et al., 1991, p. 142); other studies have revealed that women touch each other more than men touch each other and that women touch children more than men do—but that men touch women more than women touch men (Major, Schmidlin, & Williams, 1990). It can get pretty confusing.

Even touching intended to be casual may appear to be sexual, and in an organizational setting—business, professional, academic—a person who has been touched in a sexually suggestive or aggressive way has a right to state objections and then to bring sexual harassment charges. There is more information on issues of sexual harassment on the *Communicating with Credibility and Confidence* Web site.

Personal Symbols: Subtle Influences

Here's how your nonverbal messages come full circle for your credibility and confidence: Many personal, subtle, nonverbal messages influence others' impressions of you—and when they are favorably impressed, people give you positive feedback, which contributes to your self-esteem. People with high self-esteem are less likely to fear communication (Richmond & McCroskey, 1995), so your effective personal nonverbal cues to others also can increase your confidence. Your appearance, your use of objects, and your attitude toward time all symbolize something about you to others.

■ *Appearance.* Appearance is more than physical attractiveness. The way you dress and style your hair, for example, may affect the credibility, likability, attractiveness, and dominance you convey to others (Leathers, 1992). Our best advice is to *select clothes and grooming that will both make others feel you are credible and in which you will feel self-confident.* Picture the setting, the participants, and yourself in relation to your goals.

■ *Objects.* Like the pottery that tells about ancient peoples, the things living people use to symbolize themselves are called **artifacts.** Artifacts are all the things that people wear, carry, leave behind, or spread around that symbolize who they are or what they value. Artifacts include the clothing, buttons, and perfume you wear; the bags you carry; and the pictures, posters, and flowers that decorate your room. An individual can be stereotyped or not, liked or loathed, and trusted or suspected on the basis of these symbols. That's why Kaiser (1990) suggests that people need to choose artifacts that will meet social expectations for a given situation. There's some latitude in that, and it doesn't mean that you have to lose your individuality. Just choose objects that will help you achieve your communication goals.

Artifacts Things living
people use to symbolize
themselves

Time: A Cultural Concept

It's not only the objects you can smell or see, however, that impress people with who they think you are. Time can be a big issue. Think of the North American social rules and cliches: "Time is money," "Don't be late," "Don't waste my time." An individual who is late for an appointment in the United States may be viewed as irresponsible, incompetent, rebellious, or manipulative.

Other cultures, however, might regard North Americans' slavery to time as crazy. In the Hopi tradition, for example, each person, plant, or animal has its own time system, and you can't impose one entity's deadline on another (Porter & Samovar, 1997, p. 19). In the Maasai culture, the wisdom of the past guides life, but the present and future are irrelevant. In Kenya, public transportation has no schedule. A Kenyan who tells a nervous American that the bus will leave "just now," means "when the bus is full, of course," and not before (Skow & Samovar, 2000, p. 97).

Hall (2000) labels cultures as monochronic or polychronic. In **monochronic** cultures (meaning single-time)—such as are found in most of North America—people generally attend to one thing at a time. In **polychronic cultures** (meaning multi-time)—such as are found in most of Latin America—people do many things at once. In a business meeting, monochronic individuals might be prompt and stick to the agenda so they can finish on time. The polychronic persons might be late because their previous engagement took longer than planned, and they would willingly override the agenda to deal with other concerns and social relationships in addition to the explicit goals of the meeting.

Monochronic culture
Culture in which people
attend to one thing at a
time, with focus on dead-
lines and schedules

Polychronic culture
Culture in which people
do many things at once,
with focus on relation-
ships and immediacy

Porter and Samovar (1997) note that "even within the dominant mainstream of American culture, we find groups that have learned to perceive time in ways that appear strange to many outsiders. Hispanics frequently refer to Mexican or Latino time when their timing differs from the predominant Anglo concept, and African Americans often use what is referred to as BPT (black

Shimizu, a Tokyo construction corporation, devised a unit that disperses aromas through central air circulating systems. The company found that lemon fragrance increased productivity among keypunch operators, and that jasmine and lavender had calming effects. Shimizu's customized systems cost about $20,000 a room, said Junichi Yagi, a senior vice president of S. Technology, a Shimizu subsidiary in Cambridge, Mass., that is preparing the systems for use in this country.

"If you have a high-stress office environment, you want to soothe and stimulate alertness," he said. "In a hotel you want to create a relaxed mood." At Shimizu headquarters, a subtle woodsy aroma scents the floor where the company entertains clients. "It's like an aromatic Quaalude," one executive said.

. . . Mark Peltier, founder of Aromasys in Richfield, Minn., said companies and universities have asked him to develop mood-altering fragrance systems.

The three states of mind he is most often asked to induce are alertness, relaxation, and refreshment. To perk people up, he uses a blend of peppermint, lemon, eucalyptus, rosemary, and pine. To calm, he uses lavender and clove, along with "floral notes and a whiff of woodland." He blends "citrus notes with pine and eucalyptus" to refresh. . . . "This is olfactory Muzak," he said. "This is very, very big."

From Trish Hall, *The New York Times*, November 17, 1991, pp. C1, C6.

people's time) or hang-loose time—maintaining that priority belongs to what is happening at that instant" (p. 18).

In today's diverse world, communicators must be sensitive to differing concepts of time. If your culture is monochronic and you're in a polychronic meeting—relax and go with the flow. You'll learn and enjoy a lot that you would otherwise miss. If your culture is polychronic and you're meeting with people who are monochronic, be sensitive to their need for deadlines and schedules. If you're working with a diverse group, discuss norms and work out compromises. Not only is your credibility at stake, but your communication is more effective and more pleasant when you adjust to people and circumstances.

Settings: Structures and Environments

Would you rather make a speech in a dark, dingy, overcrowded room or a well-lit, ventilated, comfortable space? Would you rather say "I love you" in a subway station or on a romantic carriage ride? Would you prefer to hold an important business meeting in an elegant conference room or on your front porch? You would choose the best venue for your purposes, of course, because your surroundings exert their own nonverbal effect on the quality of your communication. The environment can affect these three human responses:

1   *Emotions* are influenced through form, shape, line, space, color, sound, smell, and so on. Color, for instance, can affect interpersonal communication by calming or inciting people. An old story has it that legendary football coaches Amos Alonzo Stagg and Knute Rockne gave their teams pep talks in locker rooms painted an arousing red but housed visiting teams in rooms painted a soothing blue.

2   *Power and control* can be symbolized and exerted through arrangements of space, sound, and aesthetic elements in a room. We saw that in the presidential debates of 2000, which used three different arrangements to equalize power and control factors. The first debate posed each candidate at a lectern in a traditional arrangement, facing Tom Lehrer, their questioner, and the audience. The second put each man in a discussion arrangement, each seated and facing Mr. Lehrer. And the third pitted the two against each other, "extemporaneously" answering people's questions in a town-hall meeting arrangement. The candidates needed to prove their credibility, to be confident under pressure, and to respond flexibly to varied situations that directly affected the power they could show as candidates and the amount of control they could take.

3   *Communication accessibility.* The ability to see, hear, and respond to messages can control the way people communicate. The nonverbal presence of electronic media in contemporary society often exerts an important influence on communication transactions, too. In your classroom, for example, you may be videotaped giving a speech. The camera becomes a major element of your audience, perhaps making you nervous at the beginning (but helping you develop your skills through its use). Or in your workplace, you might be using audio- or videotape, computer databases, or teleconference facilities to share information, diagrams, or notes with electronic blackboards, telewriting, or remote slides— all electronic methods by which you can reproduce a message on a board or screen from one site to another. You might be a "telecommuter," working in your home and communicating with others through various media. Williams (1987) points out that electronic communication gives people a "connectivity" by placing humans around the world on a grid of communication. Connectivity opens up possibilities for sharing information that never before existed. People, therefore, are accommodating media as yet other nonverbal features that influence their communication.

Nonverbal Development: Credibility and Confidence

Even though nonverbal communication is cultural, complex, and often unconscious, a good communicator can both use it and interpret it effectively. Here are some hints for becoming more effective on both fronts.

Receiving Nonverbal Cues

You can't "read people like a book." Anyone who thinks that's possible probably is nonverbally illiterate. You can, however, interpret messages much more effectively if you do the following:

1   *Don't jump to conclusions* about others' nonverbal behavior on the basis of what you or people you know would do. Recognize that variables such as culture, age, gender, status, and context may influence nonverbal cues. At the same time, don't assume you know how those influences may be manifested in an individual's behavior. Be careful to avoid stereotyping. Keep an open mind, observe, and listen.

2   *Observe nonverbal cues in clusters and over time.* One nonverbal cue on one occasion won't tell you much, but as you observe a person, you may see patterns in the same individual over time. If Kailyn always smiles, it doesn't necessarily mean she's happy; if she smiles, her eyes wrinkle up, her posture straightens, her gestures widen, and her laughter tumbles out, then you have more evidence of her joy. If you get to know her and see these cues frequently when she has reason to be happy, you can use this pattern as a basis for knowing when she is in fact happy.

3   *Look for consistency and inconsistency.* What nonverbal cues are consistent with each other and with verbal cues? When do nonverbal cues contradict one another or the verbal message? If Kailyn says, "I'm happy," and she smiles—but her eyes, other facial features, and body don't move—then there's a contradiction that makes you wonder what's really going on.

4   *Be tentative.* Formulate hypotheses carefully, and watch to see if they seem to be supported. Often, a person's nonverbal cues reflect many internal thoughts and feelings or are responses to multiple cues from several other people. Suppose, in a group, you express an opinion, and Stan scowls. Is he responding to you, or to a sarcastic remark from someone else, or to a thought about his job? Notice the cues, but be careful in interpreting them.

5   *Ask for clarification.* If verbal and nonverbal cues are contradictory, or if you are puzzled by a nonverbal response, you may be able to inquire about a person's feelings. When you observe Stan's scowl, you might say, "Stan, maybe you disagree? I noticed you didn't look too happy when I said . . ."

Sending Nonverbal Cues

You've been developing your verbal and nonverbal communication habits since you were born, and improving them is a lifelong challenge. Good actors, however, learn to use nonverbal communication so it is expressive and appropriate to the verbal message—and so can you. Here are some techniques:

1   *Get good feedback.* Ask friends and family to observe and tell you what they see and hear when you talk. You may want to do Exercise 3 in Cyberpoints at the end of this chapter to help you get the most specific information you can.

2   *See and hear yourself.* Use videotaping and audiotaping. Yes, being video-taped is awful, but it helps. Look first for what you do well and keep it up; then look for inconsistencies, contradictions, and bad habits you can improve.

3   *Visualize yourself using effective nonverbal cues.* Visualize yourself communicating consistent and dynamic nonverbal messages, write out affirmations of how you want to be, and use them in your self-talk to help you visualize your ideal nonverbal communication. See yourself as credible, dynamic, confident. Hear your voice and speech as supporting your message, your audience, the situation, and yourself. Visualize your nonverbal cues supporting and reinforcing your verbal message, so you are comfortably communicating ideas unambiguously, clearly, and interestingly.

4   *Be sensitive to listeners.* Be aware of both your nonverbal communication and other people's reaction to and interpretation of it. As you interact with others, adapt to listeners who have hearing or vision disabilities so they can pick up your cues. Think of how your cues might affect others' cultural or social norms, and avoid doing things that might dominate or offend others or cause them to stereotype you.

5   *Practice for clarity and impact.* Use voice, speech, body, and face to make your message clear and effective. Consider the conditions of the environment; if the acoustics are poor, for example, raise your volume; or if the room is small, lower your volume and shrink your gestures to fit the space.

Finally, remember two things: (1) Reading another's nonverbal cues requires your ability to observe, to be sensitive, to avoid making assumptions. (2) For every word you use, you give your listeners untold numbers of nonverbal cues. The clearer, the more engaging your nonverbal communication, the higher your credibility with others and the greater your confidence will become.

Summary

Nonverbal communication consists of cues other than words, cues that often overlap one another and the verbal messages they accompany. Nonverbal cues may repeat, emphasize, complement, substitute for, or even contradict a person's verbal message. They are used to regulate turn-taking and topic-changing in conversation, and they indicate and develop dimensions in the relationships among participants.

Nonverbal cues are more unconscious, harder to control, and much more numerous than the verbal message they accompany, so people often trust them more. Adults rely on nonverbal cues for 60–70% of their interpretation of a message, and they derive much of their impression of others' credibility from their nonverbal behaviors. Even so, people often inaccurately interpret nonverbal cues, because those cues are influenced by the situation as well as the culture, gender, and status of the participants.

Nonverbal communication includes voice and speech (vocalics); eyes, face, and body, including gestures and posture (kinesics); touch (haptics); space, including territory and personal space (proxemics); and personal communicators such as objects (artifacts) and time (chronemics). The setting, too, contributes to the mood, flow, and stimulation of communication through sensory characteristics and electronic media.

You can become a better interpreter of others' nonverbal cues by drawing conclusions with great care and being sensitive to the multiple influences that might cause particular behaviors. Becoming an effective sender of nonverbal cues requires getting both interpersonal and taped feedback, taping and analyzing messages, using good models, and practicing both privately and in interpersonal transactions so the communicator can observe and adapt to others' responses.

Exercises

1   Think about how your family uses nonverbal communication. What are the family norms for space and territory? For touching? How do family members use facial expressions, gestures, eye contact? Where do you think the family norms come from? Are there cultural or social factors that influence them? How do you think these norms affect you and your own nonverbal communication? To what extent are you satisfied with your own use of nonverbal communication? What if anything would you like to change, and how do you think you could do that? Write an essay describing your responses to these questions.

2   With one other person, carry on a conversation about any topic that interests you. As you speak, try to mirror your partner's nonverbal communication—posture, eyes, facial expressions, gestures, use of space and touch, and voice and speech. Do this for 3 minutes, and then switch roles so your partner is mirroring you. Now, discuss what effect the mirroring had on your communication. It probably seemed silly and embarrassing at first, but as you practiced it, what happened? Now, monitor your behavior as you talk with people you are very close to. Do you naturally mirror others' behaviors? Is this mirroring different from mirroring a casual acquaintance? How?

3   With a small group of students, rent or go to see a foreign film—one from a culture different from your own. Watch the way the actors use territory, personal space, and touching. Now compare your observations to the norms for using space and touch among the people you know. Where are there similarities? Where are there differences? Speculate as to how those differences might affect communication between the two cultures. As a group, present a short report to the class on what you have observed.

4   Select a piece of literature to read aloud to the class. It could be a poem you like, an editorial, or a very short story. Children's stories are excellent for this purpose. On your own, read your piece aloud and time it. Then cut it, if necessary, to be no longer than 3 minutes. Now practice it aloud on audio- or videotape. Observe yourself, and do it again and again. Work on getting the maximum expression from your vocal quality, volume, pitch, tempo, and speech. Practice making eye contact, facial gestures, and body movements so that your listeners will want to hear you. Then read the story for the class.

Cyberpoints

1   Want to improve your voice and speech? Go to the *Communicating with Credibility and Confidence* Web site at http://communication. wadsworth.com/lumsden for suggestions, exercises, and resources to help you do that.

2   Are you concerned about inappropriate touching or sexual harassment? Go to the *Communicating with Credibility and Confidence* Web site at http://communication.wadsworth.com/lumsden for information on how to avoid either being an unintentional harasser or the victim of harassment.

3   How good are your nonverbal communication skills? Go to the *Communicating with Credibility and Confidence* Web site at http://communication. wadsworth.com/lumsden and click on Form 5.1, Personal Nonverbal Communication Assessment. Print out and make two copies of the form. First, complete the assessment on your own. Then ask a friend or family member to complete the form based on how she or he would rate your abilities. Now compare your responses. When you are not sure why you or your helper chose an answer, discuss it. What specific behaviors are involved? Are they strengths? Do you need to improve them? How can you strengthen your nonverbal communication?

4   For more information on some interesting aspects of nonverbal communication, use *InfoTrac College Edition* to search on the keyword, *nonverbal*. Take a look at:

Aguinis, H., Simonsen, M. M., & Pierce, C. A. (1999, August). Effects of nonverbal behavior on perceptions of power bases. *The Journal of Social Psychology, 138* (4), 455.

Lott, D. A. (1999, Jan). The new flirting game. (Why and how humans flirt). *Psychology Today 32* (l), 42.

Marty, M. E. A nice gesture. (1999, April 14). *The Christian Century, 116* (12), 43.

Chapter 6

Verbal Communication: Connecting with Language

Objectives for This Chapter

Knowledge

- Understand the importance of language in human communication
- Identify the linguistic elements in messages
- Know factors that influence how individuals use language
- Understand how language contributes to credibility and confidence

Feelings and Approaches

- Be aware of and sensitive to uses of language
- Develop confidence in using language effectively
- Feel credible in using language

Communication Abilities

- Consider others' backgrounds in interpreting and in phrasing messages
- Use language that communicates ideas clearly and vividly
- Use language styles that increase credibility and confidence

Key Terms

verbal communication
semantics
denotative meanings
connotative meanings
syntactics
strategic ambiguity

euphemism
redefinition
DEL
style
standard language
nonstandard language

high-context society
low-context society
metaphors
images

he minute a baby says his or her first word, Mom or Dad gleefully tele-
phones the family to announce the event. They are sure their baby's grasp of
language signals genius. Maybe, maybe not, but a child does develop a picture
of the world, an identity (and, yes, self-confidence and credibility) largely
through **verbal communication,** using language, written or oral, as a symbolic
code to communicate ideas. A perfect example of someone who used words to
create a world is Helen Keller. The discovery of language released her brilliant
mind from an intellectual prison—even though her body remained in its biological prison of darkness and soundlessness. Verbal communication, for her, was
language signed into the palm of her hand; from that, she related to her world
as an author of deep sensitivity and wisdom.

Verbal communication
Using language to com-
municate ideas

In this chapter, we will examine that power in terms of how language creates different worlds for people and how people create meaning from words.
We'll look at social influences on the development of language, the impact of
language styles, and the way language evolves and changes. Finally, we will
examine ways that skillful use of language can develop your credibility and confidence in communicating.

Words Create Meanings

For humans, words shape reality. What people say may reflect what they think
and feel—but it's also true that what they say often determines what they think
or feel or even remember. According to Giles and Coupland (1991), "The language forms we use to describe a specific event . . . will distinctly affect our
memory of the original event, in a way that makes it consistent with our linguistic expressions" (p. 20). The words start to structure your reality, and soon you
can't tell where the words leave off and the reality begins.

Often without even being aware of how words might structure reality—or
vice versa—people use them to describe, categorize, distinguish, or evaluate
what they perceive.

Description. Your eyes see images—objects, events, people, actions—that
become real to others and often to yourself when you describe them with
words. The words can both limit and expand how those images are perceived.

Hablamos porque somos mortales:
las palabras no son signos, son anos.
Al decir lo que dicen
los nombres que decimos
dicen tiempo: nos dicen.
Somos nombres del tiempo.

Mudos, tambien los muertos
pronuncian las palabras
que decimos los vivos.
El lenguaje es la casa
de odos en el flanco
del abismo colgada.
Conversar es humano.

We talk because we are mortal:
words are not signs, they are years.
Saying what they say,
the words we are saying
say time; they name us.
We are time's names.

The dead are mute
But they also say
what we are saying
Language is the house
of all, hanging over
the edge of the abyss.
To talk is human.

Octavio Paz: *A Draft of Shadows*. Copyright © 1979 by Octavio Paz and Eliot Weinberger, Reprinted by permission of New Directions Publishing Corporation.

"The shirt is red" or "The shirt is a deep scarlet, washed silk, oversized slipover with balloon sleeves" may describe the same piece of clothing, but each statement creates a different picture in the mind of the sender and receiver. When you describe with one set of words, you exclude other words and the possible images they may have created.

Categorization. In giving names and definitions, words label specific categories and exclude others for discussion: "Ms. Whalen is a corporate attorney" tells us something about her education, her profession, and her status, but the label also excludes many elements of her personality and her life.

Distinction. Language makes distinctions among ideas and pinpoints ways in which they are dissimilar. As soon as people discriminate one idea or entity from another, they draw attention to differences and away from similarities. In the language of politics, for example, "He's a liberal and she's a conservative" implies great differences, when, in reality, the two individuals may be alike in more ways than they are different in their political beliefs.

Evaluation.   Language choices often imply value judgments about events, objects, and people. The old executive line, "I'll have my girl get back to your girl," for example, betrays an unconscious attitude that a secretary is a female possession who is less than adult.

Meanings Create Words

Language changes constantly as old words fall into disuse or acquire new meanings and as new words are created. Words come from many sources and change meanings for many reasons. Once, a neighbor rushed over to our house in shock at what she'd read in the newspaper. "Do you know what they're going to do?" she demanded. "They're going to change the dictionary! Now, nobody'll know what anything means!" She didn't understand that a dictionary doesn't dictate the meanings of words, it simply reflects the ever-evolving nature of a language. Words emerge from a number of basic sources, and they are developed to express a range of changing conditions in a society.

Basic Sources of Words

Trying to trace the source of a word can be both fun and challenging. In fact, there's a whole profession of language detectives, called "etymologists," who spend their lives tracking the development of words and meanings.

One way words enter a language is when people simply *imitate sounds to indicate what they mean.* "Bark," for example, sounds like the sound a dog makes. "Onomatopeia" is the technical name for that type of word.

Frequently languages use words that are *derivatives* from other languages. Languages borrow freely from one another, weaving and tangling through cultures and throughout history. English is infused with a number of languages; *mother*, for example, derives from the Latin *mater.* Many words have almost-twins called *cognates* in another language; that is, they sound similar and carry similar definitions because they derive from a common root. In English, for example, the adjective *finite* means "something measurable, defined, limited." In Spanish, the word is *finito*; in French, it is *fini*; in Italian, it is *definito*. All stem from the Latin *finite.* In German, the term is *endlich*, but that also is easy to recognize because it, too, is a cognate to the English term *end*, which stems from the Middle and Old English word *ende.*

One language frequently *adopts* a word from another, too. Listen to a foreign-language radio station and see how many English words you pick up. The expression, "She is very simpatico," for example, comes straight from Spanish. Although *simpatico* is a cognate to the English word *sympathetic*, the meaning is different and hard to define. To a North American, "She's sympathetic" might convey, "She has compassion." *Simpatico*, however, conveys a person's special ability to comprehend, to get along with people, to relate to them, to get them to relate to you.

Death and life are in the power of the tongue.

Proverbs 18:21, Old Testament of the Holy Bible

Adaptive Sources of Words   The world is changing almost blindlingly fast, and people need new words to describe all the new ideas that come with the changes. Often, people develop words or shorten phrases to express an idea more quickly or specifically to a group's understanding. Common shortcut symbols include jargon, acronyms, and slang.

- *Jargon* is language that comes out of a specialized interest or profession. It might be from inner-city slang, military talk ("grunttalk" for noncommissioned personnel), or an academic or technological discipline. Today, there's the language of the "digitally hip," or those who are developing their own computer language faster than the public can keep up with it. There now exist dictionaries (obsolete by their first printing) of digital idioms, using definitions such as the ironic one of "cyberspace: what cyberpunks and *Newsweek* say when they mean to say 'the Net' " (Revah, 1998, p. 12).

- *Acronyms* are words formed by combining the first letters of a phrase, sometimes with another letter inserted to give the word enough vowels for easy English pronunciation. A familiar example is *radar,* an acronym for "**RA**dio **D**etecting **A**nd **R**anging"—an electronic device that spots and locates an object by measuring the time it takes for the echo of a radio wave to return from it and the direction from which it returns.

- *Slang* is nonstandard, informal, lively, innovative language that reflects and defines the character of a group and the individuals within it, encoding in-group jokes or ways of saying things that would otherwise be considered unacceptable. Slang dictionaries compiled by surveying student populations, for example, mostly contain words or phrases related to drunkenness, throwing up, and sex. Student researchers in a language and discourse class at a Midwestern university found that their peers used some slang expressions that go back generations, such as "tossing your cookies" (Benoit, et al., 1992, p. 16), as well as some innovative current slang that ought not be quoted here. New slang is derived from metaphors, puns, or abbreviations for ideas. Slang can be fun; it's personal, carries inside jokes and meanings, and avoids more prolonged explanations and descriptions. Slang is inappropriate in many situations because it diminishes the speaker's credibility with others who are not part of the in-group. Other times slang is appropriate to you and your listeners and enlivens and vivifies your communication. It can be, in fact, "cool, awesome, bad, bitchin', choice, classic, intense, primo, smokin', stellar, and ultra" (Benoit, et al., 1992, p. 22).

People Create Meanings

Folks too frequently forget that what they really mean is in their heads, not in the words they use. What someone hears may not be what you thought you said at all. Or you may deliberately not say *precisely* what you mean. This is partly a matter of how a language arranges words to map people's meanings, partly an issue of how people use differing language styles.

Language to Map Ideas

For a long time, scholars have pondered how people use language to define and communicate their experience to others. Korzybski (1933) suggested an analogy for understanding this process: Words relate to ideas in the same way that maps relate to territories. Humans look at the world of ideas and create language maps to represent what they see—the territory of their experiences. A map is *not* the territory itself, and a word is not the "thing," but the symbolic representation of the idea.

People create meanings from their word maps by using and interpreting words within the structure of sentences. Let's look at how two concepts—semantics and syntactics—function in creating and communicating meaning.

Semantics **Semantics** is the study of how people use words as signs or symbols for their ideas and perceptions. Signs are clear, concrete representations of one idea that require little mental processing. "Stop!" clearly is a command, a sign, to cease action, for example. Symbols, however, are less precise. Their meanings are drawn from unique individual experiences and may be either denotative or connotative. **Denotative meanings** generally are shared by speakers of the language. Dictionaries compile denotative definitions based on ways the words are used in the society. **Connotative meanings,** however, are personal. A word's connotations draw from an individual's experience, background, values, and needs, and they exist only for that person. For example, we once asked a class what *freedom* meant. For several white, middle-class North Americans, it meant having the privilege to do whatever they wanted to do; for two Cuban refugees, it meant escaping from oppression and poverty; for several African American students, it meant opportunity and self-esteem; for a battered wife, just then rebuilding her life, it meant not living in fear. Even as we try to paraphrase these students' connotative meanings, however, we recognize that each was so personal and so deeply held that we can only approximate what we understood to be the distinctions among their meanings.

Syntactics Every language has its own way of combining and arranging words that influences how listeners interpret them. These roadways and directions that help to convey meaning are called **syntactics.** Children usually begin to understand the syntactics of their language very early in life. For example, visualize a country road. Along that road, you see white houses. There are 20 of them. All of them are small. Now, arrange that information into one standard English sentence. Most people, even young children, would say, "There are 20 small, white houses along the road." If you are a native English speaker, you may never have been told to order adjectives from number to size to color before the subject, yet you "just knew" this was correct syntax in English.

It can be hard for someone learning a second language to order thoughts in the expected way. In Spanish, for example, you don't put ownership first; you put the object first. "I'm going to John's house" translates to Spanish as "Voy a la

---

Semantics The study of how people use words as signs or symbols for ideas and perceptions

Denotative meanings Meanings of words that are shared by speakers of the language

Connotative meanings Meanings of words that are based on an individual's personal experiences

Syntactics The way languages arrange and order words to convey meaning

casa de Juan" or, back to English, as "I'm going to the house of John." This is a small difference, yet both the words and the order must be correct, because the syntax *creates and communicates the logic and emphasis of the statement.* In the English version, John gets the emphasis; in the Spanish version, the house takes precedence.

Language of Social Identity

Language defines, to a great extent, who people think they are within their society and culture. Philipsen (1989) points out that "cultural premises and rules about speaking are intricately tied up with cultural conceptions of persons, agency, and social relations. . . . In this sense a code of speaking is a code of personhood and society as well" (p. 236).

That means that language can become a volatile issue. Not long ago, the United States was seized in an intellectual and emotional issue over the Oakland, California, school board's decision to teach *Ebonics*, which some call, "Black English or Black English Vernacular—a language, some call it slang, some call it a dialect. Some say it is just bad English, some say it is sloppy, some say it is illegitimate, some say it is wrong. . . . Others have said explicitly that Ebonics is a descendant of the language that was forced upon slaves, who were prevented from learning to speak as their white masters did" (Fox, 1997, p. 237).

Fox (1997) concludes that Ebonics "is a dialect of American English," but that it's best to use standard English in North American schools for the pragmatic reason that students need it "in looking for jobs in the future" (p. 237). Simply put, the power structure in North America uses standard English.

Throughout history, conquerors have tried to stamp out cultural identities by eliminating the language of the conquered and substituting their own. The oppressor's argument is that homogeneity—of culture, of language, of thinking—makes people and society easier to control and manage.

When Puerto Rico passed from Spanish to U.S. control in 1898, for example, the U.S.-appointed Board of Education mandated English in the schools. The board president expressed the rationale in this way: "If the schools are made American, and teachers and pupils are inspired with the American spirit, . . . the island will become in its sympathies, views, and attitude toward life and toward government essentially American. The great mass of Puerto Ricans are as yet passive and plastic. . . . Their ideals are in our hands to create and mold" (Morris, 1992, p. 3).

Aside from the obvious arrogance of the colonialist attitude, does such a conversion of a language and a people work? After almost a hundred years of this policy, "the Spanish language . . . is the fundamental tool used by most Puerto Ricans for most communication. But in this context it also serves as a symbolic marker for Puerto Rican identity, in direct opposition to the English-speaking United States" (Morris, 1992, p. 16). Puerto Ricans may speak English, but Spanish still represents *who they are.*

Many efforts to replace a people's language have been made throughout history—and have failed. The cultures in power have underestimated how vital language is to a people's concept of themselves and have overlooked the richness of thought that diversity of language can bring to the society. In Ireland, the English made it illegal to speak Gaelic, but "hedgerow teachers," secretly met at the edges of fields with little groups of students to impart the Irish language and culture. Today, Gaelic is taught in Irish schools along with English. Similarly, the Canadian battle has been resolved by an uneasy acceptance of both French and English, whereas in the United States, many people are pushing to make English the national language, believing that by eliminating immigrant languages, at least in public life, this country will be united in its norms and objectives. Switzerland, on the other hand, seems to manage with four official languages.

At the moment, common language on the Internet seems to be the enemy. The European Union has been so concerned that Internet communication will blend European languages and cultures that they established a 3-year Multilingual Information Society program "to preserve the cultural crucial languages in all their diversity," including an effort to provide translation services and dictionairies over data networks (*Communications Daily*, 1996, p. 10).

Language for Social Strategy

Within any language structure, people choose their words and their syntax with goals in mind. These goals may be conscious or unconscious, ethical or unethical, or something in between. Common language strategies use words to obscure, to redefine, and, at times, to hurt.

Words to Obscure

Sometimes a person allows more than one possible meaning because of carelessness or lack of vocabulary—but sometimes people deliberately phrase a "message which is constructed to allow for multiple interpretations in order to mask or deviate from a privately represented belief, attitude, fact, or feeling" (Feldman & Walkosz, 1992, p. 2). This is called **strategic ambiguity.** This might be a kind way to protect another person from an unpleasant truth or a subtle way to influence another person, a way to avoid an issue, to control the flow of communication, to influence how another perceives you, or to manage a potential conflict (Feldman & Walkosz, 1992, p. 2).

Strategic ambiguity The deliberate use of words that may have more than one possible interpretation

For instance, you might say, "I really have to think about your sermon today," to your religious leader, when what you really mean is, "I didn't understand a word you said." Or you could say to your friend, "I'd really like to drive my car tonight," when what you mean is, "I know *I'll* stay sober, so I'll be the designated driver."

People also often use **euphemisms,** which are words or phrases that deliberately gloss over hard or potentially offensive aspects of a message. A favorite corporate euphemism, for example, is the "golden handshake" to symbolize

Euphemism A word or phrase that glosses over offensive aspects of a message

Simon and Garfunkel sang, "The words of the prophets are written on the subway walls and tenement halls." What gives language its power? How do verbal and nonverbal cues interact in signs and graffiti? What do you suppose motivates people to express their views in public places?

J. Sohm/The Image Works

using retirement incentives to unload older employees and hire younger ones at lower wages. The goal may be to "downsize" the organization, a euphemism for cutting personnel. To minimize the negative connotations of *downsize,* corporations have coined another new term, *rightsize,* a substitution of one euphemism for another.

Euphemisms and strategic ambiguity are often acceptable, but they may be used unethically to manipulate, control, and/or oppress people. Laws containing loopholes from which certain groups benefit, contracts that are vague and easily interpreted to cheat another, language that glosses over injustice—all use strategic ambiguity for unethical purposes.

Words to Redefine

Redefinition The use of language to change perceptions by changing the words used

A **redefinition** uses language to change a perception of persons or events. Sometimes, redefinition works for positive social change. Efforts to change sexist or racist language, for example, have redefined terms to reduce stereotyping. Retitling the head of a department as the "chairperson" rather than "chairman," for example, is a small step toward recognizing that women can be leaders, too. When you refer to "people of color" instead of "minorities," your redefinition does two things: It acknowledges that you're talking about people, not objects, and that "people of color" are not necessarily in the minority—indeed, worldwide they are by far the majority. In other words, you recognize the presence and dignity of many people of varying ethnic identities. Redefinition, therefore, can be a positive step in using language to connect rather than divide people. It appears that using language that humanifies others, rather than stereotyping them, also accrues to the credibility of the communicator (Seiter, Larsen, & Skinner, 1998).

Unfortunately, redefinition can also play a major negative role in propaganda. *Propaganda* is "mass 'suggestion' or influence through the manipulation of symbols and the psychology of the individual" (Pratkanis & Aronson, 1991, p. 9). Propaganda often relies on vagueness, ambiguity, euphemisms, or redefinitions to manipulate the receiver.

In Nazi Germany, dictionaries and encyclopedias were rewritten, changing definitions to make actions of the fascist regime seem acceptable. The term *Abstammungsnachweis,* for example, had previously been defined in terms of cattle breeding but was redefined as a "genealogical certificate of Aryan origin" (Lee & Lee, 1989, pp. 134–135). Nazi propaganda then used the term to justify selective breeding of "desirable" humans (and the extermination of those considered undesirable—Jews, Gypsies, homosexuals, people with disabilities, children with alleged low intelligence or disabilities, the aged and infirm). More recently, the men, women, and children of Bosnia crumbled under the force of "ethnic cleansing," a euphemistic redefinition of genocide to justify the rape and murder of an entire population of Muslim people.

As a communicator, you may use strategic ambiguity, euphemisms, and redefinitions in your word choices, but be aware of their potential for both good and evil so that you can make ethical choices about when and how and why you use them. As a receiver of communication, particularly through the mass media, your understanding of such language use is crucial to detecting others' efforts to manipulate and control your responses. Analysis of language can be the key to making decisions and controlling your own destiny.

Words to Hurt

DEL Derogatory ethnic label; a name that attributes negative characteristics to a person or group

Sometimes words are designed to hurt. Many obscenities and most "DELs" fall into this category. **DEL** is short for a "derogatory ethnic label," a name that attributes a set of negative characteristics to a person and his or her group. These toxic labels result when members of an in-group use negative words to distance and devalue members of an out-group. DELs can be based on race, color, gender, sexual orientation, age, and abilities; in fact, over 1000 DELs are documented in the United States (Allen, 1983).

In his *Letter from a Birmingham Jail,* Martin Luther King, Jr. (1963) describes the feeling that DELs can inflict: "You are humiliated day in and day out by nagging signs reading 'white' and 'colored'; when your first name becomes 'nigger,' your middle name becomes 'boy' (however old you are) and your last name becomes 'John,' and your wife and mother are never given the respected title 'Mrs.' " (p. 81).

Words may not inflict bodily injury, but they can break hearts. DELs diminish the humanity of the targets by associating their group with subhuman categories. Even calling a woman a "chick" casts her into the role of a ditzy, fluffy, incompetent baby fowl. She's cute but relatively worthless. She's not much good when you call her a "hen," either.

Furthermore, DELs may influence the labeled members of an out-group to "develop resentment and distrust for the majority group, and, consequently, [lead to] rejection of many of the values of the majority culture" (p. 81). This, again, pits groups against one another. "Why can't they just be more like *we* are?" an in-grouper says of an out-group. Why, however, would you want to emulate someone who so labels you? (Greenberg, Kirkland, & Pyszcynski, 1988).

DELs can categorize people so that neither the labeler nor the labeled can see the real person. Because language so often defines and limits what people can perceive, labels may make it impossible to see beyond them. It's true that groups often absorb into their vocabularies and humor the very DELs that hurt them. In so doing, they diffuse the effect, and the DEL becomes an inside joke. From an outsider—even an outsider who is a good friend—a DEL takes on a different meaning. A person outside of the group should never try to usurp an inside joke; it's much better to avoid DELs entirely. They carry poison.

People Use Different Styles

Style In communication, the way a person uses language

Style, in communication, refers to the way an individual uses language—the semantics, word order, grammar, and personal or group idiosyncrasies that make up his or her speech. A person's language style reveals where she or he fits in the culture's pecking order by communicating status and power and reinforcing gender and cultural differences.

Status and Power

Societies have in-groups—those who have power or dominance—and out-groups—those who have different cultures, norms, and/or social positions and are excluded from the social world of the in-group. People are comfortable with the communication of their own groups, and, sometimes, alienated from and uncomfortable with that of other groups. Generally, higher-status people will be the major in-group, and those of lesser status will be identified with an out-group. Typically, each society's language reflects these groupings by falling into two major types: standard and nonstandard (although some cultures also have several levels of language styles within each).

Standard language the language associated with power and status within a community

Nonstandard language A dialect or style that differs from the standard language within a community

Standard language is a style "most often associated with high socioeconomic status, power and media usage in a particular community" (Giles & Coupland, 1991, p. 38). **Nonstandard language** is a style, or dialect, that uses some qualities of vocabulary, grammar, syntax, and/or usage that distinguish it from "standard" language.

Often, standard and nonstandard languages also are accompanied by high-prestige or low-prestige speech patterns. Standard American English, for example, is distinguished by "correct" grammar and vocabulary usage as well as pronunciation typical of the Midwest. Most broadcasters, actors, and high-level power brokers speak standard American English. By these criteria, most North Americans probably speak a version of a nonstandard style or dialect.

Because prestige is associated with standard language use, people tend to evaluate others who speak it as more credible, competent, intelligent, confident, and ambitious than people who use regional dialects or minority ethnic styles (Giles & Coupland, 1991, p. 38). Sadly enough, teachers sometimes judge students' personalities, social backgrounds, and academic abilities negatively when the students use nonstandard language. Even nonstandard speakers themselves evaluate standard speakers as more competent than members of their own group, even though they still find people of their own group more socially attractive (Giles & Coupland, 1991, pp. 40–45).

Kimo, for example, speaks "pidgin" with his Hawaiian coworkers. In school, teachers had scolded, "You'll never get anywhere speaking pidgin." But pidgin was quick, colorful, and expressive, and Kimo could "talk story" with his friends, who shared the norms, friendships, mutual support, and knowledge of one another that pidgin expressed. When a new worker arrived who spoke only standard English, Kimo and his friends were uncomfortable with her and were aware that she might be promoted over them, even though they had more experience, because she spoke a higher-status language. For Kimo's group, pidgin provided a solidarity and identity, but it also separated them from others and, possibly, hindered their career advancement.

Status and power are clearly linked, with language often revealing a person's degree of power in the society. People who are brought up outside of the powerful group don't develop the powerful way of speaking; communication styles in their group develop differently from that of the higher-status group. Stereotypes of people based on their language style emerge, and people use these to label one another as powerful or powerless, important or unimportant, credible or not credible (Bradac & Mulac, 1984, pp. 307–309). In this context, *powerful language* is the language of status, position, education, and success, whereas language use of lower-status groups in the society, characterized by different styles and symbologies, is seen as powerless.

Kramarae (1981) calls a group that does not share the metaphors and symbols of the power group, and therefore is not heard in the larger arenas of power, a *muted group*. Typically, muted groups are women, members of ethnic minorities or out-groups, people who have disabilities, the elderly, and the poor. Their own style may have its own strengths, but it marks them as less powerful in the society at large.

Again, as with speech patterns described in Chapter 5, the most effective strategy is to be fluent in each social strata. As African American women explained their own talk in one study, they use "style-switching to accomodate the demands of African American and dominant cultural settings" (Houston, 2000, p. 11).

Gender

Gender differences are also reinforced by language style in many cultures. Tannen (1990), for example, classifies the language of white, North American males and females into *report-talk* and *rapport-talk*. She notes that men tend to use a "report" or public-speaking style; they lecture, inform, and correct others. By contrast, women use a "rapport" or connecting style by questioning, encouraging, affirming, and supporting others with their conversation. Ironically, these differences may be why women often are perceived as talking too much when, in fact, men do the most talking. Tannen concludes that men are notoriously silent at home, where women often do the talking and the questioning to get their husbands to open up to them. "Again and again," Tannen says, "women complain, 'He seems to have everything to say to everyone else, and nothing to say to me'" (pp. 78–79).

Investigations of status and gender styles have found that subordinate and/or female communicators tend to be more *tentative, hesitant, polite, correct, and more colorful* in their rapport talk; higher status people, often male, are more *certain, commanding, confident, less polite, and more colloquial* in their report talk.

Keep in mind, however, that generalizations about male and female language styles are useful only up to a certain point. First, the best style to use—for men and women—depends on the requirements of the situations (code-switching yet again). Report-talk may be better for business meetings, and rapport-talk may be essential for sharing feelings with a friend. Ideally, men and woman should be able to adapt their styles to the listener and their communication goals. In fact, recent research "suggests that people may now accept the desirability of androgyny and flexibility in gender-based characteristics" (House, Dallinger, & Kilgallen, 1998, p. 11). Second, individual cases often contradict the traditional expectations. You may know "high-status" men who usually are tentative, proper, and hesitant in their speech and "low-status" women who usually are aggressive and powerful. Third, times are changing. As women are winning higher status, their communication is changing along with their situation.

It's true that many culture-bound language style characteristics still exist in societies around the world. The way different societies reflect those characteristics, however, may vary, with different standards for power, status, and gender than those of the United States. In at least one society, the characteristics of powerful/male and powerless/female talk are reversed. Smith-Heffner (1988) reports that "in Malagasy society women have lower status than men, but they use our stereotypical 'powerful' language; they do the confronting and reprimanding and in so doing—in direct opposition to society's nonconfrontal, conversational norms—their constant violation of societal norms is seen as confirmation of their inferiority" (p. 536). Despite the reversal of the language traits of each gender, males remain the powerful and dominant group in Malagasy.

Culture

Communication styles are closely tied to a culture's perception of members' relationships to one another, their degree of closeness and interdependence, and the extent of their information about one another. Hall (1976) suggests that societies fit along a spectrum ranging from high-context to low-context. Context, in this sense, means the amount of information all members of the society hold in common.

The **high-context society** is likely to be agrarian, with close family and community groupings. People generally have the same knowledge about one another and their environment, so they have a basic context for their communication. Many Asian cultures are described as high-context cultures. Their members are often (but not always) indirect; they are concerned with maintaining *face*, or respect for self and others. For them, a primary value is harmony, because close relationships with the entire community are woven tightly into the context of their lives. Japanese children, for example, learn early on not to call attention to themselves and not to hurt the feelings of others; their mothers teach them "the subtleties of face-giving and face-threatening behaviors through modeling their mothers' behaviors" (Gudykunst & Ting-Toomey, 1992, p. 224).

Contrast this subtlety, self-effacement, and concern for harmony with that of a **low-context society.** This type of culture is more likely to be industrialized and diverse, with scattered family, community, and socioeconomic groupings. People cannot all have the same knowledge of one another and their environment, so they have less context in common for their communication. There is little motivation to sacrifice individual wants for group harmony, because there is less closeness among people. Major U.S. cities exemplify low-context cultures, and you can easily see how this affects communication. North Americans are more likely to be direct, explicit, and focused on individual goals of the communication.

A friend of ours had an experience that demonstrates what can happen when people from each culture type interact. Peter was in the People's Republic of China on a business trip, and his host interpreter told him they would be meeting with an important state official that evening. The dialogue went like this:

Peter: Should I wear a tie?

Interpreter: You may wear whatever you wish; he is a very important person.

Peter: Then I should wear a tie?

Interpreter: Oh, you may wear anything that's comfortable for you. It will be a special evening.

Peter: So a sweater would be okay?

Interpreter: Whatever you would like to wear will be fine. He's an important person. It will be a very nice occasion.

High-context society A society with close family and community groupings, in which people share the same knowledge about each other and their environment

Low-context society A society with scattered family, community, and socioeconomic groupings, in which people do not share the same knowledge about each other and their environment

Finally, after many of these ambiguous messages, Peter asked the right question:

"Will *you* be wearing a tie?"

"Oh, yes," replied the interpreter. "He's a *very* important person."

The high-context, face-saving Chinese culture made it impossible for the host to tell his guest what he should wear. The interpreter kept the issue open until our friend asked the right question in order to elicit a polite answer that guided, but didn't demand, Peter's dress choice. Peter wore a jacket and tie.

You and Language

The difference between the right word and the almost-right word is really a large matter—it's the difference between the lightning bug and the lightning.

Mark Twain, 19–20th-century humorist, novelist, essayist

When your language is effective, you are likely to feel confident of what you say. Furthermore, when you use language effectively, you convince others of your credibility. You can improve your use of language and increase your self-confidence by developing vocabulary, choosing language appropriately, communicating with clarity, stimulating listeners' thinking, and making messages vivid.

Building a Vocabulary

Students occasionally tell us they lack confidence in their vocabularies. Certainly, you will be less confident in speaking if you can't find the right words. Admittedly, English vocabulary looks overwhelming. The average high school student graduates knowing about 80,000 words (Anderson & Nagy, 1992, p. 18) out of the million or so words in English, including specialized fields (McCrum, Cran, & MacNeill, 1986, p. 19).

You already have expanded that base, however, and as you proceed through your college classes, you'll acquire more vocabulary from general education courses and from your major. If you want to embark on a vigorous effort to expand your vocabulary, many excellent programs are available. You can improve your vocabulary without a commercial program by using these guidelines:

1   *Cultivate a curious and playful attitude.* Become conscious of words— their nuances, their sources, their uses. Words give color, emotion, and impact to ideas. Look on new words as puzzles to solve and potential tools to make your own.

2   *Read as much and as widely as you can.* The real secret to building vocabulary is reading (Anderson & Nagy, 1992). As you read your textbooks, think of them as vocabulary sources and start using some of the new words they teach you. In addition, read a variety of well-written literature or news magazines from which you can learn new words and phrases.

Remember when you entered the E-mail fray, and it felt so novel . . . ?

Electronic mail was more personal than faxes or snail mail, but not so intrusive as a telephone call. Conventions quickly evolved: You usually addressed people by their first names, for example, and signed off with—well, there seemed to be different ways. I mimicked my boss and used "Cheers," even though I felt a little foolish (he's British and could get away with it). When the E-mailing public adopted "Regards," I felt much more comfortable. It was businesslike. It was polite.

Sometime thereafter, the popular so-long became "Best regards." I reserved that sign-off for more personal E-mail—people with whom I had some kind of working relationship and sincerely meant, well, best regards. That the Internet equivalent of direct mailers used it in a feeble attempt to achieve an up-close-and-personal dynamic seemed rather pointless (if predictable). It wasn't, though, such a turn of phrase that improper use of it turned my stomach.

"Warm (or Warmest) regards" is a different story. Sure, it's just one word different. But it ratchets up the expression one very important notch on the intimacy scale. It crosses the business/personal line. Warm is evocative of a human touch, of a friend squeezing your arm . . . that feeling inside when you've connected with someone, intellectually or emotionally. E-mail from strangers is none of those things. And before long, it's all one contiguous mass of gibberish to shovel through and fork over to the next guy, and we're too numb from the volume and sameness to remember there might be a person (rather than a list server) at the other end of the Reply button. And when there is a person, we have no way to acknowledge it, to make our message stand out—a raft of emoticons, capital letters and exclamation points aside.

"Warm regards" might not be quite lost to the officious E-mailers among us yet. Let's do our part to make sure it isn't. Use of E-mail might continue to evolve, but some things are sacred. Language is one of them.

Anne McCrory, When E-mail greetings shouldn't be warm. *Computerworld*, Dec. 15, 1997, p. 33.

3   *Listen for language.* Tune in to words that most effectively and clearly communicate concepts. Listening to lectures, sermons, broadcasts, and friends, and notice the words that work. When a word is new to you, grab it and make it your own. Making a word your own involves much more than just looking it up in the dictionary—although that's an important part. You can understand new words and incorporate them into your own vocabulary by doing the following:

■   *Look for the context.* Some words are easy to figure out from their context; others are not. If you hear someone say, for example, "Of *course* he didn't contribute. . . . He's a parsimonious jerk," even if *parsimonious* is new, you could infer that it means the subject is stingy and money-grubbing.

- *Ask someone who might know.* Your college is filled with experts (your professors and instructors) in a wide range of fields, and they often can give you the definition, the possible contextual interpretations, and the history of a term. The more you learn about a term, the easier it is to remember and to use.

- *Dissect the word.* Look for familiar roots (usually from Latin or Greek), prefixes, and suffixes that tip you off to part of the meaning, and parts of the word that are similar to other words you know. A wonderfully complicated sounding word, for example, is *antidisestablishmentarianism.* You know that *anti* means "against"; *dis* also means "opposition" (as in to *disbelieve*); an *establishment* is a permanent institution; *arian* is a familiar suffix indicating that a person subscribes to the concept (such as *vegetarian*); and *ism* is a suffix indicating a philosophical position. When you take the pieces apart, you can get a hint that *antidisestablishmentarianism* refers to opposing the position of withdrawing support from institutions.

Communicating with Clarity

The ideal is to provide a message that is clear to your listeners, using concrete language and minimizing ambiguities. Although you might sometimes use ambiguity deliberately, it's usually far preferable to eliminate ambiguities by paying attention to words, phrases, and sentence structures that might be misconstrued. Some sources of ambiguity:

- *A single word can be interpreted with more than one meaning.* Consider the statement, "She's such a perfect model." Does this mean she's a great person to emulate, or that she models for *Vogue* magazine and makes a lot of money?

- *A phrase may be interpreted with more than one meaning.* The statement, "That teacher really has high standards," may mean she's a tough grader, or she is extremely ethical, or she works very hard at her job.

- *The syntax, or arrangement, of a sentence may suggest more than one meaning.* One form (called "amphibole") goes like this: "The board solved the problem with money." Was the problem financial, and the board solved it? Or, did the board use money to solve some other problem?

The best way to eliminate ambiguity is to consider the possible interpretations of your words and your phrases from your listeners' point of view and pay attention to their nonverbal and verbal feedback. If you're preparing a report or speech, ask someone to listen to your rehearsal and let you know when parts are ambiguous.

It helps people understand when you use *concrete terms.* As symbols, words range from concrete to abstract. A concrete term is specific and simple, dealing with just one idea. Words that embrace broader sets of ideas are more abstract, as they have less specific detail associated with the meaning. You might

Figure 6.1 *Abstraction Circles*

Sarah

Little girls with Down's Syndrome

Girls with Down's Syndrome

Children with Down's Syndrome

Down's Syndrome patients

Genetic disorder patients

Medical cases

represent this as a sphere, with layers or levels of abstraction that move out from the center, as shown in Figure 6.1.

At the center, you have a concrete core of specific meaning about one idea. As you move outward through successive rings, each term provides more room for other ideas or things to be included in the category. The words become more abstract and more general. Although the core term is still part of the broader category, the specific individual would be hard to identify. Consider how both denotative and connotative meanings may change at each layer.

At the core, Sarah is a unique individual. Her family can see Sarah clearly in their minds when they say her name. For them, the name "Sarah" is filled with personal feelings and understandings. The next layers become more abstract. At Layer 2, Sarah is a little girl, and the term could apply to other little girls as well as to Sarah. Layer 3 puts her among girls of all ages and sizes, and at Layer 4, Sarah is one of all children without reference to gender or age or character.

Then, to the medical establishment, at Layer 5, Sarah becomes even more abstract—a Down's syndrome patient. At Layer 6, she is even less human and specific—now she's a genetic disorder. How impersonal, how unreal—but yet, how handy an abstraction for conveying a wealth of information about Sarah's condition among medical experts. Connotations now revolve around medical questions rather than individual ones about the girl herself. Finally, at Layer 7, Sarah is a medical "case." She has lost personality, gender, age, character, even her specific condition. She is simply a file folder full of records to be discussed at health-care team meetings.

Only if members of her health-care team can get back to talking about Sarah—the concrete, real, person—can that group of professionals begin to understand all the subtleties and connotations of the human being as well as the medical facts and implications of the case. Abstractions are essential to discussing complex and specialized ideas—but concrete language is crucial to understanding individual and specific issues among people.

As a communicator, concrete language can determine how effective and how credible you are. Sometimes, an abstraction *is* the perfect word for what you want to say and for the listener. A good rule, however, is to go down through those layers of abstraction in your mind and choose the least abstract term that will express what you mean. If you were Sarah's doctor, for example, you might say to another doctor, "The Down's syndrome child I talked to you about last week." To Sarah's parents, it's far better to say, "In reviewing Sarah's situation," instead of, "In reviewing the case."

When you must use an abstraction, define the term for anyone to whom the word might be unfamiliar. Sometimes, in a presentation or work group meeting, you can quote a dictionary or expert source to define a term. Other times, such as in personal conversation, you wouldn't want to insult people by waving a dictionary at them. Here are some ways you can define words within the context of your conversation:

- *Build the definitions into your discussion* with clarifying phrases or examples, for instance, "It seems to me the problem with the attrition policy—that when someone leaves she or he won't be replaced—is that . . . "
- *Clarify an idea with comparisons and contrasts* to other ideas, as in, "This is a global plan—it doesn't focus only on national problems, it addresses more general worldwide problems."
- *Use analogies* to draw the similarities between a more familiar concept and the one you want to clarify, for example, "Feeling empathy for another is like walking in that person's boots" is a familiar analogy that helps to define empathy.

Stimulating Thinking and Senses

The best communication occurs when a listener gets a flash of insight—when she or he grasps the idea at a personal level. When you use language using metaphors and images, you can provoke others' thinking processes and make them truly "see" the ideas.

Whoever would love life and see good days must keep the tongue from evil and the lips from speaking deceit.

1 Peter 3:8–11, New Testament of the Holy Bible

Metaphor The comparison of two things by calling one the other

Metaphors compare two things by calling one the other, providing a powerful way to connect ideas in the listener's mind. One management writer suggests, "A CEO proposing a joint venture may frame the opportunity by using the metaphor of 'a train leaving the station.' To fail to jump on board is to be left behind. A manager opposing the venture may frame it as 'hopping on the bandwagon,' highlighting the foolishness of joining without the benefit of careful analysis" (Aaron, 1999, p. 2).

The insight a metaphor brings to you becomes your own, taking on power and dimensions that you would never see without the help of the metaphor. To develop skill at making metaphors, practice by comparing two concepts in your mind and then develop a metaphor to express it. We heard a counselor refer to a desperately needy, impossible-to-satisfy client as an "energy vampire." With these two words, she conveyed the idea that her energy was being sucked from her by her voracious client.

Images Vivid "pictures" drawn with words

Images are vivid "pictures" drawn with words, often including metaphors, that arouse the receivers' senses. In so doing, the picture becomes real in their minds, and, once again, the listeners "own" the ideas. This is, in part, because people have sensory memories that can be triggered by smells, sounds, tastes, feelings—or your descriptions of them. If you say, "The evening was cold," the listener gets a flat bit of information. If you say, "I could feel ice daggers cutting through my forehead, my fingers were too stiff to bend, and I trembled like a tuning fork in that 50-mile-an-hour wind," the listener can conjure up his or her own similar experiences and *feel* what you were feeling.

The importance of metaphor and imagery in language cannot be exaggerated. Often, they work together and even can trigger a redefinition of old ideas. Sometimes, a new metaphor helps people to see ideas and people in an entirely different light. In Jesse Jackson's presidential campaigns, for example, he used the metaphors of the "rainbow" and the "patchwork quilt," as a new way of seeing American society, a fresh vision of diversity in the United States. These metaphors, with the images they brought to mind, replaced the old concept of the "melting pot," which implied that all Americans would merge into precise sameness. Jackson's metaphors gave a new sense of working together in a design of many cultures and ways of being (Moore, 1992) and have extended beyond his campaign to enter the national vocabulary, enlarging the national perception of this society.

To develop skill at creating images, practice identifying and describing all the sensory elements in an experience. Brainstorm every sight, sound, smell, taste, and feeling in an experience, and then combine them into a description.

Summary

Language develops a person's sense of identity and shapes his or her perception of the world. People create their own meanings for words; the study of this process is called semantics. Humans locate the meanings of ideas on mental maps of their thoughts and perceptions. They connect these words through specific arrangements dictated by the language. The study of how words are ordered and arranged is called syntactics.

The language of a people reflects their understandings of life and determines their sense of identity and pride. Language connects or divides people on the basis of similarities and differences of social status, gender, power, and culture. In-groups and out-groups within the society influence how people use language. Each language has a standard and nonstandard style that reinforces stereotypes and expectations based on position and power. In most societies, social positions create powerful groups and less powerful groups, called muted groups, who do not know and use the language of power and are therefore kept in subordinated positions. In the United States, powerful, high-status, and "masculine" communication generally is competitive, assertive, direct, and report-style. Less powerful, lower-status, and "feminine" communication often is cooperative, less direct, and rapport-style. This may be because girls and boys are conditioned as if they lived in different cultures, even within the same society.

Across the world, low-context cultures, such as the United States, rely on direct, assertive communication because little information is universally shared among people and individual effort and goals are highly prized. High-context cultures, such as those of Asia, use indirect, tactful, face-saving communication to preserve harmony because people hold much information about one another in common and rely on cooperation and harmony to get along.

Language changes constantly, with new words being generated and old ones changing to provide ways for obscuring or softening ideas through strategic ambiguity, for setting others apart through derogatory ethnic labels, for redefining concepts in the minds of others—for good ends or bad—and for shortcutting ideas to present them conveniently and quickly.

The effective use of language increases a person's credibility and confidence. A successful communicator builds vocabulary (through reading and becoming conscious of words); communicates with clear, unambiguous, concrete terms; and stimulates listeners' thought processes with such language strategies as metaphors and images.

Exercises

1   Select five advertisements from magazines or videotape five television commercials. Analyze the language used in the messages by answering the following questions:

What words are used that are concrete or very specific?

What words are used that are abstract and ambiguous?

In what ways is the language adapted to the specific audience?

What words are intended to stimulate thinking and imagery?

2   With another classmate, talk about ways in which derogatory ethnic labels (DELs) affect communicators. Analyze the impact DELs have on individuals. Consider these questions:

How do DELs relate to denotative and connotative meanings?

In what ways might DELs affect members of the target group?

What do DELs reflect about those who use them?

How does the use of DELs relate to a dialogic ethic of communication?

In what ways do DELs affect each of you at a personal level?

3   With a small group of classmates, create a vocabulary game from terminology used in this textbook. You might consider a board game, a quiz format, or any other approach your group creates. First, write the rules for your game in clear, concrete, nonambiguous language, and select the terms to be used. Then arrange for each group to play at least one other group's game. Analyze this activity by considering the following:

Were your game rules specific enough to cover all issues that arose while playing your game?

Did creating your game or playing that of another group actually increase your vocabulary?

4   Prepare a one-minute presentation in which you talk about a special occasion in your life, such as a social event, a trip you have taken, or a surprise encounter. Develop the presentation relying extensively on imagery and metaphors to express your ideas and feelings.

Cyberpoints

1   Are you interested in how technology is affecting language use? Use *InfoTrac College Edition* to locate the following articles:

McCrory, A. (1997, Dec. 15). When E-mail greetings shouldn't be warm. *Computerworld, 31* (50), 33.

Revah, S. (1998, April). The language of the digitally hip. *American Journalism Review, 20* (3), 12–14.

2   For a couple of chuckles and insights on issues of metaphors and cliches, Use *InfoTrac College Edition* to locate two short articles:

Bing, S. (1998, Oct. 12). Can't we just get along . . . without these? *Fortune, 138* (7), pp. 71 & 72.

Rothstein, L. (1999, May). The war on speech. *Bulletin of the Atomic Scientists, 55* (i3), 7.

CCC

WEB SITE

3   Many people are too lazy or just don't know how to make their language nonsexist and nonracist, that is, inclusive of all rather than exclusive of gender or groups. For some hints on how to make your language inclusive (in speech or in writing), go to the *Communicating with Credibility and Confidence* Web site at http://communication.wadsworth.com/lumsden and click on "How to Be Inclusive in Communication."

Chapter 7

Relationship Climates: Creating Communication Environments

Objectives for This Chapter

Knowledge

- Understand communication climates, causes, and effects
- Identify supportive and defensive communication behaviors
- Know how communication game-playing affects relationships
- Understand causes, effects, and strategies for managing conflict

Feelings and Approaches

- Be confident and motivated to create and maintain positive communication climates
- Feel comfortable in using assertive communication
- Have confidence in managing conflicts and game-playing situations
- Be confident in building relationships and solving problems

Communication Abilities

- Self-monitor and adapt communication to build good communication climates
- Be supportive and assertive as appropriate
- Use appropriate communication to manage game-playing or conflicts
- Develop credibility through positive communication

Key Terms

communication climate

supportive climate

humanified

objectified

defensive climate

self-disclosure

assertive communication

aggressive communication

passive communication

passive-aggressive response

empathy

confirming response

rejection response

disconfirming response

game-playing

conflict

O ur student, Dashawn, says her office is an awful place to work. Management is secretive and unpredictable. Workers don't dare speak to their boss about a problem because neither managers nor workers trust one another. The climate feels heavy and threatening, like a tornado is about to hit. In contrast, Dashawn describes her grandparents' home as "warm and breezy," like the gentle, playful relationship they've had for 46 years. The warm climate reflects how confident Dashawn's grandparents are in themselves, in each other, and in their relationship. Each is credible in the eyes of the other; each can be open and trusting of the other.

In each case, people's words and actions have created a **communication climate**—a set of conditions, ranging from supportive to defensive, that affect the quality of communication and relationships. This chapter explores what supportive and defensive communication climates are like, how people create them, and how you can improve climates even when they involve conflict or game-playing.

Communication climate A set of conditions that affect the quality of communication and relationships

Developing Supportive Communication Climates

Often, others have already established a climate, and you walk right into it. Are you stuck with it? No, not necessarily; it is possible to change a climate when you have self-confidence, credibility with the other persons, and skill in self-monitoring and adapting (Anderson, 1990).

To influence a climate, you start by mentally standing outside of the transaction and observing the way it is developing. When you identify the communication characteristics of a situation, you can use self-disclosure, assertiveness, empathy, and confirming others to develop the climate supportively.

When indeed shall we learn that we are all related one to the other, that we are all members of one body?

Helen Keller, 20th-century American author

Characteristics of Supportive and Defensive Climates

In a **supportive climate,** you know others respect your ideas and feelings, so you are free to communicate about them. A supportive climate reflects what philosopher Martin Buber (1958) called the "I-Thou" relationship, in which

Supportive climate An environment in which listeners respect a speaker's ideas and feelings, allowing for open communication

Humanified Viewed as a person with feelings, rights, values

Objectified Treated as a thing rather than as a person

Defensive climate An environment in which listeners disregard a speaker's feelings and importance

Self-disclosure The act of sharing information about yourself with another person

In order to see I have to be willing to be seen.

Hugh Prather, 20th-century philosopher

people are **humanified**—they see themselves and others as people, not as objects. When someone humanifies you, you feel acknowledged for your uniqueness, your value, and your rights; you feel safe in receptive, dialogic, supportive communication. Humanifying helps reduce defenses, so that "receivers become better able to concentrate upon the structure, the content, and the cognitive meanings of the message" (Gibb, 1961, p. 141). When communicators support each other, then, they are better able to negotiate genuinely shared meanings.

When someone treats you as an "it," however, what do you feel? You've been **objectified,** treated as a thing that can be owned, measured, or manipulated; a thing without feelings and importance (Stewart, 1990, pp. 13–19). In a **defensive climate,** people are likely to objectify one another; perhaps they fear being criticized for some flaw they see in themselves (Stamp, Vangelisti, & Daly, 1992). In feeling threatened, people behave self-protectively, feeding into a circular, progressively more defensive set of interactions. Figure 7.1 shows how communication behaviors influence a climate to develop supportively or defensively.

Any transaction begins with some risk. Even asking a clerk for help risks a rude "Whaddayawant?" Conversations usually entail a larger risk with some **self-disclosure**, or sharing information about yourself with another person. At first, you may disclose no more than your name and, perhaps, your occupation. As relationships develop, you and the other person learn more, because one self-disclosure draws a return bit of information. Suppose you've just been introduced to a stranger, and you say, "I'm a college student." That isn't an earth-shaking disclosure, but if the stranger snipes, "Another college student, huh?" you might become defensive and either snap back with your own sarcasm or walk away. However, if the person responds, "Really? That's great. I never went to college, but I've been thinking about starting," then each of you has contributed something, and you have reason to trust each other with more information. As you talk, you start a cycle of deepening trust in which you both are willing to disclose more.

Self-Disclosure

Used sensibly, mutual self-disclosure helps to increase both credibility and confidence. Used unwisely, self-disclosure risks responses that can damage your self-concept and your effectiveness. That's why it's important to understand what self-disclosure can accomplish, what influences it, and when and how you should use it in your transactions.

Effects of Self-Disclosure When you disclose information about yourself appropriately you can reap intra- and interpersonal benefits. For example:

■ *Your self-disclosure can enhance how much someone likes you.* People tend to share information with people they like to begin with, but they also learn

FIGURE 7.1 *Communication behaviors and cycles of supportive versus defensive communication*

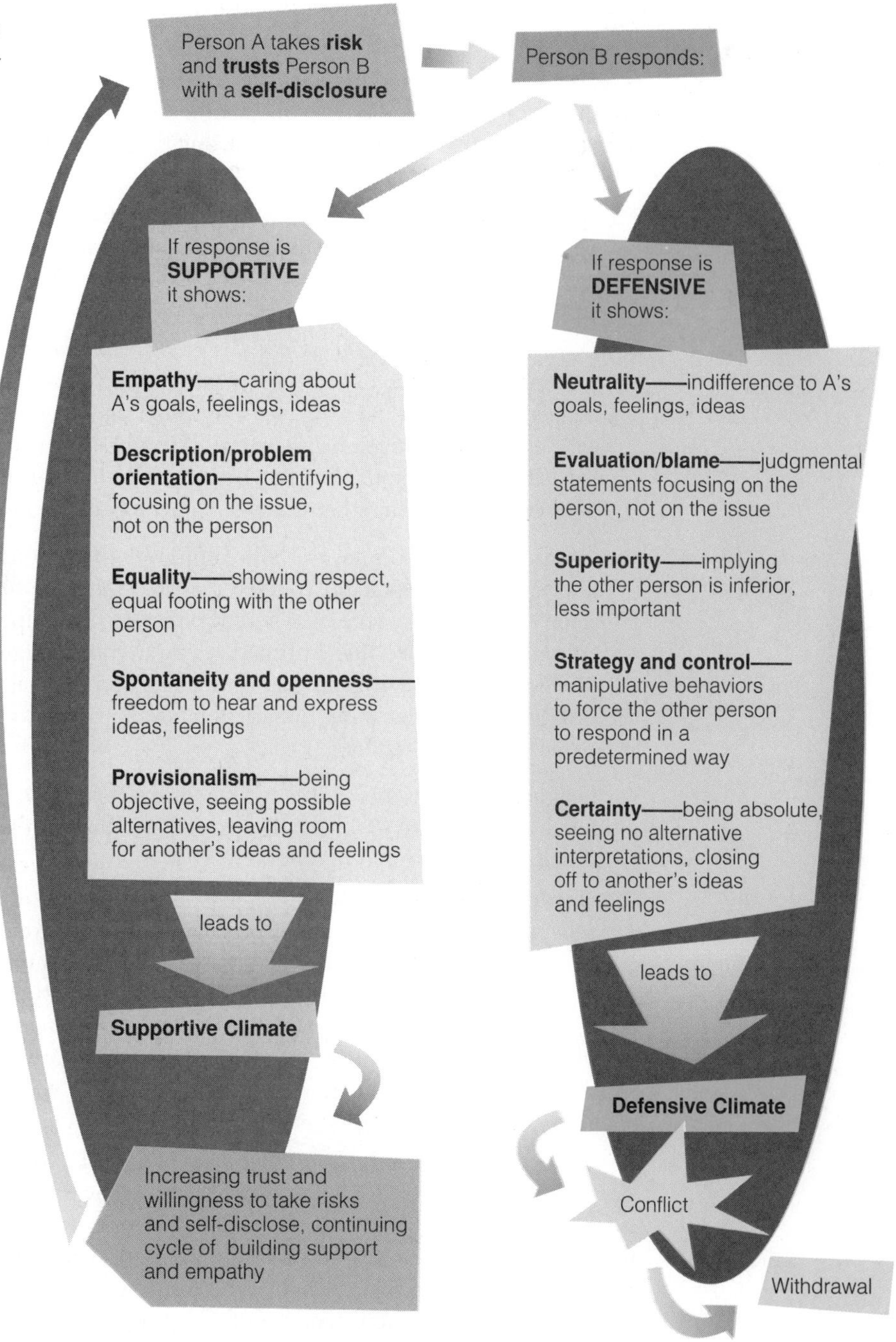

Person A takes **risk** and **trusts** Person B with a **self-disclosure**

Person B responds:

If response is **SUPPORTIVE** it shows:

Empathy——caring about A's goals, feelings, ideas

Description/problem orientation——identifying, focusing on the issue, not on the person

Equality——showing respect, equal footing with the other person

Spontaneity and openness——freedom to hear and express ideas, feelings

Provisionalism——being objective, seeing possible alternatives, leaving room for another's ideas and feelings

leads to

Supportive Climate

Increasing trust and willingness to take risks and self-disclose, continuing cycle of building support and empathy

If response is **DEFENSIVE** it shows:

Neutrality——indifference to A's goals, feelings, ideas

Evaluation/blame——judgmental statements focusing on the person, not on the issue

Superiority——implying the other person is inferior, less important

Strategy and control——manipulative behaviors to force the other person to respond in a predetermined way

Certainty——being absolute, seeing no alternative interpretations, closing off to another's ideas and feelings

leads to

Defensive Climate

Conflict

Withdrawal

to like people to whom they disclose information about themselves (Berg & Archer, 1983; Derlega, Winstead, Wong, & Greenspan, 1987).

- *Reciprocal self-disclosure shows you can trust each other.* Trust develops gradually when people trust one another with their vulnerabilities and when they are trustworthy in protecting the other's vulnerability (Trenholm & Jensen, 1988, pp. 279–280).

- *Reciprocal self-disclosure can develop coorientation.* When people perceive themselves as being similar in their approach to communication, they see one another as more competent and socially attractive (Waldron & Applegate, 1998).

- *Disclosing information helps people perceive you more accurately.* From what people observe in you, they make *attributions*—that is, they infer your beliefs, motivations, and values, from which they predict how and why you will act. They may even blame or credit you based on characteristics they have attributed to you (Harvey, Orbuch, & Weber, 1992, p. 2). Your self-disclosure can give another person a more accurate understanding of you.

Not only can self-disclosure help you develop relationships with others, it can also help you understand yourself. It's like seeing your feelings and ideas projected onto a mental screen, where the picture can help you to examine and understand who you are. Joe Luft and Harry Ingram designed a model of how self-disclosure affects both intrapersonal and interpersonal relationships (Luft, 1969). Figure 7.2 shows their "Johari Window" (a title that combines their two first names). It goes like this:

1   Quadrant 1 represents *shared information*—things you know about yourself and tell or demonstrate to others. The larger that quadrant is, the more open your life is to you as well as to others.

2   Quadrant 2 represents i*nformation about you that you're unaware of, but that others have observed.* You may be unaware of even your best attributes or worst ones (your beauty or your bad breath). Open communication can give you insight into yourself and into others' opinions of you. A student of ours once disclosed that she hated her voice. When other students disclosed that *they* thought her voice was beautiful, she jettisoned that negative self-concept. Her confidence rose because she now knew she had a great vocal instrument with which to work.

3   Quadrant 3 represents *things that you know about yourself but haven't shared with others.* For example, a person who is gay is going through the process of coming out of the closet. Hiding his homosexuality had been agonizing, but he had felt that it would be enormously risky to disclose this information. Would his family reject him? Would his friends abandon him? Fortunately, in this case, the man's family and friends are supporting him; he's able to share his life more openly with others, and he's drawing closer to his family.

4   Quadrant 4 represents *secluded things that no one—including yourself— realizes about you.* You may have unrecognized psychological issues or talents or desires; everyone does. Often, Quadrant 4 is where you gradually discover

Figure 7.2 *The Johari Window*

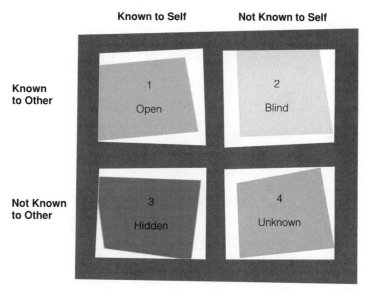

Known to Self   **Not Known to Self**

Known to Other

1 Open

2 Blind

Not Known to Other

3 Hidden

4 Unknown

From J. Luft (1969), *Of human interaction*, Palo Alto CA: Mayfield. Used by permission of the publisher.

things you didn't know before. When a student disclosed that she was unhappy in her chosen major, for example, she suddenly saw *why* she was dissatisfied. She needed a more creative field, but she had buried her creativity because "artsy stuff" wasn't valued in her family. When this student started talking about what she did *not* want, she gained an insight into what she *did* want. In this case, a simple conversation illuminated this student's dilemma. In other cases, an individual may need a support group, a counselor, or a psychotherapist to help uncover an unrecognized issue.

Disclosing information about yourself can, in this way, help you to broaden your self-perceptions. Take a look at Figure 7.3, which shows how the Johari Window "open" quadrant has grown through self-disclosure and feedback. As you discuss previously hidden areas and receive feedback, your self-disclosure helps you understand previously blind sections. With supportive transactions, you also begin to gain insight into previously unknown areas. These insights can chase away any negative perceptions or fears that may have shadowed your concept of yourself. As you know yourself better, and as you discover your own strengths, you gain confidence in yourself and in your ability to express your ideas.

Personal Preferences for Self-Disclosure How much you want to self-disclose may depend on several factors, including the way you've been socialized as a member of an identity group. In one study people in the United States disclosed the most, Japanese disclosed the least, and the French were somewhere in the middle (Ting-Toomey, 1987). These findings support the idea

Figure 7.3 *The Johari Window with expanded "open" area*

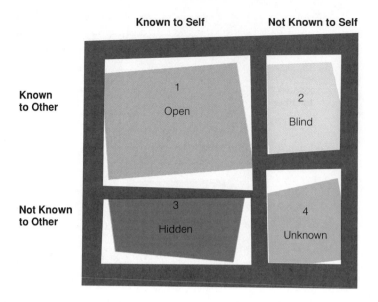

discussed in Chapter 6 that people in low-context cultures such as the United States want and give specific information, whereas people in high-context cultures such as Japan expect to know more from intuition and less from being told. In France, a middle-context culture, people might use some self-disclosure and expect others to intuit the rest.

Similarly, gender roles can influence your self-disclosure habits. From early childhood, females tend to form more intimate, disclosing friendships. By contrast, males tend to stay in more competitive, less intimate groups, sharing interests and reciprocating favors but revealing vulnerabilities to one another less than women do (Rawlins, 1993, p. 53). This might be why, when they *need* someone to talk to, both men and women tend to look for women as listeners (Buhrke & Fuqua, 1987).

Many people, however, are *androgynous*, meaning men or women who use either "masculine" *or* "feminine" behaviors as appropriate to the situation. Androgynous male and female high school students were found not only to disclose more to others but also to be less lonely than students who were stereotypically feminine or masculine in their traits (McDowell & McDowell, 1991). It may be that a student who shares more openly makes friends more easily than one who is closed—and, perhaps, an individual of either sex who can be tender or tough according to the circumstances may be more likable and interesting than one who always acts as either a "dainty girl" or "macho boy" stereotype.

Guidelines for Self-Disclosure It may seem odd that most conversations between friends, and even between intimates, are fairly low in the amount of self-disclosure (Duck, et al., 1991). Maybe they've already shared the most important information, or maybe it's because self-disclosure *is* risky. You have to choose carefully how, when, and what to reveal to whom and under what circumstances. Following are some things to consider:

- *What are the situation and the issues?* In most transactions, self-disclosure is limited to superficial things—jobs, basic interests, general likes and dislikes. You have to know you can trust another person before you make deeper, more personal revelations. It's a bad idea, for instance, to disclose negative information about yourself to a stranger; people are more likely to want to interact with strangers who reveal positive things about themselves than those who share negative thoughts (Lazowski & Andersen, 1990).

- *To what extent has the other person disclosed information to you?* If the other person has not revealed much to you, then you should proceed cautiously. If the other person has been very open, then you can feel freer to share more about yourself.

- *What is your relationship to the other person, and how has she or he treated confidences before?* It should be, of course, that the more intimate the relationship, the more you can rely on another's support when you share information about yourself. That is not always the case, however. Sometimes, families or spouses are the quickest to judge and the slowest to understand. Before making intimate disclosures, consider the other person's track record.

Assertiveness

Assertive communica-
tion Communicating
one's needs and wants,
with awareness of self
and concern for others

Sometimes people are afraid that speaking out will offend others, but it can work the other way. In Western cultures, at least, communicators are more credible when they are assertive. **Assertive communication** means openly communicating, with awareness of yourself and concern for others, what you need or want other people to know or do. With assertiveness, you can argue for your position without infringing on the positions of others. You can disagree without being disagreeable. You can focus on the issue without judging the person because you are humanifying, not objectifying, the individual.

Agressive communica-
tion Communicating
one's needs and wants,
disregarding what others
might feel or want

Being assertive is quite different from being passive or nonassertive, and radically different from being aggressive. Suppose, for example, your employer has given you more work than you can do. If you're assertive, you open the discussion with something like, "Can we talk about my work? I'm sure I can't complete it all by the deadline." When people can't be assertive, they may objectify others by being aggressive. **Aggressive communication** reflects a "me first" position that disregards how others might feel or what they might want. Aggressors actively seek to control another's feelings and behavior. Aggression doesn't necessarily involve a punch in the nose; words can inflict psychological pain by attacking one's self-concept (Infante, Riddle, Horvath, & Tumlin, 1992, p. 116; Infante & Wigley, 1986). An aggressive approach to the excessive workload might be the comment, "Well, I see that, as usual, you've made yourself look

Deborah Tannen, linguist, says,

"I challenge the assumption that talking in an indirect way necessarily reveals powerlessness, lack of self-confidence, or anything else about the character of the speaker. Indirectness is a fundamental element in human communication. . . . For speakers raised in most of the world's cultures, varieties of indirectness are the norm in communication . . ."

Deborah Tannen (1994), *Talking from 9 to 5*. New York: Morrow, pp. 75–85, 96.

Amy Tan, Chinese American novelist, says:

There was nothing discreet about the Chinese language I grew up with. My parents made everything abundantly clear. Nothing wishy-washy in their demands, no compromises accepted: 'Of course you will become a famous neurosurgeon,' they told me. And yes, a concert pianist on the side.

In fact, now that I remember, it seems that the more emphatic outbursts always spilled over into Chinese: 'Not that way! You must wash rice so not a single grain spills out.'

Reprinted in John Stewart (1999), *Bridges Not Walls*, pp. 11–104, from "The Language of Discretion" by Amy Tan (1990).

good by loading me up with work so I'll look bad." That's even worse if you speak loudly, because others may also think you're trying to dominate them (Tusing & Dillard, 2000).

Sometimes, people avoid assertiveness or aggressiveness by being passive; they care about their own rights but are fearful of how the other person might respond if they speak up. **Passive communication** involves hiding behind silence or false agreement, appeasing others while possibly building up resentment or frustration. A passive response to the ever-increasing workload might be to huddle behind the stack of work, silently grinding away, knowing that the issue will come to a head when the work isn't done on time.

When people are anxious about what they want but can't make direct statements for fear of a negative response, they may use passive-aggressive communication. A **passive-aggressive response** may find ways to block other people, halt progress, or punish someone without being caught at it. The passive-aggressive individual, faced with a mountain of work, might "lose" part of the boss's data in the computer or "just mention" to other workers how the boss has been padding the expense account.

Figure 7.4 shows how these four communication behaviors work. When you are *assertive* (upper left-hand corner of the grid), you are open and self-disclosing, you try to influence others, *and* you are very concerned for their rights. This behavior fosters an open climate. By contrast, the other three com-

Passive communication Using silence or false agreement to appease others while building up resentment or frustration

Passive-aggressive response Acting like one agrees and accepts, but seeking to undermine the process with later behavior

Figure 7.4 *The communication climate/assertiveness grid*

	Self-Disclosing (Influencing Others)	Self-Protective (Influenced by Others)
High Concern for Rights of Others	Assertive — Open climate	Passive — Closed climate
Low Concern for Rights of Others	Aggressive — Hostile climate	Passive-aggressive — Anxious/hostile climate

munication responses contribute to closed and hostile climates. When you are *aggressive* (lower left-hand corner), you are open and self-disclosing and are willing to influence, but you have low concern for others. This behavior contributes to a defensive climate. When you are *passive* (upper right-hand corner), you allow others to control the interaction and are too concerned about how others react. This behavior fosters a closed climate. When you are *passive-aggressive* (lower right-hand corner), you won't try to express feelings or influence others directly, but you may be hostile and behave with passive-aggression to punish others. This behavior contributes to a hostile and/or anxious climate.

Empathy

Empathy Understanding the ideas and feelings of another person

As people create trust through self-disclosure, they also develop empathy for one another. **Empathy** is understanding "the other's values, meanings, symbols, intentions" (Broome, 1991, p. 239). Empathy, too, relies on humanifying another person, perhaps by sharing joys or sorrows, understanding someone's excitement over a new job or frustration in trying to make a difficult decision, or feeling the pain of losing a loved one. Empathy often is described as walking in another person's moccasins.

In a supportive climate, empathy develops as you give people a chance to know and understand you and as you get to know them. You develop empathy by listening and questioning, looking not just for a person's feelings but for the context that colors them. How, for example, do an individual's background and experiences, culture and identity groups, and wants and needs affect the person? As you understand these elements, you develop your empathy more fully (Broome, 1991).

Ofttimes you want your expression of empathy to convey support as well. Interestingly, it seems that a person-centered, caring way of expressing support is what people—male and female—respond to as comforting, even though such supportive behavior is stereotyped as "feminine" behavior, and women do tend to use such messages more than men do (Kunkel & Burleson, 1999).

Human beings simply need other people to confirm them—to acknowledge that they are worth something. Confirmation is such a simple thing to give, and

The older man is looking at a square of the Names Project quilt— a square that has been handmade by friends and family to memorialize someone who has died of AIDS. The project assistant seems to be comforting him. What is it about this picture that shows the empathy one man brings to the other?

R. Lord /The Image Works

Confirming response
Message that acknowledges worth of the receiver

Rejection response
Message that discards the worth of the receiver or the receiver's ideas

To feel valued, to know, even if only once in a while, that you can do a job well is an absolutely marvelous feeling.

Barbara Walters, broadcast Journalist

yet it's also easy to withhold without even realizing the need. A **confirming response** carries a message that makes you feel recognized as a worthwhile person, with worthwhile ideas and feelings. Confirming responses may be nonverbal—such as warm eye contact, an accepting body posture, nodding, or perhaps touching to indicate understanding—or verbal—acknowledgment ("That's a good idea"), support ("You've earned the right"), clarification ("Do you mean . . . ?"), or a positive expression ("You said that so well").

The opposite of this supportive communication is a **rejection response,** a lack of confirmation or even an aggressive reaction that discards you or your ideas. Rejection may take the direct form of superior, sarcastic, know-it-all refutation of what you say; or the person may simply walk away without a word or interrupt you in midsentence. Sometimes, you get a pseudoconfirmation ("That's great, now let's eat") or an irrelevant statement that has nothing to do with what you said. People may give rejecting responses because they are distracted or absent-minded or because they have aggressive personalities, rather than because they intend to reject you. The result, unfortunately, is still a feeling of having been left standing alone and wounded.

Disconfirming response Message that renders the receiver invisible or undesirable

Similarly, a **disconfirming response** makes you feel almost invisible or, worse, undesirable. A disconfirming response may be *impervious*, revealing the listener's indifference to what you have said—for example, "That's not my problem." An *impersonal* response also disconfirms you through detachment—for example, "Those are the rules and I just follow them." Or there's the *incongruous response*, revealing contradiction between the words themselves and the nonverbal cues (Watzlawick, Beavin, & Jackson, 1967)

It's simple. When people feel acknowledged and confirmed, they usually feel free to communicate. When they believe that another person is rejecting them—even if their perception is inaccurate—people become defensive. Confirming others demonstrates your coorientation with them and your interest in what they have to say. It increases your credibility and it opens up communication. Even when you disagree with the message, you can confirm the person.

Identifying Defensive Communication Climates

They are playing a game. They are playing at not playing a game. If I show them I see they are, I shall break their rules and they will punish me. I must play their game, of not seeing I see the game.

R. D. Laing, 20th-century psychologist and poet. From *knots* (1970), London: Tavistock, p. 1.

It's terrible to be trapped in a struggle for control that becomes a game of many innings, or an ongoing conflict. While conflict and competition are a part of life, they don't have to run it. When the need to "win" shapes a communication climate, personal as well as professional relationships can suffer. Competitive game-playing and conflict, which are in many ways similar, can affect relationships and sometimes ruin them.

Game-Playing

Ruth and Mel are talking about the dance they just left:

Mel: Raoul was his usual suave and debonair self tonight, wasn't he?

Ruth: Yeah, he's fun to be around.

Mel: Well, he's got more money and education than I have.

Ruth: Oh, Mel, that's not important. Anyway, Raoul isn't all that terrific.

Mel: Tell the truth. You'd rather be with him than me.

Ruth: No, Mel, I love *you*. Raoul's not my type. Actually, I think he's kind of fake . . . you know, like . . . you're much more *real*. . . .

Mel: Yeah, right.

Game-playing A competitive manipulation of communication so that one player can achieve a personal goal

Mel wants Ruth's reassurance, and Ruth will keep on trying to satisfy his need. Ruth and Mel have played this scene before and will again. They are trapped in **game-playing,** a competitive, win-lose approach to manipulating communication so that one partner can achieve some personal goal. Game-playing can be disastrous for relationships because it hinders the individuals' ability to relate to one another on an intimate level.

Figure 7.5 *Game-playing versus cooperative communication*

Competitive Games-Playing	Cooperative Communication
Win-lose goals	Win-win goals
Not trusting	Trusting
Defensive strategies	Supportive climate
Manipulative	Open

There are such things as cooperative games, but *competitive* games assume that if there's a winner, there also must be a loser, so each participant has two alternatives: *win* or *lose*. Figure 7.5 shows the strategies and consequences of competitive versus cooperative communication.

In competitive interpersonal games, each person's goal is to win. Defensiveness results, because participants try to manipulate each other's vulnerabilities. Trust is impossible. Winning requires anticipating another's moves, taking calculated risks, and choosing moves that will counteract or defeat the other's moves. A win-lose orientation is perfectly appropriate in games such as team sports, boxing, and chess. Similarly, a debate pits two well-prepared advocates against each other so a judge can determine the winner based on the best arguments and the best evidence. Competition is fine when victory is the objective. Competition, however, is inappropriate in interpersonal and professional relationships.

In cooperative communication, the goal is for everyone to win, so people must trust one another and work together. People share control and develop mutual understanding through open communication in a supportive climate, because it is unnecessary to worry about protecting themselves. Obviously, cooperative behaviors are appropriate to experiences in which the objectives are to develop relationships and to achieve the goals of all involved.

When people take a competitive approach to a communication situation that should be cooperative—say, a marriage—one person may start a game by manipulating the other's responses to "win points." The other partner abandons cooperation, because it won't work in the competitive climate. Neither person wins; the outcome is *lose-lose,* and the climate is seriously damaged. Yet, many relationships are trapped in competitive games. Let's look at why and how people get into game-playing situations.

There are several clues, besides your generally reliable gut feeling, that somebody's playing a game. These include the gimmick, the repeated script, and the payoff (Berne, 1966).

- *Gimmicks* are a game-player's predictable approach or phrasing that gets others to respond in a particular way. Suppose you hear a supervisor say sarcastically to the secretary, "Didn't you go to secretarial school?" Having witnessed this situation before, you know that this statement starts a series of snide remarks that makes the secretary defensive. The secretary "loses points" (self-esteem and increased subservience), and the supervisor "wins" by intimidating the secretary into working overtime or doing personal favors.

- *Scripts* are consistent ways the game plays out from the gimmick. The script may not be word-for-word every time the gimmick starts it, but it has an observable structure. Like the script for a play, a game-playing script may include victims and villains and heroes in some plot, action, and climax. We once knew a woman who played a game that could have been called "Poor Me." She would open a conversation with "You'll never believe what he did *this* time." If we fell for this gimmick and asked, "What?" she would spin an involved tale of woe describing her husband's transgressions. Then she would repeatedly state, "I just don't know what to do." If you fell into the trap and made a suggestion, she would tell you why your idea wouldn't work. As the conversation continued, you realized that she was the victim, her husband was the villain, the plot involved her travails, and she was looking for a hero to rescue her. Nothing but the fantasy hero would do. The climax of the game was her tearful acceptance that this was her lot in life.

- *Payoffs*. These are rewards defined in terms of what the person needs, wants, expects, and can handle emotionally. Sometimes, the reward seems negative—such as building up to a fight with someone—but it is predictable and therefore secure for the game-player. As the script develops, a plot emerges—and the climax is the payoff. How can you tell what the payoff is? It may be something tangible; Lucy Ricardo gets Ricky to put her in his show by playing a game at the end of which he has no choice. Sometimes, the payoff is less tangible, perhaps a rejection that confirms someone's low self-esteem or expressions of love extorted by tapping into feelings of guilt. Payoffs are individual, complex, and powerful motivators for playing games.

Conflict

Conflict refers to the tension people feel between them when they perceive that they have mutually exclusive goals or feelings. Conflict isn't an argument; you can argue once about an issue and resolve it. Conflict goes on through a series of events, sometimes changing over time. The tension often has "little to do with the behaviors occurring in any single interaction, but, rather, may be strongly associated with previous relational experiences" (Stamp, Vangelisti, & Daly, 1992, p. 186).

At home, with friends, or in the workplace, people often clash over one or a combination of these issues:

- *Information*. Individuals may have insufficient, contradictory, or conflicting interpretations of data. If data are the only problem, conflict can be

Coexistence or no existence.

Piet Hein, 20th-century poet

Conflict The tension people feel in a relationship when they perceive that they have differing goals or feelings

managed by using a good problem-solving process to share, analyze, and discuss the information.

- *Resources.* When time, money, materials, or support are in short supply, people may struggle over who gets what for what purpose. Some couples fight endlessly over money or time. Resource conflicts are difficult, but they often are manageable through negotiation and compromise (Roloff, 1981).

- *Expectations.* Wives and husbands often clash over personal or societal expectations of their roles. Employers may conflict with workers who don't meet their expectations—not only in terms of job performance but also in terms of race, gender, or social status. Tension over expected behavior may be manageable with self-disclosure, honest examination of expectations, empathy, willingness to change behaviors, and acceptance of one another.

- *Needs.* People naturally feel defensive and anxious when their needs are blocked by someone else. For example, an individual who has shaky self-esteem and needs support may be in conflict with someone who constantly uses put-down humor. Need conflicts can get wrapped up in other issues, so they are hard to identify and harder still to solve. To manage need conflicts, people must take risks and be open about what their needs are.

- *Power and control.* Control conflicts may surface over any other type of issue, but the underlying clash is who controls whom. Often, people who have a high need to exert power over others prompt defensive reactions. Conflicts over power relate to other issues such as personality, expectations, resources, information, or needs, so they need to be managed within other parameters.

- *Values and ethics.* When people clash over issues of good and bad, or right and wrong, the conflict relates to their concepts of who they are. Often, these conflicts can be managed with discussion and negotiation, but sometimes value-laden issues are deep, long-lasting, and irreconcilable.

- *Personality.* People may irritate one another with behavior linked to their personalities. Self-disclosure and supportive communication can lead to deeper understanding and acceptance of one another's traits, and sometimes individuals can change specific behaviors with honest feedback and encouragement.

Changing Defensive Communication Climates

We'd go so far as to say that most defensive climates can be improved; some can be reversed. Doing so demands full commitment to the goal, and awareness of some of the approaches you can use to change either game-playing or conflict situations.

Nonviolence is the answer to the crucial political and moral questions of our time; the need . . . to overcome oppression and violence without resorting to oppression and violence . . . a method which rejects revenge, aggression and retaliation. The foundation of such a method is love.

The Rev. Martin Luther King, Jr., in his speech accepting the Nobel Peace Prize, December 11, 1964.

Approaches to Conflict Management

How do you handle a conflict? Do you always react the same way? Probably not; an individual's approach to managing conflict varies according to the situation and personal influences such as age, sex, culture, and self-concept.

Take age, for example: One study found that in intimate relationships, young couples tend to be both direct and expressive in alternatively fighting, analyzing, and joking about their conflicts. Middle-aged couples avoid conflict if possible; if they can't and the issue is important, they go at it as younger couples do. If they can't avoid it but the issue is unimportant, they do what the older, retired couples do—deal with it with as little energy expenditure and expression as possible (Zietlow & Sillars, 1988).

People's cultural backgrounds and self-construals (how they see themselves) also affect conflict management styles. A person from a high-context culture might prefer to be more collectivistic and self-effacing in a conflict, to maintain harmony and save face, whereas a person from a low-context culture would be more assertive and direct (Ting-Toomey, 1988). Even more important, however, might be the individuals' self-construals, which may or may not be linked to their cultures. One study found that people who see themselves as independent are more prone to use dominating styles and people whose self-construal is interdependent with others are more likely to use avoiding, compromising, and integrating conflict-managers (Oetzel, 1998).

Whatever your age, gender, culture, or preference for dealing with a defensive climate, game or conflict, the best thing you can do is develop the ability to choose an approach that's best for the situation. Here are some alternatives:

Postponing the issues.   Occasionally it's reasonable to delay facing an issue until the time, place, or situation is better—or until someone has cooled down. You don't want to ignore a conflict or game for long, however, if the person or issue is of value to you. Carrying around anger or frustration can contribute to stress diseases and/or interpersonal disaster.

Indirectly influencing participants. People often take an indirect approach in order to "save face" or avoid retribution. A coworker might say, "The boss was griping because *we* aren't working hard enough around here," when what she really means is, "I feel that *you're* not carrying your weight." Many families and cultures prefer indirect approaches to problems. A Western Apache, for instance, might bring a child into line by saying to another adult, "Girls are butterflies." The little girls who hear the comment know that it is an indirect rebuke for chasing "around after each other, like they had no work to do" (Basso, 1990, p. 67). Or often Asian families will have an intermediary speak privately to each participant in a conflict and work out face-saving ways to resolve the problem (Ting-Toomey, 1988).

Reversing the trend. You may defuse an escalating conflict by not buying into it—by being open and supportive no matter how someone else behaves. In a game-playing situation, you might give responses that reverse the predicted script and change the pattern (Wilmot, 1979, p. 128). Suppose your friend digs for compliments with the gimmick, "I can't believe how stupid I am," and your scripted response is, "You're not stupid; in fact, you're really smart. . . ." You might change the pattern with "Sometimes I really feel stupid, too." That eliminates the payoff and surprises the game-player into thinking about your response instead of automatically following the usual script.

Directly confronting and negotiating the issues. With an important issue, the best option may be to confront it and negotiate a compromise. You must prepare carefully and communicate with keen awareness of both the other person and yourself. A point may seem crucial because your adrenaline is pumping, but when you settle down, you see it really was not that important. Sometimes, however, a potential sacrifice in a conflict situation might involve betraying your ethics or your values in a way you'd regret. A cool assessment of those issues can give you a more realistic position from which to start a complex process. Confrontation takes dedication and effort.

Withdrawing from interaction. At times, you have to separate yourself from the people involved in a conflict. You may choose to end a relationship or to quit a job to avoid communication with others associated with the issues. This should never be the easy route; withdrawal is not justified just because confronting the issues is hard. Sometimes, however, withdrawing is the only reasonable solution when you have carefully analyzed all alternative options and concluded that none of them offers the potential of a positive solution. Some Native American cultures, for example, remain silent around *any* angry person, because the people consider expressed anger to be a kind of unpredictable, dangerous craziness (Basso, 1990, pp. 88–90).

Seeking professional help. It's possible, and often useful, to get professional help to manage a conflict. There's no guarantee that this approach will work, but it can be the only effective solution for interpersonal or professional conflicts. There are many private and public counselors for individuals and families, and organizations today frequently employ counselors to work with individuals, departments, or teams in managing conflicts and building cooperation. Additionally, professional negotiators and mediators are available to help work out organizational or political struggle.

Communication for Conflict Management

Communicating your way through a conflict means creating a new climate. It demands an expectation that you can, in fact, make this situation work for everyone—a truly win-win attitude.

As you work through a conflict, you need to identify what each person wants and needs, to look at the sources and symptoms of the problem, and to work out satisfactory compromises. "A compromise is one type of win-win solution, although it requires that both parties give up something in order to solve the problem. In the long run, however, giving up something can really be like getting something if the conflict is solved" (Rafenstein, 1999, p. 30).

You have to state what you want, think, and/or feel in assertive ways that respect your own character without impugning someone else's. Use language that takes responsibility for your own feelings, and resist the all-too-human temptation to hang responsibility around the neck of the other person. For example (Satir, 1990):

- *Use "I" statements.* Say, "I think," "I feel," "I want," and so on; avoid saying, "You do," "You think," or "You feel." Using "I" acknowledges your responsibility for your position or feelings and helps avoid attributing blame or judgment, asserting certainty, or manipulating another's response.

- *Avoid "all" statements.* Use language that allows room for degrees of probability, and avoid language that is absolute and know-it-all. Saying, "I believe," or "Probably," leaves room for people to disagree and still communicate. Saying, "Always," "Never," or "Impossible!" undermines the negotiation process.

- *Use specific language.* If you mean yes, say it; if you mean no, say it. People often fog over affirmatives and negatives out of politeness or dread of dealing with issues. For example, "I'm sorry, but I won't do that," is clear, whereas, "I am very hesitant to take such an action," is ambiguous.

- *Use definite pronouns; avoid indefinite ones.* Two common culprits are *it* and *they.* "It seems to be a problem." What does? "They said we had to." Who did? People may feel defensive because they simply don't understand the point.

- *Use words that indicate control of your own choices; avoid the language of guilt or helplessness.* Avoid *ought* and *should;* they may imply guilt and induce resistance. Substitute *can, want, will,* or *might,* or *won't, don't,* or *refuse to.* If you say, "I don't want to," or "I will," you assume responsibility.

- *Use the active voice.* Say, "I believe," rather than, "It is believed"; say, "I have decided," instead of, "It has been decided."

When you use language responsibly to express your feelings and allow others to express theirs, you keep control of your own responses. It's essential to be calm and controlled, and that requires that you monitor your nonverbal cues and use positive self-talk. Is your heart beating too fast? Are you becoming flushed and angry? Then take deep breaths, focus on the issues rather than your anger at the other person, and tell yourself, "I'm cool, I'm okay, I'm dealing with this."

Monitoring your own responses and watching feedback is crucial. What you say or do might seem like aggression to others, even if you don't mean it that way. Ask yourself if your words or actions attack others' competence, character, background, and/or appearance or threaten them in some way. Sometimes, even teasing can be interpreted as an aggressive attack on an individual's weak points and sense of self-worth. Nonverbal cues, too, such as crowding another's space or using threatening postures or gestures, can be construed as aggressive. Aggression makes people feel embarrassed, inadequate, humiliated, hopeless, desperate, and/or depressed. It can even damage an individual's self-concept (Infante, Riddle, Horvath, & Tumlin, 1992, p. 116). What's worse, verbal aggression can escalate to physical violence, compounding psychological with physical abuse (Infante, Sabourin, Rudd, & Shannon, 1990). Aggression can backlash, too, by lowering your self-esteem, increasing your frustration, making you feel inadequate, and reducing your credibility with others. Observers tend to see an aggressor as lacking credibility, character, and competence, and a person who has been attacked as all the more credible (Infante, Hartley, Martin, Higgins, Bruning, & Hur, 1992).

As you monitor your own responses, also watch others' nonverbal and verbal cues. So much depends upon the sequence and interaction; for example, conflict might escalate if you give someone unsolicited advice, but the same advice that responds to another person's request for it may be seen as your positive regard for that individual's face (Goldsmith, 2000).

In fact, creating a better climate, reversing a game-playing situation, or managing a conflict may all come down to your regard for others as well as yourself.

Summary

The climate in which people communicate and the way they communicate interact continuously. A climate may be supportive, freeing people to communicate openly, or it may be defensive, causing people to clam up or to escalate tensions into hostility and conflict. In a supportive climate, communicators are able to disclose information about themselves, which helps to develop trust and empathy. This makes the climate increasingly supportive. Transactions can be assertive and, at the same time, confirm the worth of others and their ideas.

In a defensive climate, lack of self-disclosure, empathy, and trust are often related to poor management of conflict and competitive communication patterns. Relationships may develop conflicts involving what participants perceive as mutually exclusive goals, creating ongoing problems in the relationship. Although conflict is inevitable and sometimes can be constructive, it often becomes a continuing condition that needs to be managed. Game-playing, related to conflict, occurs when participants play out predictable scripts involving some gimmick at the start and a payoff at the end. Communicating to reverse games and to manage conflict requires people to work cooperatively, good-humoredly, and supportively, using assertive, nonthreatening behavior and descriptive, responsible, and nonevaluative language.

Exercises

1 Compare and contrast the climate in two situations you have experienced (in a relationship, your family, your workplace, your school, an organization, and so on). Describe what the climate is like (stormy, cloudy, sunny, balmy . . .), and identify the communication behaviors you have observed participants using in that climate. Try to pin down specific examples of supportive and/or defensive communication, and trace the way you think the communication has contributed to the climate.

2 Recall an occasion when you have had a defensive response to something another person has said. With a partner, do the following:

a Work out a short skit that uses defensive communication to show what that experience was like and how you reacted.

b Work out a revised skit that shows how the climate could have been changed to a supportive one with different communication behavior.

c Play the first skit for the class (you can play yourself and your partner can play the other person in your experience).

d Ask the members of the class to identify which behaviors were defensive.

e Now, play the revised skit for the class.

f Ask the class to identify which behaviors were supportive.

3 With a group, identify what kinds of communication behavior are exemplified by the following statements, and speculate on how they might make the hearer feel defensive. As a group, write a more supportive way of

expressing the idea for each one, and share your ideas with the class.

"Well, when you've lived as long as I have, dear, you'll know how important your education is."

"You're always late, and it's because you just don't care about me."

"Yeah, yeah, I know. So you had a bad day. Didn't we all?"

"Well, of course you'd think that—people like you always do, don't they?"

"I'm sure you'll want to contribute for the party, since you didn't for the last one, even though everybody else did."

"Why do you always do that? You know how you make me feel when you talk about my parents that way. You just hate them, that's all."

4 Find an example of defensive or supportive communication; it could be a short scene from a play, a poem, an excerpt from a story or a novel, an editorial, even a comic strip. In a 2-minute speech, share the piece you've found with the class and explain how it exemplifies supportive or defensive communication. Relate the analysis to Figure 7.1 to identify specifically what kinds of statements are involved.

Cyberpoints

CCC

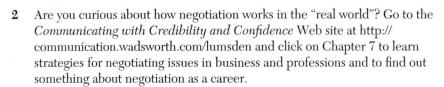

WEB SITE

1 For a range of articles on conflict management, including some interesting case studies, use *InfoTrac College Edition* and the keyword, *conflict*.

2 Are you curious about how negotiation works in the "real world"? Go to the *Communicating with Credibility and Confidence* Web site at http://communication.wadsworth.com/lumsden and click on Chapter 7 to learn strategies for negotiating issues in business and professions and to find out something about negotiation as a career.

3 Do you think you see a game going on in your life? Go to the *Communicating with Credibility and Confidence* Web site at http://communication.wadsworth.com/lumsden and click on Chapter 7 for more information about game-playing and how to cope with and/or change it.

Chapter 8

Personal Relationships: Growing with Another

Objectives for This Chapter

Knowledge

- Know the factors that influence initial conversation
- Identify issues that affect developing relationships
- Understand communication in families
- Know how conversational skills reflect credibility and confidence

Feelings and Approaches

- Feel confident in conversing with strangers and others
- Feel positive about developing and maintaining personal relationships

Communication Abilities

- Self-monitor, adapt, and achieve goals in communicating interpersonally
- Develop trust and empathy in intimate relationships
- Communicate effectively in relationship systems
- Enhance credibility in conversations with others

Key Terms

person-centered messages   intimate relationships   relational themes

affinity seeking   turning point   family

social penetration   depenetration   dysfunctional relationship

interpersonal bonding   relational "rules"   codependency

Human beings are social creatures. Even as you stand alone, awed by a blazing sunset, you might wish for someone to share that aesthetic high. Through communicating interpersonally, humans share themselves, and, sometimes, develop deep bonds that may last a lifetime.

In Chapter 1, we defined interpersonal communication as a dynamic process that touches people emotionally and psychologically (Miller & Steinberg, 1975). This process, of course, may stay at the social level, or develop further into a deeper relationship—perhaps from acquaintanceship to friendship to courtship to commitment to rearing families. That's what this chapter talks about—the interpersonal communication in all those stages of interhuman relationships.

We'll start at the beginning—getting to know people—and move through conversation to developing relationships to couple and family communication.

Getting to Know People

Many kids and most puppies "never know a stranger," but few adults can be that open. Still, any stranger *could* be a potential best friend. Indeed, most relationships—other than with family—start as stranger-to-stranger encounters.

You might meet someone on the Internet, perhaps in a chatroom, maybe through an electronic newsletter. A couple we know met through a special electronic newsletter for professional people with similar values. Several years and a baby later, their relationship seems to be going along quite well. But note that they did, at some point, meet face to face.

What draws you to someone? The first element in connecting with someone is the situation that provides the opportunity to meet people, affects how you see them, and structures your transactions (Hauser, 1988).

The situation in which you meet shapes those initial encounters. Say you join a ski club—you might just meet someone you find attractive. You talk, mostly about skiing, and find out you both love winter sports. You agree to go to a movie together, and later, as you discuss the film over coffee, you gain an entirely new slant on who this individual really is. At each step, the situation affects your transactions and your impressions.

If you are attracted to this person, that feeling may well start with physical characteristics and/or with a sense of similarity. Yet, even though similar views might be attractive, they aren't enough to motivate a relationship—nor do differences necessarily keep people apart once they get a chance to interact (Capella & Palmer, 1990; Sunnafrank, 1992). You might initially regard someone as unattractive and strange, but your conversation may start a wonderful friendship when you discover how bright and funny he or she is.

Getting a Conversation Started

Have you ever been bewildered when someone answered your, "How are you?" in great depth, when all you thought you were doing was saying, "Hello"? That's because there really are different types of conversations, and it helps to recognize what you're getting into:

- *Phatic* communication involves those quick, brief moments when people make connections with others. This isn't meant to be a conversation, just an acknowledgment of sorts, such as "Hello," "So long," or "How are you?"

- *Ritual* communication situations are symbolic structures of tradition, and your credibility can rise or fall on your sensitivity to others' rituals. When friends of ours went to mainland China on business, they discovered how essential it is to share a tea ritual before conducting a conference. At one factory in a very poor district, there was no money for tea. Before the conference, the guests sat down at the table and attended to every nuance of graciously sharing tea with their hosts—except that *unflavored hot water* was poured. The ritual proceeded as if it were with the finest tea; not a word was said about the water. Without that "tea," the hosts would have lost face—and their guests would not have been able to move on to the next step in their conversation.

- *Exchange* conversations use talk to share information, ideas, and, sometimes, feelings. An exchange may involve little emotional commitment but serve the goals of each individual. For example, a couple talks about their schedule for the day—who will stop by the store, who will walk the dog, and whether they should visit a sick friend that evening. This basic interpersonal talk is essential to daily life but engages participants at a relatively superficial level.

- *Bonding* conversations include ritual and exchange, yet go deeper to develop relational process and feelings between persons. You bond with someone as you disclose, support, and adapt to each other. For instance, you care that your friend is sad, so you listen empathically and share your own feelings. As you do, you strengthen the emotional glue that holds you and your friend together.

You might find yourself in a conversation that meets several of these descriptions at once, or in sequence. Understanding the structure and how to choose topics helps you move it along smoothly.

Is this any way to say good morning?

I walk into the office after a long, unplugged weekend, turn on the computer, log onto e-mail and up pops a message: You have 554 new unread e-mails. . . .

In the new 24/7 economy, the door is never locked on the mailroom. "You've got mail"—all the time. The helpful assistant has become the sorcerer's apprentice.

I read a study the other day showing the average corporate e-mailer spends two hours a day doing e-mail. The figure has grown by 50 percent in just one year. . . . I'm sure we are communicating more and thinking less.

This is the story of the new world. The ease and the speed of the Internet has come up against the 24-hour day.

Ellen Goodman in *The Tribune,* Thursday, October 19, 2000, p. B4.

Structure There's a reason for the phrase "the art of conversation." Like a painting or a novel, conversation usually reveals a structure, and it develops themes or topics. If you're intensely involved in a conversation, you may not think about the pattern you're following, but it's there. Good conversationalists understand how to open a conversation, how to feel the flow of talk and keep it moving along, and how to end it.

Opening a conversation is easy if you know this three-step process:

1 *Provide identification or show recognition.* Here strangers introduce themselves or acquaintances give verbal or nonverbal signs they know each other. A wave, a smile, and a "Hi, how ya doin?" might start the process.

2 *Indicate accessibility.* Show you're open to a conversation—make eye contact, smile, turn your body toward the other person, perhaps ask questions such as, "What are you doing these days?"

3 *Initiate or respond to a topic* from which to build a conversation by offering a question or thought but leaving plenty of room to change or build on it according to the other's response. You might say, "I haven't been to a movie in so long. What's worth seeing?"

Keeping a conversation flowing involves trying out, changing, and developing topics; building on one another's responses; and establishing unspoken rules for interacting. In a casual conversation, this may mean no more than taking turns speaking or figuring out how to adapt your style to the other person.

Closing a conversation can be tricky. Who hasn't felt trapped in a conversation long after it should have been over? Closing a conversation requires three steps:

1   Recognize cues that it's time to move on, such as looking at a watch or packing up books or saying, "I didn't know it was this late."

2   Make summary statements that highlight the most important points of the conversation ("Well, I really am glad to hear about your award . . . ").

3   Express positive closures that indicate an up-note. Languages the world over use some variation of "Go with God" or "Good fortune," or, in North America, "See ya!" or "Take care, now." Even e-mail often ends with a happy face.

Topics   The idea is to find something that can stimulate an exchange of information or ideas. The first step is to be interested in your partner; the second is to be interesting yourself. Be ready to share information from your life—classes, talents, hobbies. Do some conversation homework; use magazines, newspapers, television, radio, and lectures to acquire a range of information. Your talk will be more interesting and credible; besides, your confidence increases when you know you can discuss events and issues.

Getting others to talk is pretty easy, too, if you take these approaches:

■   *Explore topics at a safe level.* Move gradually from exchanging basic information to learning more about one another. Disclosing something about yourself will encourage your partner to respond, and each such exchange builds on the previous one.

■   *Try a variety of approaches.* Some people are more shy and less willing to communicate than others, so it may be up to you to get them talking.

■   *Ask good questions.* To help identify interesting ideas and topics as well as to encourage your partner to talk, ask open-ended questions such as, "What do you think about . . . ?" or "How would you . . . ?"

■   *Use free information.* Pick up ideas from people's verbal or nonverbal cues (Garner, 1981). Maybe someone's wearing a button that says, "It takes 100 dumb animals to make a fur coat, and only one to wear it," so you open with, "Great button! I guess you're opposed to wearing fur?"

Keeping a Conversation Moving

Conversational success starts with your approach. Conversations work when you want them to, when you are aware of your own participation, and when you are sensitive to others' feedback.

Your Own Participation   One scholar identifies four important elements in a good conversation (Grice, 1989) that can guide your input:

1   *Quantity of information.* Talk enough but not too much. Be sensitive to another's nonverbal cues, and monitor your own talk. If you tend to be shy or quiet, practice developing ideas with description and detail. If you are

Communication affects growth and change in relationships.

Skjold/The Image Works

enthusiastic and want to give *all* the details, ask yourself how much you really need to share—and watch for signs of boredom or overload in your listener.

2   *Quality of information.* Tell the truth. Truth-telling is a matter both of ethics and credibility. At the same time, be sensitive to the situation and your listener. Don't disclose more than is appropriate, and be tactful. Along with telling the truth, be open-minded and objective, so others feel free to express dissenting opinions.

3   *Relevance.* Stay on the topic. Don't distract the other person with irrelevant comments. Especially if you're responding to a question, keep the focus on its intent—but allow topics to develop and evolve as you talk. Sometimes, you have to give up something you really wanted to say in order to keep the conversation moving smoothly.

4   *Clarity.* Communicate coherently. Think about what you are saying from the viewpoint of the listener. Take time to express your ideas so they are organized, clear, and specific.

Culture and Gender Influences   Conversation is a give-and-take process, so being aware of influences on others' responses as well as being aware of their nonverbal and verbal feedback to you helps you adapt your end of the talk appropriately.

For example, an individual's approach to conversation may be influenced by culture and gender. You recall from Chapter 7 that people from high-context cultures might consider less information to be sufficient, while people from low-context cultures might require more (Reisner, 1993, pp. 30–31), so, for instance, a Japanese person might give you less information than a North American. Don't overgeneralize, however. Within "low-context" North America are, for example, traditional Apache and Navajo high-context cultures. Those who grew up in these cultures avoid conversation with strangers, getting to know them only by being in the same place and observing them for awhile within that context (Basso, 1990, pp. 84–85, 97).

Sometimes, too, you need to allow for your partner's conversational objectives, and these may be linked to gender. Men seem to approach conversation more as a direct information exchange, with less concern for harmony and feelings than women do (Duck, Rutt, Hurst, & Strejc, 1991). "For women, talk *is* the essence of relationships. Consistent with this primary goal, women's speech tends to display identifiable features that foster connections, support, closeness, and understanding" (Wood, 2001, p. 125). A man may think a woman's "off topic" when she is creating those connections and giving support.

Tannen (1990) goes so far as to say that "communication between men and women can be like cross-cultural communication. . . . Instead of different dialects, it has been said they speak different genderlects" (p. 42). Remember that in Chapter 6, we noted that Tannen has distinguished men's talk as *report-talk* (explaining, directing, describing information) and women's as *rapport-talk* (sharing feelings, ideas, and support to build mutual understanding). Perhaps that's why both men and women often prefer a woman as a conversational partner (Duck, et al., 1991), finding women to be better conversationalists than men (Reis, Wheeler, Nezlek, Kernis, & Spiegel, 1985). Still, these differences in style can be frustrating for both sexes. A woman may talk about a problem, expecting a man to empathize; the man may give suggestions, expecting that she wants concrete help with solving the problem. Both are contributing from their own perspectives; neither understands the other.

Give-and-Take   Some cultures—including the United States in general—value talk highly. People want conversations to flow smoothly, evenly, and interestingly. To make your conversation do that, you need to:

1   *Reciprocate and cooperate.* Keep participants roughly equal in amounts of talking and sharing. Even in talkative North America, people are more attracted to and satisfied communicating with people who listen to them and who don't dominate the conversation (Wheeless, Frymier, & Thompson, 1992). Your credibility goes up when you keep the conversation balanced.

2   *Share the conversational focus.* Doing so enables partners to feel equal. When you focus your messages on the other person, you recognize that person's uniqueness and worth, and vice versa. Using these **person-centered messages** keeps others involved and satisfied with the conversation and increases your credibility (Zorn, 1991).

3   *Demonstrate interpersonal involvement.* Show your interest in your partner

Conversation is the socializing instrument par excellence, and in its style one can see reflected the capacities of a race.

Jose Ortega y Gasset, late 19th–early 20th-century Spanish writer

Person-centered messages Conversational behavior that recognizes each participant's worth

and the conversation with your nonverbal closeness, attentiveness, alertness, animation, and concentration on the other person.

4   *Use humor appropriately.* Humor is a superb way to make a point, reduce stress, and connect with people. What's funny and what's not can be a close call, however. Funny people sometimes find humor in something that leaves others unamused (Booth-Butterfield & Booth-Butterfield, 1991). Appropriate humor depends on the situation, the individual, and the nature of your relationship with the other person.

Developing Relationships

Friends can love one another, and lovers can be friends—yet, love and friendship are not entirely the same. Friendship and love both are privately negotiated personal relationships requiring a "considerable investment of emotional energy" (Rawlins, 1993, p. 52), loyalty, fidelity, trust, affection, and commitment. Romance, however, adds a sexual component, so it is more volatile, more urgent, than friendship; friends share greater equality and generate less tension than do lovers.

So much of building a relationship is just day-to-day sharing; most of married couples' communication occurs in interactions that combine activities, such as fixing dinner while discussing the day's events. Yet, couples consider the most important interactions are those that express affection (Dainton, 1998).

Both friendship and romantic love develop as people get to know one another through communication behavior called **affinity seeking,** as they look for ways to feel similar and close. It takes communicating for people to find the ways in which they are similar, and therefore attractive, to each other (Duck, 1994a; 1994b). They try to present themselves well, show their credibility, and engage with the other person by looking for common interests, being polite, and getting involved (Bell & Daly, 1984). It seems, in fact, that trading self-disclosures and learning to see the other person's point of view is important to being satisfied with romantic relationships (Meeks, Hendrick, & Hendrick, 1998). As they grow closer, people take more risks, disclose themselves to each other, and begin to build empathy and trust. If all this sounds familiar, that's because it's part of the positive climate building we discussed in Chapter 7. You can see this process represented in Figure 8.1.

Affinity seeking Communication behavior in which participants look for ways to feel similar and close

Social penetration describes the gradual widening and deepening of a relationship as two people trade self-disclosures and develop mutual trust and empathy (Altman & Taylor, 1973). People start with exchanging information, move to exchanging understandings of emotion, and progress to exchanging and sharing activities in their lives. As their relationship develops, they make deeper disclosures about themselves to each other, which leads to interpersonal bonding. Altman and Taylor liken this process to peeling an onion, but to us it's more

Social penetration The process of gradual widening and deepening of a relationship as two people develop mutual trust and empathy

Figure 8.1 *Process of interpersonal relationship develoment and bonding*

like an artichoke. Each person's personality becomes better known to the other as, through self-disclosure, they peel away layer after layer until they reach the heart.

Building and Bonding

Interpersonal bonding
The process of forming individual relationships

Intimate relationships
Mutually supportive, trusting, enduring associations between partners

True friendship and genuine love are rare and wondrous bonds between people. Bochner (1984) defines **interpersonal bonding** as "the process of forming individualized relationships, affinities that are close, deep, personal, and intimate" (p. 544). **Intimate relationships,** which may or may not include a sexual component, are mutually supportive, trusting, enduring associations in which partners know and care about each other and talk about things they would not share with other people. Such relationships take time and effort to develop through the following stages:

1   *Initiating* is the introduction and start of conversation.

2   *Experimenting* involves asking questions, volunteering small disclosures, getting to know one another, and sharing information and activities.

3   *Intensifying* is a period of emotional awareness and developing commitment in which partners begin to care genuinely about each other. People at this

Will Schutz, psychologist, says that these three elements are necessary for successful interpersonal relationships:

- Self-regard—to understand, respect, and like myself

- Truth—the great simplifier of personal and interpersonal difficulties

- Choice—I empower myself when I take responsibility for myself.

From Will Schutz (1984), *The Truth Option: A Practical Technology for Human Affairs*. Berkeley, CA: Ten-Speed Press.

point often try to ingratiate themselves (with gifts, affection, attention), explain their feelings, and directly request a deeper closeness with the other person (Honeycutt, Cantrill, Kelly, & Lambkin, 1998).

4   *Integrating* deepens the relationship as partners begin to feel and confirm their relationship. If they become deeply connected, close, and interdependent, people may begin to think of themselves almost as one person instead of two.

5   *Bonding* occurs when people feel fully committed to each other and to the relationship in the present and the future (Knapp, 1984).

Initiating in romance is much like a dance of courtship. One person uses appearance, talk, and/or movement to attract the other person's attention while "looking good." There is much back-and-forth, ambivalent, "Maybe I like you, maybe I don't" nonverbal behavior during this stage—drop eyes, glance back—move closer, pull away—smile, go blank. Each person signals interest—pulls in the tummy, straightens the shoulders, makes eye contact, smiles, grooms, primps. An interested couple position themselves face to face, closing themselves in and others out. They lean forward, make eye contact, and may exaggerate laughing and gesturing, showing invitation and sexual arousal. They often act like parent and child, touching, stroking, nuzzling, and cooing, all to communicate potential physical intimacy and availability. A flirtation might not end in a sexual liaison, but it is a consistently implied goal of a courtship dance (Burgoon, Buller, & Woodall, 1989, pp. 325–329).

Cultural differences and changing social norms deeply affect this dance. In the 1950s, for example, society approved the attention-getting, recognizing, and positioning stages, but invitation and sexual arousal were theoretically limited to "necking" (contact from the neck up) for a dating couple or "petting" (stroking and fondling) if they were "engaged to be engaged." "Going all the way" (resolu-

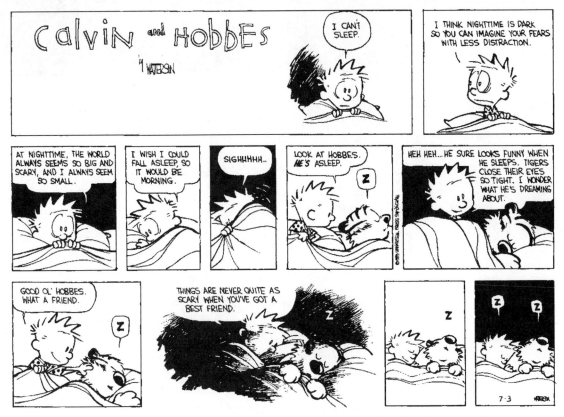

tion or sexual intercourse) was socially acceptable only on the wedding night. Not every couple waited until then, of course. Today, even with the AIDS crisis, many people go through a quick courtship process in a singles bar and wind up in bed. However, many individuals, cultures, and identity groups still advise saving sex for marriage. In fact, in some cultures, courtship is an unknown concept, because marriage partners are selected by parents, and premarital sex is forbidden.

Changing and Dissolving

Turning point Moment when a relationship undergoes an incremental change

Over time, relationships change. Romantic partners may identify **turning points,** specific moments at which something has caused an incremental change in their relationship. Turning points don't occur in any specific order or stages, but they do seem to occur in certain contexts, such as the moments of *early dating and time together*, or times of *physical separation and reunion*. A turning point may come when people are *psychologically separated* through conflict or avoidance and then become reunited. Other turning points may be occasions of *intense positive or negative experiences*, or when there is some *external competition* and a couple chooses to *see each other exclusively*. A relationship may experience a turning point, too, when a partner *sacrifices individual interests or needs* to provide support, help, or gifts to the other (Baxter & Bullis, 1986).

Turning points may improve the quality and depth of a relationship or quite the opposite. Altman and Taylor (1973) use the term **depenetration** to describe the process in which partners find less reward in their relationship and start closing off to each other (Knapp, 1984). They go through a process of *differentiating*, when partners perceive differences between themselves and judge them negatively; *circumscribing*, in which partners put fences around communication, limiting it to safe, impersonal topics; *stagnating*, when partners have nothing to say and don't much care; *avoiding* each other; and, finally, *terminating*, when one or both partners call it quits.

Understanding the phases of penetration and depenetration can help you evaluate where a relationship is, where you want it to go, and how to get there. Consider, for example, Malachy and Francis. They are extremely close and caring, but one day, Malachy begins to see Fran's neatness as "compulsive," compared to Malachy's "healthier" casual style (differentiating). Irritated by Malachy's "mess," Fran closes off communication on all issues related to lifestyle (circumscribing). Gradually, Malachy and Fran stop talking, and Malachy becomes too busy to spend time with Fran (stagnating). Fran begins to develop a new relationship that provides excuses for staying away (avoiding). Finally, inevitably, Malachy and Fran end their relationship (terminating).

Depenetration The process through which partners end a relationship

Being a Couple

As you and a partner develop a long-term relationship, you begin to build a kind of emotional house within which you'll live. Making that house strong takes caring, commitment, communication—not to mention a lot of giving, sharing, and forbearance. And often forgiveness.

Any couple consciously or unconsciously creates a structure for their relationship both of unwritten rules and communication themes. **Relational "rules"** are expectations of how couples should relate to each other, negotiated between each person's expectations of how a relationship should be (Bochner, 1984). Some rules are common to the society, such as the norm in mainland China that a young wife does as her husband's mother tells her. Other rules are idiosyncratic to the couple, for example, "We never call each other at work." A third set of rules are implicit or explicit agreements, some of which are mutually set ("We take turns doing the dishes"). Some are consciously understood but not discussed ("We don't talk about our mothers"), and others are unconscious or unacknowledged, even though an observer might perceive the pattern ("She always makes the decisions; that's how they operate").

Relational "rules" Expectations of how couples should relate to each other

Relational themes
Aspects of their relationship that emerge from
couples' conversations

Relational themes emerge from what the couple talks about—the weather, work, the news—their gossip, playing, fighting. Analyses of couples' communication has shown seven general themes that often weave through their discussions (Burgoon & Hale, 1984). These include discussions of:

- *Dominance/submission*, when partners jockey for control
- *Emotional arousal*, when they express feelings about the context of the discussion
- *Composure*, when they talk about the stress in a relationship
- *Similarity/difference*, as they talk about their commonality or difference
- *Formality*, to set guidelines for their behavior and style
- *Task/social orientation*, to address the focus of the relationship, and
- *Intimacy*, which addresses relational issues between them.

Here's an example of one statement that brings all of these themes together in a troubled period in a couple's life: "You're trying to force your point of view again [dominance/submission], and I feel so frustrated [emotional arousal]—I know we're both working too hard [composure], and I know I just get upset and you just work harder [similarity/difference], but we've got to make a rule that we take time off [formality]; pay more attention to each other [task/social orientation]—we've got to find each other again" [intimacy].

All couples have their problems—some small, some large. It isn't a big deal, perhaps, when people can't agree on who takes out the garbage, but it can be a serious issue when they conflict over intimacy or loss of trust or when they resort to aggression to feel powerful in the relationship.

Expectations of Intimacy

Building intimacy can be comparable to trying to reach over a 10-foot wall of people's expectations; when one person is disappointed and wants the other to change, the couple often goes into a cycle of one demanding change and the other withdrawing (Coughlin & Vangelisti, 1999). The relationship can be injured or destroyed when communication fails in any of four areas: self-percep-tions, self-disclosure, expectations and fears, and expressions of intimacy (Borisoff, 1993).

Meaning of the self. The objective of intimacy is interdependency and close-ness. Two people who are unequal in ability to depend on and support each other may find intimacy to be elusive. Men typically learn to think of themselves as independent, competitive, strong, intelligent, and rational, and women to think of themselves as cooperative, nurturing, and emotional. "As women strive to get close to the men they love, the men, for whom too much closeness signals suffocation, begin to retreat. This retreat creates the desire in women to 'clasp' further, which results in greater distancing" (Borisoff, 1993, p. 20).

The ability to self-disclose.   When self-disclosure is reciprocal, intimacy and bonding develop. When it is not, barriers to intimacy develop. Although men "more readily disclose views and attitudes . . . women are more likely to reveal fears and feelings" (Borisoff, 1993, p. 21). So women, feeling that men hold back their feelings, may believe that men fear the intimacy that women want in a relationship, while men may feel that women talk too much about personal issues.

The meaning of personal relationships.   Partners may not be supportive because they don't understand the other's fears. "What may be a desirable, safe situation for one individual may be perceived as a threat to another" (Borisoff, 1993, p. 21). Some research indicates that men are more likely to feel threatened by close personal affiliation and intimacy, whereas women tend to feel threatened more in impersonal and competitive situations (Gilligan, 1982).

The expression of intimacy.   Once again, as a general rule, men give information and ideas but tend to share emotion less than women, whereas women are more likely to express emotional bonds. Communication styles are changing as women open the doors to competition and careers and as men take over more family and nurturing roles. Nevertheless, their expressions and interpretations of intimacy still seem to be in conflict and to block empathy and understanding.

Hold faithfulness and sincerity as first principles.

Confucius, 5th-century B.C. Chinese philosopher

People in any committed relationship, whether it is friendship or romantic, heterosexual or homosexual, need to work hard at understanding and adapting to each other. Maybe that's the most important part of all—communicating with care.

Loss of Trust

The mortar that holds a relationship together is trust. Trust is built slowly, developing bit by bit when two people put their relationship first; when they are able to share themselves and their feelings; when each chooses behaviors and actions that will build the bond with the other.

Once trust is lost, though, it's well-nigh impossible to regain. Oh, people do succeed in rebuilding relationships, but it's a long, hard road to get back from such trust-busters as infidelity, deception, and suspicion.

Infidelity is prevalent and deadly. Pittman (1993) says that "without the expectation of fidelity, intimacy becomes awkward and marriage adversarial. People who expect their partner to betray them are likely to beat them to the draw, and to make both of them miserable in the meantime" (p. 35).

Deception is a part of infidelity, of course, but it can also be a game or a strategy for avoiding conflict. Suppose Cassie's worried because Kurt didn't show up last evening, and she asks, "What happened? Was something wrong? You didn't even call." If Kurt is fully honest he might say, "I know; I meant to, but . . . well, the truth is, I was hanging out with Leah and Rudy, and we decided to get something to eat and we got to talking and the evening just got away from me."

That's not bad. Cassie may be annoyed, but they can work that out together. Ah, but if Kurt is unwilling to cope with the disagreement he might deceive Cassie in one of these four ways (McCornack, Levine, Solowczuk, Torres, & Campbell, 1992, p. 17):

1 *Quantity deception.* "Well, you know how it is. You get busy and time slips away." A quantity deception is a "half-truth," deceiving Cassie by concealing part of what happened.

2 *Quality deception.* "Yeah, Pete had an accident and I had to go to the hospital with him." A quality deception is, in other words, a lie.

3 *Relevance deception.* "How about we go out to dinner tonight?" The relevance deception diverts attention from the issue, so that the truth need not be faced.

4 *Clarity deception.* "Yeah, like, I had stuff to do, you know, like, I've been really busy, and like, this is a rotten week, and . . . " A clarity deception is equivocation. By mumbling around, Kurt might confuse and deceive Cassie into assuming he was just "doing other stuff."

Deceiving a partner can have several effects, all bad:

- *Deception hurts credibility.* The deception is worst when it's a violation of quality—the lie—but all deception is damaging (McCornack, et al., 1992; Burgoon, 1992).

- *Deception creates and feeds on suspicion.* Deceivers give nonverbal cues that make their partners suspicious, and suspicious partners reveal how they feel by being more dominant, assertive, formal, and manipulative. The deceivers react by increasing their deception cues (Burgoon, 1992). That, of course, feeds the suspicion, and the relationship spirals down into a morass of distrust.

- *The deceived partner may terminate the relationship.* When the lie is about important information, and/or when the deceived person considers lying to be immoral, and/or when she or he already is suspicious because of previous experiences, the lie may destroy trust entirely—and the deceived partner is likely to end the relationship (McCornack & Levine, 1990).

Physical Aggression

People who lack communication skills to handle interpersonal problems may resort to force in sheer frustration (Infante, Sabourin, Rudd, & Shannon, 1990). They may be predisposed to violence because they suffer from low self-esteem, repressed shame, and anger (Scheff & Retzinger, 1991; Infante, et al., 1990), often because they grew up in violent families. And, frequently, substance abuse feeds violent responses to frustration and anger; alcohol is involved in 80% of murders, 70% of serious assaults, and 50% of family conflicts requiring police intervention (Metcalf & Felible, 1992, p. 202).

When people resort to violence to vent their frustration and to gain power over their partner, the result may be rape. Rape has nothing to do with loving, with caring, or even with sexuality. Rape is about power and control. When a person forces sex on an unwilling partner, it's rape, whether the two are strangers, dating partners, or spouses. Sadly, as aggression and violence increase, so does the incidence of rape. And so does its "acceptability." Surveys reveal some alarming findings. For example, 33% of college males say they would rape a woman if they thought no one would find out, and 50% admit they have gotten a woman drunk and/or coerced, manipulated, or pressured her to have sex (Wood, 2001, p. 312). Moreover, up to 66% of women have been sexually abused before they are 18, and up to 75% of college women have been coerced into having sex one or more times.

Wood (2001) observes that "rape is most common in societies that embrace ideologies of male toughness and that disrespect women. . . . " Noting that in many societies rape is almost unknown, she concludes that, "violence against women is not innate in male sexuality and acceptance of violence is not inevitable" (pp. 332–333).

Communication plays a serious role in preventing date, acquaintance, and spousal rape. "No" has got to mean no, and the aggressor has to understand that. One problem is that men tend to perceive more sexuality in interactions than women do (Abbey, 1991), and they interpret as invitation behavior that women construe as mere friendliness (Mongeau & Yeazell, 1992). Rapists, in particular, seem unable to differentiate a woman's nonverbal cues. There used to be a convenient rationale for seducers and rapists—that "when a woman says no, she means maybe; when she says maybe, she means yes." Perhaps the old expression should be turned around: Men should assume that if a woman says, "yes," she means "Maybe," and if she says, "Maybe," she means "Absolutely not."

Violent partners and victims both need help to stop the cycle and alter their communication patterns. Help *is* available. Most communities have organizations to help battered partners as well as batterers. Every community has branches of Alcoholics Anonymous and Narcotics Anonymous to provide assistance for alcohol and drug problems. In addition, colleges, religious organizations, communities, and police departments offer programs to help battered and abused women, children, and men. Hotlines can refer individuals to family service and support groups that help batterers, rapists, and their victims. Often, there are safe houses where a person who is afraid of a partner's violence can stay until an alternative living situation can be arranged. Violence can be stopped and people can be helped before all involved are both physically and emotionally damaged.

Marriage Vows!

Lee Anne Knight and Scott Bukofsky exchanged these vows at their wedding on November 6, 1992.

Presider: Hello. Welcome. Thank you for coming. We are gathered here tonight to celebrate the marriage of Scott and Lee Anne. They have come here tonight to express their love for one another. It is fitting that you are all here to share this moment with them since you are the ones who have helped shape their lives. All that you have taught them and every experience you have shared with them have in some way led them to this moment. I will now ask them to state their intentions.

Vows: (In turn) I [Scott/Lee] take you [Lee/Scott] to be my [wife/husband]: to love, honor, and cherish all the days of my life. I will be considerate of your wishes and desires, and respect your integrity and intentions. I will support your dreams and aspirations and strive to keep our lives full of laughter and joy. I do this at peace with myself and the world, secure in my decision, aware of your uniqueness, yet strong in the conviction that it is only together that we can achieve our fullest potential.

Being a Family

Every family is part of a culture—perhaps more than one—and every family has an internal culture of its own, made up of the ways the family is structured and the rules and images that make it work.

Samovar and Porter (2000) observe, "Keep in mind that at the moment of birth, a human being's development can take any number of paths. A child born in India perceives many people living together in one house and is learning about extended families. By being in the same house with elderly people, the child is also learning to value the aged. In most of Africa the entire village raises a child, and the child thus learns about the extended family" (p. 12).

Family An interdependent couple or group that creates its own structure within a larger culture

Within the larger culture, then, a **family** is an interdependent couple or group whose communication organizes its existence. Family members depend on one another to meet both physiological and psychological needs, from doing the laundry to supporting one another in times of grief. Family members might include spouses, cohabiting couples of the same or opposite sex, parents and children, a single parent and children, and/or siblings or even friends who share a home (Trost, 1990). Many contemporary families are "blended," as parents have brought their children into new relationships from previous families.

Each family creates itself in its own unique way. People bring previous experiences to a new relationship, and this history shapes the way members communicate and the patterns they develop in an optimal or dysfunctional family existence.

Family Development

People sometimes wail, "I'm becoming my mother!" or, "I heard my father's voice coming out of my mouth!" This comment can be both a lament and a celebration, as people see the threads of their childhoods in the fabric of their adult existence. Each family is unique, but each is affected in its development by these factors:

Time. As years go by, families change; jobs and living places change; children are born, grow, and leave; parents age and die. Each change influences family communication and development.

Relational prototypes. Individuals start new families with expectations based on previous experiences and on social stereotypes, despite recent changes in family structures. A man who expects a warm dinner on the table every night may be disappointed when his wife works until seven and expects him to do the cooking.

Irrationality. Family communication may be irrational but logical at the same time, with emotion and reason being "implicit collaborators" in determining communication behavior (Planalp, 1993, p. 6). For example, a teenager regularly prefaces her exits with a smart remark that precipitates a fight with her mother. The girl marches out, and the mother throws up her hands in angry defeat. Irrational, yes, but the emotional confrontation has an internal logic. The teenager insults her mother to assert her independence. The mother must learn to accept her daughter's independence but feels guilty about losing control. When it's clear that the teenager will no longer accept parental control, her mother has a logical reason to "give up" (Vangelisti, 1993).

Both mother and daughter are playing out their roles, for every family has role expectations for each member. Families may identify their roles with comments such as "Mom's the disciplinarian" or "Dad keeps the books." Epstein, Bishop, and Baldwin (1982) identify necessary family roles such as provider, nurturer, sexual partner, personal development facilitator, decision maker, disciplinarian and guide, finance manager, and health director. Members may share some roles, or a specific person may fill a given role exclusively, but if no one meets these needs, individual members or the family as a whole may suffer. As families develop, roles often need to be changed, too, and this may contribute to family conflict.

Roles are, in fact, changing as society changes. In the United States, fathers used to have little to do with their children; parenting was the mother's role. Today, while mothers still are responsible for most of a child's care, North

American fathers are spending an average of 2.5 hours per weekday and 6.2 per weekend day with their children (August, *USA Today Magazine*, 2000, p. 4).

Families, like couples, develop their own rules and themes, as well as images of the family that all members recognize. For example:

- *Rules.* Members know who can talk to whom about what topics, when, and under what circumstances. Perhaps sex is an acceptable subject of conversation with your grandparents, for example, but you don't dare mention it in front of Aunt Harriet.

- *Images.* Families can identify their mental pictures, concepts, feelings, metaphors, and myths of the family that members share: "My family is a circus," or, "Our family is a safe haven." An image both reflects and defines roles and rules for family communication. It can provide a sense of cohesion and uniqueness for the family as a whole, but previous family images must be negotiated when partners enter a new relationship. The new family won't be like each of the partners' old ones, so they have to build a new image that will be healthy for all the members.

Optimal Family Functioning

We would like to tell you exactly how to create a "happy" or "normal" family, but we can't. Yerby, Buerkel-Rothfuss, and Bochner (1990) point out that it's impossible to define a "normal family," because definitions are so culture- and value-laden. Certain factors, however, are characteristic of families that function at an optimal level (pp. 312–313):

- *Members support one another.* They are not oppositional, hurtful, manipulating, or defensive.

- *Members enjoy themselves and one another.* They are spontaneous, playful, humorous, and witty. They do not take life too seriously.

- *Members are directed toward one another.* They are not self-involved and do not focus excessively on analyzing problems and motivations.

- *Members maintain conventional boundaries.* Children are respected and nurtured but not treated as peers to their parents. That is, family roles allow children to develop at a normal pace, guided by boundaries that protect the process.

As families develop, they face opposing forces that members must find a way of managing. Consider how the following issues might have affected your own family experiences:

- *Stability and change.* Change is certain, but people are uncertain when they face change. A healthy family helps members to maintain their sense of family and, at the same time, to adjust to the stress of changing circumstances (Yerby, et al., 1990). A dysfunctional family may teeter constantly on the brink of crisis, unable to achieve stability or to embrace change.

- *Integration and separation.* A family needs to integrate members' roles, interests, and needs into the family system. Yet it is normal for people to leave. When someone leaves the home or when a member dies, a strong family can help members to integrate and deal with separation without losing the sense of family and support (Yerby, et al., 1990). A dysfunctional family may fail to integrate its members, responding to one another with fear, jealousy, or competition; yet, members may be unable to adjust relationships when a member leaves the home.

- *Power and control issues.* Power in families normally is asymmetrical, and adults control family functioning as the children develop. That's a secure situation. If, however, adults fear that they are controlled by the children, there's a problem. Physically abusive parents often "attribute high levels of power to children, and children are themselves placed in a parenting role" (Bugental, 1993, p. 288). The consequence can be a violent and dysfunctional family, as parents who think their own power is threatened try to control their children.

Dysfunctional Family Relationships

Dysfunctional relationship Interactions in which participants play games and manipulate one another, which breaks down the optimal relationship

Codependency Patterns of behavior that "enable" participants to behave in dysfunctional ways

In a **dysfunctional family,** members may play games, manipulate one another, and enable one another's self-destructive behavior. Instead of interdependency, they may act with codependency. In **codependency**, members become "enablers," enabling one another to behave in dysfunctional ways. The family hangs together because no one knows what it is like to be otherwise. With codependent partners, for example, the husband of an alcoholic may rant and rave but clean up her mess and lie to the boss to cover her absence, then make up, take the blame, and set the stage for the next episode. A codependent family member is characterized by "an overdeveloped sense of responsibility, a fear of personal criticism, a fear of abandonment, and a need for control" (Policoff, 1987).

Members of dysfunctional families frequently play specific roles that enable others to escape facing issues. For example:

- *The identified patient:* The person with a problem who becomes the focus of the family's attention and draws attention away from others in the family. This protects the family from facing issues. Suppose a mother is an alcoholic, for example. Everyone may focus on her problem and on covering for her so the neighbors won't know. In the process, they have an excuse to ignore a child's increasing depression or the chaos in the household.

- *The scapegoat:* The "bad" person on whom all misfortunes are blamed so the family won't have to take responsibility for itself. Perhaps, for example, the eldest son constantly is told he is a "bad boy," and he fulfills that prophecy by regularly getting into trouble at school. The parents are always rushing off to see the principal and figure out ways to discipline their son—

According to a new survey released last week by the National Center on Addiction and Substance Abuse at Columbia University (CASA), the quality of a teenager's relationship with his or her father directly affects the likelihood of the teen's using drugs or alcohol.

In its first analysis of family structure and substance abuse risk, CASA found that children living in two-parent families who have only a fair or poor relationship with their father are at a 68 percent higher risk of smoking, drinking and using drugs than are all teens living in two-parent households. They are at higher risk than teens living in a household headed by a single mother, who are at a 30 percent higher risk of substance use compared to all teens in a two-parent household.

The safest teens, according to CASA's analysis of its fifth annual CASA National Survey of American Attitudes on Substance Abuse, Teens and Their Parents, are those living in two-parent homes who:

- Have a positive relationship with both parents
- Go to both parents equally when they have important decisions to make
- Have discussed illegal drugs with parents
- Report that both parents are equally demanding in terms of grades, homework and personal behavior.

Alcoholism & Drug Abuse Weekly, Sept. 6, 1999, p. 5.

---

and they don't have time to figure out why their relationship is deteriorating or why they can't pay the bills. By attending to the scapegoat, the family avoids taking responsibility for any other problems.

- *The hero:* The "good" person who does everything right. The hero often is the child who cooks dinner, gets good grades, wins awards, is amiable and kind, and covers up for her parents' bad behavior. This child is a miniature adult who must keep the family together, no matter what. Despite all her or his successes, this "hero" child can never feel adequate because no one can be all things, and no child is an adult.

> *Becoming a father, that is no achievement. Being one is, though.*
>
> Less Murray, 20th-century Australian poet

An adult child of an alcoholic writes, "There are approximately 28 million of us in the United States alone—probably more, because one of our characteristics is that we try to deny there was ever anything wrong with our parents. Yet we were shaped by their alcoholic way of life" (Hobe, 1990, p. 18). As a child, this woman's task was to care for her father and mother when they were drunk, to keep the secret, to cover the guilt. She was reared to be a codependent, an enabler, playing "the hero" to her parents' roles as patients. As an adult, she had to let go of those roles and learn new ones for a healthy relationship.

The bad news is that people who grew up in dysfunctional families often bring codependent patterns with them into their new relationships. The good news is that dysfunctional family patterns do not have to be repeated. Self-help programs, books, and counselors can guide the grown-up children of dysfunctional homes to relinquish these patterns and create healthier ones. If you grew up in such a family, or if you are close to someone who did, you can find assistance or referrals in most college counseling centers. If the dysfunction was related to alcohol or drug abuse—as it often is—groups such as ACOA (Adult Children of Alcoholics) can help you change those patterns for yourself. For many people, breaking dysfunctional patterns is the first step to building good relationships and healthy families for the future. It's worth the effort.

Summary

Interpersonal communication ranges from a relatively superficial level of social relations to the much deeper level of interhuman relations at which people are touched emotionally and psychologically, influencing changes in individuals and their relationship over time. Getting to know people starts with attraction and opportunity. The conversation process starts with casual talk and exploratory communication to develop commonalities between participants. Keeping a conversation moving requires going beyond topics related to the setting and into topics of interest to the participants.

When you start developing friendships, you explore more about one another in a gradual process of interpersonal bonding in which you form deep and personal affinities. This may lead to friendships, which may become enduring intimate relationships in which friends support, trust, and care for each other. Romantic relationships may start with a courtship ritual that moves from attention-getting strategies to sexual invitation and activity. As the romance develops, the couple may go through a number of turning points that define their relationship and its stages.

As two individuals become a couple, they develop a mutual identity with unwritten rules that govern communication and conversational themes that define their relationship. Problems may arise due to gender-expectation and -role barriers that affect the openness of communication between the partners. Worse problems may arise when partners deceive one another, destroy trust, and/or resort to violence.

Families evolve from members' previous family experiences and the relationship. Families establish roles to serve functions of the family, rules to structure communication among members, and images that portray the nature of the unique family. In optimally functioning families, members are mutually supportive, enjoy one another's company, are directed toward one another rather than self-involved, and maintain appropriate boundaries and structure in which children can develop.

When families become dysfunctional, members may be codependent, enabling one another to act in ways that are destructive to themselves and/or the family. People can turn around dysfunctional behaviors—and create healthier families—with assistance from a wide variety of sources such as books, self-help and support groups, counseling groups, and agencies.

Exercises

 1 Think back to a relationship you have had (this could be a good friendship or a romantic relationship). Do the following:

 a Analyze the stages your relationship went through.

 b Identify the turning points in your relationship.

 c Apply the diagram in Figure 8.1 to your relationship. How were—or were not—the levels of communication described in that diagram reflected in your relationship?

 2 With another student, do the following:

 a Make up a description of a situation for a blind date. Write the roles for two characters; explain what their characteristics are, and what the setting is for the date.

 b Each of you take one role, and role-play for your class the opening conversation for your date.

 c With the class, discuss how the conversation developed.

 3 Browse through anthologies, magazines, or song lyrics to find a poem or short essay that expresses your beliefs and values about friendship, romantic relationships, or families. Practice reading the piece aloud until you can read it with excellent eye contact and feeling for the words. Then read it to the class.

   In a small group, discuss the selections your classmates read. What did they have in common? What important ideas did they share? From this discussion, create a list of "principles of interpersonal communication in prose and poetry" with your group. Report your list to the class.

   Together, integrate the lists into one, eliminating any repetitions.

 4 With a small group, observe a play or television show that portrays a family. Do the following:

 a Identify the image you think members might have of their family.

 b Identify the roles each member plays.

c   Identify how rules seem to work in this family.

d   As a group, present your observations to the class.

Cyberpoints

CCC

WEB SITE

1   For further information to help with family communication problems, go to the *Communicating with Credibility and Confidence* Web site at http://communication.wadsworth.com/lumsden and click on Chapter 8.

2   Go to http://www.interchg.ubc.ca/nikolai/conbeg.html and explore issues related to conversation openers.

3   Are you interested in families in a variety of cultures? Use *InfoTrac College Edition* and the keywords *family* and *culture*.

4   Use *InfoTrac College Edition* to locate and read the article by Stacy L. Norris and Richard L. Zweitenhoft, "Self-monitoring, trust, and commitment in romantic relationships."

Chapter 9

Professional Relationships: Transacting for Success

Objectives for This Chapter

Knowledge

- Understand how to communicate professionally in organizations
- Know how roles, stereotypes, and expectations affect workplace communication
- Identify ways to manage workplace harassment
- Recognize elements of intercultural communication competence
- Identify the types, functions, and goals of interviews
- Know how to prepare for and conduct interviews

Feelings and Approaches

- Approach college and career communication professionally
- Be aware of stereotyping and expectations in college and the workplace
- Feel comfortable in communicating with colleagues of diverse cultures
- Have confidence as an interviewer and interviewee

Communication Abilities

- Communicate appropriately with people in different organizational roles
- Develop intercultural communication competence
- Communicate credibly in professional situations
- Prepare and conduct interviews credibly

Key Terms

professionalism	primary question	job-qualification question
organizational culture	secondary question	behaviorial question
goal conflicts	open-ended question	situational question
stereotypes	closed question	simulation
interview	leading question	

Why are you putting all this investment of time, energy, and money into college? Our guess is that you have a vision of your future that includes a satisfying, productive, and successful career. We believe that a key to both your credibility and your confidence is **professionalism,** communication that shows your involvement, competence, pride, and ethical standards in what you do. Being professional helps you move from promising student to effective employee and leader.

At this moment, you are involved with at least one organization—your college—and probably others. In your future, you will communicate within numbers of organizations, often at the same time. That's why this chapter discusses issues in organizational life and ways to communicate professionally and effectively within it. Then, because you may often be an interviewee or an interviewer, this chapter presents several ways to develop your professional communication skills so your interviews will help you reach your goals.

Professionalism
Communication that shows involvement, competence, pride, and ethical standards in one's work

Communicating in Organizational Cultures

When you enter a new organization—whether in college or the corporate world—you may feel as if you're a stranger in a new land. In a way, you are. There are new people, new ways of doing things, new expectations. No matter how excellent your academic or technical qualifications may be, you can rise or fall on the basis of your understanding of the system and your communication within it.

You will begin to sense, early on, the way things are done in a specific organization—the **organizational culture,** in which, "as in all cultures, all facts, truths, realities, beliefs and values are what the members agree they are— they are perceptions" (Ott, 1989, p. vii). Members develop norms and expectations that both reflect and reinforce their ways of communicating (Weick, 1979), using communication as "the 'means' to create, maintain, and facilitate change in the culture of an organization" (Benjamin & McKerrow, 1994, p. 36).

Frequently, an organization has multiple cultures: an official and an unofficial culture, as well as subcultures within specific departments or offices.

The "official" culture is the leadership's ideal, often published as a "mission" or "vision" statement of organizational goals and values. The statement should provide a rationale for policies and actions. If, for instance, a college mission state-

Organizational culture
The way things are done within a specific organization

ment includes serving a diverse population then the college should develop active recruitment and retention policies to encourage the enrollment and success of a diverse student body.

The "unofficial" culture is developed over time by members' interactions. You probably have a good idea of what your college's unofficial culture is like from hearing stories about past events, teachers, students, and athletes. Your interactions teach you how people relate to one another at different levels in the hierarchy as well.

Subcultures grow within the larger culture in teams, offices, and departments. Perhaps on your campus, faculty in one department work well together and are helpful to students, whereas in some other department professors compete against one another and have little time for students. Such norms reveal departmental subcultures, which reflect not only members' individual personalities but the experiences and attitudes they have built together as a separate group within the larger organization.

As you become a part of an organizational culture, you will need to build positive relationships, to show your commitment, and to become an active part of the communication network—because these contribute to success and tenure in the job (Feeley, 2000). Sometimes, too, you will need to cope with conflicts, pressures to comply, and such problems as stereotyping, bias, and harassment. Let's look at those issues here.

Goal Conflicts and Compliance Pressures

Ideally, what you want from your work will mesh with what your organization wants from you like gears in a clock. But as you try to achieve your *personal* and *career* goals, your boss is trying to fulfill *management* goals. Often, these differing objectives create **goal conflicts.** Your career goals may take time from your personal life; management goals may coincide with yours, and they may not. Here's an example: Ali, a physical therapist, requests funds to attend a two-week workshop to improve his skills. Meanwhile, management has told Ali's supervisor, Jan, to increase the patient load without increasing the number of therapists, so she can't spare the time for Ali to go to a workshop. Ali is an outstanding therapist, and Jan has supported him in the past, yet this time she turns him down. Ali is perfectly justified in feeling this is unfair, but the decision goes to management goals.

In any organization, a manager's success relies on the effectiveness of subordinates, so it's necessary to get people to comply with procedures, rules, orders, goals, and so on. A manager may try to get compliance by explaining what is wanted in a friendly but persuasive way, or perhaps hint indirectly, get someone else to talk to the person, or even use coercion or threats.

Most supervisors say they prefer a friendly approach (Levine & Wheeless, 1990), and, at least in the United States, a direct, cooperative strategy of

Communication is very, very important. It should not, however, be confused with memos.

Dave Barry, American humorist

Goal conflicts When your personal and career goals differ from each other or from your management's objectives

reasoning and friendliness to gain compliance from their subordinates (Sullivan, Albrecht, & Taylor, 1990). Women supervisors, particularly, seem to prefer a cooperative, accommodative, open, trusting approach, but men tend to be more competitive and less trusting. When put in a defensive position, however, women are likely to forgive violations of trust less easily and to use more competitive strategies than men (Conrad, 1991).

Most people are aware of the need to save embarrassment for oneself and others by using *facework* (Goffman, 1967), that is, "a variety of communication devices available to interactants for preventing face loss (both their own and others'), restoring face if lost, and facilitating the maintenance of poise in the advent of disrupted interactions" (Metts, 1997, p. 375). Facework is part of politeness, courtesy, simply making interaction comfortable for all.

Facework often is associated with Asian cultures, and it may be that an Asian supervisor who was concerned about your performance might ask your uncle if, perhaps, something was bothering you, thereby alerting your uncle to a problem, and causing him to privately remind you that your brother works very hard. You'd get the point. A North American supervisor might be more prone to say directly, "Look, I don't like the way you're doing this."

Nonetheless, facework is important in any culture, and it appears that when the supervisor and subordinate build a relationship of similar, cooperative communication behaviors, and when the supervisor uses positive facework in a compliance or reproach situation, subordinates view the interaction as being more fair and the supervisor as more credible and competent than when negative approaches are used (Carson & Cupach, 2000; McCroskey & Richmond, 2000).

Stereotypes, Bias, and Harassment

Stereotypes Screens of expectations and judgments through which people filter their perceptions

In organizations, just like in neighborhoods or schools, people filter their perceptions of a "new kid on the block" through a screen of expectations and **stereotypes** to infer "additional 'knowledge' of what else is likely to be true of the individual" (Hamilton, Sherman, & Ruvolo, 1992, p. 137). One of our students, Janet Sweeney (1994), a registered nurse in an urban hospital, writes, "I am frequently asked, 'Do you have many foreign doctors?' The person who asks this question usually uses a certain tone as if to say, 'Are they qualified and as skilled as American doctors?' I think it is unfortunate that these prejudices exist. It is even more disturbing that people are unaware of these preconceptions."

Such judgments from stereotypes can amount to bias against individuals. A fine doctor might be rejected on the basis of gender; an excellent prospect for leadership might be overlooked because of bias toward an ethnic group. Bias is not only unfair and illegal, but also self-defeating, because it deprives organizations of the talents a diverse workforce can contribute.

That's why many U.S. organizations have been working to recruit and retain people who have suffered from such bias in the past. DuPont uses ombudsmen to track the careers of women and people of color; Xerox and AT&T actively seek advice and critiques from groups who traditionally experience bias; and

A bureaucrat is just someone who works in a bureaucracy—a person who is tired, frequently abused, often lacks real authority, and has "heard it all." The beleaguered bureaucrat may hide behind "Write a memo," or, "It isn't in my job description," or, "See so-and-so," or, "It's time for my break."

How do you dissolve the bureaucratic wall?

- *Be friendly*. Make eye contact, smile, talk person to person, show that you aren't on the attack. A brief personal comment, such as, "You folks are really busy today, aren't you?" or, "I really appreciate you taking time with me," or, "I like your poster up there," can put both of you at ease.

- *Expect to cooperate in solving a problem*. Look to the person behind the desk as a source of information and help. Show that you are taking a win-win approach to the discussion. But remember that the client before you may have been rude, so your bureaucrat may already be defensive. Your cooperative attitude may come as a surprise. Keep a problem-solving, win-win attitude, and she or he will come around.

- *Prepare and organize your approach*. Know

exactly what you want and whom you're supposed to see. Take everything you might need with you, arranged so you can put your hand promptly on exactly what you need. And carefully plan how you will explain what you want.

- *Stay focused*. Keep your attention on the goal, not on reacting to the other person's tone or style. Explain carefully, ask precise questions, confirm your understanding by paraphrasing what you heard.

- *Be persistent*. If you're not clear on what you have to do, or you're not satisfied with the answer, keep after it. Rephrase, ask for explanation, make sure it's right. If you have to go to another source or a higher authority, be nice about it, but be assertive and clear in explaining what you need.

- *Show appreciation*. Even if the encounter's been a bit hairy, try to wind it up with appreciation. Bureaucrats don't get many "Thank you's," or, "You've really been a big help" comments. Your appreciation will make both of you feel good—and your bureaucrat will have a better attitude toward the next client to come along!

many organizations have instituted training to diminish bias in the workplace (Deutsch, 1991, p. F25).

Sometimes, stereotyping by sex or race, combined with competition for power and control, leads to harassment that results in enormous pain to the victim and cost to the organization. A few years ago, Denny's Restaurant chain was "making amends to the black community. And every employee, especially managers, must attend sessions on the advantages of a multiracial clientele"—why? Because Denny's was slow in noticing a de facto policy of systematically ignoring and embarrassing African American customers until the company had to pay a $54 million class-action settlement (Goleman, 1995, pp. 155–156). And in 1998, there were 15,618 sexual harassment complaints to the Equal Employment Opportunity Commission (EEOC). In the same year, Mitsubishi paid $34 million to 500 women workers to atone for sexual harassment; in 1999 Astra Inc paid $10 million in a settlement for 120 women (Stephen, 1999). Organizations are trying to face the issues, but there's a long way to go. We hope you never have to deal with harassment, but it's well to be prepared. Here are some basic guidelines:

1   *Keep a journal* of events that relate to the problem you're experiencing.

2   *Note any witnesses* who may have observed the events.

3   *Determine your organization's guidelines* for dealing with harassment.

4   *Assertively confront your harasser* with a clear, direct, descriptive statement of what she or he must do and must not do to take the discomfort out of your relationship (if the harasser is your boss, you may have to try an indirect approach first).

5   *Prepare documentation.* Write a complete account of what has happened and mail it as a registered letter to yourself. When you receive the letter, keep it, unopened, for future documentation.

6   *Discuss your problem privately* with someone whom you can trust and who will be willing to come forward for you later.

7   *Ask witnesses if they would be willing to substantiate your claim* if necessary.

8   *Follow your organization's guidelines* for the full process of protesting.

Communication Connections

When you communicate in an organization of any kind, a first objective is to find ways of working cooperatively with others, of becoming an integral part of the group. You try to build bridges that connect you to others in working with diverse goals and needs as well as diverse cultures.

Bridging Goals and Needs   If you can understand where someone is coming from, you're halfway there. If your communication gains cooperation, you're all the way there. When you need to talk to someone who is important to your success, it helps to:

Get to know the other person.   Talk with people and learn to understand them as human beings, sharing yourselves, creating respect. Even professors are just people who loved school, and/or their disciplines, so much that they never left. Or a supervisor probably is in that job because she or he was really good at doing what you're doing now. The more you learn about any person, the more you can become credible and confident in communicating.

Identify the other person's goals. Teachers, supervisors, and administrators—all have goals for you to accomplish, so review the syllabus and requirements, or the job description, or your organization's mission statement, before you discuss your work. Try to identify how your task can help to fulfill the other person's goals. Consultant Geoff Bellman (1992) points out that if you can identify management goals and ways you can help achieve them, you make your boss look good, and that usually also advances your objectives.

Identify your own goals and needs. You enroll in classes or take a job intending to do it right, but something may go awry. In our own work, both as professors and as supervisors, we can tell you that we like to be kept informed. Whether talking to a professor or a supervisor, you don't have to publicize your private life, but you do need to discuss barriers to your effectiveness. Together, you may find ways to surmount them.

Work within the structure of the organization. As soon as you enter a new system, even a new class, find out where to go and whom to consult for help, know exactly what you want to achieve, and familiarize yourself with the organizational processes. Then you can plan ahead and avoid a lot of frustration in trying to find people and get help.

Find out how you're doing. You need to know if you're on the right path, so ask professors and supervisors for a regular assessment of your work. Suspend ego, shelve defensiveness, communicate cooperation. Keep your attention on the goal, not on reacting to the other person's tone or style. Explain carefully, ask precise questions, paraphrase back—and keep building a supportive transaction. Then you can find ways to solidify your successes and correct any problems.

Establish relationships for the future. Every communication transaction can be important to your résumé and influence your letters of recommendation—and your ability to impress future interviewers. Even more, you might find a *mentor*, someone in a position to help who encourages, guides, and serves as a model for you—someone who finds you credible and takes an interest in your future. Many successful people attribute their success to having connected with a professor or a supervisor who mentored them through colleges and careers, so keep an eye out for *your* mentor. She or he could be any one of your professors or supervisors.

Your success often depends ultimately on your credibility and confidence in maintaining professional connections between you and other people. It's a matter of teamwork that wins for everyone.

W e generally think of corporate culture as the cumulative result of a lot of things a company does that have little or nothing to do with running the business—dress codes, policies concerning pets, company outings, Friday-afternoon beer blasts, and the like. At many companies, moreover, that's about all there is to it. Culture is an add-on. It has only a tangential relationship to the hard logic of profit. . . . When the company gets into trouble, moreover, it often jettisons the very practices it's been using to define its culture. . . . But a growing number of companies like Setpoint have figured out how to build a vibrant corporate culture with a rigorous attention to the financials. The camaraderie, the sense of all-for-one-and-one-for-all, actually grows out of the company's management system.

Not that these companies are lacking in the kinds of rituals and practices we usually associate with corporate culture. Setpoint has enough to put any Silicon Valley start-up to shame. For one thing, almost half of its workforce—including its two founders—are dirt-bike fanatics, and they regularly go riding together in the mountains around Ogden, Utah, where Setpoint is located. On the bulletin board in the shop are photographs of various employees flying through the air on their motorcycles. . . .

At Setpoint, such extracurricular activities work in tandem with the management system to create a culture that gives business a kind of inner strength, allowing it to weather crises that would sink most other small companies and quite a few larger ones as well.

From Bo Burlingham, "What's Your Culture Worth," *Inc Magazine*, September 2001, p. 128.

Bridging Cultures   To a great extent, your career and the quality of your work life will be influenced by your ability to build bridges between cultures and to turn strangers into colleagues and friends. Building these bridges can be a special challenge.

Stephan and Stephan (1992) note that "individuals often experience intergroup anxiety before interacting with people from a different culture. [Intergroup anxiety] is also common within cultures, for example, in contacts between members of different racial and ethnic groups, and between members of nonstigmatized and stigmatized groups" (p. 17), such as people who are old, who are gay or lesbian, or who have disabilities. The prospect of interacting with someone "different" can challenge people's self-confidence—they fear that they will embarrass themselves or feel incompetent or be frustrated or even threatened by the other person's evaluation, rejection, and perhaps aggression. They might also fear their own identity group's sanctions against interacting with an individual from that other group (pp. 18–19).

	Bill	Muhammed
Description	He stands close to me.	He backs off from me.
Interpretation	Maybe he's pushy.	Maybe he's prejudiced.
	Maybe he's friendly.	Maybe he's cold.
	Maybe he's trying too hard.	Maybe he's thinking about something else.
	Maybe Arabs get closer than North Americans.	Maybe North Americans don't get as close as Arabs do.
Evaluation	I'm uncomfortable, but I'll try to understand.	I need to be close, but I'll try to back off a little.

Figure 9.1 *Steps in achieving intercultural understanding*

It takes a supportive, open climate and intercultural communication competence, self-monitoring, and adaptability to reduce the anxiety of intergroup communication. Remember in Chapter 3 we discussed the important perception differences among observing, inferring, and judging. Gudykunst and Kim (1992) similarly note that when you observe and listen to someone from another group, it helps to "differentiate among a description of what we observed, how we interpreted it, and our evaluations" (p. 369). For example:

- *Description* recognizes specific actions without qualifying them in any way.

- *Interpretation* includes hypothesizing a series of possible explanations for the described act but not reaching a hasty conclusion about what it means.

- *Evaluations* should be withheld until sufficient information is available to weigh the quality and meaning of the person's behavior.

Suppose, for example, Bill (a white man from the United States) is talking with Muhammad (a brown man from Saudi Arabia). Muhammad gets very close, face to face, and gestures broadly. Bill becomes uncomfortable and backs off. If Bill jumps straight to evaluation—as people often do—he may think, "This guy is pushy." Muhammad is concerned because Bill backs off, and if he also leaps straight to evaluation, he may think, "This guy is cold and he doesn't like me." If each can separate his description from interpretation and evaluation, however, the thinking might go as shown in Figure 9.1.

If Bill and Muhammad can keep their thinking and responses clear in this way, they can reduce intergroup anxiety and open up intercultural communication. Good advice for adapting to people from other cultures and with different interests is to use "an unconditionally constructive strategy" in which you behave with rationality, understanding, consultation, reliability, noncercion, openness, and acceptance . . . to create a situation that is good for both parties *and* good for the relationship (Fisher and Brown, 1992, p. 398).

Communicating in Interviews

To use everything we've discussed so far, you have to get into the organization—and that usually requires successful interviews. Interviews are challenging and essential tools to help you accomplish many of your goals, both in and out of college. Like other communication events, interviews occur in various contexts; they are directed toward specific objectives; they have openings, middles, and endings; and they rely on effective verbal, nonverbal, and listening skills. Also, like other communication events, you are more likely to achieve your goals if you understand interview processes and if you carefully plan and prepare for the transaction.

Interview A goal-oriented conversation in which participants follow a question-and-answer structure

Interviewing is similar to conversing, but an **interview** is a goal-oriented transaction in which participants follow a structured process of questioning and answering in order to achieve some specific purpose. Participants have clearly defined roles as questioner and answerer, each with responsibilities for the success of the interview, although they may switch roles as they talk. Even so, the interviewee may do 70% of the talking (Stewart & Cash, 1991, p. 5).

Interview Types

How you play your role as either interviewer or interviewee is determined, in part, by the type of interview. Each type pursues specific goals that you need to reach in order to develop a career, resolve issues in your life, or influence other people to act in ways that meet your objectives.

- *Information interviews* get information for purposes of problem solving, research, or media news or entertainment. You might interview experts for your research paper in college or subjects for a research project in your job.

- *Selection interviews* determine which individual is best qualified for a particular position. As interviewer, you ask questions to determine if the candidate fits your criteria; as interviewee, you answer with information that shows how you meet those requirements and ask questions to determine, "Is this the right place for me?"

- *Performance appraisal interviews* evaluate a person's work and set objectives for future performance. In college or on the job, a performance appraisal interview may influence decisions about grades, promotions, raises, transfers, or training opportunities. Sometimes, the interview is for disciplinary purposes—to document, clarify, and correct problems. Although it sounds intimidating, a well-conducted discipline interview can be a fair, ethical way to clarify goals and help a person do a better job.

- *Exit interviews*, conducted with an individual who is leaving an organization, serve the interests of both the organization and the departing employee. The interview identifies reasons for the departure and both positive and negative aspects of working for the firm, and sometimes it helps the interviewee to identify alternative options for the future.

A news team from a Spanish-language television station conducts an interview to gather information about an automobile accident.

Bob Daemmrich/The Image Works

- *Needs analysis interviews* reveal "employee feelings, causes of problems, and expectations and anticipated difficulties" (Pace & Faules, 1994). Organizations use needs analysis interviews to increase satisfaction, productivity, and quality in an organization, frequently by planning training programs to meet the needs identified.

- *Persuasion interviews* are efforts by an interviewer to influence an interviewee to comply, cooperate, change an attitude, or take some action. A sales presentation, for example, may, through careful questioning and listening, seek to find out what the customer needs and to show products or services that may meet those needs. Other types of interviews may include persuasion, of course, in that participants try to convince each other of their credibility and the logic and value of their positions. For an employment candidate, for instance, the selection interview is a persuasive communication opportunity.

- *Helping interviews* assist an individual to solve or cope with a problem through listening and questioning, diagnosing, advising, and counseling. The interviewer may be a health care worker, counselor, advisor, teacher, or someone in a personal relationship who tries to help another by listening and questioning empathically.

Interview Homework

Picture this: You're in an interview. You know what you want—but not what the other person wants. You know who you are—but not who the other person is. Now picture this: You clearly understand the other participant, the goals, and the issues surrounding the interview. Obviously, that's a much more pleasant experience than the first scenario, but it does rely on doing some homework, starting with research:

1   *Collect necessary information.* As an interviewee, organize information that you may want to show, quote, or document. In a job selection interview, for example, the interviewee needs a résumé and, perhaps, a portfolio or samples of work. The interviewer may need brochures, job descriptions, and procedural guidelines to show the candidate.

If you are the interviewer, prepare any information the interviewee may need; this could be brochures, process and schedules, requirements, and so on.

2   *Review everything you can find about the other person and/or organization.* If you are the interviewee for a job, you might want to know if the organization is economically sound and if it practices socially responsible policies, or if it has problems. The library has many sources to help you get information about organizations, such as *Dun and Bradstreet's Book of Corporation Management, Standard and Poor's Register of Corporations*, and many business-oriented newspapers and magazines. It's always a good idea to carefully review the Company's Web site and to look at the latest annual report to corporate stockholders (or to donors if you're interviewing for a position with a not-for-profit charitable organization). Knowing about the organization helps you to present yourself in a favorable light and also to make an informed decision about your future. Think about how the organization's reputation and policies mesh with *your* career and life criteria.

If you are the interviewer—whether to select a job applicant or to prepare for a television exposé—if you have received a résumé, application, or file, review it carefully. If the person has written a book, read it. If the person has held positions of responsibility or taken controversial stances on important issues, familiarize yourself with them.

3   *Understand procedures and issues for both the interviewer and the interviewee.* If you're interviewing subjects for a research project, for example, know precisely what questions you will ask, what order you'll ask them in, how long they'll take, and how you'll approach and close the interview. In performance interviews, both interviewer and interviewee need to know the background, the student or employee's actual performance record, and policies and procedures that affect the process and outcome of the interview.

As you do your homework, try to get as clear an idea of each person's primary and secondary goals as you can. Ask yourself, first, *What do each of us want as the major outcome of the interview?* The interview questions and responses directly or indirectly lead to these ends. If you're being interviewed for a job, for example, the interviewer may ask, "What can you do for my organization? Why are you a better bet than other candidates?" If your goal is to get that job, you try to show just how your experience, background, and personality can contribute qualities the organization wants.

In addition, ask yourself, *What else might each of us want out of the transaction?* These secondary goals are extra dividends from the interview. As a student, for example, you might interview a professor with the primary goal of getting information that will produce an "A" project, but a secondary goal might be to develop a contact for the future. Your interviewee's primary goal is to help you with your project, but a secondary one could be to recruit you as a major in that department.

Interview Planning

From the moment you've identified your goals for an interview, you need to think through the process carefully, because each step affects how you impress the other person and how effectively you accomplish what you want to do.

Arrangements You know what people say about the importance of first impressions. That first contact must be organized and professional. Sometimes, the interviewer sets up the meeting; sometimes, an interviewee requests it. In either case, follow these steps to arrange an interview:

1 *Contact the interviewee.* The initial contact may determine whether you get the interview or not, so it needs to be done right. You can start with either a letter or a phone call. The impression you make in this first step matters, even if your first contact is with a secretary or assistant, considering that 91% of executives surveyed said they count their assistant's opinion as important in selecting an employee (*Black Enterprise*, 2000, p. 49). Be sure that your letter or your call courteously and confidently explains who you are, why you want the interview, and how long you think the interview will take.

2 *Set up the interview.* Accommodate as much as possible to what is most convenient for the other person. If a face-to-face meeting is impossible, a telephone interview might work. In either case, set up a specific time that is convenient for the other person so you can both concentrate on the interview without interruptions.

3 *Confirm the arrangements.* Before the interview, write a note that thanks the interviewer in advance, restates your purposes in the interview, and confirms the time and place. Then, the day before the interview, call to confirm your appointment. This prevents embarrassing errors and shows your consideration and competence—both vital to the credibility you wish to convey in the interview.

If you don't get your interview on the first try, don't give up. A New York radio station manager made this point in telling us how she had hired a new disc jockey. On the day a DJ quit, the applicant happened to call. The résumé he had sent in was on the top of the manager's file. She noticed it, listened to the applicant's audition tape, accepted his call, gave him his interview, and awarded him the job. Was it luck? Only if you consider it luck that this applicant had sent in a fresh résumé and made follow-up calls once a month for two years. The station manager said, "He put himself at the right place at the right time with the right qualifications for what I needed." This wasn't luck. It was organization, persistence, and determination.

Strategy and Structure   Good interviews are planned. They are based on a carefully outlined structure that ensures you won't miss important points but still have room to pursue ideas. How an interviewer develops that outline depends on its purposes.

1   *Exploratory strategy interviews* allow participants to identify and examine a range of ideas. The interviewer may start with one or two questions, allow the interviewee to take the discussion in any direction, and then follow up by probing more deeply into the interviewee's ideas. Exploratory strategies can be excellent for helping or general information interviews, but not for interviews in which all issues must be addressed or those that require clear bases for making judgments.

2   *Objective strategy or structured interviews* are useful for selection or research interviews. A structure is consistently applied with all applicants or subjects, and the interviewer asks a series of carefully prepared job- or goal-related questions for which there are predetermined rating scales for evaluating answers. Interviewers must "stay on script" but still be able to formulate probing questions that will follow up an interviewee's answers, to listen, and to assess nonverbal cues (Hollwitz & Wilson, 1993, pp. 45–49). In selection interviews, these steps lead to more reliable decisions (Cortina, et al., 2000) by ensuring that the interviewee can present essential information on specific criteria (Weekley & Gier, 1987).

If you're the interviewee, understanding how each type of interview works will help you prepare so you're ready to supply whatever the interviewer needs. If you're the interviewer, an outline will keep you on track. Perhaps you're writing a newspaper article or a term paper about a political issue and you interview your state senator about it. You might have an outline like the one shown on the *Communicating with Credibility and Confidence* Web site at http://communication. wadsworth.com/lumsden. With this outline, you build a personal rapport, you guide the exploratory interview, and you leave room to follow up on ideas.

Any type of interview should include at least the following information:

- What procedures your interview will follow
- How information from the interviewee will be used
- What next steps are necessary
- What procedures are to be followed in the next steps

For example, in selection interviews, the introduction should include a precise description of the organization, the job, and the steps the hiring procedure will follow. The conclusion should outline exactly what the next steps are. If an interviewer does not provide this information, the interviewee should ask for it.

Question Functions and Forms   If you're the interviewer, you need to think carefully about what questions to ask. If you're the interviewee, you need to prepare a list of information that's important to give or get from the interviewer. Then, if you're not asked the right question, you will remember to work in the relevant information.

It is better to know some of the questions than all of the answers.

James Thurber, 20th-century American humorist and novelist

In both roles, questions serve two functions: to get *objective information*, which "includes unbiased and testable facts . . . names, dates, locations, and circumstances," and to find *subjective information*, which "includes personal feelings, attitudes, and beliefs" (Donaghy, 1990, p. 6). An effective questioning strategy can help an interviewee give the information the interviewer needs and help the interviewer interpret that information accurately.

A common questioning strategy is to start with a **primary question,** one that the interviewer has planned in advance. Often, an interviewee can anticipate some of these and plan answers. "What was your most important experience in college?" might, for example, be a primary question in a selection interview.

A primary question frequently leads to **secondary questions,** ones that probe the respondent's answers for more in-depth information. If you answered our sample primary question with, "Being president of my major department's club," a secondary question might be, "What was it about that experience that was important to you?" or, "What did you learn from doing that?" As an interviewee, you can't be sure what secondary questions might be asked, but you can think about what the interviewer is looking for, what kinds of probes might reveal that information, and how you might answer them.

Frequently, interviewers miss important information because they don't know how to formulate primary or secondary questions. And sometimes they fall short because they don't use the best question *form*. Here are two good basic question forms and one bad one:

- **Open-ended questions** are useful because they allow the respondent to answer in a variety of ways. They often start out with "What," "How," or "Why." "How did you become interested in this field?" for example, lets the interviewee develop an answer from almost any starting point. An interviewee who has really thought about how previous experience fits what the interviewer is looking for can formulate an answer so it demonstrates these qualities.

- **Closed questions** are either/or, yes/no, or multiple choice questions that limit the options of the respondent. They should be used only when the possible answers are genuinely limited to those the question suggests. "Did you graduate from college?" is a legitimate yes/no question. "Did you go to college or straight to work out of high school?" however, excludes options. Maybe you went to a technical school, or an art or drama academy, or into the military. If there is some other option to a closed question, the interviewee can respond with something like, "Well, neither one. Actually, I . . ."

- **Leading questions**—also known as "loaded" questions—can be misleading, manipulative, and unethical because their wording forces answers based on erroneous assumptions. Leading questions make people defensive and may lead them to answer awkwardly or inaccurately. As an interviewee, you can avoid falling into this question trap by analyzing the question and choosing your answer carefully. Suppose, for example, you've said you were active in a service group that helped the homeless. If the interviewer then

Primary question
Question that interviewer has planned in advance

Secondary question
More focused question that follows from respondent's answers to primary question

Open-ended question
Question that allows the respondent to answer in a variety of ways: How? What? Why?

Closed question Question that limits the answer of respondent: Yes/No, either/or, multiple choice

Leading question Misleading, manipulative, or unethical question whose wording forces a respondent's answers

asks, "What political bias was behind your decision to join that group?" you would recognize a leading question. However, instead of defending your politics—a losing proposition—you could *confront the implication tactfully*: "I don't think I had a political bias. I got into it because I saw these people who needed help. . . ." Or, you could *sidestep the implication* entirely and simply explain your unbiased motivation for participating in this group, for instance, "My friend was involved and she asked me to help."

Questions for Selection and Performance   Selection and performance interviewers use questions specifically to learn about your qualifications and personality. If you're the interviewer, you need to phrase these carefully. If you're the interviewee—when your potential or present career is on the line—you can plan ahead to answer these types of questions credibly:

Job-qualification question Question intended to assess one's ability to meet the criteria of a job

- **Job-qualifications questions** probe beyond the résumé to assess your ability to meet specific criteria for the job. Respond with examples from your experience to demonstrate what you know and how it meets the organization's needs—and make clear your ability and willingness to learn.

Behavioral question Asks respondent about ways they have acted in previous situations

- **Behavioral questions** ask interviewees to recount ways they have acted in previous situations so the interviewer can see how they'll act on the job. These can be powerful predictors of future success or failure (Janz, 1982, 1986). An interviewer who wants to know how you handle defensive people might ask, "Describe an occasion when you had to deal with someone who was nasty. How did you feel? How did you handle it?" You'll be ready to answer if, in preparing for your interview, you've analyzed both job and related experiences. When you're asked such questions, you'll have a reservoir of ideas. Answer with a specific description of the situation and your responses to it, and show how it relates to your qualifications for this job.

Situational question Asks how respondent would behave in a hypothetical situation

- **Situational questions** ask about a hypothetical situation and how the candidate would handle it. An interviewer might ask, "As a supervisor, what would you do if you discovered someone was punching in for another employee to cover up chronic tardiness?" As with behavioral questions, prepare by reviewing your real experiences in your mind; then answer by describing what you would do so it shows your confidence and ability to solve the hypothetical problem. You might say, "I would talk to both workers privately to see what was going on. When I was sure of the facts, I would choose a disciplinary action consistent with company policy."

Simulation Demonstration in which interviewee role-plays a job-related situation

- **Simulations** have interviewees role-play a situation so the interviewer can observe the action. Simulations often are used to assess leadership, problem solving, people management, and presentational skills. In fact, some of your instructors may have been asked to present a simulated lecture when they interviewed at the college to demonstrate how they would present information in the classroom. To prepare for simulations, review what you know about the skills important to the job, and conduct some role-playing practice sessions with friends and peers. Videotape, analyze, and improve your performance so you're comfortable with role-playing when you're asked to do it.

An interview should serve the needs both of the interviewer and the interviewee, but there is a line into a person's private life no interviewer should cross, and the Equal Employment Opportunity Commission (EEOC) requires that selection procedures and questions be relevant to important job qualifications. Interviewers are barred from asking questions about marital and family status, age, race, religion, sex, ethnic background, credit rating, and arrest records unless they can prove that the information has a direct bearing on job qualifications (Donaghy, 1990, p. 165).

An interviewer who is ignorant of the law, or disregards it, may ask questions that serve not to assess the applicants' qualifications, but to eliminate them from consideraton because of their nationality, race, religion, gender, or sexual orientation.

This can create a dilemma. If you answer even though the question is unlawful, you might lose the job opportunity. If you confront the issue, you might also lose the job opportunity. You might not want to work for an organization that uses such tactics—but what if you do want the job, anyway? Start by assuming that the question is based in ignorance rather than malice, and choose a response that allows the interviewer to leave the issue gracefully. Your options are to:

- *Bridge the question by moving from it to something else.* An interviewer who asks, "What church do you go to?" might just be curious—or might want to screen out people with certain religious beliefs. A bridging response might be, "That brings up a great experience that taught me the leadership skills I need for this position. For 2 years I was a youth counselor . . . ," thus ignoring the specific religious question but speaking to your experience.

- *Confront the issue tactfully.* You might respond, "Is that relevant to my job qualifications? Could we go over the criteria?"

- *Confront the issue bluntly.* Simply say, "I never answer this question in an interview because the EEOC lists it as unlawful." If you have to use this response and it costs you the job, you're probably better off without it.

Interview Confidence and Credibility

Good interviews don't just happen. They're good because you are confident, you know what you're doing, and you demonstrate your credibility as you talk. When you've prepared thoroughly, you can build your confidence by training like an athlete—that is, both mentally and physically. Use visualization and affirmation to see the interview and your behavior exactly as you want it to be. Get a friend to role-play the interview with you, preferably with videotape. Discuss the goals and situation of the interview and then practice both asking and

I'm a great believer in luck, and I find the harder I work, the more I have of it.

Thomas Jefferson, Founding Father of the United States of America

answering questions. This will help you not only improve your fluency and verbal presentation but also identify question areas for which you need more information or analysis.

Here are a few guidelines for managing a credible interview:

1   *Dress appropriately.* The generally accepted advice is to dress a bit more formally than you normally would for work. Consider carefully how your appearance might affect your credibility, but dress so you feel confident in yourself as well. One consultant says that applicants "need to wear the uniform of the team they want to be a part of. . . . Initially people are more comfortable with people who look like they do in their dress" (Ballard, 1999, p. 68).

2   *Keep your focus.* Think of both your own and the other person's goals. An interview should reach both sets of goals, so you must keep both in mind.

3   *Communicate nondefensively and cooperatively.* Both interviewers and interviewees may feel awkward because of inexperience and defensive because they are being tested in one way or another. Assume that you both mean well, and strive to make the other person comfortable.

4   *Stay on top of your own stress.* Take slow, deep breaths to reduce defensive responses. In addition, recognize the sources of tension. Frequently, employers structure selection interviews to put the interviewee under stress. In a second or third interview, one interviewer may play the "bad cop" role, intentionally being hostile or rude to the interviewee. They want to see how candidates stand up under pressure and criticism. Here, again, if you understand the interviewer's purposes, you have a better opportunity to maintain a positive approach and to control your responses.

5   *Be honest and direct.* An interview, although brief, is a relationship. As soon as deception enters into it, trust and credibility are lost. Goldhaber (1990) says, "Do not try to be what you are not. If you know the answers, give them. If you do not know the answers to some of the questions, be smart enough to say so" (p. 434). When you ask or answer a question, use language that is clear, direct, open, and appropriate to the situation.

6   *Listen carefully to questions and answers.* Listen actively to ensure that you know what you are being asked and what responses you get. Listen interactively as well; if a question is unclear, ask for clarification or definition, with responses such as, "Could you give me an example of what you mean?" or, "Are you referring to . . . ?" or, "I'm not exactly sure what you're asking. Could you please rephrase it for me?"

7   *Monitor your own and the other's nonverbal communication.* The eyes, face, body, voice, and use of space indicate a lot in an interview. Notice how others respond to you and adapt your behavior accordingly. If, for example, you are leaning close and the other person draws away, you can assume that you're inside the person's territory. Respect that difference in communication style, and back off a bit. In the United States, it's generally true that people establish rapport, openness, and credibility with direct eye contact; a warm, firm hand-

shake and forward-leaning posture; relaxed gestures; and a strong, confident voice.

Finally, the way you wind up an interview and the actions you take to follow it up can make or break your credibility. Be sure you do these three things:

1   *Summarize and confirm what you have learned.* Ensure that the other person is comfortable with your conclusions.

2   *Ask permission to call if you have further questions or need to confirm information.*

3   *Follow up appropriately.* Write a thank-you note for the interview and, if your next step involves a phone call or sending information, be sure to follow through promptly.

Summary

A professional attitude that reflects involvement, competence, pride, and high ethical standards is the foundation for your communication in college and in your career. In any type of organization, people must learn to understand organizational cultures with their unique norms and roles and to communicate with people such as faculty members, supervisors, and bureaucrats who have their own goals and pressures.

Workplace tensions can result from differences among organizational goals, workers' goals, and managers' needs to motivate and direct subordinates to comply with management preferences. Unfortunately, people's expectations and stereotypes can result in bias based on an individual's gender, race, or identity group, or in harassment. People can avoid being harassers by screening their own messages and may be able to stop others' harassment with carefully selected communication strategies. A professional attitude allows all members of an organization to communicate freely and integrates strangers into the organization. A professional attitude includes intercultural competence, whereby individuals are adaptable and seek to understand and work with people from other cultures.

Both in college and in careers, skill in interviewing involves understanding requirements that vary according to the specific goals—information, selection, performance, persuasion, or helping. Building confidence and credibility in interviewing depends on identifying goals, researching, arranging, and planning the strategy and structure of the interview. Interview questions may be open-ended or closed and may probe more deeply into responses to previous questions. Often, questions are behavioral or situational, and sometimes they are simulated situations so the interviewer can observe the interviewee. Interviewers should avoid questions that are loaded or that make unlawful inquiries into the interviewee's personal lives.

You can become more confident in interviews if you train for them through preparation, stress management relaxation and visualization, and role-playing. Your credibility is enhanced by your preparation and interaction.

Exercises

1 Go to the student center and strike up a conversation with a stranger who differs from you in culture or ethnicity. Try to talk for awhile. Then reflect on these questions:

a   How did it feel to approach a stranger?

b   Did you feel intergroup anxiety, and if so, what was it like?

c   What did you do differently than you might in talking with an acquaintance or a stranger who appeared to be from your own identity group?

d   What did you learn from the encounter?

e   How can you use it in your future communication?

2 Most organizations, including your college, should have an office that deals with issues of bias and harassment in the institution. Set up an appointment and interview an officer in such a department. Find out what the legal issues are in preventing or correcting bias and harassment problems and how the office goes about ensuring that the organization complies with their obligations. Report your findings to the class.

3 With a small group, do the following:

a   Decide on one topic about which you want to get information.

b   Together, design an interview outline for your topic.

c   For each person in your group, identify someone as an expert on the subject to interview. (These could be anyone from professors to local politicians to members of organizations dedicated to your topic.)

d   Decide which one of you will interview which expert.

Separately, do the following:

a   Do your background homework, revise your outlines as necessary, and arrange an interview.

b   Conduct your interview. Use a tape recorder if possible, and take good notes.

c   Write a thank-you note to your interviewee.

Together, do the following:

a   Compare and contrast the information each of you obtained and the process each of you went through in the interview. Where are they similar? How are they different?

b Discuss what factors may have created differences between your interviews. Consider your preparation, organization, and questions, as well as the way you and your interviewee approached and interacted in the interview.

c As a panel, report to the class what you found out about your topic and about interviewing from this experience.

4 Search through the classified ad section in a major newspaper to find an advertisement for a job in a field that interests you. Imagine that you are going to apply for the position and do the following:

a Identify the interviewer's goals. What criteria do you think an interviewer would use to judge an applicant?

b Consider what would contribute to an appropriate background for an applicant. Think about courses, extracurricular experiences, attitudes, abilities, and so on.

c Research the background of the organization and consider how what you have learned might affect an applicant's interview.

d Consider what objective questions an interviewer might ask.

e Consider some subjective questions an interviewer might ask.

f Make a 3-minute presentation to the class explaining your findings.

Cyberpoints

CCC

WEB SITE

1 Do you want more information on dealing with racial or sexual harassment? Go to the *Communicating with Credibility and Confidence* Web site at http://communication.wadsworth.com/lumsden and click on Chapter 9.

2 For a sample interview outline, go to the *Communicating with Credibility and Confidence* Web site at http://communication.wadsworth.com/lumsden and click on Chapter 9.

3 You can get sources on interviewing from Quintessential Careers at http://www.quintcareers.com/general-job-sites.html. To get insights on how employment interviewers approach the selection interview, go to http://job-interview.net.

4 Do you have some interviews coming up? Use *InfoTrac College Edition* and the keyword *employment*—you'll find current articles written by personnel professionals that will help you prepare.

Chapter 10

Groups and Teams: Communication and Leadership

Objectives for This Chapter

Knowledge

- Understand the role of working groups and teams in contemporary society
- Identify elements that transform a group into a team and a superteam
- Distinguish among task, group-building, and individual roles and processes
- Know what makes leaders credible
- Describe leadership roles in groups
- Understand styles and approaches to leading groups
- Know how to prepare and lead group meetings

Feelings and Approaches

- Feel comfortable working in groups and teams
- Develop confidence and credibility in fulfilling leadership functions
- Enjoy helping a group develop and succeed
- Be confident when exercising principled leadership

Communication Abilities

- Communicate effectively in group-building and task roles
- Help other members to communicate in a group setting
- Work with others in developing goals and strategies for solving problems and making decisions
- Serve leadership functions in groups and teams

Key Terms

panel	midpoint crisis	laissez-faire leadership
symposium	leadership	authoritarian leadership
forum	leader	democratic leadership
group	emergent leader	transactional leadership
team	shared leadership	transformational leadership
superteam	group-building roles	visionary leadership
cohesiveness	task roles	situational leadership
synergy	individual-interest/	hidden agenda
syntality	blocking roles	agenda
	principled leadership	

G roups can be lots of fun. Groups can be productive. Groups can be frustrating. The one sure thing is that you will work in groups and teams. In your career, community, church—in your life—your personal skills in teamwork and leadership can make or break the experience.

These days, teamwork is critical to solving problems and managing in just about every business and social venue. Why? Because "two heads are better than one"? That's one reason. In one study, groups outperformed even their best individual members 97% of the time (Michaelson, Watson, & Black, 1989). Each member of the group brings a unique background, set of experiences, and viewpoint; when the members interact, they can draw new insights from one another and develop new approaches that no one of them could have generated alone. People of diverse genders, cultures, and backgrounds can create a richer field of ideas and knowledge than one person alone might bring to solving a problem or achieving a goal.

This chapter examines why teamwork is so important and how your group can become a team and even a superteam. It then prepares you to share leadership or to be the designated leader in groups, as well as ways to get a specific group or team started on its work.

Groups, Teams, and Your Future

At this time, in this century, it is essential to work well with groups and teams, for two reasons: First, as a problem-solving, creating, or management tool, teams are used extensively by the organizations with which you inevitably will work. Second, teamwork gives you an opportunity to excel and achieve your personal goals, too.

Members Work Together to Attain Goals

As a member of an organization or as an individual, you are often focused on attaining specific goals. Often those goals interact in some way toward your personal success, but they can be examined separately for the sake of understanding why they are important.

Organizational Goals   Why are contemporary organizations emphasizing small group and teamwork so heavily? We've already mentioned that a diverse group of people usually achieves better ideas and solutions than do individuals. There's another important reason groups can be enormously effective: *Participants in a group are involved in their own learning and decision making—and that leads to greater satisfaction and agreement with the group's decision. This means that people are more committed to a decision they themselves have made* (Gouran, 1969).

Not only do organizations bring together people from a wide range of backgrounds to serve on teams, but employers now actively seek managers and workers who have teamwork skills. Managers' jobs are shifting rapidly from the traditional functions of organizing work and increasing individual production to focusing on "team motivation and output . . . [and] the functions of coaching and facilitating" (Kinlaw, 1991, p. xix).

Of course, group work takes time, effort, and the right abilities from members. Furthermore, some problems really only take one talented individual to solve them. If you have a sophisticated math problem and one mathematical genius, let the genius solve it. If there's a fire in a wastebasket, go ahead and put it out—don't wait for a committee. But anytime you want diverse insights and talents, a group is best.

Groups Help to Achieve Personal Goals

In school, on the job, in your community, in your religious organization—working in a group can help you, personally. For example:

- *Leadership development.* Groups provide opportunities to develop and demonstrate your leadership abilities to employers.

- *Career advancement.* One General Foods employee stated that her work on a company subcommittee "exposed more people to my past and present skills and led to my being called in on some new product development projects" (Serant, 1992, p. 39).

- *Personal satisfaction.* Studies and experience show that high-performance team members see "their teams as special and their experiences as having participated 'in something bigger than myself' " (Katzenbach & Smith, 1993, p. 81).

One of our students described the satisfaction he and his teammates felt after completing a very successful class project. They stood in the college parking lot for an hour, he reported, basking in the knowledge that they had accomplished more together than any one of them could have done alone.

Such satisfaction results, in part, from knowing you've communicated well. Group communication draws on all the knowledge and skills developed throughout this book, including the ability to speak, listen, question, and adapt to nonverbal cues. When all members don't have these capabilities, the group process can break down, but when you master these abilities, you can enjoy your teamwork. Further, nothing gains you credibility and the respect of others like the ability to manage group communication successfully.

Leadership is not manifested by coercion. . . . Greatness is not manifested by unlimited pragmatism, which places such a high premium on the end justifying any means and any methods.

Margaret Chase Smith, former U.S. senator and author

Members Adapt Formats to Attain Goals

Although we will be focusing on problem solving and managing work or study in small groups, it's important to recognize some of the ways you might use groups for other functions. Some group sessions take place in person or are broadcast before an audience to inform, persuade, or entertain the listeners. You have seen, for example:

- a **panel**: A group, often with a moderator, that exchanges information through members who share ideas and ask and answer questions in a relatively informal manner.

- a **symposium**: A more formal group session in which each participant gives a speech without direct interaction among the members. Often, the members interact in a panel discussion following the individual speeches.

- a **forum**: An open meeting where the audience may make comments or ask questions. Forums often are combined with other meeting formats, such as a panel, symposium, or speech, by opening up the floor after the presentations.

Such group formats are relatively brief public communication opportunities, but they result from careful planning and management by a small group (a committee, perhaps) or a team that meets over some period of time. That's only one possible product of group work. Whatever their goals—to develop a product, to publicize an idea, to build a new church, to elect a senator—small work groups and teams can become superteams with excellent communication and leadership skills.

Groups, Teams, and Superteams

A group may be people who meet for anything from going to a hockey game to studying scripture to planning a corporate merger. Shaw (1981) defines a **group** as "two or more persons who are interacting with one another in such a manner that each person influences and is influenced by each other person" (p. 8). If your group is specifically focused on achieving some kind of task goals, it is possible that good communication might mold a high-powered team out of an ordinary group of people.

A **team** is more than a group. It is "a diverse group of people who share leadership responsibilities for creating a group identity . . . to achieve a mutually defined goal" (Lumsden & Lumsden, 2000, p. 13). A team's identity often depends on its task. A pit crew at the Indianapolis 500 race, for example, changes tires, fills gas tanks, and makes adjustments on the cars with little talk but with split-second timing and accuracy. A creative team at an advertising agency, however, might talk for hours to bring radically different concepts together into the one idea that will satisfy the client and appeal to the public.

Panel Group that presents information to an audience through members who share ideas and ask and answer questions informally

Symposium Formal group session in which each participant gives a speech to an audience, without interaction among group members

Forum Open meeting in which audience makes comments and asks questions

Group Two or more persons interacting to influence and be influenced by each other

Team Group of people who share an identity and have a mutually defined goal

What these teams have in common is their drive toward fulfilling specific goals, yet each has unique characteristics of critical work processes, interpersonal communication, and leadership.

Not every group becomes a team—or needs to—but "every work group can become a work team and every work team can become a superior work team" (Kinlaw, 1991, p. 12), and some, ones that achieve exceptional results, may become **superteams** (Hastings, Bixby, & Chaudhry-Lawton, 1986). There are five levels of group achievement (Katzenbach & Smith, 1993):

Superteam Team that achieves exceptional results

1   *Working groups:* Short-term groups that will have no opportunity to become teams.

2   *Pseudoteams:* Groups that have the opportunity to become teams but have not yet made any attempt to excel and are, in fact, weaker than working groups because their interactions are ineffective at best.

3   *Potential teams:* Pseudoteams that are trying to improve but need more clarity about goals, more discipline in developing a common working approach, and a sense of collective accountability.

4   *Real teams:* Teams whose members share a genuine commitment and responsibility for their goals and to their transactions as a team.

5   *High-performance teams:* Real teams that *also* share a common concern for one another's personal growth and success. The high-performance team is close to being a superteam.

Effective Team Characteristics

Perhaps few groups attain superteam status, yet any group that adopts high-achievement communication will enhance the quality of their group's performance. Even short-term study groups gain more from the same limited amount of time when each member's contributions are of a high quality. Superteams have a number of characteristics in common (Hastings et al., 1986; Katzenbach & Smith, 1993):

■   *Vision:* A sense of purpose and direction, a "clear and elevating" inspirational quality (Larson & LaFasto, 1989) that expresses "deeper aspiration than just near-term goals . . . themes that are particularly meaningful and memorable. . . . Members feel it is important, if not exciting" (Katzenbach & Smith, 1993, pp. 62–63).

■   *Goal-orientation:* Specific outcomes or results of the team's effort that all members describe in the same way. Successful groups establish goals early on. Groups without clear goals usually cease to exist, because people won't continue to devote time and effort to a group that lacks a clear purpose. Superteam goals are endorsed by all members, with a commitment that overrides personal objectives, even though team goals may differ from individuals' original preferences. Superteam members use their goals to keep on track by continuously asking, "What are we trying to achieve?"

Many tasks are more successful when you use teamwork.

Paul Barton/corbisstockmarket.com

- ■ *Commitment:* To one another, to success, and to quality. Superteam members work *with* others, rather than for or against them, with a "win-win" attitude that accepts the achievement of one to the credit of all. Members respect knowledge, competence, and contributions over status and position. They have very high expectations of themselves and of others, and constantly look for better ways to do things.

- ■ *Diversity:* Seeking out and respecting members who vary in gender, ethnicity, background, and expertise, because diverse members find more and better problem-solving strategies and solutions (Nemeth & Kwan, 1987; Wood, 1987).

- ■ *Open communication:* Being willing to listen and to share, being accountable for contributing to the team whether members are apart or together. Superteam members are quick to respond, positive, and optimistic even when things are not going well; they are able to confront people and issues to eliminate roadblocks, and they build formal and informal relationships that include people who can be helpful to them. They seek feedback as a desirable, shared, helpful process for improving their team.

- ■ *Creative and critical thinking:* Distinguishing priorities and choosing flexible, creative, or routine approaches, taking legitimate risks to achieve significant gains but carefully analyzing options and potential outcomes before taking action.

- ■ *Culture and image:* Developing a unique, positive team culture and image. Although influenced by society, the organization, and members' backgrounds, team culture ultimately is the members' unique creation. Different though members may be, they develop shared values, beliefs, and assumptions as well as their own image—a strong identifying set of characteristics. (Sometimes, a team decides on an image and creates a special name, logo, or symbols to represent that character. The "Fly-by-Nites," for example, was a team within the Xerox Corporation that had responsibility for improving the overall quality of overnight air shipments. Their name communicated both their humor and their togetherness as a team (Bowles, 1990).

■ *Cohesiveness:* The degree to which members are attracted toward each other and the group. Other phrases describing **cohesiveness** are "esprit de corps," "groupness," and "team pride." Cohesiveness is like a glue that holds members together, creating a "one for all and all for one" good feeling. Members of strong teams know they're good (but they must avoid becoming arrogant or overconfident as a result).

■ *Synergy:* **Synergy** is a combination of the energy, drives, needs, motives, and vitality of the members. With high synergy, members work intensively together, multiplying their effectiveness and reaching their goals with mutual effort. With low synergy, individuals who are motivated to do well for a grade or a promotion work themselves to a frazzle, do other people's work for them, and meet frustration at every turn.

■ *Syntality:* **Syntality** is to a group what personality is to an individual and is more than the sum of the individual members (Cattell, 1948). A given group might, for example, reveal a dynamic, aggressive syntality in interaction even though individual members' personalities, taken alone, range from extremely shy to extremely pushy.

Effective Team Developmental Phases

Teams, like people, progress through stages to reach their full potential, and the process of moving from working group to superteam is not necessarily either smooth or predictable. Groups tend to go through five general stages, although not always in this order:

1 *Forming.* Members organize and orient themselves to one another and the group.

2 *Storming.* Conflicts—perhaps minor, possibly major, arise.

3 *Norming.* Members develop norms for communication and conflict management.

4 *Performing.* Members complete work, feeling a sense of satisfaction.

5 *Adjourning.* Members end their work and say good-bye to the team. (Tuckman & Jensen, 1977)

Different groups go through different stages, but it is likely that teams of all types experience one critical stage in common: a **midpoint crisis,** a point when

Cohesiveness The degree to which group members are attracted toward each other and the group

Synergy Combination of team members' energy, drives, needs, motives that affect how successful the team is

Syntality Personality of the group

Midpoint crisis Moment when team members realize that time is half-gone but work is less than half-finished

members suddenly realize that their time is half-gone but the work isn't half-finished. Some may immediately reassess and refocus their work; some may panic before settling down and getting on with it. Some groups may even break up and then return, motivated and committed to their goal (Gersick, 1988).

Leaders and Leadership

Must every group have a formally designated leader? No. Does every group need leadership to succeed? Yes. There is an important difference between "leader" and "leadership":

Leadership Verbal and nonverbal communication behavior that influences team processes to achieve goals

- **Leadership** is verbal and nonverbal communication behavior that influences a team's processes to achieve members' and the team's needs and goals (Lumsden & Lumsden, 2000, p. 29). This definition emphasizes that leadership is achieved by communication, and it recognizes that both individual and team interests are important. Members with leadership skills influence the group because others respect their credibility and responsibility.

Leader Person holding a designated title or position in a group

- A **leader** is a person holding a designated position. An individual may be elected or appointed as president, chairperson, or department head. These titles imply status and the expectation that the person will fulfill specific functions as a leader.

Of course "leaders" ought to provide leadership, but sometimes they don't. You've often heard people complain because their workplace or government "lacks leadership"—even when there clearly is a manager or an elected official. *"Leader," therefore, describes a title; "leadership" describes behaviors that help the group.* It would be wonderful if all leaders knew how to lead. Leaders are not, however, always the best-qualified individuals. People outside the group or the group members themselves may select leaders because they have higher rank or status, wield political influence, or are just popular.

In some cultures and organizations, age or seniority may determine who is the leader. In many cultures, elders are thought to have greater wisdom and thus to deserve more respect than younger people. The Japanese, for example, consider age seniority the primary criterion for selecting a negotiation team leader (Hellweg, Samovar, & Skow, 1994).

Emergent leaders People who become leaders by helping groups develop effective processes

Frequently, people are not appointed or elected, but become **emergent leaders** by providing information and leadership that help groups develop effective task and group-building processes. Unfortunately, however, groups may overlook a potentially good leader because members look for stereotypes of leaders based on socioeconomic status, education, class, race, culture, age, gender, or special abilities or disabilities. Nye and Forsyth (1991), for example, found that "despite identical performance information for the male and female . . . leaders, some subjects exhibited less liking and expressed less desire to work for female leaders" (p. 376).

Shared Leadership

Shared leadership
Group situation in which all members take leadership responsibility

Whether a group has a designated leader or not, it will be most effective with **shared leadership,** when *all* members take responsibility for leadership. Katzenbach and Smith (1993) state that in every high-performance team they investigated, "leadership is shared. . . . The leader's role remains, but is mostly ceremonial or for the benefit of outsiders" (p. 80). Gouran (1982) points out that many individuals must provide leadership to counteract problems that block a group as it works toward its goal. When such leadership is absent, groups often make bad decisions and take harmful actions (p. 148).

When you work in a team, therefore, you can't ignore leadership needs by saying, "Well, *I'm* not the leader." With these obligations in mind, let's examine how you might provide leadership roles in your groups.

Leadership Roles

Leaders empower others by making them feel significant, helping them to feel their learning and competence are important, making them feel a part of a community, and instilling them with a sense of excitement about their work.

Warren Bennis, a leading American theorist and writer on leadership

Just as your roles in life vary from the way you behave as a friend to the way you act as a family member, so do your roles vary in how you contribute to a group. Each member may fill several roles in the transactional processes of building the group and completing its task. You might hear members describe a meeting in terms of people's roles:

"She took the role of leader."

"He was the secretary."

"He was the class clown."

"She played the mom when we argued."

The roles members play are part of a group's development of syntality and help them to achieve the group's goals. Group communication experts traditionally divide roles into three categories: group-building, task, and self-interest/blocking.

Group-building roles
Functions that help manage members' feelings and create harmony in the group

Group-Building Roles   Members who help to manage feelings and create harmony in the group are playing **group-building roles.** They help create a sense of groupness, an open climate, and a mutually supportive and cooperative attitude. Without their help, other members may be uncomfortable about offering creative ideas or arguing a point for fear of being judged. Group-building roles help members to think and work together; they empower individuals and, in so doing, empower the team.

As you provide group-building leadership, you demonstrate the coorientation and trustworthiness that also build your credibility. Here are some suggestions to help build your group (Benne & Sheats, 1948; Pavitt & Sackaroff, 1990):

- *Suggest and encourage positive norms.* Set an expectation of openness, mutual concern, cooperation, and responsibility. Openly state your preference for a supportive climate, and ask for other members' agreement.

- *Encourage the involvement of each member.* Ask for information, ideas, opinions, and feelings; support others through agreement or open-ended questions; confirm the worth of others through attentive listening and your verbal and nonverbal communication.

- *Encourage trust and openness.* Take a few risks and disclose a little about yourself. Suggest group norms for confidentiality, expect it, and protect others' disclosures.

- *Help manage conflicts.* When conflicts arise, remind the team that conflict is normal and can be helpful; stay objective and find ways to support negotiation and compromise.

- *Make connections.* Help people to support one another; look for things they have in common and state your appreciation for others' contributions. Encourage open-mindedness and interest in others' points of view.

- *Create a sense of teamness.* Orient members toward mutual goals; support team processes, discuss the ways in which the team works, and comment on what it does well; suggest positive ways to assess and improve the quality of teamwork.

- *Work actively to deal with team stress.* Acknowledge stressful situations, help to diagnose causes of stress, and find ways to relieve it; use humor, "time-out," and negotiation to ease tensions.

People in a hurry may feel that group-building roles take time away from getting the task done. Actually, group-building roles make it possible to reach the goal by creating the essential positive communication climate.

Task roles Functions that help a group establish structure, develop flexibility, and set goals and objectives.

Task Roles Roles that help a group agree on its structure, develop flexibility and adaptability, and set clear goals and objectives are **task roles.** In working through a process of fulfilling its task together, a good team researches and shares information and cooperates in open and creative critical analysis, problem solving, decision making, and task achievement.

Managing the processes of group building *and* task achievement can be a bit of a juggling act—but an exciting one to perform. Further, your credibility increases in the eyes of your teammates as you show them your competency and objectivity. These guidelines will help you provide task leadership (Benne & Sheats, 1948; Pavitt & Sackaroff, 1990):

- *Be sure meetings are organized.* Suggest and confirm meeting arrangements, agendas, records, and assignments. Remind group members when the discussion gets too far off track.

- *Discuss and confirm team goals.* State goals for the team and ask for confirmation that everyone agrees with them.

- *Identify what the team needs for its work.* Suggest that the team consider needs for information and resources, and identify ways to get what's needed. Guide discussion of individual expertise and interests; suggest ways to divide up research and other outside work.

- *Orient the team toward task processes.* When attention wanders, call it back. Summarize what's been done, suggest next steps, and check to see if people agree before moving on.

- *Make sure information is shared.* Ask for, summarize, review, and analyze information. Ask for others' analyses and opinions, too.

- *Provide information and ideas.* Take it on yourself to get good information and to explain it clearly to the team.

- *Contribute creativity and critical thinking.* Share ideas and encourage others to do so. Ask questions and make suggestions. Cooperate with others to analyze logic, reasoning, and proposed solutions.

- *Test conclusions for ethicality.* Ask questions that stimulate thinking about how ethically members treat one another. Examine the value and acceptability of all suggestions, decisions, and possible actions.

Individual-interest/ blocking roles Functions that draw attention away from group tasks or goals to serve individual member's needs

Individual Interest/Blocking Roles   **Individual-interest/blocking roles** can destroy a meeting when a member draws attention away from task or group-building processes to serve his or her own wants or needs. Blocking roles include aggressor, blocker, recognition-seeker, self-confessor, fun-seeker, dominator, help-seeker, and special interest pleader (Benne & Sheats, 1948).

Of course, it can be healthy to express anger, to be humorous, or to be playful. These behaviors may help to manage a conflict or relieve tension. When someone persistently shifts the group's focus away from the issues, however, that person loses credibility and blocks both group-building and task processes.

Specific roles also can interact, even within a simple transaction. Perhaps a member says, "I'm really tired," and someone responds, "Who cares? We've got work to do." This response is related to the task, all right, but it's also an individual, aggressive attack. Of course, the victim will react defensively. This interaction will impede both group-building and task performance. Someone must exercise leadership to harmonize the tension between these two members and move the task forward.

Principled Leadership

Principled leadership Leadership that works to promote ethical values in communication and decision making

As effective as group work can be, it has its drawbacks. One danger is that a group of people may forget to consider what is right or wrong, simply swept away by the desire to conform or by the anonymity of being "just one of the group." It is imperative that each member provides **principled leadership** to maintain ethical values in communication and decision making. Each individual should be asking, "Is this right? Is it ethical?" Not only are there ethical issues about decisions the group might make, but also about your relationships with one another. Perhaps, for example, it is against your principles to manipulate others to do something that clashes with their values. Then you would apply that principle by not allowing yourself or others to manipulate a member of your team.

Larson and LaFasto (1989) identify principled leadership as a critical component of outstanding teams (p. 125). Principled reasoning raises the quality of members' thinking and the potential for better decisions. What's more, after working with someone who has provided principled leadership, other members tend to use more principled reasoning for themselves (Dukerich, Nichols, Elm, & Vollrath, 1990). And lest you think that ethics are irrelevant to teams in the workplace in this day of disenchanted competition, think again. Some hiring personnel "now are more likely to scrutinize a candidate's reputation and actions through the lens of ethical ideals" (Gauss, 2000, p. 89).

It may take courage to apply your principles to group work; sometimes others will disagree, even want to override your point. If it's important, don't let it go. You have to live with what your group does after the meeting is over and the anonymity of it is gone.

Designated Leaders

Groups are most effective when all members share leadership responsibilities, but members may choose to have a specific leader, an organization's bylaws require one, or a corporation designates a manager as group leader. In such cases, a designated leader takes certain roles and faces certain expectations other group members may not share. Here we explore personal qualities that make designated leaders effective and specific responsibilities they face.

Effective Leader Qualities   The qualities effective leaders need depend partly on both the group's goals and its members. Thornton (1990), for example, identified traits most important for leaders working in the "global marketplace" as flexibility, a sense of humor, patience, resourcefulness, positive regard for others, and technical competence (pp. 22–23). In another study, students identified enthusiasm, forcefulness, understanding, supportiveness, intelligence, creativity, friendliness, and organization as qualities of effective leaders (Pavitt & Sackaroff, 1990, p. 380). Chinese people see interpersonal competence as most important, but also see personal morality, goal efficiency, interpersonal competence, and versatility as key characteristics to good leadership (Ling, Chia, & Fang, 2000, p. 729).

We can condense all these effective leaders' qualities to these:

Credibility.   Chapter 2 defines credibility as the extent to which one person sees another as competent, objective, trustworthy, cooriented, and dynamic. Interpreting these attributes as leader qualities, however, depends in part on cultural outlook. North American businesses, for example, select their negotiation teams more for technical expertise and less for status or socioeconomic background than some other cultures do. Mexican negotiation teams are most influenced by personal attributes and *palanca* (leverage, connections, "clout"), which may or may not be connected with formal status. For Japanese, Chinese, French, British, and Saudi Arabian teams, an individual's status is a high priority. The Japanese, however, also value knowledge and age, while the French value interpersonal ties and similarities (Hellweg, Samovar, & Skow, 1991, pp. 286–292).

Proactivity and preparation. A proactive person reaches beyond the moment and creates opportunities, as compared to the reactive person, who waits for someone to say something and then responds. The proactive person anticipates, thinks of possibilities and contingencies, plans ahead, and acts. Your proactivity shows when you're prepared, you're organized, and you come to meetings with information and ideas. You have already anticipated needs and acted without being asked.

Communication abilities. All leadership relies on communication. The individual likely to emerge as leader is the one who shows self-assurance, directs and summarizes, and orients the group toward the goal (Schultz, 1986). Even just being talkative and involved makes others feel that you have the potential to be a leader (Riecken, 1975). You also need to be able to laugh, to think creatively, to play with ideas, to enjoy people, and to get other people to do the same. These communication abilities all help to build self-confidence, which is important in your willingness to serve as leader.

Effective Leader Responsibilities The contemporary leader is, in a sense, a supermember, working to empower the team to reach its goal. One writer defines the best leader as "teamplayer: [one who] unites others toward a shared destiny through sharing information and ideas, empowering others and developing trust" (Kinlaw, 1991, p. xvi). In successful research teams, effective leaders fulfill these responsibilities (Kolb, 1991):

- Speaking and acting as representative of the group
- Maintaining cordial relations and having influence with superiors
- Keeping the group in good standing with higher authorities
- Exhibiting trust by giving team members meaningful levels of responsibility
- Providing team members with the necessary autonomy to achieve results (p. 9)

By any standard, a leader's job is demanding. We'll add the following to Kinlaw's and Kolb's lists of essential responsibilities:

Developing others' self-leadership. "In many modern situations, the most appropriate leader is one who can lead others to lead themselves" (Manz & Sims, 1991, p. 18). As leader, get to know team members' strengths, suggest areas in which they can take special responsibility, encourage their progress and leadership, and express appreciation for their successes. As organizational teams take on more responsibilities, the role of "coach" becomes more critical. At one company, supervisors—now called "team facilitators"—who once spent 10% of their time coaching now *spend 60% coaching and training* (Wellins, Byham, & Wilson, 1991, p. 130).

In your classroom project group, coaching may mean no more than understanding group and task processes and explaining, encouraging, and helping others to assume responsibility for themselves. One of our students used her theater background to coach her class project team in presenting skits to represent principles the team had chosen to present for the class. She did a great job, the team did a great job—and they got that "A."

Setting standards. People often look to a leader to set the standards for both the work and the ethics of the group. Lead others to brainstorm and set standards for their group and task processes. Express high standards of your own and manage your own behavior to model those standards. Prepare yourself for meetings. Encourage others to bring in information, and set standards for analyzing it effectively. Help to create the image of a team that develops expertise in its area and takes pride in its work. Be willing to take risks that help create a star-quality team.

Ensuring meeting processes. As leader, you also are responsible for making meetings function well. Here's a list of reminders:

- Organize and communicate the purpose and structure of each meeting with an agenda and minutes.
- Establish a climate of openness, empathy, and trust.
- Establish norms for full participation and support.
- Encourage self-evaluation of the team's processes.
- Respect the diversity and differing needs of members.
- Maintain high standards for working with information.
- Maintain norms for critical analysis of information and ideas, but not of people.

Leadership Styles

You may have used one or more leadership styles at some time. Certainly, you have noticed the leadership styles of people in roles such as teaching, counseling, coaching, managing, and holding political office. Their style is influenced by their culture or gender socialization and often fits into one of three classic categories (White & Lippett, 1960):

Laissez-faire leadership Neutral, uninvolved leadership style

- **Laissez-faire leadership** is a neutral, uninvolved style in which the leader simply lets the group do what it wants. The laissez-faire leader must already be designated for the job, because being this laid back will rarely get anyone the position. This style works well for a team of experts who are comfortable sharing leadership and want to charge ahead. In other circumstances, however, productivity, quality, involvement, and satisfaction decrease.

Authoritarian leadership Rigid leadership style in which leader makes all decisions and may use coercion or reward to get results

Democratic leadership Open leadership style that facilitates discussion and shares decision-making power

- **Authoritarian leadership** is a rigid style in which the leader keeps tight control, makes all decisions, runs things by the book, sets schedules, and may use coercion or reward to get results. Authoritarian leaders often increase short-term productivity, but they can also increase dissatisfaction, aggression, and turnover rates among members.

- **Democratic leadership** is an open style in which the leader makes sure everyone's heard, guides and facilitates discussion and decision making, and shares decision-making power. With a democratic style, meetings may take longer, because members have genuine input to a decision, but members are less likely to be absent or leave the group and are more likely to generate good ideas, participate, and be committed to their decisions.

Although these terms still serve to describe how many leaders work, newer concepts describe the ways a leader can empower groups and individuals to move forward on their own. Whether in your classroom or on a self-managing corporate team, the ideal is for members to take responsibility for their own development. Researchers and theorists have used the following labels to describe these newer concepts of leading styles:

Transactional leadership Leadership style that uses rewards in return for effective performance

Transformational leadership Leadership style that motivates, inspires, and develops members to meet goals

- **Transactional leadership** avoids coercion or punishment (unlike authoritarian leadership) but does use rewards in return for effective performance. Rewards may be actions that fulfill members' needs for interpersonal communication, satisfaction, quality of work life, or personal wants and values, including promotions or pay raises. Groups pull together better when rewards are for the entire team rather than for individuals (Hackman & Walton, 1986, p. 84).

- **Transformational leadership** is an ideal that promises "extraordinary individual and organizational outcomes" (Pillai, Scandura, & Williams, 1999, p. 763). The transformational leader elevates, motivates, inspires, and develops members to meet their individual, team, and organizational goals. Bass (1990), who has studied transformational leaders in the business world, reports that they are highly charismatic. Transformational leaders provide vision, instill pride, and inspire and stimulate team members to use their own intelligence, rationality, and problem-solving skills. They coach and advise on an individual as well as a team basis (p. 22). As a result, teams work harder for transformational leaders than they do for transactional leaders.

Visionary leadership Leadership that shapes and gains a team's acceptance of a long-term goal

Situational leadership Style that adapts to needs and maturity of individual groups

- **Visionary leadership** goes even further, shaping and gaining a team's acceptance of a long-term vision. A visionary leader is a direction setter, change agent, spokesperson, and coach, a person who leads superteams to success by providing clear and uplifting goals (Nanus, 1992).

- **Situational leadership** addresses the unique requirements of each group. Fisher (1986) notes that leaders "behave differently with different people; they behave differently at different stages of group development; and they

Manz and Sims label leadership styles in terms of four personae:

1   The "strong man," who commands through power and coercion

2   The "transactor," who exchanges rewards for cooperation

3   The "visionary hero," who inspires members through close, relational communication

4   The "superleader," whose personal modeling is such that she or he leads people to lead themselves.

Although these terms almost beg for a video and a comic book of their own, they do describe vividly the varying approaches a leader might take.

From C. C. Manz & H. P. Sims (1991, Spring) Super-leadership: Beyond the myth of heroic leadership. *Organizational Dynamics*, pp. 18–35.

behave differently when the task situations differ" (p. 205). A leader may adapt to situations according to the stage the group is in (how self-motivating and directed it is) (Hersey, Blanchard, & Natemeyer, 1979) and, as well, according to the type of task the group must accomplish (Hollander, 1978).

A Group's First Steps

When you start a brand-new group, you are thrown together with people in a collaborative relationship, and each of you must develop some understanding of how to work with all the others. Making the relationship effective takes an investment of time: to get to know one another and to build rapport, as well as to decide the group's approach to leadership and standards for participation.

Getting to Know One Another

Taking enough time and effort to get to know one another is essential. A group that meets just once may have only 5 minutes for making connections among members; a team that will meet for weeks (or even months or years) may take an entire meeting or two to build mutual rapport. Members need to know something about one another, to identify abilities they can bring to their task, and to discuss their expectations for the experience. Even in a brief meeting, however, you can make a conscious effort to move the group through a getting-acquainted process this way:

1   *Take the initiative.* Suggest spending a few minutes on introductions. Say something like, "Could we take time to find out something about each other? I think we'll work together better if we do."

2   *Learn—and use—everyone's name.* Attaching a name to a face, after all, is the first step to seeing another person as a distinct individual. This makes communication more comfortable.

3   *Create dialogue.* Show interest in people and ask them questions; disclose something about yourself. Start, of course, with basic information, such as where you're from, what you do, and so on.

4   *Identify special strengths.* Each individual brings particular strengths to the group, such as access to important resources, relevant talents and interests, or experience in a related topic. Say something like, "Why don't we each make a list of what we think we can do for this team? For example, does anyone have contacts with people who can give us information on the subject?"

5   *Share your values.* Individuals start out with personal feelings about the team and its task. Members' feelings may reflect the importance they attach to the work, their particular needs or wants, and their expectations about how the group will interact. To explore values, ask questions such as, "What do you think is important about the issues facing the team?" "What kinds of ethical issues will we face?" and, "How will we deal with them?"

6   *State personal agendas.* Members often bring their own personal agendas, or individual goals and objectives, that may be hard to detect. Often, these are **hidden agendas,** based on motives that the individual would rather not talk about but that may affect the team's interactions. Although people may keep their agendas hidden, a group's early discussion of individual issues and expectations can create a norm for sharing information that allows members to meet both individual and group needs.

Hidden agenda Member's personal goals that affect the team's interaction but that the member does not share with the group

Deciding on a Leader

Maybe someone has already appointed a leader for you, maybe not. Do you want to choose one?

Discuss the issue early on and decide whether you want to select a leader immediately or not. If time is crucial and you need someone to take charge, you may want to go ahead and choose a leader. Or, you may want to take some time to assess individuals' abilities to fulfill leader functions. One who seems like a dynamo right now may turn out to be full of hot air on closer scrutiny. Designating one person may make it too easy for a group to dump all responsibility on the leader, and other members might fail to provide the group-building and task leadership needed to develop a real team.

If there is any doubt, we suggest waiting for a few meetings before choosing a leader. You have some alternatives:

■   Distribute all leader functions among various members according to their inclinations and talents.

- Distribute some leader responsibilities for specific functions, and share the rest among the entire group.
- Take turns as primary leader according to a specific schedule.
- Wait and allow a leader (or leaders) to emerge as the team works together over time. Frequently, someone who voluntarily fills leadership functions gains the group's confidence and emerges as the leader.

Whatever alternative you choose, discuss precisely what the team expects of a leader or of people fulfilling leadership functions. Potentially good teams can fall apart when everyone "just assumes" that others will take care of the agenda, minutes, resources, and so on. Assumptions don't work for leadership.

Setting Standards and Procedures for Work

Norms are the usual, expected ways of behaving that a team will develop over time. However, some norms shouldn't wait. You need immediately to set standards relating to members' commitment and accountability to the task, as well as to set meeting times and places. Such norms need to be discussed and agreed to at the beginning—you can reassess and modify them as your group progresses.

Commitment and Accountability   A sensitive, and crucial, issue is members' understanding of their responsibility to the group. Suppose you've worked hard on your group's task only to have someone say, "I haven't worked on this because it isn't that important to me," or, "I don't have the time." A discussion early on about time and task commitments can help to avert these blockades to progress. Ask—and answer—the following:

- How much time (per day, per week, per month) can each member reasonably commit to meetings and to outside preparation?
- What problems with time does each member have to solve? School, family, or job conflicts? Habitual tardiness or late assignments?
- What happens if a member misses a meeting or does not produce work on time?
- How will you deal with unanticipated problems such as illness or a family crisis? You might set up a system for communicating among members and taking responsibility for sharing information.

Many conflicts in teams arise because of individuals' different expectations. Question one another, understand these expectations, and decide on norms.

Meeting Times and Places   If anything can make or break a group, it's the meetings. If you are specific about meeting times and places, people will be more likely to attend, and you can plan meetings with a clearer picture of when, where, and how they'll be conducted. Discuss these details at your first meeting.

Meeting times. Share all members' schedules and identify potential meeting periods. Set specific meeting times, with a few alternatives in case of unforeseen glitches, for the entire stretch of the team's work. Ask members to put those meeting times on their calendars, but also get someone—the leader, the secretary, or a volunteer—to send out reminders.

Meeting places. Your meeting environment affects the processes of the group. Consider not just accessibility for all members, comfort, and, perhaps, available resources, but ambience, too. If someone offers a living room, will the hominess facilitate discussion or will it be so comfortable it gets you off the task? If you meet in a classroom, will the accessibility of the library and a blackboard be advantages? Or will everybody be so burnt out with school that the classroom ambience will be deadly?

Preparing Agendas

Agenda Written plan for a meeting

An **agenda** is simply a written plan to guide the order of discussion for a meeting, but what an important plan it is. The agenda can be simple and straightforward or creative and artful. Meetings should have an agenda—formal or informal—designed, ordered, and phrased to identify participants, purposes, issues, and time needs of the meeting. Team members need to prepare for the meeting, so they should have the agenda early on. Some groups make it a rule that the agenda is prepared and copies sent to the members by a specified time before each meeting.

Formal and Informal Agendas   Large organizations and their committees often use formally structured parliamentary rules such as *Robert's Rules of Order* (Robert & Evans, 1990). Parliamentary rules are established with the realization that democratic bodies are set up on adversarial, political premises; that members can engage in every possible means of persuasion; and that interactions must be guided by rules or the weakest voices will not be heard and meetings will be bedlam. The formal, parliamentary agenda usually guides meetings in which there are officers, regular committee reports, and a variety of issues or plans to discuss and bring to a vote.

An informal agenda is custom designed for the purposes of a specific meeting, which could be anything from a short, one-time discussion to a workshop extended over several days. Even a group that is meeting only once should have some discussion of an agenda. The group needs a road map. Suppose you're meeting with a group of students to plan a class project. You might use an agenda like this:

1   Introduce yourselves.

2   Ask someone to take notes if necessary.

3   Ask someone to lead if necessary.

People from varying cultures may come to a meeting with very different expectations, as meeting planners have found out. Advice for meeting planners points out that lower-context cultures, which tend to be high-technology, industrialized, and competitive cultures, are likely to follow their agendas rigidly, whereas higher-context members might prepare an agenda—or, preferably, a simple list of items—and change it at the meeting according to their need. Sandra Mumford Fowler, a Washington, D.C., consultant and trainer, says that lower-context folks, such as Germans, would be offended at the idea of changing an agenda. Higher-context people, such as some Asian groups, are more comfortable letting things evolve.

Lower-context cultures also want to begin and end meetings promptly at the scheduled moment, whereas people from higher-context cultures are happy to let the time adapt to the situation. "I was at a meeting in Sweden when an African speaker started telling stories to illustrate his point and went overtime," recalled Margaret Pusch, president of the Intercultural Press in Yarmouth, Maine. "People thought it was so rude."

From R. Reisner (1993, June). How different cultures learn. *Meeting News* 27(6), 30–32.

4 Decide on your goals—what you must accomplish by the end of the meeting.

5 Plan steps to achieve the goal.

6 Get all the information about your task on the table.

7 Analyze the information in terms of the goal.

8 Summarize what you've accomplished.

Although this general agenda must be adapted to your group's task, it provides a checklist to help your group work through its task efficiently.

Formats for Agendas A team that meets over a period of time usually needs specifically designed agendas for the various purposes of its meetings. How you phrase ideas can structure the way you think and talk about them. One format lists topics; another lists discussion questions.

Topical agendas. These are brief and to the point. If everyone has a clear sense of where you're going, and your purpose is only to review and discuss some information, the agenda need only list the order of topics. For example:

1 Review information from the last meeting.

2 Get a report from Bob.

3   Discuss information relating to Dale's proposal.

4   Set up the next meeting.

Discussion question agendas. This format stimulates thinking and discussion. It guides the order and kicks off the discussions but leaves plenty of leeway for thinking critically and creatively. Suppose your college task force has created a proposal to solve the parking problem, for example, and this meeting is to evaluate that proposal. You might use a question format:

1   How well does the proposal meet our goals to provide better parking?

2   What are the advantages and disadvantages of the proposal?

3   What are the ethical implications?

4   What are the legal implications?

Managing the Meeting

Members sometimes are shockingly grateful when a leader or member simply manages and moves the task. Yet these are probably the easiest skills to learn and to provide for a team. They include the steps we've just discussed for planning the meeting and ensuring the process of the meeting itself. A good set of standards to keep in mind is that suggested by Larson and LaFasto (1989):

- Avoid compromising the team's objective with political issues.
- Exhibit personal commitment to the team's goal.
- Do not dilute the team's efforts with too many priorities.
- Be fair and impartial toward all team members.
- Be willing to confront and resolve issues associated with inadequate performance by team members.
- Be open to new ideas and information from team members. (p. 123)

According to Barge (1991), the most important functions and skills in a leader's task competence are to:

- *Facilitate participation.* Encourage, motivate, and get members to participate. Ask for and give information on the problem, solution generation, evaluation, and implementation.
- *Define roles.* Regulate participation and structure role expectations for ensuing meetings. Make sure everyone gets a chance; keep people from dominating; consider differences and needs of members.
- *Keep discussion coherent.* Make connections among ideas. Refer, when appropriate, to previous information or to related information from other experiences. Synthesize concepts, identify relationships, or find new interpretations or applications of ideas within the discussion topic.

- *Control discussion inhibitors.* Try to keep people from sidetracking the discussion, withdrawing, criticizing negatively, or contributing to confusion in the group.

The idea is to draw the best of individual and collaborative effort from the group—to achieve your goals as a "superteam."

Summary

Careers today involve working in groups and teams, as organizations have discovered how much more effective groups often are in accomplishing tasks. Developing group communication as a student helps you to practice and demonstrate the leadership abilities that employers want. The ideal is for your work groups to evolve into teams and then into superteams—highly committed, collaborative groups characterized by clear vision, firm goals, excellent communication, and solid teamwork. Members develop a team culture and image as they move through developmental phases and face midpoint crises.

In effective teams, all members share leadership responsibility by fulfilling roles that build the group and accomplish its tasks. Leaders are people appointed or elected or who emerge as leaders because of their contributions to the team. Good leaders are credible, adaptable, proactive, prepared, and effective communicators.

Leadership styles vary from classic laissez-faire, authoritarian, or democratic guidance of group processes to more contemporary approaches such as transactional, transformational, or visionary leadership, that seek to empower team members. Leaders often must adapt their styles to situational contingencies revolving around circumstances, tasks, purposes, or members.

Getting a good team started requires getting to know one another, deciding whether to choose a leader immediately, and setting standards and procedures for work, including personal commitments, accountability, and meeting times and places. The group should prepare and distribute an agenda prior to a meeting and modify it at the beginning of the meeting as needed.

Exercises

1   To assess your leadership skills, complete the form in Activity 4 in the Cyberpoints that follow these exercises. Then make an additional copy of Form 10.1 and ask a friend to rate your leadership behavior on that copy.

Discuss the completed forms with your friend. What does your friend see that you do not? How can you use that feedback? List your strengths and the skills you'd like to develop.

2 Select one behavior from the leadership survey that you would like to use more often (summarizing issues for the group, for example). For a couple of weeks, consciously use the new behavior in group meetings or in classes. Keep a journal of how you use the behavior, how you think it affected the group, and how you feel about expanding your repertoire of group behaviors in this way. When you feel comfortable with this new skill, select another one and use the same process to develop it.

3 The student organization has appointed a new committee to consider student groups' requests for funds. The committee is meeting for the first time. A portion of some of the committee's discussion is shown below. In a small group, discuss this meeting and then respond to the questions following it. Report your findings to the class.

Chris (the chairperson): Let's get this over with, I've got a date in 10 minutes. We've got five requests here. I think the first one's legitimate. How many are in favor of it?

Sue: Whoa, I don't even have a copy of these requests. What are they?

Chris: Oh. Well, this one is from the Spanish Club and they want a hundred dollars to help with their banquet.

Shawn: Are there other ethnic clubs who want money, too?

Chris: I don't know. Let's see—here's the Irish Club. They want money for the St. Patrick's Day parade in the city. And here's one from . . . who cares? Let's just go through and decide. . . .

Nicola: Wait, wait . . . how much money do we have to allocate? Are there any policies about how we decide?

Sue: What other requests are there?

Shawn: Is this the whole committee? I don't know any of you . . . and who else should be here?

Chris: I have to go in five minutes. Can we just say these are all granted?

- What is happening with the leadership in this group? Who's the leader? Who is trying to provide leadership? What could be done to improve it?

- Will this group become a team? Can it become a superteam? Why or why not? Think of the characteristics of a group versus a team versus a superteam. How does this group fit right now?

- What should have happened at the outset? What could happen now to make this group work more effectively?

4 Think of a group to which you currently belong (social, religious, school—whatever). Create an agenda for the next meeting of your group, considering all the issues described in this chapter for good agendas. Then make a short presentation to the class in which you describe your group, its goals, and the agenda you have designed for the meeting. Explain why you chose the type of agenda and the order of items that you did for this group.

Cyberpoints

CCC

WEB SITE

1   Use the *InfoTrac College Edition* and the keyword *leader* to locate current articles about leading and leadership. How would these articles relate to information in the text?

2   Go to the *Communicating with Credibility and Confidence* Web site at http://communication.wadsworth.com/lumsden and measure your leadership skills by clicking on Form 10.1, Self-Assessment of Leadership. What do you think you do well? How can you improve your skills to help a group or team experience more effective and less frustrating?

3   Are you interested in groups for personal development and problem solving? You could access one of these Web sites to see how some groups provide support for people: http:www.alcoholics-anonymous.org; http://www.overeatersanonymous.org; or http://emotionsanonymous.org.

4   Would you like to find a group that focuses on a particular interest of yours? Go to http://www.meta-list.net and search by keyword or category for your interest. Then subscribe to their newsletter and find out how the organization operates. Are there small groups that meet face to face? How do electronic meetings occur, if at all, and what are the goals and norms of the group?

Chapter 11

Problem Analysis and Decision Making: Achieving Group and Team Goals

Objectives for This Chapter

Knowledge

- Understand the functions of goal setting for decision-making groups
- Know steps in a decision-making sequence
- Identify criteria for analyzing possible solutions and instilling confidence in team decisions

Feelings and Approaches

- Sense the importance of thorough analysis in decision making
- Want to be vigilant in problem-analysis and decision-making activities
- Appreciate the value of group approaches to decision making
- Feel confident about using group problem-analysis and decision-making processes

Communication Abilities

- Be a credible communicator in group problem-analysis and decision-making situations
- Guide your group through decision-making tasks
- Apply critical and creative thinking in group problem analysis and decision making
- Use analysis tools and techniques when investigating problems and possible solutions
- Recognize and minimize groupthink conditions in decision-making groups

Key Terms

group goals

charge

instrumental objectives

team inquiry

brainstorming

applicability

practicality

advantages

disadvantages

risk

desirability

consensus

groupthink

I f you're like most of us, you'd probably like to enjoy your work with others and to feel that what your group produces is worthwhile, but you probably know from experience that sometimes it's extraordinarily difficult just to get several people to talk and listen to one another, let alone to get them to come to the same conclusion. How can you reduce frustration and improve both relationships and productivity in your group or team experiences?

Most of your work with decision-making groups will extend over some period of time. These groups usually have the opportunity to move from being short-term "working groups" (as described in Chapter 10) to becoming real "teams." In this chapter, we use the term *team* throughout to reflect the qualities that contribute to effective collective decision making by working groups that become more than just "pseudoteams."

This chapter shows the steps teams can use for good decision making, including identifying goals, finding needed information, and systematically selecting a solution. It also examines ways that a team might make poor decisions because of groupthink, and provides ways that members' vigilance can protect your team from groupthink's negative effects.

Identifying Your Team's Goals

Group goals Results that a team has been assembled to achieve

A team project can be compared to taking a trip—you need to know where you're going to know if you've arrived. A team has to set **group goals** early to clarify its destination, to know what both other people and the members themselves expect of the team. The team needs to develop a plan for accomplishing its work. These steps involve identifying the purposes for creating the team and defining its goals.

Identifying the Purposes

Why has your team been created? Usually the team is to do one of the following:

- *Information gathering:* Research and investigate a specific problem or issue and prepare a report, often as a first step toward other purposes.

- *Problem analysis:* Investigate, report, and often provide recommendations upon a specific problem, to determine its scope, causes, and impact. In a college setting, a problem-analysis team might focus on anything from parking to plagiarism.

- *Decision making:* Conduct the full range of information-gathering and problem-analysis processes to arrive at specific decisions that will be implemented. The same team might implement decisions, or it might pass them along to others to implement. For example, an organization's quality teams might be instructed to "identify areas that can be improved and implement changes to improve them." Such teams might be responsible for their ideas from creation through implementation and assessment.

Defining the Goals

Charge Task or assignment that defines the purpose of a team

The people who established your team presumably told you its purpose, usually by a task description or assignment called the **charge.** The charge may or may not be specific. On a college committee, for example, your charge might be to "look into the problem of low involvement in student activities." At work, you might be assigned to a task force with the vague charge to "improve community relationships."

Both of these charges are very general; they do not give you specific tasks. The team must define the specific goals for itself. Early on, the team will need to say to its founder, "This is what we think we should do; is that what you want?"

Your team needs to write a goal statement that states, in clear, unambiguous terms, *what* will be done, *who* will do it, *when* it will be accomplished, and what the *criteria* for success are. A goal statement for a written report might be:

- *Major goal.* On October 1, the team will present to Ms. Fernandez, Director of Community Relations, a written report on the investigation and recommendations of the Task Force on Community Relations.

- *Criteria.* The report will be approximately 20 pages, complete, well written and documented, and professionally prepared.

Instrumental objectives The lesser tasks that lead to achieving a team's goal

To move from a goal statement to final results, the team needs to identify **instrumental objectives,** all those smaller tasks that will lead to reaching the ultimate goal. Identifying instrumental objectives and planning how to reach them forms a blueprint for achieving major goals. For example:

1   Major goal: Written report

2   Major goal: Oral report

3   Instrumental objective: Get information on current relationships between the company and community

4   Instrumental objective: Get information on what citizens see as a helpful corporate role

5   Instrumental objective: Design and suggest ideas for what your company can do

6   Instrumental objective: Write and edit report

7   Instrumental objective: Plan and rehearse oral presentation

You now have two major goals with five instrumental objectives: two information-gathering tasks (3 and 4), one problem-analysis, idea-generating task (5), and two report-preparation tasks (6 and 7). Each instrumental objective is essential to reaching your major goals (1 and 2). Each instrumental objective may also have still smaller steps. For example, to find out what current relationships are, other tasks might include designing a survey, surveying local organizations and institutions, and analyzing the survey results. Each instrumental objective should be constructed just as carefully as final goal statements, with clear terms and criteria for achievement.

If you set clear goals and instrumental objectives at the outset, you can save a lot of trouble later. You may need to clarify, alter, expand, or reduce some of your goals as you go along, but at least you know what you're trying to do and how to go about it. We've seen, for example, a team carefully research, design, and duplicate a survey—and then discover they should have gotten the institution's permission to distribute it. What a terrible waste of time, energy, and money.

Understanding and Committing to Goals

Often, members think they are in agreement and then find out they don't understand one another at all. You can reduce confusion by confirming what people intend by their goals. These communication techniques can really help:

1   *Paraphrase the stated goals and discuss whether the paraphrase is accurate and complete.* Sometimes, discussion will unearth differences you didn't know were there; other times, you confirm that everyone has a similar understanding.

2   *Hypothesize interpretations, examples, or applications for the goals.* One member might say, "Okay, we've said we want this report to be well documented. Would an annotated bibliography be one way we'd do that?" Someone else might say, "Good grief, no! I thought we'd just list any sources we used!"

This way, you can negotiate a mutual meaning about your goals and objectives. Still, the team's effectiveness is diminished if some people will work hard for those ends and others will not. You may need to negotiate everyone's commitment to the goals, both by asking members to state their commitment and by building expectations of involvement into the team's norms as you go along. One method is the *census-taking* technique, asking each member to what extent she or he can take responsibility for achieving these goals. Every member has his or her own needs and approaches, and you'll never have a total match among members, but you do want to be sure everyone's in the same boat, rowing at approximately the same pace.

Technology meets human interaction: Two groups of people, meeting at different places, can interact via videoconferencing that allows them to talk, to see one another, and to study the information they need to make good decisions—all without leaving their workplace.

Jon Feingarsh/corbistockmarket.com

Planning Your Team's Inquiry

The work performed between setting the goals and reaching them usually determines the team's success. Nobel Prize-winner Herbert Simon (1977) has done extensive research on decision making in organizations. He divides the decision-making process into four broad phases of how people actually work through information to reach a conclusion: intelligence, design, choice, and review. We'll talk about that first part, intelligence (meaning information), now, and then we'll discuss the other parts as they fit into the rest of the chapter.

Very quickly, your team recognizes the need for specific information and must plan the **team's inquiry** for getting it and sharing it in their analysis and decision making.

Team inquiry Plan for gathering and sharing information

Information: What, Where, and How to Get It

Nobody can make good decisions without information; as Hirokawa and Scheerhorn (1986) write, "A group's information base is directly or indirectly tied to all phases of the decision-making process. Therefore, any errors occurring within the base are likely to contribute to faulty decision-making" (p. 74).

Your team's immediate task, then, is to discuss what information you need. Think about this in terms of your goals and your instrumental objectives. Make an open-ended list of the things you need to get. Then consider who should get what.

You can start with the team members. What expertise may have contributed to selecting specific team members? In addition, what do the members know, what can they do, and how can they apply their expertise to your team's goals?

The McDonald's Corporation and the Environmental Defense Fund (EDF) joint task force provides a good example of information-gathering approaches. The two organizations made an historical breakthrough by bringing together representatives from a corporation and environmental activist into a cooperative team to reduce waste and increase recycling in McDonald's restaurants. The members already had extensive expertise relating to this project from their own organizations' perspectives, but individually they consulted books and materials to gain information about the other organization. In addition:

Team members spent numerous hours in various McDonald's restaurants to understand operations. Each EDF member worked a day in a restaurant. . . . The team toured facilities of two McDonald's food suppliers, five packaging suppliers, and one of McDonald's largest distribution centers. They also visited a polystyrene recycling facility and a composting facility. Most visits included tours, formal presentations, and extensive question and answer sessions with top management and technical experts. McDonald's brought in experts from various departments to discuss issues in depth. Likewise, additional EDF staff as well as experts from other environmental organizations provided background on issues beyond solid waste.

Environmental Defense fund/McDonald's Corporation Task Force Report, 1991, p. iv. Used by permission.

Once you have identified what the team already has available, you can plan a strategy for getting the other information you will need. Your goals may demand specific research, using public resources such as print and media materials in libraries, public offices, museums, and archives, computerized databases and indexes, or interviews with experts on the topic.

Now what? Every good idea comes down to hard work. This is where many teams slip up. Everybody gets an assignment; half of the people do it, half don't. Of the half who do it, half do it halfway. The team winds up lacking some of the information it needs, drastically undermining its effectiveness.

Before anyone leaves the meeting room, do these things:

1   Determine who will do what, set deadlines, and establish guidelines for presenting the information to the team. First, divide the information-gathering tasks. Consider each person's talents, interests, contacts, and time—but also, as a team, consider equity and balance in getting the work done. Then assign appropriate tasks to each member.

2   Create a work plan—a complete list of assignments including *who, what,* and, if you're doing the work in subgroups, *with whom* and *by when.* Calculate the time needed for research, discussion, and planning, and *leave yourselves*

Figure 11.1
Research assignment worksheet format

Research Planning Form				
What information is needed?	Resource location	Reporting format	Possible resources	Date needed

room for the unexpected. Set deadlines for the completion of each piece of work as well as individual progress reports. Use a form such as the one in Figure 11.1 to create your work plan covering all responsibilities and deadlines. Give everyone a copy.

3   Set guidelines for documentation. These guidelines can be simple. Just be sure that everyone gets full documentation for sources (author, date, title of article, title of book or journal, edition, publisher, page numbers). Not only does documentation show the credibility of both you and your source, but it also ensures that if you need to go back for further information, you'll know where to find it.

When members report to the team, each should provide brief, concise handouts that clearly summarize the critical information, including glossaries for new terms. If you run across information that could be useful for someone else on the team, copy the material for the other person or provide a full bibliographic citation and where they can locate the resource.

Information: How to Share and Analyze It

A team that has done good research will have gathered a lot of information that the team must *work through together*. When your team meets to share information, that may well be the only item on your agenda, because all members need to understand all information well enough to analyze it, draw conclusions, and make applications to achieve the team's goals. This requires allowing time for feedback and questions.

Information sharing is important for two reasons. First, if there is a change in membership, the team can pick up the threads and weave the work back together more easily. Second, information is essential not only for achieving goals but also for developing a team's vision and cohesiveness. When all team members share and understand the information, the synergy of the team has a more consistent focus. Sharing information effectively is one of the ways you become a superteam.

Reporting information to your team requires skills similar to those needed for presentations to other audiences. You should organize material carefully, present it in an interesting and direct manner, give clear and believable supporting evidence, and supplement data with appropriate visual aids. When you share information with your team, you need to keep everyone's attention focused on the ideas. One useful technique is *posting* information—that is, using visual displays so everyone else can see the data while you talk about it. You can present information visually with printed handouts, overhead projectors, or flipcharts to refer to a specific item or to identify relationships among ideas so everyone can focus on ideas and recall the meaning.

Making Team Decisions Systematically

Vigilance is a key word for good decision making. The degree to which members are vigilant about the quality of their decisions determines the degree to which they will be successful. Vigilant critical thinking and analysis proceed through a series of smaller decisions at four stages: examining the problem, clarifying objectives, developing available choices, and examining potential consequences (Gouran & Hirokawa, 1983; Hirokawa & Scheerhorn, 1986).

For our discussion, we have combined these decision stages with Simon's four-stage decision-making process (intelligence, design, choice, review) and the reflective thinking stages John Dewey (1910) developed years ago. The result is seven task activities to guide your decision making. These activities are useful in three ways: as strategies for work plans, as items for meeting agendas, and as reminders of essential elements so you don't miss important angles when thinking through decision-making tasks.

1 Analyze the problem.

2 Establish criteria for solutions.

3 List possible solutions.

4 Evaluate possible solutions.

5 Decide on the most appropriate solution(s).

6 Implement the decision.

7 Evaluate the effectiveness of the decision.

These tasks may provide the agenda for a single meeting if the problem to be solved is relatively simple, or they may guide a team's work over a period of months or even years. Because problem solving is so detailed, however, and because the team decision making does not always occur in this order, agendas may be modified considerably as meetings move along. Teams often overlap the tasks, loop back, and jump forward in vigilant analysis and achievement.

A systematic plan doesn't guarantee clear thinking. As you move through the decision-making tasks, you might use **brainstorming** to create multiple

Brainstorming Process of generating solutions by thinking of as many ideas as possible without constraint

perspectives and options. Brainstorming helps produce more ideas to improve your chances of making the highest-quality choices.

The best way to brainstorm is with a group, so you get a lot of ideas from diverse sources, but you can use the same process alone. The goal is to think of as many ideas as you can. Reach to the outer limits for wild and crazy thoughts. Look at the problem from every angle. Here are some guidelines:

1   Appoint someone to facilitate if you're in a group.

2   Don't stop to evaluate ideas.

3   Keep the flow of ideas moving fast.

4   Write down as many ideas as you can.

5   Do not "own" ideas, good or bad—keep egos out.

6   "Piggyback" or "hitchhike" ideas onto previous thoughts.

7   Sweat out silences and plateaus; sit quietly and let your brain incubate until something emerges.

8   After many ideas are on the list, analyze and winnow them down.

9   Start serious selection from the remaining possibilities.

Try it. You'll discover ideas you didn't dream you could have.

Analyzing Problems

Dewey (1910) states that when people "feel difficulties," they have taken the first step in problem exploration. They sense that something is wrong, such as when students complain about their choices of classes or the final exam schedule. Sometimes, there are as many explanations of the problems as there are students lamenting.

The first task is to move from intuitions about difficulties to identification of the nature and scope of the specific problems. The team must ask questions, gather information, and think analytically, critically, and creatively to identify the problems and to find their causes and effects.

Problem Identification   Identifying problems is not as easy as it sounds. From "feeling the difficulty," you move to exploring the general area of concern to find trouble spots. Then you start isolating problems by tracking them. You analyze how things presently *are* functioning and compare that with the ways things *should* work.

Assume you have been appointed to a college task force charged with improving registration procedures. First, your team might track the registration process as staff and students actually experience it. To track through the issues, you could create a step-by-step flowchart to help clarify the team's thinking and identify the problem spots. A flowchart can be used at any stage of information sharing or problem solving, but it is particularly useful for identifying problems. Figure 11.2 shows a flowchart that might illustrate the registration process.

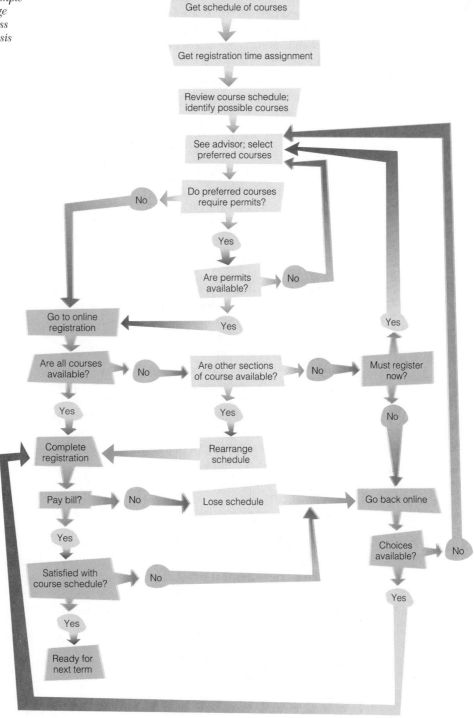

Figure 11.2 *Sample flowchart of college registration process for problem analysis*

Get schedule of courses

Get registration time assignment

Review course schedule; identify possible courses

See advisor; select preferred courses

Do preferred courses require permits? — No

Yes

Are permits available? — No

Yes

Go to online registration

Are all courses available? — No — Are other sections of course available? — No — Must register now?

Yes

Yes

Yes

No

Complete registration ← Rearrange schedule

Go back online

Pay bill? — No — Lose schedule

Yes

Choices available? — No

Satisfied with course schedule? — No

Yes

Yes

Ready for next term

Next, compare your flowchart to registration procedures as described by established policies. Your task force can use the comparison to identify possible problem areas in the process and to isolate the policies that need more careful examination. Your analysis can begin by seeking answers to some of these questions:

- What difficulties are people experiencing? Where are the bottlenecks? At what points are many people encountering obstacles?

- What harms are being done? What is the scope of the problem? How many people are affected? How seriously?

- What conditions are relevant to the difficulties? Are the policies, procedures, objectives, or criteria missing or inappropriately applied?

As you start to analyze the registration problems, your task force may detect some patterns. One difficulty may be lack of sufficient classes at times convenient for students. The negative results are clear: Students can't get into classes or must take them at inconvenient times; they may have trouble completing requirements or getting course prerequisites.

Causes and Effects   Tracking problems helps you see possible causes for them. Analysis of causes and effects makes or breaks problem solving. If you don't have the correct causes, you're not going to solve the problem—and you may create new ones. It can be difficult to determine whether one factor causes a problem or just happens to occur at the same time, possibly as another symptom rather than the cause. Chapter 3 develops guidelines for logical cause-effect reasoning, and those principles should be applied in your team's problem analysis.

A fishbone diagram, created on a flipchart or large board with all members participating, assists you in identifying, tracking, analyzing, and visualizing multiple cause-effect relationships (Ishikawa, 1982). See Figure 11.3 for an example.

You construct a fishbone by drawing a long line—vertical or horizontal—to represent the problem on which you're working. You then draw diagonal lines—like the ribs of a fish—off the problem line, labeled with the issues that the team identifies as related to the problem. For example, as shown in Figure 11.3, your registration fishbone could list students, departments, resources, and methods as potential components of the registration problem. Next, you might draw shorter horizontal lines off the diagonal lines, labeled with subordinate issues or categories that affect the larger problems. Now you have a diagram showing relationships among issues pertaining to the problem. The fishbone doesn't solve the problems or even prove the causes, but it does make the relationships among the issues much clearer.

Establishing Criteria

To make quality choices from many options, you have to know the requirements of the solution. Criteria are those standards by which you will judge potential solutions to determine if you are selecting wisely. You can't assume you'll "know

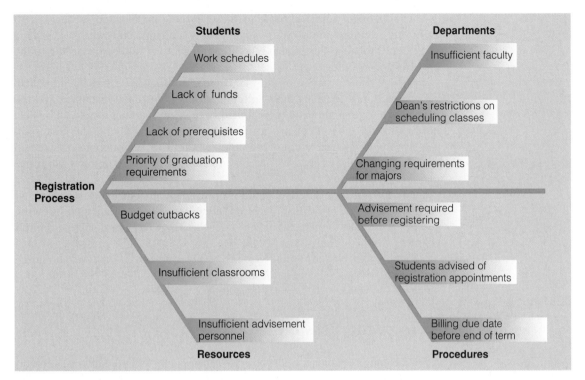

Figure 11.3 *Sample fishbone analysis of registration process to identify problems' causes and effects*

it when you see it." You might not. Establishing clear criteria is extremely important to your success.

To set criteria, first brainstorm a list of what conditions would be like if you had the perfect solution. If your task is to create a class project, for example, your criteria will include meeting the objectives of the assignment, the objectives for learning and grades, and the conditions that you, as a team, have decided to include in your project. For example, suppose you're on a creative team for a film-making class. Your criteria for an "ideal" project could look like this:

- Be original and unique.
- Involve each member in a specific role.
- Deal with a controversial or timely topic.
- Demonstrate skill in each area listed on the syllabus.
- Write a good script.
- Use graphics effectively.
- Cut and edit smoothly.
- Achieve demonstration quality for each member's portfolio.
- Have fun.
- Earn an "A" for each member.

As you might surmise, some of these criteria are dictated by the assignment, but some are the product of the team's thinking about what will make a good film. Probably, this team would add and subtract criteria according to the possible projects they might do.

Once you've drafted your criteria, try to *visualize* what things would be like with a solution that meets those criteria. All members need to understand the team vision of their work—a mental picture of what that final result will be like, how it will feel, what it will provide. As you visualize and discuss the ideal solution together, you clarify any misunderstandings or assumptions that could cause problems later on. Further, the vision you hold in common motivates members to achieve it.

For any potential solution, you'll want to consider four issues in particular: (1) applicability, (2) practicality, (3) advantages versus disadvantages and risks, and (4) desirability and ethicality. We'll develop these in more detail later in this chapter.

Finally, and very importantly, *record your criteria*. The criteria should be written clearly and unambiguously and posted—possibly in big print on a flipchart—so you can check potential solutions against your criteria.

Generating Possible Solutions

After carefully documenting a problem's causes, describing the effects, and noting the seriousness of their impact on people and operations, it's time to consider solutions. Generating possible solutions requires time, energy, and dedication. You need teamwork and creative thinking from all members to gather every imaginable solution. Use idea-generating approaches such as brainstorming to enlarge your list. Hold off judgment and criticism until you get as many ideas as possible on the table. Don't be afraid to get silly. You want quantity now; later, you'll evaluate the quality of the ideas.

When your team has a list of possible solutions and criteria, you're ready to make some decisions. It's easier to select the most appropriate solution when you use charting methods to visualize how each proposal measures on each of several critical issues. One useful technique is to prepare large charts of both the solution options and the criteria—on flipcharts, the blackboard, or taped-up butcher's paper.

Analysis Tools Two approaches to analyzing possible solutions can help your team work through these tasks together.

T-chart. One simple and effective way to keep everyone focused on the comparison is a T-chart. On a large sheet of paper or the blackboard, draw a T and label one side "Pros" and the other "Cons." As members make their observations about the merits of a solution, record them in the appropriate column. Figure 11.4 shows a sample T-chart for one possible solution for registration problems.

I have a few ideas. Together with yours, we may have something.

Max DePree, corporate founder, developer, CEO, and author

Figure 11.4 *Sample T-chart for analysis of one solution to registration problems*

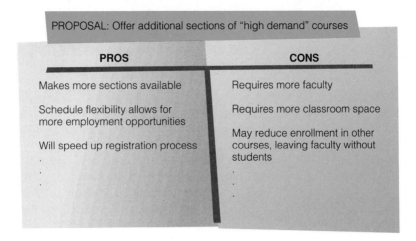

PROPOSAL: Offer additional sections of "high demand" courses

PROS	CONS
Makes more sections available	Requires more faculty
Schedule flexibility allows for more employment opportunities	Requires more classroom space
Will speed up registration process	May reduce enrollment in other courses, leaving faculty without students

Decision matrix. When you're comparing the merits of several solutions, a decision matrix lays out the information and jogs members' memories. As Figure 11.5 shows, a decision matrix is simply a large grid. Across the top, you label each column with one criterion from your list for the ideal solution. Down the left-hand side, you label each row with a designation for one possible solution. Then, as a team, you fill in the cells with notes as to how each plan meets each criterion. When you've completed the grid, you have a concise, easily comprehended set of comparisons for the proposals.

Once criteria are clearly established and visualized, your team can start examining critical issues. You need to focus on four areas: applicability, practicality, advantages versus disadvantages and risks, and desirability or ethicality.

Applicability How well a solution meets the criteria for solving a problem

Applicability Different solutions have varying levels of **applicability**—how well they may meet your criteria for solving the problem. For each possible choice, you want to predict the outcome against each criterion. You could consider:

- Will the proposed step solve the entire problem?
- If a proposal solves only part of the problem, how significant is that part?
- How does the idea compare to others on goal achievement?

Suppose your sorority wants to send the officers to a national meeting and needs to raise $5,000. Your brainstorming list of solutions includes a bake sale. Somebody will have to bake a lot of cookies for that solution to solve your problem. At this point, some proposals will clearly be inadequate and therefore be eliminated or at least combined with other possibilities.

Practicality The likelihood that a solution to a problem can be implemented successfully

Practicality Every possible solution can raise sticky issues of **practicality** that could keep them from being implemented successfully. These issues center on several areas:

Figure 11.5 *Decision matrix for comparing possible solutions*

Possible Solutions	Criterion #1: **Reduce waiting**	Criterion #2: **Use classroom space efficiently**	Criterion #3: **Have students get classes when needed**
Register by phone	Shorten wait Etc.	No effect Etc.	Immediate confirmation Etc.
Register online	No waiting Etc.	Yes—rooms assigned after all requests in Etc.	Little control over 2nd and 3rd choices Etc.
Register without advisors	Less wait, but reduces personal attention Etc.	No effect Etc.	Negative impact— may take wrong courses Etc.

- How much time and money will be required, and will they be available?
- What kinds of support from others (teams, agencies, parent organizations, individuals) will be necessary?
- What kinds of barriers will have to be overcome?
- Will it be possible to sell the idea to those who will implement it?

If any of these issues are significant barriers, then the idea can't be implemented. Sometimes, however, you see ways to adapt a proposal to solve practical issues. In these cases, evaluate whether the adapted proposal weakens the effectiveness of the plan and whether it is still superior to other plans.

Advantages, Disadvantages, and Risks Aside from simply solving the problem, implementing a solution may bring with it extra advantages, disadvantages, or risks. A proposal may solve the immediate problem but also have other positive or negative consequences. To identify both **advantages** and **disadvantages,** consider what could occur if the project were implemented. Some questions you could think about include:

- What effects would the implemented proposal have on individuals or groups other than those it is intended to affect?
- Would the advantages flow automatically from implementing the idea or require some other action?
- Would some minor modification eliminate some disadvantages?
- How do the advantages and disadvantages weigh against each other?
- How do the advantages and disadvantages weigh against those of other proposed solutions?

These questions clarify the advantages and disadvantages, as well as perhaps revealing some previously unconsidered risks in the proposal. **Risk** refers to the potential gains achieved in solving the problem weighed against the possi-

Advantages Positive effects of a solution to a problem

Disadvantages Negative consequences of a solution to a problem

Risk Potential gains of solving a problem weighted against potential losses

ble adverse consequences, such as costly or damaging results or even failure. Any innovative and potentially successful idea involves some risk. By definition, the new idea isn't proven by long experience, so it necessarily carries the possibility of failure. Without risk taking, therefore, there would be no new ideas, no progress, no exciting possibilities. The reality, however, is that people have to weigh the risks and make the most informed choices they can.

Desirability No matter how perfect a proposed solution may appear to be in terms of applicability, practicality, and so on, it may rise or fall depending on its desirability. **Desirability** judgments are based on the character of the proposal and the value systems of the team members involved. That is, you examine the relative worth of probable outcomes and the values and ethical choices that affect the decision. Here, values and goals come into play, as the decision makers debate how valuable and how worthwhile the goals are in terms of what it takes to implement a given plan.

Desirability The relative worth of a solution to a problem

A few years ago, an automobile manufacturer had considered, and rejected, a proposal to recall cars because the number of people *killed* due to its safety defect was not enough to justify the expense of recalling the cars. Management had weighed the number of deaths and the cost of possible lawsuits against the cost of recall and human lives lost. One may wonder how many lives would have been needed to tip the scale.

As your team looks at its proposals, ask some of these questions:

- How desirable are the probable effects of the proposal?

- Will the implemented proposal serve the team's vision?

- Will the proposal harm anyone spiritually, psychologically, physically, economically, and/or socially?

- Is any team member uncomfortable with the ethics of the proposal?

As you discuss ethical issues, you will find that some answers are easy. "No, that's against our values," or, "Yes, that's ethically defensible." Some issues, however, are not simple at all; they may present a dilemma when choices are among competing people and competing values (Toffler, 1986, pp. 21–22). You have an ethical dilemma, for example, when one team member believes a specific solution is unethical while another's values are violated by the only other practical alternative. How do you handle these competing values? First, team members must recognize that a dilemma exists by listening to and analyzing one anothers' ideas. Then, they must discuss the ethical issues and the relevant values and try to reach a consensus. Sometimes, resolving dilemmas requires a more objective outsider to facilitate the discussion.

As a team, consider in what ways alternative responses to the dilemma can be justified, and examine each set of reasons in the context of both individual and social codes of ethics. Jaksa and Pritchard (1994) point out that "seeking exact points of difference can help solve disagreements by eliminating false distinctions and evasions" (p. 17). Above all, don't brush the dilemma off with "Everyone's entitled to an opinion," or, "Value judgments are subjective." Such statements tend to bring a discussion to a quick end. Although these statements seem to express an attitude of tolerance, they also suggest that you do not have much to learn from one another.

Gouran (1982) suggests five questions that help a team examine the ethics of both its decisions and the processes by which it made them:

1 Did we show proper concern for those who will be affected by our decision?

2 Did we explore the discussion question as responsibly as we were capable of doing?

3 Did we misrepresent any position or misuse any source of information?

4 Did we say or do anything that might have unnecessarily diminished any participant's sense of self-worth?

5 Was everyone in the team shown the respect due him or her?

Decision Modes

Although a team could go on analyzing alternatives indefinitely, at some point it has to make some decisions. Take time to be sure everyone's clear on the merits and characteristics of each proposal and to clarify questions. This lets you get second thoughts out in the open and check whether everyone's in agreement.

Your method of deciding affects the fairness of the decision and members' satisfaction with it, so your team needs to consider your approach. All too often, teams fall into making "twofer" decisions: two people speak for a decision and the silence of other members is interpreted as consent. Twofer decisions lead to disgruntlement and lack of commitment. Better modes include decision by consensus, voting, and even decision by authority.

Consensus Agreement of all group members achieved by intensive discussion and negotiation

Consensus decisions. Theoretically, consensus represents the full agreement of every team member. Actually, **consensus** represents some degree of agreement by all members achieved through intensive discussion and negotiation. Individualistic North Americans are trying hard to learn the consensus techniques of the Japanese because they clearly work so well. Japanese teams typically hammer out decisions in exhaustive round-the-clock discussion until everyone agrees. This is a harrowing process, but once consensus is reached, decisions move swiftly with full support of all concerned. Striving for consensus is worth the effort, even if the final decision has to be made by another method. A team that achieves a high degree of consensus develops stronger commitment to its decisions and is more likely to follow through than a team that does not.

Voting. When the team, because of time constraints or strong disagreements, cannot reach consensus, voting is an option. Most North Americans are accustomed to a vote as a quick and easy method to decide between alternatives. If discussion has been thorough, and all individuals concerned have had an opportunity to express their ideas and feelings, most people are willing to accept a majority decision and go with it. Much too frequently, however, a majority vote is a cop-out, a lazy way of pushing to a conclusion without vigilant and vigorous problem analysis. Voting is quicker, but it leaves more people dissatisfied and results in less cooperation down the road than does a consensus decision.

Decision by authority. This means that the team only makes recommendations, and does not determine actions. In some cases, the team's function is to do the inquiry, think critically and creatively, make the recommendations, and wait for a decision. Someone with higher status, perhaps a manager, an executive committee, or the president of an organization, has the final say.

Creating Implementation Plans

Teams often have superb ideas, but when plans get put into action, some details are missing that prevent the solution from working. Successful implementation of an idea requires a carefully developed plan.

Implementing a proposal starts with reviewing the original goals and vision for the team's work. Maintain a mental picture of what the final product will look like while planning the implementation so that the end does not get obscured by the means. We suggest the following steps for developing your plan:

1   *Brainstorm a checklist.* Include everything that must be done to implement the proposal. Use the formula "who does what, when, where, how, and from what resources."

2   *Divide the checklist into categories.* For example:

- Resources needed: Money, information, technological support, permissions and cooperation from authorities, agencies, and organizations

- Actions that must be taken: Contacts, communication needs, materials to be obtained, applications for permissions or licenses, arrangements for space, guests, equipment, and so on

- Instrumental objectives for each action, step by step

- Person(s) responsible for each action

- Time required for each step

3   *Decide precisely who is responsible for completing each step.* Be specific, make sure each member commits to his or her responsibilities, put the list in writing, and make sure everyone has a copy. When you have implementation meetings, go over the checklist to see if things are being done and if revisions are necessary. Humans have a touching faith in their memories; unfortunately, it is often unjustified. No matter how many previous times a flight crew has flown a Boeing 747, we expect them to scrupulously review the flight safety checklist each time we are on board.

4   *Plan how to evaluate the proposal.* You will need objective, systematic feedback to know how well the solution works. Evaluations could include questionnaires and surveys directed to people affected by your plan and assessments by objective, expert observers.

Avoiding Groupthink

Even the best of teams can slide into what Janis (1983) calls **groupthink:** "a mode of thinking that people engage in when they are deeply involved in a cohesive group, when members' striving for unanimity overrides their motivation to realistically appraise alternative courses of action. . . . Groupthink refers to a deterioration of mental efficiency, reality testing, and moral judgment that results from in-group pressures" (p. 9). Groupthink is a kind of mindlessness, or perhaps single-mindedness, that blinds team members to everything except what they assume and want to be true.

When the space shuttle *Challenger* exploded just after takeoff, people were thunderstruck and wondered how this tragedy could have happened. As the inquiry proceeded, it became painfully obvious that information about a possible defect in an O-ring had been available, but the decision makers were shielded from the analysis that might have delayed the blast-off to correct the fatal flaw.

These people were not stupid; they were both the perpetrators and the victims of groupthink. Groupthink undermines the credibility of your work and reduces confidence in your decisions. Teams need to know how groupthink happens, how decisions are affected, and how to reduce its chances of occurring.

How Groupthink Happens

Groupthink can develop from certain previous team experiences or "antecedent conditions" involving cohesiveness as well as the structure and situation in which the team functions (Janis, 1989).

Cohesiveness. We have identified cohesiveness as a characteristic of outstanding teams, but cohesiveness can become a barrier to good decisions when members protect it at all costs. If nobody wants to introduce anything that could be disruptive, an unwritten "group harmony rule" silences dissenting members and problems are not discussed (Janis, 1989, pp. 56–58).

Structure. Structural conditions that make it easy to develop groupthink include homogeneity, inadequate group processes, and insulation from the outside world. Without diversity, like-minded members tend to think in narrow channels. Without vigilant decision-making processes, the team shortcuts critical-thinking steps and neglects impartial, principled leadership that could encourage members' openness to ideas and dissent. Insulation from outside information leaves members unaware of data and perspectives that might affect their decisions.

Situation. Situational stress can pressure a team into groupthink. Members are more likely to remain closed to new or different ideas when facing a crisis, threat, or high-stakes competition. This is particularly true if the team's leader advocates a solution and the members see no viable alternative. Situational stress is worse if the team's self-esteem is low because of recent failures or if the team faces an impossible task or a moral dilemma for which no solution meets members' ethical standards. A team in this depressed situation may accept alternatives that, as individuals or under other circumstances, the members might reject.

What Groupthink Does

Not all teams that experience some or all of the "antecedent conditions" fall into the groupthink trap. If they do, however, it shows up in their decision-making processes. Here are some warning signs of groupthink:

- *Illusion of invulnerability.* Members feel that their team is stronger than any counteracting forces. This leads them "to become over-optimistic and willing to take extraordinary risks and causes them not to respond to clear warnings of danger" (Janis, 1971, p. 225).

- *Belief in the team's inherent morality.* The team assumes it has "right" on its side, so anyone who is in opposition must necessarily be with the forces of "wrong." This belief builds a "we against them" mentality by stereotyping others as incompetent, inferior, or immoral.

- *Closed-mindedness and collective rationalizations.* Members resist new ideas and information and build rationalizations for their preconceived positions. They exclude or fail to get information that could increase their understanding, paying attention only to those facts that support a position they favor.

- *Self-censorship.* Team members rationalize their positions and don't allow themselves to say, or sometimes even to think, something that counters the team's thought or that might "rock the boat."

- *Pressure on dissenters.* Members exert pressure to conform on anyone who expresses a dissenting thought. Leaders may encourage this pressure by ignoring, downplaying, or even ridiculing a dissenting view.

- *Mindguards.* Just as bodyguards protect people from harm, mindguards protect leaders from hearing anything that might disturb or upset their viewpoint. Members deflect bearers of bad news and filter, distort, or hide information that might disturb groupthink illusions.

■ *Illusion of unanimity.* Members have an illusion that they all agree, which comes around full circle to reinforce all of the behaviors that led to the illusion in the first place (Janis, 1983, 1989).

These behaviors, which certainly protect a team's sense of self-esteem, superiority, cohesiveness, and strength, also create a stranglehold on the members' abilities to think rationally and critically. Scary, isn't it, when you consider that the failed U.S. invasion of Cuba in the Bay of Pigs fiasco, the Watergate scandal that led to the resignation of President Nixon, the Iran-Contra affair, the *Challenger* tragedy, and many more disastrous decisions were precipitated by groupthink (Jaksa & Pritchard, 1994).

Groupthink also besets less earth-shaking policies and actions. We remember a group of students who got together to study for an exam. Under stress but overconfident, they failed to research their topic and relied on one student's recollections without confirming them. As they talked, the students created a rubric of misconceptions that all members then used to write their exams. Their professors were boggled at the extent of the inaccuracies—and the students were shocked that they had done so poorly. Groupthink had convinced them that they had the right information.

How to Reduce Groupthink

Here are some groupthink-busting approaches to help avoid this blight on teamwork:

1 *Set norms.* Value openness, the right of dissent, and principled leadership.

2 *Test assumptions.* Examine assumptions about facts, values, or people. Look for evidence of illusions of invulnerability, moral superiority, or unanimity. Check for stereotyping of other groups and assumptions about others' behaviors or values.

3 *Scout for information.* Aggressively seek outside resources, experts, and relevant information to challenge members' views. Make it a team expectation that each member will discuss ideas with outside groups and communicate the responses to the team.

4 *Challenge ideas.* Have all members take the role of "critical evaluator," regularly challenging ideas, information, and suggestions. Appoint someone to be devil's advocate, arguing as persuasively as possible for the "other side" (Janis, 1989).

5 *Shift the structure.* Set up outside groups or subgroups to work separately on the same issues, and compare deliberations. Then regather the full team and hash out the results.

6 *Hold focus meetings.* Set up special meetings to focus on single issues when policy decisions may involve serious risks (Janis, 1989).

7 *Review.* Hold "second chance" meetings for people to review decisions and to raise new ideas or concerns about them (Janis, 1983).

At every stage, review and assess team processes to be sure that everyone is heard and that pressures to conform are within bounds. If all members are vigilant in avoiding groupthink traps, you can develop a cohesive, productive team that investigates and analyzes issues openly, clearly, and critically.

Summary

Good group decisions depend on every member's credible, principled leadership to help the group identify its purposes, define its goals specifically and clearly, plan and execute research, share information, and follow systematic, analytical steps to identify potential solutions.

An orderly process includes analyzing the problems and identifying possible causes and effects; establishing clear, specific criteria by which the group can later judge its potential solutions; and generating a range of ideas. The group then applies analytical techniques to determine whether each proposed solution will be applicable, practical, and advantageous or disadvantageous. This analysis must also examine possible risks and the desirability, or value, of the proposed decision. The group then decides on the best plan by consensus, majority vote, or authority. Finally, the group may make plans for implementing the decision and for following up with an evaluation.

Throughout this process, members must vigilantly avoid groupthink. Especially if the group is under stress, members may be highly cohesive and strive too hard for harmony, and this can lead to groupthink that blocks out information and hinders analysis. Members may believe they are invulnerable and morally superior to other groups, rationalizing their attitudes, becoming closed-minded, censoring themselves and others to block contrary ideas, or "mind-guarding" their leaders from hearing contradictory information. They may agree on a disastrous decision under the illusion that they are unanimous. Members can avoid groupthink by setting norms for vigilant analysis, testing assumptions, seeking full information, and challenging ideas, information, and suggestions. It helps to have someone play devil's advocate or to use outside groups, sub-groups, or focus meetings to shift the group's structure and expose different analyses. Finally, it is important to have special follow-up meetings to review, and possibly to revise, a decision after it has been made.

Exercises

1   Recall a time that you've been in a group (school, work, family, community) that had a problem to analyze and a decision to make. Using what you've learned in this chapter, reflect on the ways your experience relates to effective processes of analyzing problems, generating and analyzing solutions, making decisions, and implementing and assessing decisions.

2   With a group of classmates, select a recent procedural or legislative decision that has been made at some policy level (for example, student government; college administration; local, state, or federal government). Investigate the process by which the decision was reached using interviews, articles, minutes, and so on. As a group, analyze the process and answer these questions:

- How effectively did the decision makers use the steps of problem solving and decision making?

- To what extent did you see signs of groupthink in the process? What were the signs? What were the causes? What were the effects?

Prepare a report of your investigation to make to the class.

3   Form a small classroom group. Assume you are a task force in a large corporation. Your attention has been called to issues related to these facts:

- The plant is in a rural industrial park.

- The closest town is 10 miles away.

- Sometimes, people who have families seem distracted.

- The town has one small day-care center.

- Two churches have preschools that operate until five o'clock.

- The company has no maternity/paternity-leave benefits.

- Many employees live 20 or more miles away.

- Parents of small children are frequently late or absent.
- Parents of older children miss many school holidays.
- Some personnel have left the company when they started families.
- Recent productivity declines are primarily among people ages 25–45, normally a productive age group.
- Morale in the company is low.

   a   Using this information, analyze the problem(s) these facts suggest and create a fishbone diagram to illustrate the causes and effects of the problems.

   b   Using the cause-effect diagram you created, set goals your task force would like to achieve and establish criteria for a satisfactory solution. Then generate possible solutions to the problems and create an implementation and assessment plan.

   c   Report your analysis and plans to the class.

4   Observe a group or team as the members try to solve a problem. This could be a college or community committee, a work team, and so on. Click on Chapter 11 at the *Communicating with Credibility and Confidence* Web site at http://communication.wadsworth.com/lumsden. You will find Form 11.1, which you can use as a guide to analyze the team's processes. What worked well? What didn't? Where did members seem to conform to what you've learned in this chapter? Where did they not?

Make a brief oral report to the class on your findings. Identify the most important thing this group did well and the processes it used to achieve it. Also identify one place where the decision-making sequence broke down and what members might have done to work through the difficulty.

Cyberpoints

CCC

WEB SITE

1   Need some help with researching your topic? Go to http://trochim. human.cornell.edu/index.html—Bill Trochim's Center for Social Research Methods at that site provides a full range of information and help.

2   Looking for additional library resources? According to Morreale (April, 2001), the following are the top ten libraries on the Web: (1) Internet Public Library: www.ipl.org; (2) LibWeb: sunsite.Berkeley.edu/libweb; (3) Library Spot: www.libraryspot.com; (4) Stanford Univ; www-sul. Stanford.edu; (5) Univ. of CA: infolib.berkeley.edu; (6) Harvard College Library: www.hcl.harvard.edu; (7) Yale Univ: www.library.yale.edu; (8) UCLA Library: www.library.ucla.edu; (9) Carnegie Mellon: www. library.cmu.edu; and (10) Penn State: www.libraries.psu.edu. Morreale, S. Morreale's Mailbag, (April, 2001) Morreale's Mailbag, *Spectra, 11*, 4.

Chapter 12

Research and Development: Creating Public Speeches

Objectives for This Chapter

Knowledge

- Understand how speech preparation affects credibility and confidence
- Know the steps for preparing and organizing a public speech
- Understand approaches for selecting and refining a speech topic
- Know how to research and use supporting material for speeches

Feelings and Approaches

- Recognize the importance of research and development for a speech
- Feel confident in your abilities to research and develop a speech
- Appreciate a speech as a creative product resulting from extensive work
- Value the confident feeling generated by thorough preparation

Communication Abilities

- Select and refine a topic for a speech with a specific purpose
- Identify audience characteristics relevant to a particular speech occasion
- Research and organize material to reach the goals of a speech
- Develop speeches that increase self-confidence and credibility

Key Terms

speech to inform
speech to persuade
thesis statement
audience analysis
demographics

psychographics
research
speech body
organizational pattern
speech introduction

speech conclusion
transition
supporting material
visual message

A good speech is like a good business—both rely heavily on research and development. Known as R & D in the business world, research and development is the key to creating new ideas or products to stay competitive.

R & D also is critical to your success as a public speaker. You will be more confident when you are thoroughly prepared and know what you're talking about. And you'll certainly be more credible with a speech you've structured clearly with well-supported ideas.

Effective presentations are products of intensive preparation. President Woodrow Wilson, who took pride in his public speaking, was once asked by a reporter, "How long does it take you to prepare a 10-minute speech?" Wilson thought for a moment and replied, "About two weeks." "How long, then, does it take you to prepare an hour's speech?" the reporter probed. Wilson answered, "About a week." The reporter pursued it further. "What about a two-hour speech?" "I could make that right now," Wilson quickly responded.

The "public" in public speaking provides an important perspective. You "go public" through your speeches, providing a window through which others see you and assess your competence and credibility. Of course, that's one reason public speaking creates such high anxiety. But speeches are also opportunities to demonstrate your command of information and situations. That's why your R & D requires serious attention.

Speech R & D follows a simple process—simple, but not easy. Preparation uses your analysis and creativity through nine essential steps; a shortcut at any point will make success less likely.

1   Determine your topic and purpose.

2   Analyze your audiences.

3   Gather research information.

4   Select material to include.

5   Organize your ideas.

6   Develop your ideas to achieve your goal.

7   Plan visuals to supplement your text.

8   Prepare speaking notes.

9   Rehearse your presentation.

This chapter guides you through the first seven of these steps. Chapter 13 covers the last two R & D stages.

Determining Your Topic and Purpose

If you're like our students, you wish you could find the "perfect" topic for your classroom speech, something to seize the audience's interest and hold them spellbound. "Perfect" topics are not discovered, however; speakers create them. You no doubt have heard dull speeches about potentially fascinating issues and mesmerizing speeches about seemingly boring subjects.

Your subject selection depends partly on your goals. This section guides you through selecting the topic and clarifying your purpose.

Selecting a Topic

In the "real world," a speaking commitment usually includes some expectation about your topic. Students have a wider choice for their classroom speeches, but they may wrestle so long with selecting a topic that they have too little time to develop their speech adequately. Here are some ideas to help you in your quest for a topic:

Your own interests. Consider your hobbies, reading interests, work experiences, organizational memberships, or places you've visited. One of our students, a dedicated mountain biker, spoke on the sport and the controversies that impinge upon it.

Family background and heritage. Everyone's roots provide unique ethnic, cultural, and historical issues that you could research further. A student of Irish heritage, for example, might speak on historical, religious, or geographic topics relating to Ireland.

Ideas from other courses. You might use this chance to delve into something a professor said that sparked your interest. A geography instructor once mentioned that there is still more gold in the California mountains than was mined since the Gold Rush years. That led a student to speak about the current status of gold mining in the state.

Social or political issues. Look for a topic that interests you in media coverage of social causes and pending legislation. One student, inspired by discussion about roles in the military for people who are gay or lesbian, developed her speech about the need for laws protecting equal rights for people with different sexual orientations.

The topic you select should meet six important criteria:

Time limits. Usually, you have a time limit, and you need to plan a talk you can really communicate within that limitation. For instance, in five minutes you might be able to explain finding a good travel buy on the Internet, but you couldn't describe a two-week tour of Europe.

Resource availability. Research materials should be readily available to you. Some sources may be available through interlibrary loans, but you'll want to avoid subjects for which essential materials are in special collections some distance away.

Spirited interest. You need enough enthusiasm about your topic to communicate interest, concern, or involvement to your audience—if you're bored, your audience will be, too. Find something you think is exciting or intriguing.

Occasion. Frequently, the topic is dictated by the circumstances of the event. A holiday celebration, your fraternity's or sorority's anniversary dinner, or a wedding toast dictate your topic but allow creativity in your approach.

Purpose. If you want to inform your audience, you start with what they know and expand it from there; if you want your listeners to *change,* you need to give them reason and motivation to shift their attitude or behaviors from their present status.

Adaptability to audience. A topic may be new to your listeners, but you need to draw on their backgrounds and motivations to interest them, perhaps taking them to another level of understanding without stretching them impossibly far beyond their present knowledge or attitudes.

Even a very good subject may be too broad for the time limit on your speech, so you'll need to narrow it. (Skipping this step is one reason President Wilson required less preparation time for a longer speech.) You narrow a topic by getting more and more specific until you reach a manageable scope. Think of the process as an inverted pyramid, moving from broader, abstract to very concrete issues. Figure 12.1 provides three examples of narrowed topics.

Let's develop the broad subject of "crime" into a workable speech topic and then identify a specific purpose for the speech. The topic of crime can take us in several directions, so we'll start with rehabilitation of prisoners. Refining the topic might begin with the general level of *crime* and narrow to the more specific topic, *repeat offenders*. You might narrow it with more specificity to *lack of rehabilitation for offenders* and even further to *how prisons prepare inmates for independent living and self-management,* and, more specific yet, *training prisoners to take greater financial responsibility.*

Determining Your Purpose

People often describe a speaking task in terms of what they have to *do*. They say, "I have a report to give," or, "I have to prepare a five-minute speech." These statements focus on the task or the product rather than on the intended

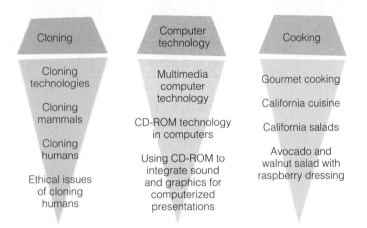

Figure 12.1 *Three broad topics narrowed for speech time limits*

Cloning
- Cloning technologies
- Cloning mammals
- Cloning humans
- Ethical issues of cloning humans

Computer technology
- Multimedia computer technology
- CD-ROM technology in computers
- Using CD-ROM to integrate sound and graphics for computerized presentations

Cooking
- Gourmet cooking
- California cuisine
- California salads
- Avocado and walnut salad with raspberry dressing

effects. You'll be more effective if you focus on the *results* expected from your presentations. The critical issues are these: *Why* do you have a speech to prepare, and *what* do you want the speech to accomplish? Even if getting an "A" grade is your personal goal, you need a focused purpose for your speech topic, perhaps, "To get the oversight committee to approve our proposal for prisoner training."

No matter what the specific purpose, all speeches have the goal of getting listeners to change in some way. That change may be to increase listeners' knowledge (when you speak to inform) and/or to influence them to shift their attitudes, values, beliefs, and/or behaviors (when you speak to persuade).

These two goals—informing and persuading—often overlap. All persuasion must provide some information so listeners can understand your arguments, and all informative speaking must in some way persuade people to listen and value what you are teaching them. Nonetheless, we will talk about informative and persuasive speaking separately to help you learn how to approach each task.

Speech to inform Public speaking that provides listeners with information or shows relationships among material

Speeches to Inform A **speech to inform** provides listeners with new information or shows them new relationships among known material. These speeches may teach a process, a skill, or ideas; they may provide background and facts that let people mentally experience new places or that increase their understanding of a subject.

You seek to inform when you coach a team, report on your research, talk about a trip you took, or discuss a book you read. Managers explain health benefit plans to employees; religious workers teach their doctrine to potential or actual followers; judges instruct juries; people give directions for getting to specific locations; and parents share the family history with their children. Chapter 14 focuses on special considerations for these speeches.

Speech to persuade Public speaking that seeks to alert listeners' attitudes, values, beliefs, or behavior

Speeches to Persuade A **speech to persuade** seeks to get listeners to alter their attitudes, values, beliefs, and/or behaviors—to influence new thinking and actions. You provide information, but you take your listeners further to convince

When you get people to listen to what you believe, you get on fire yourself—big fires, little fires—that never do go out. I met Everett Dirkson in the airport in St. Louis, one of the greatest speakers of the day. He said, "You are a great speaker. I know. I've heard you."

"Where was it?" I asked.

"I forget the circumstances," he answered, "but you said the following. . . ." and he repeated what I had said verbatim. That is the greatest compliment you can have as a speaker. It lights a real fire in you.

I remember a young fellow who wanted me to advise him on how to be a good speaker! I told him, "Be interesting, be enthusiastic, and don't talk too much!"

Norman Vincent Peale, from L. Walters, *Secrets of Successful Speakers*, p. xiii. Copyright © 1993 The McGraw Hill Companies, Inc.

---

them that established ways of thinking or doing things must change; that your proposals provide best ways to satisfy that need, and that the proposed changes are consistent with their attitudes, values, and goals.

Persuasive communication is an essential part of democratic societies and capitalistic economies. Politicians influence voters to elect them, lobbyists work to influence legislators, and legislators seek to influence one another. Salespeople influence buying decisions, teachers influence students to complete assignments, to aspire to higher goals, and to develop self-esteem. Chapter 15 develops strategic approaches particularly suited to persuasive speeches.

Speeches for Special Occasions We mentioned earlier that speeches often are for particular occasions. Let's look at a few special occasions:

Introducing a speaker. Usually the audience knows who is to speak, but your job as introducer is to talk about factors that enhance the speaker's credibility. It's best to summarize (briefly) the speaker's expertise as it relates to the occasion, mention special awards or recognition the speaker has received, and refer to the speaker's background, experiences, perhaps special projects, that may provide common ground with the audience.

Presenting an award. The critical information to include in presenting an award are the criteria for earning the recognition and a brief summary of how the recipient's achievement demonstrates them. If the audience doesn't already know who the award winner is, you may want to build suspense by withholding the person's name until the end of your presentation.

Accepting an award. Receiving an award is an honor, but it focuses the spotlight on you in ways that can make you especially nervous. You've probably watched media award winners, such as for the Oscars, go on and on with disorganized thank-yous. Short and sweet should be the rule here. If you're surprised, say so, but also express your pride—don't cover it under a cloak of humility. Thank those who confer the award and *very few* others who are important to this recognition, and indicate any ways in which the award might challenge you in your future efforts.

Entertaining. Most speeches should have some entertainment value to keep audiences listening, but some presentations are purely to entertain. They can range from stand-up comedy to a dramatic reading. Each requires you to have a sense of your role and the audience's expectations.

Speaking after dinner. Combining a meal with a presentation is challenging for the speaker. People tend to relax after eating—perhaps even to want a nap—and that makes them a tough audience to engage. You need dynamism and appropriate humor to grab and hold attention. Frequently, an after-dinner speech serves as entertainment, and the audience expects lighter, more humorous fare. When you can, get your audience involved in your speech in some way: give them a task to perform, solicit questions, or interact with them to keep them energized.

Making a business presentation. At work or in class, you will present research findings and proposals—often as part of a team, so you need both teamwork skills (covered in the previous two chapters) and presentational skills. You and your team will cooperate to develop the content, assign specific responsibilities for each part of the speech, and rehearse together. An advantage is that you can take turns speaking, and this variety can help keep your audience's interest.

Stating Your Thesis

Thesis statement
Declarative sentence that states the central idea of a speech

The refinement of your topic and clarification of your purpose leads you to a **thesis statement,** a clear, concise declarative sentence stating the central idea of your speech. The thesis expresses the idea you want your audience to understand or to act on. The statement must be specific enough to identify the precise ideas, yet general enough to summarize the speech's content. The speech on the refined topic of crime, for example, might have this thesis: "Prisoners need to develop greater financial responsibility while incarcerated."

A thesis statement can include more details about the speech's main points—for example, "Prisoners should develop greater financial responsibility by paying for some of their living expenses while in jail, by reimbursing victims, and by planning financially for their release." The statement is still general, but specifies the three main points that will be developed in the speech.

A clear thesis statement helps you identify specific issues you will need to develop in your speech. An examination of our sample detailed thesis statement suggests the following issues you may need to cover:

- Is developing prisoners' financial responsibility desirable?
- Does greater financial responsibility enhance self-esteem?
- Does greater financial responsibility reduce recidivism (chances of returning to prison)?
- Can prisoners pay any part of their living expenses?
- Can prisoners reimburse victims?
- Can prisoners plan for their finances after release?
- Does paying for one's living expenses help develop financial responsibility?
- Does reimbursing one's victims help develop financial responsibility?
- Does financial planning for one's release help develop financial responsibility?

Analyzing Your Audience

The more you know about your listeners, the better you can tailor your messages to win their understanding and acceptance of your ideas. Corporations spend large sums to research customer preferences for marketing a new product. Political campaigns take daily polls to track subtle shifts in voters' attitudes. You might not be able to use these audience analysis techniques for your speeches, but you will need to get as much information as you can about your audience's characteristics and expectations.

Audience Characteristics

Audience analysis
Process of examining the characteristics of proposed listeners

Demographics External characteristics of a group: age, sex, ethnicity, income, education

Psychographics Internal characteristics of a group: attitudes, values, needs

Audience analysis examines the demographic and psychographic characteristics of your listeners. **Demographics** categorize people according to external attributes: age, sex, ethnicity, income, educational level. **Psychographics** categorize people based on internal factors: attitudes, values, needs. These analyses tell you what to include and what angle to take in your speech. Be careful not to make assumptions about people based on stereotypes about their identity groups, but try to learn about their:

Knowledge. How much does the audience know about the topic? What they already know helps you determine how much background to give your audience for a clear frame of reference. Obviously, well-informed individuals with a prior interest in the topic require less introductory material than do those who know little about it.

Audiences differ widely. In which of these photos would you suspect the audience members to have the most in common? Why? How many different audience characteristics can you identify in these groups? What characteristics can you not identify in a photo? What does the presence of cameras and microphones suggest to you about audiences?

Spencer Grant/Photo Researchers, Inc.

Bob Daemmrich/The Image Works

Attitude. What is the audience's present attitude about the subject? If listeners already tend to support your position, then you need to focus more on reinforcing and strengthening their attitudes. If you intend to "sell" a proposal to people who might oppose it, however, then your presentation must change their attitudes with more documentation and strategic appeals.

Values. What audience values are relevant to the issues? People try to act in ways consistent with their values, and sometimes you have to show the audience that your ideas are grounded in their values. For example, if you propose to the college president and board of trustees that the college invest in its music program, you might choose to spotlight the economic value of potential alumni contributions, or the public relations benefits that might accrue—depending on how important to your audience you believe each approach might be.

Expectations. What does your audience expect of this presentation? Brief or long? Formality or informality? If you speak for 30 minutes to a group that expected a 15-minute presentation, for instance, or if you are breezily informal in a more formal situation, your audience may be annoyed and your credibility may suffer. Before you prepare a speech, ask what is expected. Start with your speaking assignments for this class. Suppose you present a brilliant 10-minute, memorized persuasive speech—but your instructor is grading you on an assignment for a five-minute informative speech, using notes, that includes three different sources and visuals. You might be disappointed in your grade.

Sensitivity. What issues are sensitive? The approach and the language of your speech should always reflect sensitivity to issues of gender and culture. We've seen well-meaning people undermine their presentations with tasteless jokes, thoughtless cartoons, and inappropriate examples. Sexist or racist language and material offensive to members of other cultures or identity groups both reduce your credibility and adversely affect the listeners' response to the content.

Audience Analysis Sources

Getting reliable information about your audience requires the application of good research techniques. Here are some ideas:

Asking. Talk with people who know your audience members. Start with the person who arranged for you to speak. For example, one of our colleagues was asked to talk to the student council about using parliamentary procedure. He prepared by asking several council members and the group's advisor about procedures they used, problems they encountered, their familiarity with the topic, and their level of concern over the issue.

Reading. Obtain literature—newsletters, mission statements—from the group to gain insight into the organization's values and priorities, as well as other activities to which you can relate your material.

Observing. Think about your classroom speeches. You spend time with this audience each week. What have you learned about their interests and backgrounds? What do they know that you can use as a foundation for enhancing their understanding of your topic?

Researching Your Speech

The computer term *GIGO* (garbage in, garbage out) applies to building a speech as well—you only turn out a good speech when good information goes into it. You build a speech on finding, evaluating, and recording good information.

Finding Research Information

Facts do not cease to be because they are ignored.

Aldous Huxley, 20th-century American writer

Before you even start your research, please, please plan your approach to documenting what you find. Remember that you will need to quote and attribute your sources accurately, and you may need to go back and check something. With that in mind, keep a clear, well-organized record of your notes and their sources—these could be on note cards, a voice recorder, a photocopy, or a print from a scanner/computer. Every note needs to include the name of the source, qualifications, author of the material (if it's a secondary source), article title, publication title, date, page numbers, publisher, and specific information from the material; if the source is electronic, you need the name of the production, the artist, director, or creator; copyright date; and specific information from the material.

Research Process of finding answers to questions through information from various sources

With that plan ready, you can start your **research,** which is simply the process of finding answers to questions through information from various sources. Good research asks penetrating questions and finds credible sources of information to answer them. Earlier in this chapter, we discussed how your thesis statement leads you to identify the issues you need to consider for your speech. That analysis also provides you with questions to answer with research (and sometimes, research leads you to modify your thesis).

Credible information can come from a variety of sources—electronic, print, and human.

Electronic Sources of Information   Most libraries have collections of films, videos, and audiotapes, including CD-ROM discs that incorporate many of the other resources listed here, as well as multimedia resources that can be accessed with a computer.

As for the Net: We have to acknowledge up front that the e-world is changing so fast that anything we write about it will be obsolete by the time this book is in print. Anything, that is, except problems with using it, which will not be resolved that quickly.

Nonetheless, the Web is a vast source of information on just about anything and probably, like many students, it's your habit to go there first when you need information. Useful sites to look for are:

Organizational and government Web sites for information on products, issues, research, or enterprises.

News groups that maintain bulletin boards for various topics, transmitted through an electronic bulletin board system, *Usenet*. There are over 20,000 News groups (Carlson, 1997, p. 1049). "News groups are organized in categories called hierarchies, in which each level is separated by a period. These levels become more specific after each period. For example, "soc. culture. african.american" is a social news group with an interest in African American cultural issues" (Muhammad, March, p. 37).

University files and programs that provide anything from library indices to departmental or university information. Many universities now have developed special discs to guide students through research methods in given fields or across the university, and some of these, such as those at Cornell University or Purdue University, are available to you on the Web.

Advertised addresses that organizations relevant to your interests have published in newspapers, magazines, journals. You may or may not find what you want, but there's a better chance that the site address will be current if you find it advertised in a current publication.

Print Sources of Information   Some things actually are not available electronically and some are easier to read and ponder in print. Most libraries list research sources in computerized databases; these include:

Books.   Still "best friends" for some of us, books are great for discovering just the right quotation, insight, or reference for a speech.

Reference works.   These include encyclopedias, atlases, almanacs, and related resources, many or most of which also are available electronically.

Documents.   If anything exists, some governmental agency has probably studied it and reported the findings. Some libraries are designated as depositories and receive all documents published by the federal government. Again, most of these are available online or on library discs as well.

Periodicals.   Indexes, including many on computer discs (such as Socio File and Psych Lit), lead you to resources from professional journals, magazines, and newspapers. You will need to identify the key words for your subjects to guide your search.

Human Sources of Information   People can help you enormously in finding and understanding information. For example:

Reference librarians.   These people are experts on tracking down resources, and most of them get great satisfaction from applying their expertise to help a student.

Yourself. You may have taken a course, traveled to a relevant location, or developed knowledge through a hobby that relates to your topic. This gives you a lively, interesting view that you can supplement with other resources to give you a broader sample.

Surveys. You can expand your knowledge with a survey of your classmates, fellow employees, or a larger group. Focus your survey directly on the questions you seek to answer for your speech. Although you usually can only generalize your findings to the group you survey, when that group is your audience the responses are directly relevant.

Interviews. Your campus is filled with experts on a wide range of subjects—professors—who, as well as experts in the community, are willing to talk to students. Interviews, either face to face or by phone, can give you firsthand information. Sometimes, you can get permission to tape-record your interview and use a short excerpt in your speech.

Evaluating Research Information The challenge is to sort through the information you get so you aren't putting garbage in. We talked about some of this in Chapter 3, but we want to remind you, first, to examine a source's qualifications, reputation, and ethical behavior; if any of these is questionable, so is what the source says.

Remember, too, that Web sites are not necessarily reviewed by anyone; information could be accurate, or it could be fabricated. One authority says that articles on the Internet can be considered reliable if they are "written and/or issued by an authoritative source such as the federal government or a reliable organization . . . authenticated as part of an editorial or peer review process by a publisher . . . [and/or] . . . evaluated by experts, reviewers, or subject specialists/ librarians as part of collection development" (Brandt, 1996, p. 44). Check the header, body, and footer on a Web page to find out the author, the source, and whether the source is a moderated or unmoderated list, or even an anonymous site. You also can check online directory sources to find out about the source's affiliations and biographical information (Brandt, 1996, p. 46).

When it's possible, use a *primary* source, the first publication or person to provide information. A *secondary* source (one that repeats or summarizes the original material) is an abstraction or compilation of information and, because it's one step or more removed, it may contain inaccuracies or biases. For example, *Readers' Digest* articles often are abstracted from other publications. Newspaper articles and television reports are the writer's synthesis and interpretation of events. Examine your information to see if it is consistent with other findings or if it stands out as an exception. Differing points of view should be noted and evaluated, but, generally, the thinking that has greater consistency with other findings tends to provide more dependable answers to your research questions.

Finally, check the timeliness of the information. Sometimes, old information is fine—for example, contemporaneous reports of historical events and

The Internet makes name-calling too quick and easy . . . and online critics rarely let the facts stand in the way of a strong opinion.

Joe Henderson, in Screen Ravers, *Runner's World,* November, 1997, p. 20.

quotations from original sources. More recent information, however, is often more reliable than older data. Research findings grow, and later studies may build upon or contradict earlier studies. Information about television in the 1980s, for instance, may not apply to today's programming.

Organizing Your Ideas

Speech body Main content or substance of a speech

All the good stuff you've collected must be sifted and framed in such a way that your audience can understand it and accept it. Your intuition may be to prepare the introduction, body, and conclusion in that order, but ignore your intuition. The best way is to start with the **speech body,** the substance of it, structured with main points and subpoints.

Only after you have clearly delineated and organized your main points do you create an introduction to prepare the audience for what follows and a conclusion to provide a strong closing. Then you develop transitions to communicate clearly the relationships among these major sections as well as among the main points, subpoints, and supporting material.

Speech Body

As you'll recall, well-organized messages are easier for listeners to process and understand. Miller (1956) explains that people process information in "chunks," or groups of related items. This concept should guide your approach to organizing the body of your speeches.

Organizational pattern Structure that shows how ideas relate to one another and lead to a conclusion

Organizational Patterns . An **organizational pattern** is a structure that shows how ideas relate to one another and lead to a conclusion. The main ideas that support your thesis may be organized in a linear order. Or they may follow a more conceptual approach that relates various parts of the topic to a larger whole, or use a psychological strategy designed to move the audience from where they are to where you want them to be. Patterns include:

Chronological organization is a linear design that links ideas or events sequentially, such as past to present to future or through a step-by-step process. A speech that teaches or demonstrates how to do something normally has this structure.

Spatial or geographic organization relates ideas in terms of space. A report on the U.S. economy could be organized by major regions (Northeast, South, Midwest, and West) or you organize a speech about your college in terms of the activities in various buildings: Travis Hall, Williams Lounge, and Melendez Center.

Parts-to-whole or topical organization develops related ideas under the same main topic. If a speech answers the who, what, when, where, why,

Figure 12.2 *Sample
division of a thesis
statement into its
main points*

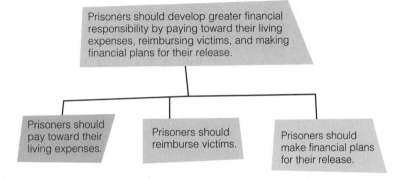

and how of an issue or event, it uses this structure because each answer is a
"part" of the whole story. Or dividing an issue into political, economic, and
environmental aspects of an issue uses a parts-to-whole pattern.

Ascending or descending organization orders ideas in numerical order, size,
or status. David Letterman's "Top 10" lists are always presented in ascending order—from Number 10 to Number 1—the "top" of the hierarchy. Or
a descending-order speech about taxes could flow from federal to state to
county to local governments.

Problem-solution organization divides the speech in two main ideas: a perceived problem and ways to solve it. Sometimes, you can add a third main
point, the advantages or benefits of the proposed solution.

Logical format organization subdivides the ideas into in a sequence that
reflects a pattern of reasoning. For example, the points could be divided
between cause and effects (or effects and causes).

Organizational Process Developing the organization of your speech is
detailed work. The first step is to sort your research notes into groups, one for
each general idea. The theme of each group suggests main points for the body
of the speech, as shown in Figure 12.2.

The next step is to structure the material within each main point. Take the
notes for each main division and separate them into subcategories. This provides the subpoints for the main points. Figure 12.3 gives an example of the
results of this step.

The process of creating subdivisions continues until all material you want to
use is in place. As you divide the information into categories, keep these principles in mind:

■ *Use no more than five major chunks for any division.* That's about all people can process when they hear it; after all, there is no instant replay. So the
speech should present a maximum of five main points, and each main point
should contain no more than five subpoints.

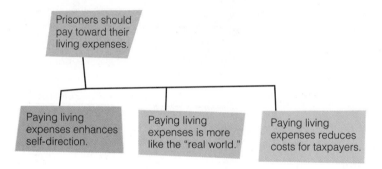

Figure 12.3 *Sample subdivision of a main point into subpoints*

Prisoners should pay toward their living expenses.

Paying living expenses enhances self-direction.

Paying living expenses is more like the "real world."

Paying living expenses reduces costs for taxpayers.

- *Show clear relationships among the parts within any subdivision.* All "chunks" within a group should link clearly to one another in keeping with the organizational pattern. You would not organize main ideas into "past, present, future, and implications," for example, because the first three chunks are chronological and "implications" is inconsistent with the time sequence pattern. Mixing the categories upsets the relationships and makes it harder for an audience to follow and comprehend.

Under each main point, however, you could use a different pattern of sub-points. That is, a first main point, "the past," might fall into subpoints of who, what, and where in a parts-to-whole pattern. Under the second main point, "the present," you might use another pattern, such as spatial; just follow the basic principle that each grouping or subdivision should include only subpoints that are clearly related to one another.

At this stage in developing your speech, look over your structure to find any gaps in information or logic. Often, you will find that you need more informa-tion on some issue, and this is the time to go get it. Even so, because you have been intensely involved in the topic, you could know much more about it than the audience. That can lead to underestimating the amount of explanation and supporting material your listeners will need to understand connections that are obvious to you. You don't want to insult the intelligence of your audience, but neither do you want to overestimate their level of prior knowledge.

A final consideration is whether your speech will be the right length for the time allotted. You may need to cut some material. If so, first look for entire sec-tions to eliminate rather than bits and pieces throughout. Even if you must cut an entire main point, that's usually better than trying to cover too much in too little time to develop each idea sufficiently.

Speech Introductions

Now that the speech is mapped out, you can think about the introduction. It's like the first class day of a new term when the professor asks you to introduce someone to the class. Don't you need to meet the person first and find out some things about him or her? That's why introductions should be prepared *after* developing the body, when you are familiar with what you are introducing.

Furthermore, when you have a plan for the speech you have a better idea of how to get it started. As a general guideline, your introduction should take about 10% of your total speaking time. In a five-minute speech, you have only about 30 seconds to achieve several important objectives.

Objectives An effective **speech introduction** is an opening that gets the audience's attention and sets them firmly on the path into your thinking. For most speeches, four goals are paramount:

Gaining the audience's attention. You need to pull the focus away from whatever might be on the listeners' minds and involve them immediately in your speech topic.

Motivating the audience to stay tuned. Many years ago, Borden (1935) warned that listeners are always thinking, "So what?" or, "Who cares?" So the presenter must find ways to tell the audience "what's in it for them" and make them see how they will benefit from listening to you.

Establishing your credibility. You may show your goodwill and coorientation with the audience by sharing a common experience relevant to the topic and by showing your sincere interest in your audience and topic. You can also demonstrate your competence by relating, subtly, your experience with the topic, perhaps referring to how your interest has led to careful research.

Focusing your topic. The introduction should point out where your presentation will take the audience. It helps an audience if you *preview the specific main points of the speech.* For example, you might say, "I'll first discuss the scope of the trade deficit with Japan, and then look at ways it might be reduced." You might tell your audience what you will *not* cover, for instance, "I won't cover all aspects of the U.S. international trade deficits—I will look only at those with Japan." This represents the first step in the proverbial advice to speakers: "Tell them what you are going to tell them, then tell them, then tell them what you've told them."

Types of Material If you don't hook your audience in the first few moments, you might never get them. Recall that human beings can pay attention to only one thing at a time (Howes, 1990, p. 71). You have a brief moment when listeners pay attention simply because you've gotten up and faced them—and that's the moment you must bring their attention directly to your speech.

You can select your introduction from a wide variety of options:

Reference to the occasion. Tie your speech to the circumstances surrounding the speaking event. A college recruiter speaking to a high school senior class, for example, might say, "They tell me this is 'college week' at Hampton High. This is the week you go crazy, trying to decide about the next four or five years of your life. Maybe I can help."

Speech introduction
Opening of a speech, designed to get the audience's attention and prepare them to listen to the topic

---

The Romans said, "Exemplum docet," which translated means, "The example teaches." And it teaches best. . . . Fill your talks with examples and illustrations.

Robert Montgomery, motivational speaker and communication consultant

---

Reference to the audience. Comments about your audience can help establish coorientation and goodwill. In a classroom speech, you might recall experiences from your class that relate to your topic or offer sincere compliments to class-mates. At a meeting of professionals, a speaker commented, "As I talked with you before dinner, I was impressed by the supportive feeling in this room. It's great to be with people who care about one another the way you do."

Startling or challenging statement. You can phrase ideas in surprising or novel ways to highlight the scope or impact of an issue: "Look around you. There are 50 people in this room. The statistics from a local poll suggest that 25 of you drove drunk even before you graduated from high school." This should get attention and make your audience want to know more.

Narrative. A narrative is a brief story that sets the scene or the tone for the speech. A student in her 40s used the following introduction to her speech: "About 20 years ago, Elizabeth faced a tough decision. She found out she was pregnant. Her husband had just left her and she already had a young child. She knew she could not depend on her ex-husband for any help, and she had no job nor source of support. After careful consideration and consultation, she decided to have an abortion. It was a difficult decision, but at least she was able to do it legally, privately, and with minimal additional anguish." The student then developed her presentation about protesters' harassment and violence at abortion clinics.

Quotation. A quotation can serve several purposes: to intrigue your audience, to recount a startling statement, or to relate material that appeals to audience values and needs. An appropriate quotation also helps establish your credibility on the topic. Perhaps you're introducing a speech on the need for bipartisan solutions to social problems. You might open with, "In Africa, the Kikuyu have a saying: 'When the elephants fight, it is the grass that suffers.' In the United States, the elephants are trampling on the needs of American citizens."

Rhetorical questions. A rhetorical question is phrased to focus the audience's thinking; you do not expect an answer. Rhetorical questions require careful tim-ing; following the question, you need to pause long enough for people to think, but not so long that they respond verbally. You can cue the audience with your vocal inflection—a pace and pitch that lets the listeners know they are only to think about their responses. Rhetorical questions are most effective when you use two or three in a series (even if they are only slight rewordings) rather than just a single question. You might ask, for example, "How would you feel if you found out that your best friend told a secret that you had shared in confidence? [pause] Would you feel betrayed? [slight pause] Angry?"

Appropriate humor. Humor can create a bridge into the speech with a brief ironic or witty reference appropriate to the audience, yourself, and the occasion. Once, Phyllis Diller got up to speak with her arm in a cast. She began, "I'd like to begin with a public service announcement: If there is anyone here who has just bought the new book *The Joy of Sex*, there is a misprint on page 206" (Walters, 1993, p. 127). Whatever you do, *don't* start a speech with an irrelevant or old "joke," followed by, "But seriously, folks . . ." You'll lose your audience as soon as you say "seriously."

Reference to a previous speaker. Someone who spoke ahead of you may have said something relating to your speech in some way. Take advantage of this and look for ways to adapt your introduction. The worst thing you can do is to ignore the similarities when the audience will surely see them. Your listeners may think you were not paying attention or failed to see the connections, diminishing your credibility. Suppose your speech is on the abolitionist movement of the 1800s and a previous speaker has talked about the women's rights movement of the 1900s. You might say, "The fight for human rights—both women's rights, as Randi has just described, and the rights of African Americans—goes back a long way. That fight took shape in the 1800s. . . ."

Speech Conclusions

Speech conclusion
Ending of a speech, designed to summarize ideas, propose action, and provide a strong close

Your **speech conclusion** is your opportunity to drive home your ideas or "to make the sale," but, as important as this is, conclusions are often neglected in preparation. Too often, speakers end with a limp, "Uh . . . Well, I guess that's it. Thank you." They lose the chance to give their speeches impact and aesthetic balance and to ensure their listeners remember and act on what the speaker has said.

A good conclusion isn't long—also about 10% of your total speaking time—but it needs to accomplish specific goals using appropriate material.

Objectives You have three objectives to achieve in your conclusions. To some extent, they are mirror images of the introduction's purposes.

Summarizing the speech. Here's the place to "tell the audience what you told them." A summary, which repeats the main points, may include an illustration that encompasses the key ideas of the speech.

Telling the audience what to do. You want your speech to have an impact, so give your audience specific responses they can make to your material. In what ways could they apply the information? How could they get more details if they so desired? Do you want them to approve your proposal or seek more information? Should they lobby or contact legislators? What behaviors should they change? Don't assume these steps will be obvious—give your listeners some direction.

Providing a strong finish. The first and last impressions are the most powerful, and you want the audience to remember your message. Your closing statement should finish by focusing attention on your ideas. Most speakers realize they must start the speech with strong material to get the audience's attention. You need to close it with equal impact.

Types of Material   Most types of material for introductions are also appropriate for conclusions: You can refer back to the occasion or the audience; you can sum up with a quotation; you can startle or amuse or challenge the audience. You can combine all of these to provide closure and impact. Here are three more approaches specifically for conclusions:

Synopsis.   Pulling your main points together into a concise restatement helps hammer home your thesis. For example, you could say, "In the past few minutes, I have explained how costly it is, both economically and spiritually, to neglect the problem of homelessness. I also have described the way one group is working to solve that problem, an approach that any group can take on as a service project. . . ."

Call for action.   Suppose you've just explained why you believe the Federal Communications Commission (FCC) should set stricter guidelines for children's television programming. You might conclude with a summary of your arguments, followed by this statement: "What can you do? You can write directly to the FCC and you can write to your congressional representative and senators. I have copies of the addresses here. Four letters may take you 30 minutes to write and a bit over a dollar to mail—and they may help to improve the quality of life for countless American children. It's a small investment to make."

Reference to the introduction.   Conclusions that go back to the introduction can balance the speech, bringing the ideas full circle. The student who opened her speech with the narrative about Elizabeth's abortion closed with the following: "At least Elizabeth was spared the difficulty of battling through harassing throngs to get to her doctor. Her decision to have the abortion was excruciating enough, and the additional agony would be more than she should have to suffer. I know, because I am Elizabeth."

Speech Transitions

Transitions are statements that link points, serving both as bridges between ideas and as "road signs" telling the audience when you are making turns or going in a different direction. You want to keep the audience's mind in the same place as your own, so you need to signal clearly every change. Here are examples for each connection point:

From introduction to the body.   Suppose you've just used an ironic, startling statement as an introduction: "It's nice to know we're educating the young. It seems that 10-year-olds today can name more brands of beer than they can name U.S. presidents!" Your transition might be: "Some experts—like Dr.

George Gerbner of Pennsylvania's Annenberg School of Communication—believe that marketing is creating our culture and narrowing the perspective of our people. Let me tell you why communication experts have reached this conclusion—and what they're trying to do about it."

From a main point to a subpoint. If the main point is long, it's a good idea to preview all the subpoints in the same way you preview the speech's main points in the introduction. If it's a briefer speech, less detail is needed—for example, "Three reasons support this idea. Let's look at the first."

From a subpoint to the supporting material. This transition requires short phrases to make the connections for clarity and to provide documentation as an ethical, credible communicator. If you're citing facts or statistics or quoting another source, use phrases such as "According to . . . ," "In the words of . . . ," "Senator Roberts has said . . . ," "Confucius expressed it this way . . . ," or, "Here's an example of . . . ."

From one main point to the next. This transition can remind listeners of the previous point and bridge to the next one with a preview or signpost. You might say, "We've seen that, morally, this proposal is the right thing to do. But pragmatically, is it something we can afford to do?"

From the last main point to the conclusion. This transition often leads into a summary. An example might be, "So what do we know? We have seen (summary of your main points)" or, "Based on the evidence I've given you, we can only conclude that. . . ."

Developing Supporting Material

Supporting material
Information that clarifies, proves, or makes vivid the content of a speech

The organization of your speech provides a basic skeletal structure; **supporting material** is additional information that holds the body up and gives it shape, substance, and energy. From your research base, select supporting material to accomplish three objectives:

1   *Clarify.* A statement may give your audience a fact or a position; you add supporting material to help them understand it.

2   *Prove.* Any statement may or may not be true. Supporting material provides data to convince your audience that what you say is probably true. Proof helps establish your credibility as a speaker.

3   *Vivify.* No matter how factual or reasonable a point may be, an audience needs to "see it," to understand its relevance and feel its impact. Supporting material can help to make an idea stand out over other ideas, and to gain an audience's attention and understanding.

Types of Supporting Material

In conversations, in reports, in papers—you find ways to clarify, prove, or vivify what you mean. In a speech, you have the advantage of thinking ahead and planning specific support for each point and subpoint. Some types of supporting material include:

Examples make a point real and vivid, so it's a good rule to: Let no generalization stand without an example. Several types of examples are shown here as they might be used in a speech on the subject of marriage:

- A *hypothetical example* is made up. You've just said, "Holidays can create major conflicts in a marriage," and support it with, "For example, suppose Jan's family and Terry's both insist on the couple coming for the big holiday meal?"

- A *real example* is an actual occurrence: "When my parents were married, my father's mother refused to speak to the newlyweds for three weeks because they went to Mom's mother's house for the holidays first."

- *Instances* are brief examples, usually presented in a series. "There's the matter of whose house the couple goes to; the question of when gifts are opened; the value clash over religious beliefs; the issue of how much money each family spends. . . ."

- An *illustrative narrative* is a story told from beginning to end to illustrate the point: "Family conflict almost broke up my friends, Donnell and Shoshanna, when Donnell's father proudly announced he was *taking* the couple on a honeymoon cruise. . . ."

Comparisons and contrasts show similarities to and differences from something else, using either direct comparison or analogy. A direct comparison might be, "Marriage is like a legal contract—it binds the two partners in economic and civil matters." An analogy clarifies by comparing an idea to another thing: "Marriage is like setting out in a little boat on a big sea—it takes both people working together to keep it steady."

Facts are statements that can be proven, as opposed to an opinion, which cannot. A fact would be, "There are more interracial marriages in the United States now than ever before," whereas an opinion might be, "It's a sign of progress that more people are marrying people of other races."

Statistics are useful to prove a factual point or to emphasize and clarify a value, but they need to be understood easily by the audience. You might support the preceding fact with, "According to Dr. Frazier in the book *Psychotrends*, 'Every year, about 600,000 interracial marriages are made in the U.S., about a third of which are between whites and African Americans'" (Frazier, 1994).

Testimony is quoted from an expert in a specific field or from a nonexpert who has observed or experienced something. Expert testimony helps establish the probability of a fact or the desirability of an action. "Lay" or nonexpert testimony can add clarity or vividness to a point. Both add to the power of a speech. You see both expert and lay testimony on television newscasts, where the reporter asks an expert to explain or prove a phenomenon but also interviews people on the street for their observations or reactions.

Explanations may use any of the preceding methods in the process of describing, elaborating, or detailing what a point means. An explanation can include:

- *Restatement.* Different words are used to elaborate on a previous statement. A first statement might be, "Marriage as a civil contract is one thing and as a religious commitment is another." The restatement: "That is, a civil contract should be available to all citizens but spiritual commitments should be made according to a couple's religious institution."

- *Definition* may take many forms. Dictionary definitions report common usage, but you can also define ideas with other types of support such as example, testimony, and comparison: "My mother divorced my father because, in the end, she felt he held all the power in their relationship [an example]. As gender expert Julia Wood says, 'The social view of women as less powerful than men carries over into intimacy' (Wood, 2001, p. 212) [expert testimony]. And, for many women of my mother's generation, marriage was like childhood—controlled first by dad, then by husband [comparison]."

Choice and Use of Supporting Material

Think of yourself as an artist painting a picture for a special client—your audience. You need to decide where to put strong lines, where to add color, where to create shapes so your audience will see the picture you want them to see. To do that, you have to decide what supporting material to use and how to use it most effectively. Answers to these questions will help you choose:

- What support will help reach your purpose and your goals?
- Where do you need proof? Clarification? Vivification for attention and interest?
- Which specific material will appeal to your audience's needs, goals, and values?
- Which material will best show your objectivity, competence, and coorientation with your audience?

Visuals to Enhance Supporting Material

Visual message
Graphic image that helps listeners understand the content of a speech

Spoken words usually have greater impact when accompanied by **visual messages.** A study at the Wharton School of the University of Pennsylvania (1981) found that when spoken messages were supplemented by visuals, receivers understood more of the content, and, when asked to process the information to make decisions, they arrived at better decisions more quickly.

To cool off the presentation escalation, General Hugh Shelton, Chairman of the Joint Chiefs of Staff, recently took the unusual step of ordering military personnel around the world to limit their slide shows to the basic information.

Shelton isn't the only one who's fed up. Navy Secretary Richard Danzig complains, "The idea behind most of these briefings is for us to sit through 100 slides with our eyes glazed over, and then do what all military organizations hope for . . . surrender to an overwhelming mass."

From "Friendly Fire" of the Electronic Variety. *Dollars & Sense*, July, 2000, p. 4.

Some say the presentation software explosion is part of a general decline in public speaking—as Stanford professor of communications Cliff Nass puts it, "Try to imagine the 'I have a dream" speech in PowerPoint."

Geoffrey Nunberg, in The Trouble with Power-Point, *Fortune*, December 20, 1999, p. 330.

Graphic images help people "to see relationships, processes, and problems in a way that textual descriptions do not" (Carlson, 1999, p. 182), both because the ideas take shape in graphic form and because people take in more messages through their eyes than through their ears. When the eyes are not focusing on the speaker and supporting visuals, they wander—and the mind follows. Visuals are a big help.

Remember, however, that the visual aids are not the speech, nor should they only repeat what you say in the speech. In fact, visuals can be a detriment when the speaker uses them to escape the responsibility for engaging the audience and the listeners' eyes glaze over under the onslaught of slides. The point is to enhance your oral messages with visual cues.

Visual Formats   "The ability to prepare a slide presentation has become an indispensable corporate survival skill," says *Fortune* magazine (Nunberg, 1999, p. 1). Fortunately, this skill is becoming easier and easier for speakers to learn. And the slides are easier to use, because newer versions of software packages allow the speaker to control the entire presentation alone (Toupin, 1999, p. 39).

It used to be that "visual aids" referred mostly to posters, slides seen through a projector the speaker lugged to the presentation site, or scribbles on a blackboard. Those days are past. You may well have PowerPoint available to you, and certainly most corporations do. PowerPoint, as well as other similar programs, are easily used by what one writer calls the "graphically challenged" (Carlson, 1999) to create graphics for a presentation. These programs provide templates to construct an image (charts, illustrations, drawings, business graphics, and such) that can be shown on slides operated by the speaker.

You also may have available to you the software for adding audio to your presentation (Ellis, 2000, p. 64) and for digital editing ("Make it Snappy," 1999, p. 178). The sky's pretty much the limit.

Figure 12.4 *Story-board for planning visuals to supplement a speech*

Outline	Description of visuals
I. Main point	_____
A. Subpoint 1	_____
1. Supporting detail 1	_____
2. Supporting detail 2	_____
B. Subpoint 2	
1. Supporting detail 3	_____
2. Supporting detail 4	_____
II. Etc.	

Even without all this high tech, however, it's possible to use visual aids the old-fashioned way, with overhead projectors, flipcharts, slides, and audio- or videotape segments. Whichever you use, you want your visual aids to be enough to support, prove, clarify, or vivify your information—and not enough to overwhelm your presentation or your audience.

To plan your visuals, you need to consider the audience size, the formality of the situation, and your available resources. Chapter 13 develops ways to use your visual materials effectively. Whatever format you choose, remember that your credibility is enhanced by high-quality visuals.

Guidelines for Creating Visuals   Whatever the production method, each visual needs to meet three criteria:

1   *Big.* Be sure the visual can be seen easily from any point in the room. Check this with the equipment and in the room where you will be speaking.

2   *Bold.* Give your visuals life and interest. Use vivid colors, engaging graphics, appropriate humor, and audience-involving formats.

3   *Brief.* If your visual uses text, use only key words or phrases of four or fewer words. In both text and graphics, limit each visual to five or fewer key ideas; use multiple slides for complex ideas, laying one over the other if necessary to bring multiple "chunks" together. Round off numbers where possible and set up figures so there's plenty of room for relationships to be seen vividly.

Plan for your visuals as you develop your speech, although final decisions must wait until you're closer to completion. A visual should supplement your oral text, not substitute for it, so coordinate the two carefully. A storyboard is a good way to plan for visuals by providing space—a box or a column—for identifying visuals in your speech notes. Figure 12.4 shows an example.

A good speech is a work of art that uses your thinking, your language, your graphic representations to create a message that will inform or persuade your audience to reach the goals you have set.

Summary

Research and development for a speech begin with identification of your specific purposes and preparation of a clear, concise thesis statement. Your goals will be achieved through the thinking and/or actions of the audience, so you need to analyze their demographics and psychographics to know how the listeners' knowledge, attitudes, and values might influence their responses.

Speakers build and demonstrate their credibility by delivering a speech that has a clear structure, contains sound evidence and careful reasoning, and uses a style and format that command attention. You develop the speech's content from your research, selecting the appropriate information and organizing your ideas strategically. An organizational structure moves the listener from point to point with appropriate transitions—from a purposeful introduction, through a cohesive body, to an effective conclusion.

Ideas need supporting material to clarify, to prove, and to vivify them for an audience. Examples, comparisons and contrasts, facts, statistics, testimony, explanations, and repetition increase your effectiveness when speaking to inform or seeking to persuade listeners to change their attitudes, values, beliefs, and/or behaviors. Effective visuals, whether prepared through specialized software or by hand, present your information in ways that provide variety and clarity.

Exercises

1   Choose four of the following and refine the general subject to a specific speech topic. See Figure 12.1 for examples.

Politics	Television	College life	Careers
Technology	Friendship	Civil War	Waterways
Religion	Agriculture		

Next, select any two of your refined statements and write a thesis statement that could be used for a speech on the topic.

2   With a partner, select one of the thesis statements that either of you prepared in the previous exercise.

a   Create an organizational structure for a speech developing that thesis statement by creating main ideas, subpoints, and possible supporting material.

b   Use either an organizational chart or the traditional outline format to develop the structure.

c   Use a specific organizational pattern (chronological, spatial, parts-to-whole, and so on) for each subdivision you create.

3 In a small group, brainstorm as many possible resources for information as you can for the following speech thesis statement:

Visiting Hong Kong provides great opportunities for sightseeing, shopping, and dining.

4 Prepare a brief presentation for the class in which you do the following:

a State an idea in a single declarative sentence.

b Provide one item of supporting material to clarify the idea, identifying the source of the material as you use it.

c Have your audience identify the type of supporting material you have used (for instance, example or testimony).

d Discuss with the audience the quality of the material and its effectiveness in terms of achieving your goal. Would you need different material or sources depending on whether you're using the support to prove as opposed to clarifying or vivifying a point?

Cyberpoints

1 Do you want to investigate some interesting Web sites? Here are some available at this writing:

Current News groups lists (http://www.dejanews.com) (Muhammad, March, p. 37).

Cybersoc.com, "an online resource for social scientists interested in the study of the Internet, cyberspace, computer-mediated communication, and online communities," as well as issues of *Cybersociology* magazine and links to bibliographies and reviews of pertinent Web sites and software (http://www.cybersoc.com/home.html) (Morreale, 2000, October, p. 11).

E-mail discussion lists and public newsletters that you can "search by keyword or category and in thirteen different languages" (http://www.meta-list.net/) (Morreale, 2000, February, p. 8).

The Invisible Web, "the search engine of search engines," indexes "over 10,000 data bases, archives, and search engines offering links to targeted search sources instead of hundreds or thousands of web pages. Users can search by keyword, perform an advanced search, or browse a list of entries organized under 'Hot List.'" (http://www.invisibleweb.com/) (Morreale, 2000, February, p. 13).

"The *Media Beat*, a publication of the *Communication Initiative*, electronic magazine that features selected articles from developing world newspapers relating to communication, development and change trends, programs and policies" (http://www.comminit.com/news.html) (Morreale, 2000, February, p. 13).

"The *National Data Book* of the Census Bureau offers a collection of statistics on social and economic conditions in the U.S." (http://www.census.gov/prod/www/statistical-abstract-us.html) (Morreale, 2000, July, p. 7).

"*1stHeadlines* links to thousands of headline news stories each day from over 300 newspapers, broadcast, and online sources . . ." (Morreale, 2000, July, p. 7).

2 To see some sample speech outlines and storyboards, go to the *Communicating with Credibility and Confidence* Web site at http://communication.wadsworth.com/lumsden and click on Chapter 12.

3 For up-to-the-minute sources on software for creating visuals, use *InfoTrac College Edition* and enter the keywords *PowerPoint, visuals*, and *public speaking*.

Chapter 13

Rehearsal and Delivery: Speaking to Audiences

Anne Dowie

Objectives for This Chapter

Knowledge

- Identify the characteristics of different modes of speech presentations
- Know techniques for rehearsing and refining a speech
- Understand how to get set for the moment of presentation
- Know what makes a speech presentation credible to an audience

Feelings and Approaches

- Enjoy preparing, rehearsing, and presenting a speech
- Feel confident in presenting a speech
- Feel that the listeners are partners in a conversation

Communication Abilities

- Select the best presentation mode for an occasion
- Rehearse and polish a speech through visualization and practice
- Manage notes, media, and visuals effectively
- Speak confidently and credibly
- Manage feedback and questions effectively

Key Terms

impromptu speaking   manuscript speaking   memorized speaking

extemporaneous speaking

At the end of every term, we teachers are impressed and gratified when a student who started the class scared, trembling, and inarticulate delivers a confident, credible, well-prepared speech. That successful speaker has prepared the material, *and* chosen the best mode for presenting the speech, *and* visualized and rehearsed—out loud, with the visuals—until she or he is confident of success. That's what it takes to make a successful speech.

With the right approach to developing and rehearsing your speech, you can go to the podium with confidence and deliver your speech so that your audience engages with you and with your ideas. This chapter discusses how to select your mode of presentation and to rehearse so that it will be second nature for you to use your notes, manage your visuals, and respond to your audience confidently and credibly.

Selecting Your Mode of Presentation

Think about some of the best speakers or lecturers you've heard. Consider them as models for what you want to do. Study their content and their behavior. What made you sit up and listen? What made you feel these speakers were talking directly with *you*? Chances are, you were drawn to their vitality and energy and involvement. Successfully reaching your audience depends partly on the type of presentation you choose.

There are four basic modes of speech presentation:

Impromptu speaking Presenting your ideas in an organized and thoughtful fashion without formal preparation or rehearsal

1   **Impromptu speaking** is presenting your ideas in an organized and thoughtful fashion without formal preparation or rehearsal. You might give a short impromptu speech to support a position or provide information when you're at a meeting. The quality of an impromptu speech depends on how much you already know and have thought about the topic, as well as on your skill in organizing and presenting ideas quickly and articulately. Impromptu speaking is appropriate only for a quick, to-the-point response to a situation; the lack of preparation quickly undermines your effectiveness in longer impromptu presentations.

Extemporaneous speaking Presenting a speech using notes that has been prepared and rehearsed

2   **Extemporaneous speaking** is a well-prepared, well-organized, and well-rehearsed—but not written-out—presentation for which the speaker has first prepared a complete outline but speaks from a few, key-word notes. The

wording is developed through repeated oral practice—"talking it out"—rather than writing it out, so the precise words may change every time the speech is presented. Extemporaneous speaking is the most flexible, adaptable, and dynamic method for engaging your audience. Usually, the extemporaneous speech gives you the best opportunity to be a credible communicator by showing both your careful preparation and your direct involvement with the audience.

Manuscript speaking
Reading aloud a speech that has been written

3 **Manuscript speaking** is reading aloud a speech that has been carefully written with specific wording and prepared as a manuscript with indications for emphasis and gestures. Newscasters—and political speakers—read from a manuscript or from a TelePrompTer, which is a monitor that scrolls up the words for the speaker to read. A manuscript may be required when the event is formal, when the speech contains crucial information for a large audience, or when the slightest mistake might have serious repercussions. Speakers often think they will be safer with a manuscript, but they are wrong—a manuscript is difficult to use well, and it creates a wall between the speaker and the audience.

Memorized speaking
Speaking a written text from memory and rehearsal

4 **Memorized speaking** takes manuscript speaking to a more difficult preparation level through memorization and rehearsal of the written text. Not only is it difficult to memorize a speech, but when you do, you lose the spontaneity and flexibility of an extemporaneous presentation. If you forget a word, you're likely to forget the entire flow of the speech.

You can make an extemporaneous speech more polished and professional than an impromptu speech, of course, and even more important, you will be able to communicate more directly and comfortably with the audience than if you are using a manuscript. Generally, the way you speak normally—your *oral language*—is more dynamic and interesting to listen to than an essay you have written, no matter how well you might recite it. Oral language is likely to be more direct, informal, concrete, spontaneous, and often, more believable. Written language is usually more formal, uses a more complex vocabulary level, and often seems more remote. As soon as listeners feel they could more easily read your speech for themselves than listen to you speak it, you've lost credibility—and their apparent boredom will undermine your confidence.

Another advantage in using an extemporaneous preparation is that a speech is a living, dynamic event—so it is not entirely predictable, no matter how well you have planned. With an extemporaneous presentation you can adapt to the unexpected more easily than if you are reading from a manuscript. When using only a few notes, you are able to observe the audience's responses and to monitor your own. You know your organization, your goals, and your information, but you are not locked into a word-by-word development. When necessary, you can explain further, omit a point, or add an illustration to help your audience understand and connect with your ideas. You can change your wording on the spot, shifting from abstract words to concrete words—or vice versa—to build coorientation with your audience. If you forget a word or an idea, you can fill in or shift direction without anyone knowing that you missed something. Further, you have the freedom to move around, to gesture, and to maintain direct eye contact, because you don't have to battle with a manuscript.

Figure 13.1 *Extemporaneous versus manuscript speaking*

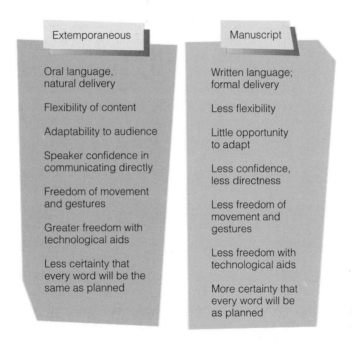

Extemporaneous	Manuscript
Oral language, natural delivery	Written language; formal delivery
Flexibility of content	Less flexibility
Adaptability to audience	Little opportunity to adapt
Speaker confidence in communicating directly	Less confidence, less directness
Freedom of movement and gestures	Less freedom of movement and gestures
Greater freedom with technological aids	Less freedom with technological aids
Less certainty that every word will be the same as planned	More certainty that every word will be as planned

With a manuscript, you've set and practiced precise words in a specific order. You're boxed in, and if you lose your place, you have to scramble around to determine what you need to say next. A manuscript burdens you in other ways as well. Reading or memorizing takes much more preparation and skill than working from notes and usually results in a less effective performance. Further, if a problem arises with a manuscript—such as misplaced pages—you may have to shift to extemporaneous speaking anyway. When former President Clinton presented his 1993 health care speech to Congress and the nation, the wrong speech started scrolling on the TelePrompTer. He looked at the screen, realized that the speech was wrong, and proceeded extemporaneously until the problem was corrected. Fortunately, Mr. Clinton is an adept extemporaneous speaker, and he knew his material well.

Figure 13.1 compares manuscript to extemporaneous speaking.

Because we so strongly believe that extemporaneous speaking is the place for you to start, we do not develop manuscript speaking in this text. If, however, you absolutely must use a manuscript for a specific occasion, you might want to consult the *Communicating with Credibility and Confidence* Web site at http://communication.wadsworth.com/lumsden and click on Chapter 13.

Visualizing Your Success

We've emphasized the impact visualization can make on your effectiveness and self-confidence throughout this book. Once again, and with feeling, we say:

Envisioning yourself as an effective speaker is important from the moment you start preparing. Too often, people do just the opposite: They see themselves as nervous and ineffective. Research reveals a circular relationship: Speakers who are very anxious are likely to "see" their upcoming speech negatively (Ayres & Huett, 1997), and negative images of a speaking situation make a speaker more anxious (Fanning, 1988). Your anxiety can undermine you from the moment you start preparing, let alone at the moment you get up to speak. Visualizing yourself as confident, credible, and communicative, however, stresses positive images and helps you direct your energy to speak effectively (Ayres & Hopf, 1987, 1991, 1993). You manage your anxiety *and* improve your speaking ability.

Although we have discussed positive visualizations and writing affirmations before, we want to stress these things:

1   Take time out to sit down, relax, close your eyes, and focus on positive images of your presentation, both before you practice and before you actually present your speech. Choose a quiet place where you won't be disturbed.

2   Mentally create a visualization for the entire day of your speech (Ayres & Hopf, 1993, pp. 31–47). See yourself getting up in the morning, dressing appropriately—so you feel and look good—and preparing for an excellent experience. Develop an image of the entire speaking experience. Envision the room; sense what it's like; see yourself entering the room, feeling comfortable and confident. Visualize yourself in front of the audience communicating dynamically and engagingly. What are you doing? What is the audience doing and how are they responding? Create clear, moving pictures—mental video previews—of yourself succeeding in the presentation and gaining the audience response you desire. Take your visualization all the way through your successful conclusion. Replay the scene in your mind in full living color; concentrate on your positive emotional responses as the successful presentation proceeds.

3   Write out an affirmation—a complete, positive, present-tense description— of your image, feelings, and the audience response you are receiving. Eliminate the negatives—no suggestion of anxiety or inadequacy. Make it terrific.

4   Read your affirmation over to yourself before each practice session, and focus your imagination on just how positive the experience will be.

Preparing and Using Notes

Your notes really do make a difference. Notes have a place in actually developing your speech, in rehearsing it, and certainly in presenting it to an audience. Brief, to-the-point notes unobtrusively remind you of what you want to say without distracting you or the audience and allow you to be communicative and spontaneous in your delivery.

Good notes will remind you of where you are and what you're talking about but *will not tell you precisely the words to use*. Your original outline will use complete sentences and annotations, but your notes will be brief and adapted to changes you make during your rehearsal. Here's our advice to make your notes work for you:

1   Avoid using sheets of paper or large cards—they are awkward, noisy, and distracting to your audience.

2   Put your notes on cards: If you might not have a lectern, use 4″ by 6″ cards that fit easily in your hand. If you know you will speak at a lectern, you can use 5″ by 8″ cards that you can put down in front of you.

3   Use large print so the notes are easy to see if nervousness clouds your vision.

4   Use only *key words* in the notes, not full phrases or sentences.

5   Start every new main point on a new note card; it helps to maintain a better sense of your organization during the presentation.

6   Indicate clearly on your notes where you will use visuals or other aids.

7   Number the cards so you won't have to shuffle them to find your place.

Figure 13.2 shows three sample note cards for an extemporaneous presentation. You can see how these note cards would remind you of your main points, ensure that you quote another source correctly, and still give you freedom to adapt and change as you speak.

Rehearsing and Adapting Your Speech

You are ready now for the next three stages of preparing a speech: Practice, practice, and practice. Mark Twain once said that the only way to prepare a speech is to *talk* it. That is, to speak it out loud, feel how it flows, hear how it sounds, and change it to make it better. Good rehearsal is another stage of developing your speech, because *your speech continues to change as you develop your notes, practice, revise, practice, and polish it with a clear image of an effective presentation and with good feedback to help you.*

When you rehearse, practice using your notes as reminders while you talk out loud about the ideas. As you "talk" the speech, you may well modify it by adding supporting material, eliminating a joke, or embellishing an idea, until the speech sounds natural, confident, credible, and communicative. If, after repeated practice, you find that the key words on your note cards don't serve your memory well, add a word or rephrase.

Here are some guidelines to help you get the most from your practice time:

Practice out loud. If you simply look over your notes, you're practicing only part of the actual presentation. Silent rehearsal is like practicing with only two balls for a three-ball juggling act. Moving from idea encoding to transmitting is a significant leap in the communication process.

There are two kinds of speakers: those that are nervous and those that are liars.

Mark Twain, 19–20th-century North American writer

Figure 13.2 *Three sample notecards for an extemporaneous speech*

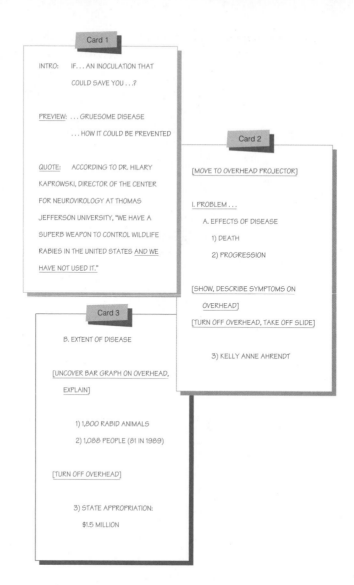

Rehearse in sections. Every practice session doesn't have to start with the introduction and end with the conclusion. Sometimes, your rehearsal may be more productive if you work repetitively on short sections with which you're having difficulty. In 10 minutes, you might run through an entire speech once, but you could work through a 20- to 30-second segment 20 times.

Use visual and/or audio support as you practice. You want to be sure that any aid you use flows smoothly with the presentation so it supplements your talk rather than distracts the audience.

Time yourself. As you develop your presentation, you may add or subtract material. You also will develop a good pace as you "talk it out." Time yourself frequently, and be sure that you are within the allotted time limits.

Rehearse with eye contact. Even if there's no one in the room but you, a tape recorder, and a mirror, talk to imaginary people. Move your eyes to focus on different places in the room, as if there were people there. (We'll discuss more about this shortly.)

Practice in the most realistic location. Ideally, you would rehearse your speech in the room where you are to present it. If this isn't possible, try to familiarize yourself with the site. You can then use the place for your visualization *and* look for as similar a place as possible to rehearse. Consider:

- *Size and sound.* Get a feel for how much you need to project your voice to reach everyone in the room and how much space you have to move around in without landing in someone's lap.
- *Lighting.* Find out how much light there is, where it falls, and how to control it. If the lighting in the room is dim, you need to be more dynamic and active than if it's bright, because people's attention drifts in low light.
- *Equipment.* Figure out precisely how you will present your audio or visual aids. Know where the electrical outlets are and ensure that the equipment you need is there.

Rehearse with feedback. When you get and use feedback, you perform better (Mills & Pace, 1989). You can get helpful feedback with:

- *Videotape.* If videotape is not available, use audiotape. In either case, focus on what you do well and how you can do it better. Listen for places where you could increase vocal inflection, or pick up or slow down the pace, or pause for greater effect. Find specific things you can do to improve. For instance, don't just look at a tape and say, "My hands are awkward," and then glue them to your sides. Awkward might be better than rigid. Instead, try putting one hand into a pocket briefly, or gesturing to emphasize a point as you would in a conversation with a friend.
- *A friendly audience.* Even video replay can be more useful if you combine your own assessment with that of a skilled observer to coach you. Ask people to listen to you who are on your side—who will give you feedback that honestly helps you to improve your performance.

"Getting Set" for Your Speaking Opportunity

"On your marks—get set—go!" Public speaking is much like running a race. You've been "toeing the mark" as you developed and practiced your speech. When the day comes, you have to get set before you go. This means, first, managing your anxiety, and then getting yourself involved in the entire event and analyzing ways in which you need to adapt—and finally, taking command of the room.

Managing Your Nerves

An effective speaker is so busy being audience-centered, he/she has no time to be self-centered.

Azriela Jaffe, journalist, So Long, Stage Fright, in *Success*, June 2000, p. 70.

With all that practice and preparation, will you be completely calm? No. You're a reasonable person. You know that your presentation can affect your credibility and possibly your grades or your career. Of course, it's natural to be apprehensive when you are about to make a speech, but the flow of adrenaline can be a positive force for you. In fact, an overly calm person is usually a boring speaker. Who wants to listen to someone who doesn't seem to care? Your challenge is simply to manage your nervousness and use its energy to enliven your performance—that is, to get all those butterflies to fly in formation.

Here is our advice:

1   *Dress so you look both attractive and professional.* Even for a classroom speech, think of yourself as a career person. How you look affects your credibility and confidence.

2   *Eat a nourishing—but light—meal.* You want the energy food gives you, but you don't want to feel bloated or sleepy.

3   *Do some loosening-up exercises.* Do what actors do. Before you enter the room, go to a private spot—possibly, the restroom—and stretch all of your muscles, one at a time. Consciously work to relax the muscles in your throat, shoulders, and neck. Breathe slowly and deeply. Wiggle your face around, blow air through your lips, make open-throat sounds—"ah, hah, ho"—and think about relaxing your throat and breathing from your diaphragm. Your body is your instrument for speaking, so it must be both relaxed and alert.

4   *Rerun your affirmation statements and visualizations in your mind.* Be sure your mental picture of yourself giving your speech is complete and fresh.

5   *Focus your thoughts on your purpose.* You have a message to share with the audience; so concentrate on it.

Finally, keep the focus on *communicating.* Your listeners aren't there to criticize you—they are there to hear what you have to say. If you're a little less than perfect, that's okay. The audience knows you're human, and so are they.

Adapting to Circumstances

When you arrive at your speaking site, become involved with the people and the event. Talk with others prior to the meeting, and participate if other activities are scheduled. When other speakers are making their speeches, concentrate fully on their delivery and their message. This does four things:

1   Keeps your mind off your nerves and on the moment;

2   Keeps your energy up so you can carry it into your presentation;

3   Maintains your connection with the people who will be your audience, keeping the focus on them as your listeners, rather than on yourself;

4   Gives you information that you might want to use in your speech. For example, you may decide you want to shift your visual aid from the left side of the room to the right side because the light is better, or you may learn something from another speaker that you'd like to refer to when you talk.

With even the best preparation, you may arrive at a speaking occasion and find unexpected conditions. There could be a power failure, making it impossible to use your overhead projector. There could be a change in the agenda, resulting in your speech being last when you thought it would be first—or vice versa. A previous speaker could cover some material you had planned to discuss. Or another speaker could go overtime, leaving you with fewer minutes than you expected. These possibilities require:

Preparing for the unexpected. Consider in advance where you can elaborate on information, how you can present it differently, and how you can adapt to changes of agenda or equipment. If, for example, technology should fail, it's a lot easier to adapt if you have handouts or are ready to draw on a blackboard, describe verbally, or simply cut out the parts that absolutely require visuals. Knowing you can adapt gives you confidence, and listeners either are not aware of your adaptations or are impressed by your ability to make them.

Using the unexpected to your advantage. You can mention a change, but don't complain about it. Your audience will find you both credible and confident if you deal with the unexpected calmly and smoothly. Suppose, for example, two students speak on the electoral college. The second speaker, Kira, might start with, "Shue has told you how the electoral college works—now I am going to tell you about how it worked in the last presidential election and about current proposals to change it." In this way, Kira provides a credible bridge from the previous speech into her own.

Maintaining flexibility. If someone stops you to ask a question that covers one of your points, you can answer the question, skip over the point, and save the time for other items or for more questions. The goal is to have the audience understand and respond to your speech. If you adapt your presentation—even if you omit something you had intended to cover—that's okay as long as you achieve your overall purpose.

Talking with Your Audience

When you deliver a speech, you are really talking with people—there simply are more of them than in a normal conversation. Just as in a conversation, you want each person to feel connected with you, to feel you are talking directly with her or him. Because of the larger number of people, however, your communication needs to be bigger—farther ranging and more dynamic—than it would be with one or two people. From the moment you get up to speak, you need to take command in these ways:

Remember that you're ready. At this moment, you are the expert on your topic. You've researched and prepared. That doesn't mean you know everything—but it does mean you have something to which people will want to listen.

Own the room. In your visualization and in your actions, you want to walk up there and make the audience feel that you are in command of yourself and your material. When it's time for you to speak, take a deep breath, look around, and move confidently to the speaking area. Arrange your notes or visuals so they are properly set for you to use. If you are to use a microphone and a lectern, check the microphone height and test it to be sure it's working properly. Unless you are compelled to stay at the lectern and/or microphone, however, you get a much stronger start if you step away from the lectern so you own the entire space, with no barricade between you and your audience. You can put your notes on the lectern and use it as a stage prop, but not as a crutch. If you must use a microphone that's attached to the lectern, stand behind it. The best rule is, *Don't touch the lectern*—touching leads to leaning on it, wrestling with it, and scrunching behind or over it.

   Take a moment to settle in before beginning your speech. Your listeners *want* you to succeed—they are there to hear you—so start by focusing on them. Engage individuals in the audience, eye to eye. Smile. Act friendly. Take a deep breath, and focus on what you want your audience to know or to do.

Introduce the speech firmly. Give your introduction the way you have practiced it. Don't preamble with, "My speech is about . . ." You deliberately have planned and rehearsed an introduction that will get your audience's attention and move them into the process of understanding and accepting your words. Use that introduction. If you need to adapt it to previous speakers or the situation, do so, of course—but keep your original strategy in mind, and don't weaken it with a separate preamble.

Enhance your credibility. Your listeners measure your credibility, as you know, in the way they see your competence, objectivity, trustworthiness, coorientation, and dynamism. They see it in the honesty and care with which you've done your research and prepared your presentation and in the credible support you provide. You show your credibility, too, in the competence of your preparation and in the dynamism of your delivery.

Communicate with—not at—your listeners. We talked, in Chapter 1, about a *dialogical ethic* (Johannesen, 1996, pp. 63–85); this feeling of "dialogue" is as important in public speaking as it is in interpersonal conversation. Even though you are one person speaking to many, communicating with a dialogical ethic means that you respect your audience and provide them the freedom and necessary information to choose among options. Even though they are not speaking aloud, you are listening to them—that is, you are considering their perspectives, watching their feedback, considering them your partners in communication. When you do so, you invite the listeners into a discussion on the topic. This creates genuine listener involvement, making each person a partner with you.

Keep your goals clearly in mind. Even if you forget something entirely, you can adapt and work toward your purpose—and your listeners probably won't even know you missed a point. If the point you missed is important, try to bring it in later, for instance: "But before I explain just why this is a problem, let me go back for a moment and define what I mean by . . ." Sometimes, humor can help, too.

Don't jump to conclusions about people's nonverbal reactions. Somebody's frown may indicate not displeasure, but thoughtfulness. A person who rolls her eyes may only be trying to remember something relating to what you've said. You can't be sure that such cues are negative. To the contrary, they may be positive. If nonverbal cues from one person are distracting you, look at someone else.

Effective public speaking is 95 percent mental preparedness and 5 percent technique.

Dilip Abayasekara, founder of Speaker Services Unlimited

Using Nonverbal Delivery

A consultant and trainer for political candidates says, "Think of all the memorable speakers you've ever heard. One trait they all share is their uniqueness" (Crounse, 2000, p. 64). The point is not to be like everyone else, but to learn ways to enhance your nonverbal communication so it engages the audience and fits the situation.

Although some speaking situations are more formal than others, you will feel more confident and your audience will be more interested if you start with the attitude that you're having a conversation with them. Think of it this way: If you're talking with one person, what is your nonverbal communication like? Take a look at Figure 13.3.

As you converse with one person, you feel free to express yourself and to respond to the other person naturally and easily. You easily adjust your gestures and voice to fit within a small area around the two of you, making frequent eye contact as you speak. If two other people join you, what do you do? You speak a little louder, you move your eyes from person to person, your gestures become just a bit broader, and you shift position to include the other listeners.

If a larger group of people gathers around you, then what? You simply raise the volume of your voice, expand the range of your eye contact, and use broader gestures so you can communicate with everyone in the group. Simple, isn't it?

Figure 13.3
Expanding audience size, "conversation," and amplitude of movement and voice

Conversation with one

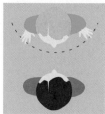

Conversation with three

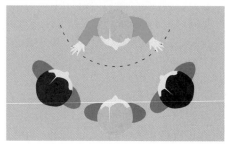

Speech/conversation with many

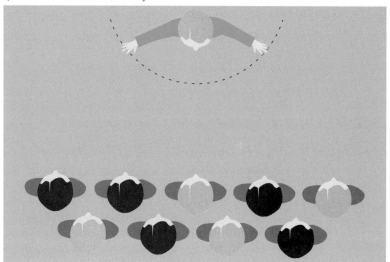

This easy expansion of space is the foundation for talking with an audience of 25 or 250. Whatever the size of the audience, it's just a collection of individual people, each of whom wants to be able to hear you, see you, and understand you.

In that context, your delivery of a speech starts with what you already know and do regularly—the art of conversation. Then it extends to skillful use of your

Most presentation software includes graphics and images that can be used as part of a presentation. A word of warning, though: Don't get carried away! While graphics can be pleasing and humorous, try to keep them to a minimum so they don't detract from the content.

But Web pages and other documents on computer monitors are another story altogether. They are designed to be viewed by one person at a distance of less than 20 inches. Ironically, some presenters fail to take this into account because even during the presentation they are staring at a 15-inch monitor or small laptop screen. Unfortunately, the audience gets seasick while the mouse glides swiftly across the screen or while a page goes scrolling by in a blur. Most trainers learn, through experience, to slow down, to tell the audience what they are about to do, and to repeat movements as needed. Project your work onto a large screen and see what it looks like.

From D. Scott Brandt, technology training librarian at Purdue University Libraries in West Lafayette, Indiana. Digital Presentations: Make Your Delivery Effective, *Computers in Libraries*, May 1998, *18* (4), pp. 35, 38, & 39.

eyes and face, your body and gestures, and your voice and articulation to make it all clear and interesting.

Eyes and Face

Your face and eyes give your audience the first impression of your credibility and goodwill. "But I'm not an actor," students say. "How do I make my face expressive? And if I make eye contact I'll forget what I want to say."

You don't have to be an actor. Expressiveness starts from within and works its way out. Beginning with your visualization, and continuing as you introduce and develop your speech, see yourself as lively, expressive, and focused on your interest in the topic and the audience. As you develop that approach, your face will reflect what you feel inside. When you ignore your self-consciousness and concentrate on your topic and your listeners, you will show your involvement and confidence. People will react with trust and interest.

The worst thing is to immerse yourself in your notes; you'll drown in them. But if you make eye contact, will you forget what you want to say? Actually, it's just the opposite. Your eyes will help you to connect personally with audience members—and that will increase both your confidence in yourself and their belief in your credibility. Here are important guidelines for using eye contact:

Sustain your contact. When you make eye contact with someone, hold it for several seconds, long enough to actually feel you are speaking to *that* person— one speaker calls that moment a "mind lift" (Walters, 1993, p. 137)—then move on to someone else. Avoid using the flicker or sweep system of eye contact. That is, don't touch on one person like a firefly and then flit off to someone else or just sweep your eyes back and forth across the room. If you've ever been in the audience when a speaker did these things, you know they're unnatural, unnerving, and uncommunicative.

Look at everybody. Be sure you make eye contact throughout the entire room. Be careful not to focus mostly on one side or the center of the room; this makes other listeners feel they might as well not be there. What if the audience is too large? That's okay; in a very large audience, your eye contact with one listener makes those behind that person feel as if you are looking at them as well. Just divide your audience into imaginary squares, like a tic-tac-toe pattern. Then focus on a front-center person in each section until you have made full contact, and move on to another section (Walters, 1993, p. 138).

Adapt to listeners' responses. Once in awhile, you have to adjust or break the eye contact rule. If, for example, your eye contact seems to make someone squirm, move on to someone else. Sometimes, culture influences a listener's responses; often, for example, people from Asian cultures are not comfortable with sustained eye contact. If you have a listener who seems hostile, you might try sustained eye contact and a smile or two to try to win the person over. If that doesn't work, just concentrate on the rest of the audience. Finally, some listeners are so friendly and supportive it's a temptation to talk only to them. Appreciate the support, but resist the temptation to carry on a private conversation for too long.

Body and Gestures

You want your audience to be vitalized by your speech—and to accomplish that, you must be vital, too. You develop energy through visualization, relaxation, exercise, and practice. You continue to build enthusiasm for and involvement in your speech just by the way you walk up and own the room. And you carry that energy through your straight, tall, relaxed, and energetic posture.

Does that mean a person in a wheelchair, for example, can't be a powerful speaker? Not at all, but it does mean that the speaker must convey energy and involvement with other cues—eyes, face, gestures, voice. Franklin D. Roosevelt used a wheelchair, but he was a powerful speaker and was elected president four times.

Here are some additional guidelines, to supplement those in Chapter 6, for using body movement and gestures effectively in a speech:

1   *Use your space.* People need change and contrast to keep their attention; your movement helps them stay involved and increases your contact with all

Al Campanie/Syracuse Newspapers

Your eyes, face, hands, and body are all part of your nonverbal delivery.

It's not about "acting" a speech, it's about getting to the "truth" of what it is you're trying to say, and what you want from your audience."

Bill Crounse, president of a firm specializing in media and speech coaching for political candidates

parts of the audience. Even in a large room, you can use a lavaliere (a small microphone that hangs around the neck) or hand mike, and move around on the stage to emphasize points and convey energy.

2   *Move naturally—but strategically.* If you were having a simple conversation, you would move naturally to emphasize your points, or to indicate your thoughtfulness, or to regulate the conversation. Often, however, public speakers stay glued to one spot or else they pace like caged tigers. To find the natural movements that will help you to communicate your ideas, think about when you want to emphasize transitions from one point to another or strengthen the importance of an idea. Then, in rehearsal and in your speech, use those occasions to walk to the other side of the room, step briefly behind the lectern to read a quotation, move to your visual, or take a few steps forward.

3   *Let your thoughts dictate your gestures.* Don't say to yourself, "I'll slam my fist into my hand here." That kind of planning produces gestures that miss a beat, look unnatural, and make you feel uncomfortable. Remember, audiences believe in you and your message when your words and gestures match (Woodall & Burgoon, 1981). So, let your gestures develop in the context of what you want your audience to know or do. Use your gestures as illustrators to show and as regulators to guide your listeners through your ideas.

4   *Adapt the size of your gestures to the size of your audience.* As you develop gestures, make sure they are appropriately large and broad for your audience— but not so grand that they draw attention away from your point.   Look back at Figure 13.3. If you're talking to one person, your gestures are relatively narrow. As your audience expands, your gestures expand as well to encompass the most distant members. A good rule of thumb is to use gestures about as wide as the distance from the person farthest to your left to the person farthest to your right. Unless you're demonstrating something, keep your gestures above your waist or the lectern so that they are visible to your audience.

Voice and Articulation

A communication trainer notes that, "in a clearing in the woods of the Green Mountains of Vermont there is a stone marker with an engraving commemorating that 'on July 7 and 8 in the year 1840, Daniel Webster spoke at this place to 15,000 people.' Without a mike!" The trainer goes on to say that speakers who can't be heard tend "to put the blame on the listener when, in fact, speaking-to-be-heard is becoming a lost art" (Drucker, 2000, p. 71).

She is so very correct. When you're speaking to an audience, remember two things. First, each listener does not have constant eye contact with you and may not be close enough—or see well enough—to read your lips or pick up your more subtle facial expressions. Your vocal inflection and pace may be the best cues to the meanings and feelings you want to convey to your listeners. Second, audience members usually won't stop you to ask, "What did you say?" Nor, as when reading a book, can they flip back to review a previous page. So clear pronunciation of your words is crucial to your success.

No one voice is best, nor is any one dialect superior. There is, however, a best way to use *your* voice, and there are ways to articulate clearly so that people understand you no matter what dialect you speak. Our advice is this:

1   *Develop the most effective use of your voice.* Remember that you have the best vocal quality and appear most confident and relaxed when your throat is open (Crannell, 2000, p. 46), although you adjust the degree of openness for the meaning you want to convey. Try some of the exercises at the end of this chapter to develop an open throat, and try to speak that way in conversation as well as in speeches.

2   *Focus on the meaning you want to convey.* Practice your words to use your voice and speech to communicate those ideas. Develop variety in your pitch, rate, and volume to help your listeners understand your meaning and to reinforce your credibility (Ray, 1986). Try various combinations of inflections of pace, volume, and pitch to best convey the emphasis, feelings, and impact you want to communicate.

3   *Pronounce your words correctly and articulate them clearly.* When you're with a group of old friends who know you well, they know how you speak and are quick to grasp your meaning. Public speaking, however, demands that you make your ideas clear for an audience that doesn't have that advantage. If people can't understand you, you lose credibility and, probably, listeners. Wolvin, Berko, and Wolvin (1993) point out that "if you say 'air' for 'error' or 'din't' for 'didn't,' you are being lazy in your use of articulators" (p. 192). Keep in mind that people stereotype others on the basis of their speech, and you don't want a prejudgment to reduce your credibility. Check the correct pronunciation of words, and listen to yourself on tape to pick up sloppy or unclear speech. Also, have others listen to you and give you feedback.

4   *Use pauses, rate, and emphasis to clarify meaning.* If you pause between thoughts, vary your rate of speech to suit your audience as well as your meaning,

Dr. Dilip R. Abayasekara, born and raised in Sri Lanka, spoke mostly Singalese as a child. But he became fascinated with public speaking and, when he came to the U.S.A. to earn his B.S. and Ph.D. in organic chemistry, he pursued his speaking interest through classes and contests. When he entered his first oratorical contest, Dr. Abayasekara says, *"It didn't even cross my mind that my accent might be an obstacle. . . .* Looking back, I think the professor who organized the contest was surprised that a foreign student entered. I placed second."

Today, Dr. Abayasekara shares his expertise in public speaking through the consulting firm founded, Speaker Services Unlimited, coaching clients from such diverse areas as professional organizations, colleges, and the Pentagon.

Summarized from Azriela Jaffe, So Long, Stage Frig in *Success*, June 2000, p. 70.

and emphasize ideas with changes in volume and pitch, you will help your listeners understand you (as well as to be interested in what you say). Some of our students whose first language was not English have been brilliant speakers—not because they lost their accent, but because they used pauses, variation in rate, and emphasis to make their meaning clear.

5 *Reduce detractors to a minimum.* Everyone occasionally uses vocalized pauses like "um" or verbalized pauses such as "y'know" instead of just remaining silent for a brief moment. Silences are usually preferable to adding such sounds, but don't worry about a random filler in your speech. If you use these detractors habitually, perhaps while you gather your thoughts or as a punctuation sound between many phrases, then they become distracting and annoying. The only way to excise them from your speech is to become aware of them (that's where video, audio, or personal feedback helps), and then consciously to edit them from your oral speech. Surprisingly, it isn't very hard to do. You have to stop yourself a few times, sometimes in mid- "um," but that's okay. Just stop and then go on with your statement.

Using Visuals

Visuals—whether old-fashioned and simple or technological and sophisticated—are only as good as you make them and as effective as you are in using them. At the year 2000 Republican National Convention, Laura Bush looked at her TelePrompTers for her speech only to find that enthusiastic delegates had besieged them with confetti—and made them inoperable. Fortunately for Bush, she was able to see a TV screen that also displayed her text (Bedard, Borger, Kaplan, & Parker, 2000, p. 64). She was lucky. Sometimes you just have to know what you're going to say and do if your visuals—or TelePrompTer—fail you.

This incident is a reminder of the need to *rehearse with your visual, audio, or demonstration aids* as well as be prepared to adapt if they fail you. Learn how much time it takes to switch from talking to presenting the visual and back again. Among other things, get a feeling for how the visual aids can help relax you as a speaker; both your focus and the audience's attention are diverted temporarily from you. Not only can this reduce anxiety, but your physical movement as you turn from the audience to the visual and back to your notes actually helps your body relax.

Here are a few other things to remember when using visuals of any kind:

Use visuals to supplement the speaking, not supplant it. The point is to keep attention on the ideas and to reinforce the oral message. The ease in creating overhead visuals by computer, for example, leads some people to project their entire speech on the screen. This makes a boring presentation, because audiences read faster than people speak.

Talk to the audience, not to the visual. A rule to guide you is "TTT—touch-turn-talk." Touch—identify the visual area you want the audience to focus on. Turn—redirect your attention to the audience by engaging them with direct individual eye contact. Talk—continue with your oral message.

Reveal only what you want the audience to focus on. If you're using an overhead projector to show a list of items, for example, only reveal one at a time as you talk. Keep the others covered. When you are finished using a visual, turn it off, cover it, or remove it so the audience doesn't continue to concentrate on the aid and miss what follows.

Beware of passing around handouts, pictures, or objects. If you must give the audience material to hold or pass, do it only as you go over it with them. Otherwise, they get absorbed in reading or looking at your handouts and stop paying attention to you.

Answering Questions

Questions can be your best friends. Even an ordinary presentation can become brilliant when the speaker responds to questions from the audience. Questions allow you to be sure your message has been understood correctly and to respond to concerns or objections audience members may have.

Before you start, be aware of how the situation, people's expectations, and cultural differences may affect questioning, so you can plan ahead. In some situations, there is little time for questioning, so you have to manage the session tightly—or there may be too much time and people aren't asking the questions you need. It's wise to think ahead so you can fill that time with added information.

Some groups, too, do not expect to ask questions or, the reverse, expect to engage in a full dialogue. You need to inquire before you speak as to what expectations an audience may have of the question session. Similarly, recognize and be prepared for cultural differences. For example, many Asian people do not expect to respond with questions—whereas the French ask a lot of questions (Allen, 2000, p. 78).

Even with the best of preparation, though, question-answering can seem a bit threatening. Martel (1989) gives this very good advice to people preparing for question-and-answer sessions: "Don't participate in the session until you have a positive attitude regarding how it can help you accomplish both your substance and image goals" (p. 156). You should, of course, adapt the presentation to anticipate questions, but time limitations may prohibit covering everything. So, during rehearsals, have your friends identify places where questions may pop up and ask questions so you can develop clear, concise responses. Anticipate both honest and hostile or trick questions so you can get a feel for potential answers. Examine your speech content and think about what your audience might ask. For example, what information, resources, or concepts might listeners want explained, and how might you do so without simply repeating what you have already said? What points might listeners want to challenge, and how might you respond to demonstrate your competence, objectivity, and trustworthiness—and still make your point?

Your credibility can be enormously enhanced by masterful responses to questions; the skills are fairly simple, but impressive in action. Do the following:

1   Assume questions are well intentioned. Even if they aren't, treating them as if they were puts the ball in your court and reflects favorably on you.

2   Listen intently and concentrate fully on the question.

3   Answer questions as concisely and directly as possible with a friendly and cooperative approach.

4   If the question is hard to hear or is long and complicated, take a moment to analyze it and restate it more briefly for the audience.

5   If the question really involves two or more questions, separate them and state your intention to answer them individually.

6   If the questioner makes a speech instead of asking a question, don't disagree or argue. Listen courteously, and then phrase a question from it or ask the speaker to phrase the question.

7   If the question is loaded ("Why would you spend money on a dead-end project?"), do three things: Point out how the question is loaded, reject it as stated, then shift to a better question ("I disagree that this is a dead-end project, and I can't logically answer that question as it is phrased. Now, if you mean what will this project do to justify the expense, I can give you three benefits it will bring to this community." ("How Do I Deal," 1998, p. 27).

8 If your answer to a question is complicated, organize the response into concise chunks and begin your answer with a preview: "Four concerns are involved here. The first is . . ."

9 If you have already answered the question, don't mention that fact. Just answer it again, perhaps embellishing your response slightly.

10 If you don't have an answer, say so; don't fake it. If appropriate, promise to find out the answer and get back to the questioner.

11 If the information for an answer is on one of your visuals, go back and show it as you discuss the answer.

You may someday face a questioner who is overtly hostile. Remember that hostility from one person doesn't cancel out the majority who are supportive and favorable to your message. The key is to stay cool and friendly; don't get sarcastic or defensive, because that's giving control to the questioner. Sometimes, you can "bridge" the question—that is, start with what the questioner said and move the topic to your ground. For example, suppose a listener asks, in response to a speech about oral vaccine for rabies, "How can you talk about spending money on this vaccine when there isn't even enough money to build new schools?" You might answer, "Whether the oral vaccine is the right priority for funds is a legitimate question. As you recall, one state spent $1.5 million to treat people who were exposed to rabies. So the issue is not whether to spend the money, but whether to spend it on prevention or on treatment."

Summary

Preparing for a speech starts with deciding whether to present it as an impromptu, extemporaneous, orally read manuscript, or memorized speech. Extemporaneous delivery uses more oral language and enables you to adapt more readily to the situation and audience, although sometimes a manuscript is essential for specificity or control of public messages.

You need to prepare careful notes for extemporaneous speaking. Use numbered cards, large print, and key words as cues. Notes allow you to "talk" the development of the speech using the key words to trigger memory while allowing oral language and a direct style to develop.

The process of rehearsing and adapting the speech starts with visualizing and affirming yourself successfully presenting it. You also need extensive practice (preferably at the site, but certainly in a quiet place) with videotape and personal feedback from friends to help you polish the presentation. Practice also involves handling the visuals until using them is second nature and identifying possible questions and preparing answers for them.

Before delivering the speech, get set mentally and physically by visualizing, relaxing, exercising both body and articulators, and becoming fully involved in the audience and the situation. Sometimes, you need to adapt your approach to accommodate changes in agenda, other speakers, or technological difficulties. Being prepared to adapt increases your confidence and your credibility. When you approach the front of the room, you want to take command and engage your audience in such a way that you demonstrate your credibility and a dialogical ethic. Maintaining your confidence as you speak is easier if you keep the focus on the audience and your message rather than on yourself.

Delivering your speech effectively involves using the same nonverbal abilities as in a one-to-one conversation, but simply expanding the range of your voice, gestures, eye contact, and body movements to accommodate your conversation to a larger group. Upright posture, good eye contact, expressive gestures, vocal variety, and clear articulation are essential to communicating well in a public speaking situation.

Finally, handling questions in a cool, well-organized, friendly manner enables you to clarify ideas and enlist the cooperation of the audience.

Exercises

1 Attend a public presentation—a lecture, a sermon, a business presentation, or the like. Evaluate the speaker's presentation. Consider:

   a The mode of presentation, the management of notes or manuscript, and the use of visuals or other aids

   b The language (Does it seem oral or written?), the adaptation to the audience, and the speaker's credibility

   c The degree to which the speaker appeared to be confident and the way she or he handled questions

   d The speaker's presentation abilities—uses of body, face, eyes, gestures, voice, and speech

   What was effective and what would you suggest the speaker do to improve his or her presentation? Report your observations to the class.

2 Select a short essay on a controversial topic from a book or magazine. Then do the following:

   a Read it over once. Then, for a small group of fellow students, make a three-minute impromptu speech with an introduction, body, and conclusion, on the essay's topic. (Don't look back at the essay.)

   b After making your impromptu speech to your group, refer back to the essay. Now take 30 minutes to select specific points to develop a thesis and supporting information. Organize, practice, and present—*in your own words, not the author's*—a three-minute extemporaneous speech with an introduction, body, and conclusion for your group.

3 *Voice and breathing.* With a partner, tape-record a session in which you take turns doing the following exercises. Listen carefully and coach each other. Then, for one week, do the exercises privately three times a day, trying to build up stronger breath support, a more open throat, and crisper articulation of sounds. At the end of the week, have another session with your partner and tape-record yourselves again. Play back the first recording and the last. Do you hear any differences in either of your performances? Do you feel any differences in the amount of breath support or in your articulation of words?

a To develop strong breath support and open throat, draw your breath in evenly as you slowly count (mentally) to six, pursing your lips so you can hear the air pushing into your lungs. Next, hold the air for another six counts, keeping your throat open. Then exhale slowly and evenly as you count (mentally) to six, again keeping your lips pursed so you can hear the exhalation. Be careful not to exhale too fast at first. Repeat once.

b To learn to control your breathing, say each of these words but try to control your breath so it doesn't all rush out at once:

hit—home—half—hot—head—heavy

Feel how the air tends to rush out because the "h" sound is made with a panting movement of air. Try to hold back some of that air so it is more evenly available for the full word.

c Try to say this in one breath:

Have you ever seen such a wonderful, splendiferous sight as a spider spinning, swirling, sending its silky, slender string amongst the stickily, prickly boughs of a tree trembling in the nebulous night?

Now, do it again, trying to parcel out enough bits of breath for each portion of the sentence.

4 *Articulation.* Reread the instructions for Exercise 3 and then do the following:

a Recite this phrase:

lots of hot coffee in a proper coffee pot

Listen for the clarity of "t" and "p" sounds; these should be crisp. Also listen for an "ah" tone in the "o" sounds. If you make an "aw" sound, try to make the sound farther back in the mouth with a more open throat.

b Try this one:

Theophilus Thistle, the successful thistle sifter, in sifting a sieve full of unsifted thistles, thrust 3,000 thistles through the thick of his thumb. Since thousands of successful thistle sifters have sifted unsifted thistles without thrusting thistles into their thumbs, Theophilus Thistle is an unsuccessful thistle sifter indeed. We wish success to Theophilus Thistle, the faithful, if clumsy, thistle sifter.

Listen for clear "th" sounds, made by pushing air through the tip of the tongue against the top teeth, and for clear "s" sounds, made by pushing air through the tip of the tongue just barely touching—briefly—the ridge behind the top front teeth. On the "s" sounds, if you make a "th" sound, the tongue is a bit too far forward and flat; if the "s" whistles, the tongue tip is placed too hard against the ridge.

c   Now try this one:

If Axelrod only would ask Askew to drop the axe nicely, Askew would act in accordance and Axelrod's accelerating anxiety about an axe-induced ache would no longer accrue.

Listen for clear "x" sounds, made starting in the back of the mouth and moving the tongue forward quickly from a "k" to an "s" position. And listen for a clear "s"; sometimes, people reverse the order of the "s" and "k" sounds in words, which substitutes "x" for "sk," resulting in "axe" instead of "ask," for example.

Cyberpoints

CCC

WEB SITE

1   Do you need to make a manuscript speech? Go to the *Communicating with Credibility and Confidence* Web site at http://communication. wadsworth.com/lumsden and click on Chapter 13 for some hints on how to prepare a manuscript.

2   Would you like to improve your voice or your speech? Go to the *Communicating with Credibility and Confidence* Web site at http://communication. wadsworth.com/lumsden and click on Chapter 13 for exercises that will specifically help you to develop your delivery skills. Or check out the Virtual Presentation Assistant at www.ukans.edu/cwis/units/coms2/vpa/ vpa.htm for further help on preparation and presentation.

3   For additional help on using visuals effectively, see the advice of the Oceanography Society for the Office of Naval Research and the Oceanographer of the Navy presentations at http:www.onr.navy.mil/onr/speak/ visual.htm.#command.

4   At http://www.lib.msu.edu/vincent, you can listen to excerpts from the speeches of a number of U.S. presidents. You'll find a wide variety of styles and ways of using the voice among these speakers.

Chapter 14

Public Presentations: Speaking to Inform

Objectives for This Chapter

Knowledge

- Identify purposes and contexts of informative speaking
- Know ways to help audiences understand and remember information
- Understand methods to help listeners to learn

Feelings and Approaches

- Feel confident in communicating information
- Approach speaking to inform with the audience's benefit as a central focus
- Enjoy interacting with audiences to help them understand

Communication Abilities

- Present information credibly
- Design a presentation that motivates others to learn
- Set measurable objectives for enhancing listeners' understanding
- Present information effectively in various contexts

Key Terms

audience motives	parallel structure	mnemonic device
learning styles	associate idea	reinforcement

Did you ever try to explain something to someone only to see the person's eyes glaze over, and you try again—and again—to find a way to make the information clear? Talk about frustrating! This happens to teachers every day, and to the rest of the world almost as often.

This is an information age, they say, and ours is an information society. From classes to study groups to researching projects, you are gathering information. From giving reports to coaching Little League to explaining an idea to a friend, you are providing information.

Sharing information is so important that some communication theorists list it as the second key role of communication, after gaining cooperation (Infante, Rancer, & Womack, 1993, pp. 25–26). The problem is that people are overwhelmed with data; it's been estimated that the amount of information available doubles about every 20 months (Koenenn, 1989, p. B5). People are presented with too much to know and remember. As a speaker, therefore, you compete for your listeners' comprehension against a multitude of unrelated facts and ideas. That's why you must be both credible as a source of information and confident of your ability to inform people effectively.

This chapter will help you develop the ability to impart information and enhance others' understanding in a variety of contexts.

Speaking to Inform

Almost any speech includes some explanation and data that informs the audience, but many presentations focus specifically on sharing ideas or information. You hear lectures—that is, speeches inform you about a topic—every class day. It's true, of course, that the same data presented solely to inform you may also serve in another speech to support the speaker's persuasive appeal to, say, vote for your candidate or donate to a cause. The design of the speech depends, in part, on the occasion and the specific content of the speech.

Occasions for Informative Speaking

The most relevant occasion, at the moment, probably is your classroom assignment. The purpose of that experience is to prepare you for future speaking opportunities, including:

If you don't have objectives for your presentation, you will probably present a talk you didn't intend to. Objectives are a security blanket to protect you from rambling.

Wess Roberts

- *Reports.* As a student, you may give research or project reports to your classmates, but just wait until you're in your career and have to give reports to colleagues or managers. Health care professionals report on treatment and patient progress to their teams; managers report on sales and marketing campaigns to executive boards; members of organizational teams report their research to their teammates and superiors; your professors report results of their research or academic projects at conferences and, sometimes, to administrative committees or boards.

- *Briefings.* Many jobs include briefing people on information about some action they must take. A briefing specifically focuses information and analysis on what the receiver needs to know. A major part of a researcher's or analyst's job is to prepare someone else to answer questions and convey information intelligently. Executives, administrators, politicians, and top newscasters often rely on briefings for the research and analysis that they will subsequently use in their presentations, meetings, press conferences, or broadcasts.

- *Lectures.* If you're good at what you do, you may find yourself lecturing about it, perhaps using slides or other visual aids to present your information. You probably will carry on a dialogue with your audience through question-and-answer sessions, and you might combine lecture with discussion and other teaching methods.

- *Training.* You may train someone else to play a sport, do a job, make a presentation, understand the way an organization works—almost anything. A primary objective of corporations these days is to train people to work together and manage themselves (Byrne, 1993, pp. 76–81). One communication career option, therefore, is in training for business, social, religious, academic, and community organizations. Such training develops not just people's skills but their understanding of theories and data so they can assume more responsibility for a wider range of individual and team activities.

Types of Content

Whatever the topic or purpose, when you speak to inform the audience you normally talk about objects, events, processes, and/or concepts (Byrns, 1981). Here's an example: Your art professor is talking about Michelangelo. Her lecture might touch on:

Objects. *The speaker describes or explains something tangible and concrete;* your professor shows you a slide of paintings on the ceiling of the Sistine Chapel and describes the details of their composition and color, enhancing your understanding of the object.

Events. *The speaker gives a description and, perhaps, a chronology of events* to clarify how a given occurrence fits into a larger context; perhaps in this case she

It's important to talk to people in their own language. If you do it well, they'll say, "He said exactly what I was thinking." And when they begin to respect you, they'll follow you to the death. The *reason* they're following you is not because you're providing some mysterious leadership. It's because you're following them.

Lee Iacocca with W. Novak (1984), *Iacocca: An autobiography*. New York: Bantam Books, p. 55.

explains events that led Michelangelo to lie flat on his back for years, painting a ceiling he never wanted to paint in the first place.

Processes. The speaker shows relationships among various components in developing some outcome; the professor might explain Michelangelo's process of cartooning, projecting, preparing, and painting a mammoth depiction of the biblical story of creation on a ceiling. Sometimes, a speech about processes includes demonstration and/or hands-on experience to help the learner internalize the information.

Concepts. The speaker defines complex ideas about theories, beliefs, values, philosophies, and viewpoints, often using a variety of perspectives to help the listeners grasp the concept. Your lecturer might explain Michelangelo's concept of how a form emerges, through the artist's sculpture, from its prison in a piece of marble—and why the artist found sculpture so much more satisfying than painting.

Audience Motivations

You set the objectives—but only your listener can reach them. Your job is to be credible and confident in shaping and presenting information so your audience can use it. Part of that job is knowing how to draw on your audience's motivations and ways of comprehending and learning.

We won't go back over the information in Chapter 3, but you can apply those principles in planning your speech. The object is to draw the **audience's motives,** their needs, wants, and values, to find their reasons for wanting to know what you can teach them. For a review of audience motivations, you also could go to the Web at http://www.speech210.com/m3c5tpc3.htm.

Audience motives Listeners' reasons for wanting to know what a speaker can teach them

Individual and Cultural Learning Styles

Learning styles Ways individuals process information, influenced by side of brain used and individual ability, personality, culture, and, perhaps, gender

Remember, too, that individuals process information differently. Each person has an individual **learning style** that uses one or both sides of the brain (McCarthy, 1990), and reflects such influences as our abilities, personalities, culture, and perhaps gender. These differences can affect your speech in a number of ways. For example:

- *Your audience's cultures affect how they respond to information.* Research finds, for instance, that Anglo and Asian learners are likely to use analytic learning, breaking ideas down into component parts. Native Americans, Hispanics, and African Americans, however, tend to use a relational style, relating ideas to one another holistically (Powell & Andersen, 1994).

- *Your listeners' styles may be different from yours.* Speakers may unconsciously reflect a cultural bias in the ways they present information (Lieberman, 1994), imitating their own teachers without recognizing that the method may not help a diverse audience to learn (Blakeslee, 1980). In North American classrooms, for example, suggest Felder and Silverman (1988), most students *need* more visual information that uses their right brains intuitively and creatively, but what they often *get* is more lectures or abstract symbols on a blackboard. This is due to a Western bias toward linear or analytic left-brain thinking.

- *Some listeners expect to interact and question; some don't.* Powell and Andersen (1994) note that in Asian cultures, students "receive information and then reflect upon it," neither disagreeing nor asking questions because "such behavior would threaten the 'face' of the teacher who is a revered and respected individual" (p. 324). Native American students also tend to learn silently, through observation and imitation, whereas North American Anglos often question, respond, and discuss ideas (p. 324). Figure 14.1 summarizes the relationship between culture and learning.

If your listeners all are just like you, maybe they learn the same way you do. If they have diverse backgrounds, your best bet is to vary your presentation so individuals can process your information in the ways best suited to them.

Methods to Aid Understanding and Memory

How can you help your audience to understand and remember? American students retain about 10% of what they read, 26% of what they hear, 30% of what they see, 50% of what they see *and* hear, 70% of what they say, and 90% of what they say *as* they practice what they are learning (Silverman, cited in Lieberman, 1994, p. 185). This is good news for your own learning; giving your presentation will teach *you* a lot. If you can design a speech that helps your audience to hear what you say, perhaps also to see it, and even to practice

Figure 14.1 *The relationship between culture and learning*

Low-Context Cultures:

- Provide information in words

- Are less aware of nonverbal cues, environment, and situation

- Lack well-developed networks

- Need detailed background information

- Tend to segment and compartmentalize information

- Control information on a "need to know" basis

- Prefer explicit and careful directions from someone who "knows"

- View knowledge as a commodity

High-Context Cultures:

- Draw much information from the surroundings

- View nonverbal cues as important

- Exchange information freely

- Rely on physical context for information

- Take environment, situation, gestures, and mood into account

- Maintain extensive information networks

- Are accustomed to interruptions

- Do not always adhere to schedules

Monochronic People:

- Do one thing at a time

- Concentrate on the job

- Take time commitments (deadlines, schedules) seriously

- Are low context and need information

- Adhere religiously to plans

- Are concerned about not disturbing conversations

- Emphasize promptness

Polychronic People:

- Do many things at once

- Are highly distractible and subject to interruptions

- Consider time commitments an objective to be achieved if possible

- Are committed to people and human relationships

- Change plans often and easily

it, then they, too, will remember what you've taught them. To help your audience understand your information, you can start by wording your points to help them remember the connections among them and by supporting your ideas with material that strengthens and clarifies the points in your listeners' minds.

Organizational Patterns

You already know the basic process and some effective patterns for organizing the body of a speech from Chapter 12. Now let's look at some additional patterns that specifically help to enhance your listeners' understanding and memory.

Extended Analogy or Example   Analogies and examples are a great way to clarify concepts—the analogy draws on previous knowledge and the example illustrates the idea. If you extend an analogy or an example throughout your speech, either one can serve as an organizational pattern.

Suppose your speech is to inform the local Chamber of Commerce of how management structures in the city's corporations are changing from vertical to horizontal organizations. The body of your speech might be an analogy comparing an urban skyscraper to a traditional Spanish home, in which case you would structure your subpoints to show spatial relationships:

    I. Traditional organizations and skyscrapers are tall.

        A. Communication from the bottom to the top is limited.

        B. Creative flow from the bottom to the top is limited.

        C. Participation from the bottom to the top is limited.

    II. Contemporary organizations and Spanish homes are horizontal.

        A. Communication among all parts of the organization flows freely.

        B. Creative flow among all parts of the organization is free and open.

        C. Participation among all parts of the organization is encouraged.

Using drawings of each type of building, you could show how the skyscraper has levels piled on one another, with the power offices at the top and specialized areas underneath them. Only elevators and staircases provide communication from level to level. You would compare this to the Spanish home, with all the rooms on one level, arranged around a central patio accessible to all areas of the house so people can interact openly and freely.

Acronym Arrangement   An *acronym* is a word you create out of the first letters of several related ideas. As an organizational pattern, an acronym is a word created from the first letters of each of the main points of a speech. This helps your audience (and you) to remember the specific ideas. If your speech is on maintaining optimal health through weight control and physical conditioning, your acronym organization might be VEER:

    I. **V** is for "Visualize yourself as thin."

    II. **E** is for "Eat sensibly."

    II. **E** is for "Exercise faithfully."

    IV. **R** is for "Reward yourself appropriately."

Your organization also gives you ideas for introducing and concluding your speech. You might start with, "How would you like to VEER from the fat lane, to drive down the thin lane, and enjoy the view in your mirror? I'm going to show you how to do that in four easy steps."

Then, you might conclude with, "So, remember—VEER from the fat lane by visualizing yourself as thin, eating sensibly, exercising faithfully, and rewarding yourself appropriately."

All your audience has to remember is the acronym to trigger memory of the rest of your message.

Journalist's Formula   In a journalism class, you learn to write stories that answer the *who, what, when, where, why,* and *how* questions. These same questions provide an excellent pattern for a briefing, report, or explanation of an event, arranging some or all of the categories to suit your topic. You might organize a report to your employer this way:

    I. What do we want to accomplish?

   II. How can we do it?

  III. Who should be responsible?

  IV. When can we implement the program?

Another way to apply this formula is in subpoints under any other pattern, such as problem-solution:

    I. We had a problem with our product's quality.

       A. The problem was a defective spring. [What?]

       B. The problem was caused by the manufacturer's error. [Why?]

   II. We solved the problem with our product's quality.

       A. We changed the contract with the manufacturer to require quality testing before they ship the springs to us. [How?]

       B. We implemented our plan at the plant during last quarter. [When?]

Demonstration   Many times, a speech to inform often demonstrates how a procedure works through a chronological, step-by-step procedure that shows as well as tells your listeners what they need to know. Methods to help your audience grasp the process include:

Grouping steps.   Group ("chunk") the steps into no more than five logical main points. Don't commit the common error of going straight down a list of 10 or so steps. They are too hard to remember. For example, one of our students spoke on how to prepare a resume. She started preparing with a long list of ideas: Brainstorm, request references, check transcripts, organize ideas, state objectives, list education, note academic and extracurricular experiences, draft, edit, type, print; it was far too much to remember. So she organized the body of the speech like this:

I. Analyze your qualifications.
   A. Identify important academic experiences.
   B. Identify important extracurricular experiences.
   C. Identify important skills and abilities.
II. Assemble the pieces.
   A. Request letters of recommendation.
   B. Order transcripts.
III. Create the résumé.
   A. List important elements.
   B. Emphasize important points.
   C. Set up for visual impact.
   D. Write for clarity.
   E. Edit for accuracy.
IV. Publish the résumé.
   A. Have the résumé professionally typed.
   B. Have the résumé professionally printed.

Using visuals. Plan your demonstration with visual aids that develop each step on the outline. Then rehearse carefully to be sure you can develop each step sufficiently in the length of time you have. Demonstrations are worse than useless when the speaker rushes through without proper equipment. The résumé speaker communicated effectively within her time limits by using an overhead projector to show her audience, step by step, how she had prepared a professional-looking résumé.

Preparing in advance. Plan ways to prepare portions of your demonstration ahead of time. The perfect example of this is when television's many cooking show hosts grate a bit of chocolate and put it on the stove to melt—but then use chocolate that was previously grated and melted. They mix the chocolate mousse and slip it into the oven as the viewers salivate—but when a lucky guest savors a taste of the mousse at the end of the show, it's a mousse that was baked earlier.

Outline Wording

The way you *phrase* the main and subpoints of your speech makes the logical connections between your ideas. It just isn't enough to have a list of topics.

"Let's see," you may say to yourself, "I'll talk about how aerobics helps the heart and respiratory system and how to do aerobics." To weave these points into a logical and memorable development you need to:

Connect phrased points logically. In this case, you may think you have three main points, but close examination shows that you really have two: how aerobics can help one's health (the subpoints would deal with benefits to the heart and respiratory system specifically), and how one can do aerobics.

Word points to help you with the extemporaneous development of the speech. You do not want a prewritten manuscript, but your talk should carry through the logical development of your outline. If you clearly state each point on the outline, you will more easily remember and develop the ideas.

Word points to help listeners follow and understand you. We can't emphasize this point enough. Plain old topics, such as "Economy—living—success," just won't do; you need clear statements of each main point and subpoint. What is your point for each topic, and how does each relate to the others?

Parallel structure
Organization or material that uses same phrasing for each of a series of ideas

An excellent way to phrase main points, as well as subpoints for each, is to use parallel structure. **Parallel structure** is repeatedly using the same phrasing to introduce or complete each of a series of new and equal ideas so the wording reinforces and intensifies the impact of the ideas. You'll notice that our sample speech outlines use parallel structure. Parallel structure doesn't just make the outline seem smooth and seamless—though it does that, too. Hearing the same phrases to introduce each idea helps your audience to see and remember the logic of your speech. Further, the very process of thinking through and phrasing points serves you in these critical ways:

Making points parallel helps you create logical categories that are equal to one another.

Making points parallel helps you remember what you want to say with few notes and freedom to adapt as you speak.

To get your outline in good form, follow the advice given in Chapters 12 and 13, and be sure that all main points begin or end with the same phrase so the relationship among all main points is equal and clear.

Look, for example, at the brief outline at the end of this chapter for a student's speech about preparing for a career in physical therapy.

As you can see, the body of the speech uses a parts-to-whole organizational pattern with main points focusing on equal topics of motivation, discipline, and involvement. With the parallel wording "*A physical therapy student* must . . . ," the speaker and listener can see each point as immediately related to one another and to the whole process of preparing to become a physical therapist. Similarly, under each main point, the parallel use of "*Your* . . ." underscores personal responsibility for developing qualifications for this major.

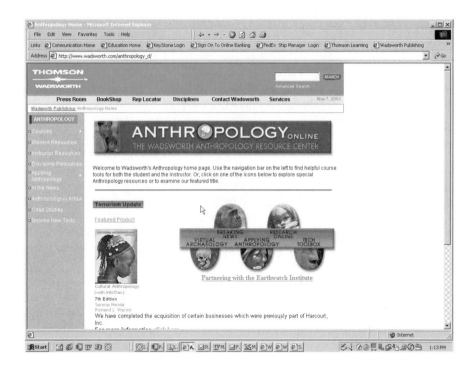

Good supporting materials can help you define terms and find interesting quotations. Researching online can lead you to a number of good resources quickly.

After the body of the speech is prepared with clear, parallel points, the introduction is easier to craft. This speech opens with a personal anecdote that leads directly into the preview and the body. The parallelism also makes the transitions easy to design so they bridge the points with a few words that summarize the previous point and preview the next one. Finally, the clear parallel structure simplifies creating a quick summary and a conclusion that brings all of these points together. In this case, that goal is accomplished by using a conclusion with a rhetorical question and a reference back to the introduction.

Support for Ideas

You already know a lot about supporting your ideas from Chapter 12. We will expand those concepts specifically for speeches to inform. The first criterion for support in an informative speech, of course, is that it be clear and specific; the first criterion for clarity is using the simplest, most concrete language possible. Sometimes, however, you will be introducing complicated concepts and new vocabulary to your listeners. Supporting such new material often involves defining terms, associating ideas, and using language that enlivens and clarifies the information in some way.

Defining Ideas Your desk or computer dictionaries are fine, but sometimes other methods of definition are more accurate or clearer—or more interesting.

Suppose, for example, you were speaking of love. You could define it by using:

Quotations from authorities. Look for experts' quotations in reference books or specialized dictionaries or articles or books on the subject. You might go to psychology textbooks or scholarly books on the nature and types of love.

Negation. Showing what something is *not* is sometimes called "definition by negation," as when Apostle Paul writes to the Corinthians that love "does not envy, it does not boast, it is not proud. It is not rude, it is not self-seeking, it is not easily angered, it keeps no record of wrongs. Love does not delight in evil but rejoices in the truth" (I Corinthians 13: 4–6, New International Version).

Comparison and contrast. Weigh the concept against other, more familiar, ideas. For instance, you could use an analogy or an example to compare attributes, such as, "Love is like a flowing stream, moving and nourishing those it touches." Or you could quote a poet's or philosopher's analogy, such as Kahlil Gibran's "Stand together and yet not too near together for the pillars of the temple, in order to hold the temple up, stand apart. The oak tree and the cypress do not grow in each other's shadow."

Components. Break the concept down to component parts and define each separately—then put them back together. Perhaps you would define love by citing psychologist Branden's (1980) concept that love involves spiritual, emotional, and sexual attachment, and then proceed to use those terms as the foundation for the three main points of your speech.

Historical roots. There are many ways to use history as a foundation for defining a concept. One way is to trace the etymology of the term in a given language and culture. Love often is defined in terms of the classic Greek concepts of filial love, spiritual love, and erotic love. You might talk about all three, or you might focus your speech on romantic love and trace that concept through the centuries. Alternatively, you might compare and contrast the views of love held by different cultures through history.

Associating Ideas Your listeners already have ideas and information that you can use to help them learn. When you link that information to new material, or **associate ideas,** the new material seems more familiar, less threatening, and easier to learn than if it were presented as something totally unfamiliar. Maybe you're trying to explain the concept of ethics to people who have never heard the term, so you start from their religious frame of reference. The study of ethics goes far beyond one religion, but understanding can start with the familiar concept.

Associate ideas New material that is directly linked by a speaker to existing ideas and information

Another aid to your listeners' memories (and your own!) is a **mnemonic device,** a memory aid that connects ideas to other ideas. It's something like remembering where a place is by remembering what you had for lunch there. Useful mnemonic devices include:

Acronyms. We talked about using acronyms as organizational patterns for speeches, but you can also use them for subpoints or to summarize a single point. Suppose you were speaking on stress management; you might say, "Remember to 'ALF'—Always Laugh First."

Similar symbols. You can relate a visual symbol to a word so the association triggers a memory. People often use this trick to remember a new acquaintance's name. If the name is "Fawcett," for example, you rehearse it mentally, picturing a faucet with the person's face. A speaker can give listeners a similar hint to help them remember a concept. You might help your listeners remember that it was Theodore Roosevelt who said, "Walk softly and carry a big stick," by telling them to think of a teddy bear carrying a baseball bat.

Metaphors and analogies. These devices express the similarities between two ideas, show logical relationships, and help an audience to associate a new concept with a strong or familiar bit of support. For example, a statistics professor helped one of your authors—Gay—by saying, "Statistical analysis is like language—it just uses mathematical symbols instead of words to show relationships among ideas." With just one analogy, that teacher melted away a mental block and opened the road to understanding statistical concepts.

Reinforcing Ideas   You can help your listeners to remember by reinforcing the important points. **Reinforcement** is a process of repeatedly underscoring an idea and intensifying its importance so it stands out in the mind of the listener against competing demands for attention and memory. You can reinforce your ideas with:

Rewards. You can link your main points to a reward—to something the audience wants or values. People find rewards in the reasons you give them for listening. Your listeners might see a reward in listening to your speech on physical fitness, for instance, if you remind them that fitness can benefit their sex lives.

Repetition. You can repeat ideas in the same words. Repetition is especially important in helping people to remember a concept by giving the idea extra importance and strength. In a speech on animal husbandry, for example, you might repeat the phrase, "The welfare of your stock is the welfare of your family," to emphasize the economic importance of learning how to care for your animals properly.

Dr. Samuel Betances

Dr. Samuel Betances, internationally known "edutainer," consults with businesses and educational institutions—teaches and entertains—writes and lectures—on how to communicate and get along in this widely diverse society. A professor of sociology at Northeastern Illinois University, Dr. Betances earned his masters and doctorate at Harvard University. He is a funny, wise, and incredibly communicative teacher, as well as an agent of change in a changing world. Dr. Betances has said, among other things:

I remember coming from Puerto Rico and going to school being intelligent and yet unskilled. My teachers looked at my generation and said, "Speak English," and we said, "Si." And they said, "Forget Spanish," and we said, "OK." But before we learned English we forgot Spanish, and soon we were illiterate in two languages. How dumb to tell us to forget what we know. . . . You need to learn middle-class English, [but] do not forget what you knew, because in order to be good Americans, you don't have to know less, you have to know more.

I came to school, I did not understand the language of English. . . . The teachers gave a demonstration of what they wanted us to know in English, . . . and I missed out on the explanation, not because I lacked intelligence, but because I lacked the symbolism. And sometimes the teacher did not know how to express something in the way that I could understand it. . . . I was failing for not knowing what I had not been taught. She . . . gave us 14 problems in arithmetic for homework. Victor told me that in Spanish. So I went home and I began to work on my 14 problems in arithmetic, and I had missed out on the explanation, and I did not know what to do. . . . By the time I got to the fourth one I was almost crying. [My mama] said, "Don't worry, I will help you," and she did the next one, and I kissed her and she did the next one, and I kissed her, and soon we were on a roll, she was doing, I was kissing, and then I copied all of them in my own handwriting, handed them to the teacher ('cuz I'm Puerto Rican, but I'm not a fool), the teacher came back, the first four that I did had four red

Ways to Use Participation and Feedback

Today's audiences are a restless bunch. As Wolvin, Berko, and Wolvin (1993) observe, "Most of us who have been raised on television have come to expect a seven-to-ten-minute viewing format, followed by a commercial break" (p. 25). People fade out or squirm when they get bored and also tend to forget anything that didn't involve them. That means the more you can get your listeners involved in ideas and feedback, the better. The extra dividend is that when you're really engaged in transactions with your audience, you are less nervous—and when you get feedback, you feel even better.

"x" marks, and then the ten that my mama did had ten red "x" marks. So I said, "Victor, come here. She marked them all wrong!" Victor said, "Teacher, Sammy's got a confession to make. He did the first four, but what you don't know is that his mama did the next ten! And you marked all wrong!" And Miss Carmel said, "Tell him his mama doesn't know what she's doing." She said something about my mama! So I said something about her father! And stupid Victor translated it. Next thing I know, I'm at the principal's office writing 500 times, something that to this day, I don't know what I wrote. But I suspect it has something to do with somebody's mama.

Listen to me. I was intelligent. Harvard-bound. Sometimes corporations today send their helicopter to pick me up. And when colleges think of freshman orientations, and think about the future, they send for me. Intelligent, yes, but unskilled. My mother loved me, but she was unskilled. The teachers worked hard, but they did not know how to communicate with us. And I'm telling you something, you who are now entering this freshman class: Learn to collaborate with other young people and those of you that know how to do it, learn how to do it better by helping those of us who are intelligent but unskilled. To give them the opportunity, to tutor, to collaborate, and to make coalitions of interest instead of coalitions of color so that we can march to the front door, all of us helping each other. The one that tutors learns it better by teaching it to those that don't know, and the ones that don't know get it from other students, because sometimes some of us teachers don't know how to do it, and some of the parents love us but do not know how to give us what we need. . . . Are you ready to collaborate and to make those coalitions of interest and to help each other out so that you can all be successful?

Amen! Well all right, let's do it.

From Dr. Samuel Betances' presentation at Kean University, Union, NJ, August 30, 1993. Used by permission.

Audience Participation

You can get an audience to participate actively in your presentation in a number of ways. For example:

1   *Ask them questions, get them to think about the topic, and open up discussion.* Keep the questions nonthreatening, and give people a little time to answer. Speakers too often ask the question and immediately proceed to the next point. If you were giving a speech on job interviewing, for example, you might ask, "What would impress a potential employer with your leadership ability?" After having listeners brainstorm ideas and write them on a flipchart or

People speak to inform in many settings. You can see how involved the audience is as this teacher explains the museum's collection.

blackboard, you could select one and then ask, "Now, how could you show this in an interview?"

2   *Give them hands-on opportunities as you speak.* In a speech on selective perception, for example, you might ask audience members to close their eyes and listen intently for 60 seconds—and then have them make a list of everything they just heard.

3   *Use guides, quizzes, or exercises as you speak.* A student reporting on gender differences in communication, for example, gave listeners a list of statements about male versus female language and had them mark "True" or "False." She then referred to the quiz as she spoke, asking her audience for their responses and opinions, and relating her research findings to the statements.

4   *Enlist audience members to role-play a situation with you.* You can demonstrate a point quickly by asking a person in the audience to be someone else for a moment. We once heard a speaker ask someone to role-play her employee. Then she asked, "Now, how would you respond if I said, 'You really do lousy work, don't you'?" Of course, the role-player answered defensively. Then the speaker said, "Right. Now, let's do it another way. Suppose you've handed me a report and I've looked at it. I say, 'I can see you've put a lot of effort into this. There are just a couple of things I'd like to go over with you.' " Naturally, the

role-player's response was much less defensive, and the speaker had effectively used her audience to make her point about using supportive communication. If you have plenty of time for your presentation, you can vary this by having two members of your audience role-play for you.

Feedback Opportunities

Everybody needs feedback in order to find out what they've done and what they want to do next time. The most effective feedback lets you know how well your objectives are being met and indicates what changes you need to make. Approaches for getting and giving mutually helpful feedback include the following:

- *A presentation assessment by your listeners.* You can use a handout sheet on which you ask for general or specific information about how effective they found your presentation. You'll find some sample feedback forms on the *Communicating with Credibility and Confidence* Web site at http://communication.wadsworth.com/lumsden (click on Chapter 14) that you may want to try or adapt for your own purposes.

- *A quiz that tests information or concepts you tried to teach.* If people are to take this quiz immediately, it should be brief, easy to read and check, and questions should focus on one point at a time.

- *A hands-on demonstration of specific skills you wanted people to learn.* You can ask people to show you what you've told or taught them; for example, if you demonstrated how to cross-stitch, you might give each participant a small bit of cross-stitch to do for you.

Feedback only helps if you can use what it tells you, either for yourself or for your audience. If you're testing listeners' learning, for example, try to summarize the results and discuss them in general terms with your audience. This can clarify and reinforce information that the listeners may have misunderstood or missed entirely. If you're asking for feedback to improve your presentations, then view it purely as potential help for you. Summarize them, read comments, and isolate one or two objectives to strive for next time. Most people give you good, honest, supportive responses. Rarely is anyone rude or hypercritical. If someone is, find whatever shred of constructive criticism you can, but disregard the rest. Any aggressive person who verbally uses you as a punching bag has a problem that is unrelated to you or your presentation.

Your Source Credibility and Confidence

When you set out to inform people, you are acting as an intermediary—someone who researches and refines information for others. Before you speak, you will have researched the topic thoroughly. You will know more about the topic than your listeners do, and have analyzed and interpreted your data for them. Most of your listeners' understanding will come from what you choose to tell them and from your responses to their feedback and questions. As the listeners' intermediary, then, you bear an ethical responsibility for what they learn.

Jensen (1981) points out that a credible and ethical speaker should always have the good of the audience in mind and be open to discussing alternative ideas. In addition, the speaker should present information that is:

Accurate: The information is specific and precise.

Complete: The information includes all important factors.

Relevant: The information relates directly to the point.

Understandable: The information is clear and to the point.

Reasonable: The information is developed logically.

Socially useful: The information can serve good purposes.

Meet these criteria and you will be both credible and confident—you will know what you're talking about, and your audience will know you're on their side.

Summary

At school and in your career, you may give many presentations to inform, including reports, briefings, lectures, and training sessions. Your presentations should be based on learning objectives—clearly stated, specific, measurable, and reasonable goals that you want your listeners to accomplish. Your confidence and credibility rely, in part, on your using basic principles of learning to tap into your listeners' motivations. Then you can get them to attend, listen, and remember through techniques of definition, association, and reinforcement.

Proper wording of your outline aids both your own memory and presentation and your audience's understanding and memory. Each main point should be carefully worded in full, declarative sentences and coordinated with each other main point in parallel structure. Each subpoint, too, should be a complete declarative sentence that parallels other subpoints under a main point. The summary of your information should be clear and focused, followed by a conclusion that reinforces the information and listeners' motivation to remember and use it.

In addition to the organizational patterns explained in Chapter 12, extended analogies or examples, the journalist's who-what-when-where-why-how formula, acronym arrangements, and step-by-step demonstrations work well in speeches to inform. Seek to involve your audience as much as possible with questions, hands-on experiences, guides and exercises, and role-playing with or between audience members. You can get and give feedback relating to your objectives by asking listeners to fill out an evaluation of your presentation, to take a quiz or test on the content you presented, and/or to demonstrate what they learned to do with a hands-on exercise.

Exercises

1   Identify a hypothetical audience (for example, a civic or religious group, a political setting, a school group). Select any chapter of this book and plan a five-minute speech for this audience to inform them about some part of the chapter's content. Remember that a five-minute time period will allow you to cover only two to four concepts from the chapter you select.

2   Get together with a partner and share the plans you developed for Exercise 1. Then work together to refine the plans. Compare your perceptions of the audiences' needs and expectations. Now create an outline together, using a specific organizational pattern worded with parallel structure. Under each point, suggest the kind of supporting materials you might use, and create an introduction and conclusion. Then work together to present your planning to the class.

3   With a small group, click on and print a Speech to Inform Assessment Sheet from the *Communicating with Credibility and Confidence* Web site at http://communication.wadsworth.com/lumsden. Then observe a short videotaped speech or a live speech on television (your college resource center or the library may have a collection of these). Now meet with your group and compare your ratings with those of others. In what places are your ratings similar? On what items do you differ? What aspects of the speech seemed to lead your group's members to similar assessments? What tended to make your responses differ? As a group, present your findings to the class.

4   Plan and present to your class a five-minute speech to inform. This can be a lecture, a report, or a demonstration of a process. Make a complete, parallel structure outline with a bibliography of the resources you used. Write a brief, objective quiz (true/false or multiple choice questions), duplicate it, and have your classmates complete it to assess how well they learned the principles you set out to convey.

Cyberpoints

CCC

WEB SITE

1   For help in creating your informative speech, click on the Speech to Inform Planning Guide at the *Communicating with Credibility and Confidence*

Web site, http://communication.wadsworth.com/lumsden. You may find additional guidance from *The Virtual Presentation Assistant* at www.ukans.edu/cwis/units/coms2/vpa/vpa.htm.

2   To help you plan a PowerPoint presentation, try: http://www.presentersuniversity.com/default.cfm.

3   Remember to use *InfoTrac College Edition* for your research to locate articles listed by keywords that relate to your topic.

SAMPLE SPEECH TO INFORM

Commentary

Topic: What is involved in preparing to be a physical therapist

Purpose: For the audience to understand the personal effort to become a physical therapist

Thesis: A career in physical therapy takes motivational, academic, and experiential preparation.

Introduction: The speaker uses a personal narrative with strong imagery and descriptive wording to get the audience's attention, to build rapport with the audience, and to develop her credibility on the topic.

Preview

The speaker summarizes smoothly the three main points of the presentation so her audience will know precisely what she will discuss. As she develops the speech through practice, she may add a brief transition, such as, "What do I mean, first, by 'motivational preparation'?"

Body of Speech

Organizational pattern: The points are organized as parts relating to the whole picture—a parts-to-the-whole pattern.

Main points: Each of the three main points is worded as a declarative sentence parallel to each of the other two, each starting with "A physical therapy student must be. . . ." This helps both speaker and audience to follow the logic of the speech.

Outline

Introduction

Three years ago, an automobile accident changed my life forever. I found myself lying in a hospital bed, twisted in pain, unable to move my legs, and scared to death. I thought I might never walk again. Today, I ride horseback, swim, run—I feel great. I feel great because 2 years of physical therapy restored my body and my confidence. That's why I've decided to become a physical therapist—so I can help others get their bodies and their confidence back, too. But I have discovered that becoming a physical therapist is nearly as hard as my recovery was.

Preview

I'm going to share with you what I've learned about becoming a physical therapist—what it takes in motivational, academic, and experiential preparation.

Body of Speech

I. A physical therapy student must be highly motivated to overcome discouragement along the way.
   A. Your ability to meet the heavy requirements is essential.
   B. Your ability to compete against many other well-qualified, motivated students is essential.

   Transition: Not only do you have to be motivated to meet requirements and compete against other equally motivated students, but you also have to be extremely well disciplined to succeed academically.

(continued)

Commentary

Subpoints: Under each main point, all sub-points are of equal type and weight, with each subpoint worded parallel to the other two. As the speaker plans the speech, she will add supporting materials to develop the subpoints. These should include examples, statistics, quotations from physical therapists or researchers, and explanations.

Transitions: Between the first and second and the second and third main points, the speaker has planned a transition that bridges the two points. The first transition ties together motivation and discipline. The second transition ties together discipline and experience. This way the "parts-to-the-whole" are woven together into the total picture for the audience.

Conclusion
The speaker weaves together four methods of conclusion: A rhetorical question (answered by her personal testimony), a brief summary, a reference back to the introduction, and a strong concluding statement. In so doing she reminds the audience of all she has said and reaffirms her convictions and her credibility.

Outline

II. A physical therapy student must be highly disciplined to succeed academically.
    A. Your social life is a dream of the past.
    B. Your professional life is a dream of the future.
    C. Your college life is a nightmare of studying in the present.

    Transition: All this academic discipline and sacrifice isn't enough, however. You also must be highly involved in the field itself.

III. A physical therapy student must be highly involved in the field to be admitted to a program.
    A. Your application must demonstrate extensive volunteer experience in the field.
    B. Your interview must demonstrate extensive knowledge of the field.

Summary
I've told you a little bit about how motivated a person must be to overcome discouragement in such a demanding and competitive field—how much discipline it takes to succeed in academic and hands-on requirements—and how thoroughly involved in volunteer activities and the field a student must be to get admitted into a physical therapy program.

Conclusion
Do you think it's worth it? I do. I think becoming a physical therapist is worth every bit of motivation and discipline and involvement it takes—because, without physical therapy, I would not be standing here today to talk about it. Now I can help someone else to have that same new chance at life. Yes, I definitely think becoming a physical therapist is worth it.

Chapter 15

Public Presentations: Speaking to Persuade

Bob Adelman/Magnum

Objectives for This Chapter

Knowledge

- Identify components of the persuasive process
- Know principles of influencing change
- Understand strategies for organizing persuasive messages
- Identify appeals that motivate audiences to change
- Know how language affects audience responses

Feelings and Approaches

- See persuasion as an artistic transaction between speaker and audience
- Feel confident in designing a persuasive speech
- Feel credible in influencing an audience to change
- Honor ethical standards in using persuasive strategies

Communication Abilities

- Analyze audiences and goals as a foundation for persuasive speeches
- Organize speeches psychologically and logically to move audiences
- Select emotional, logical, and psychological appeals to motivate audiences
- Develop an audience's belief in your credibility
- Use persuasive language that moves the audience to understand and accept your position

Key Terms

persuasion

self-persuasion

belief

attitudes

values

behaviors

social judgment theory

deductive speech pattern

inductive speech pattern

problem-solution speech pattern

motivated-sequence speech pattern

residues speech pattern

Persuasion is all about influencing others to change how they feel, or think, or act. Whether you're selling shoes or running for president, your ability to influence others is important to you in many ways—in getting a job, in advancing your career, in maintaining relationships, in making a difference in your community and in your world. Democratic societies depend on their members to advocate all sides of important issues persuasively so their audiences can make reasoned and ethical decisions that affect the good of all.

As a member of a democratic society, you engage in what Barber (1984) calls "political talk." By this he means not just talk about politics, but communication about values, options, and decisions within the political framework of your religious organization, your business, and your community. Political talk could include working with others on social or religious issues—for example, to change a school's curriculum or to get a new stop sign to protect children from injury.

As political talk, then, persuasion often is the basis for your relationships with other citizens. More than just speech, says Barber (1984), the process includes listening, thinking, setting agendas, and engaging in mutual inquiry (p. 173); this transactional communication "makes and remakes the world" (p. 179).

Although this chapter focuses on designing speeches to get public audiences to change, the principles of persuasion apply any time you try to get even one person to accept your point of view. Here we examine persuasion as a process by which speakers seek to influence change, and we discuss ways to use your knowledge about your audience to adapt persuasive messages. Then we give you some specific strategies for organizing persuasive speeches, we develop methods for achieving credibility, and we examine ways that effective language enhances persuasive messages.

Process of Persuasion

Persuasion Process of moving an audience to change willingly its beliefs, attitudes, values, and/or behaviors

Persuasion is the process of moving your audience to change their beliefs, attitudes, values, and/or behaviors—and to change them willingly. Let's consider what each part of this definition implies.

Willingness to Change

If you get what you want by holding a gun to someone's head, that's not persuasion. It is coercion. Coercion uses fear or blackmail to force someone to comply; it's usually unacceptable, often illegal, and it may win submission but it doesn't win minds or hearts or ensure future commitments. You might be compelled to hand over your money to a robber, for instance, but the experience won't persuade you to seek out another robber to whom to give money the next day.

In a democratic society, the objective is to influence people to take actions because they want to. The final decision remains with the audience. With persuasion, you are ethically concerned with the benefit and free choice of the audience. Far from manipulating your audience to do something they wouldn't do otherwise, you maintain respect for your listeners' rights to agree or disagree and give them reasons to agree with you.

Self-persuasion
Process by which an audience develops a rationale for change because of information provided by a speaker

Ultimately, any change your audience makes is through **self-persuasion.** As a speaker, your influence depends on your providing material that activates the audience members' motives—their needs, values, beliefs, attitudes, and goals. From these motives, individuals develop their own rationale for changing in some way. In that sense, persuasion is transactional, building change on elements contributed by you and by the audience itself. Centuries ago, Aristotle (1954) identified the speaker's challenge as "finding all available means of persuasion" (p. 24). He never guaranteed that any method would always be successful, because audiences still have individual choices and motives.

Beliefs

Often a person doesn't know enough about a subject, or "knows"—that is, believes—mistaken information. In persuasion, you give your audience information necessary to change beliefs as they relate to your goals. If you and your message are credible and audience members accept the information, then you have inspired them either to adopt new beliefs or to change old ones. As beliefs change, related attitudes, values, and behaviors may change as well—and that's persuasion.

Belief Degree to which a person accepts something as true

We have previously defined **beliefs** as "what people have learned or come to know through experience; they are either true or represent what they think is true" (Baum, Fisher, & Singer, 1985, p. 54). You can think of beliefs along a continuum, ranging from 0% (no belief that something is true) to 100% (total certainty that something is true).

Figure 15.1 shows a belief scale. Once you acknowledge the slightest chance something is true, you categorize it as "possible." When you have some greater rationale to support the statement, you consider it as "plausible." When you conclude that something is more likely true than not, you view it as "probable." When you have no doubt in your mind, your belief is "certain." You might believe it is highly probable that money put in Salvation Army kettles during the December holidays will provide help for people in your community who have

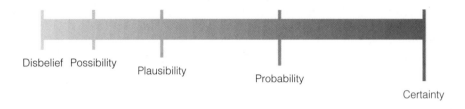

Figure 15.1 *Scale showing range for beliefs*

Disbelief Possibility

Plausibility

Probability

Certainty

needs. But are you equally confident that all money given to charitable organizations provides all the services the groups claim?

Although you may believe something is probable if it has better than a 50 percent chance of being true, you may want a higher degree of confidence than that to take action. Certainty, however, is even more elusive. You know that true/false test items that state "Always" or "Never" are usually false, because rarely is anything that absolute. You don't really need to persuade your audience that something is certain; simply persuading your listeners to be less sure or more sure—any move in either direction—represents a change. Suppose you're trying to persuade an audience to contribute money to a program for hungry children, and your audience believes it is only *possible* that this program will actually feed the kids. That isn't good enough; you have to convince them that their donations *probably* will provide the food.

Attitudes

Even though persuaders seek to change others' attitudes all the time, the actual **attitude** is an unobservable, internal degree of favor or disfavor, like or dislike, that an individual feels about people, objects, or ideas. Attitudes are, as we defined them in Chapter 3, preset responses, stable and enduring dispositions to evaluate things in particular ways. "Virtually anything that is discriminable can be evaluated and therefore can function as an attitude object" (Eagly & Chaiken, 1993, p. 5).

Attitude Scales While the continuum for describing a belief ranges from "I don't believe that" to "I totally believe it," an attitude is different. You can measure an attitude along a scale from a positive to a negative side, perhaps from "It's wonderful" down to "It's horrible." As Figure 15.2 shows, an attitude might be shown on a scale anywhere from a positive extreme of +1.00 to a negative extreme of −1.00. The "0" point on the scale doesn't mean a person has no attitude, but rather indicates that the attitude is neutral—neither favorable nor unfavorable.

Suppose that at the beginning of a new term somebody hands you a scale like this one and asks you to identify your attitude toward each class you've enrolled in. There might be a couple of classes about which you have no previous knowledge, so your attitude may be neutral. There may be one that you've heard is excellent, so your attitude is, perhaps, a +.50—you think you might like it. You may also be enrolled in a class that you've heard is boring or excessively

I see the world verbally. You say truth, you say justice, you say democracy, you say development—words don't create them, but if they do not exist in words they will never exist.

Carlos Fuentes, 20th-century Mexican writer and diplomat

Attitudes Internal degree of favor or disfavor an individual holds about people, objects, or ideas

Figure 15.2 *Scale showing range of possible attitude positions*

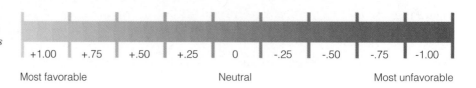

Most favorable   Neutral   Most unfavorable

difficult, in which case you might rate it −.75. Attitudes can change with new experiences, however; you may find the maligned instructor to be brilliant and would rate the class positively by the end of the term. Or maybe you'll be even more negative and move closer to −1.00.

Attitude Change You might persuade your audience to shift all the way from one side of the scale to the other, but really, an attitude change is any movement along the continuum—for example, a shift from +.50 to +.60 is change in a positive direction, and from +.50 to +.40 in a negative direction. Those small attitude shifts may be sufficient for your purposes.

Suppose you're speaking on behalf of Julie Coldwell's candidacy for mayor. One audience member, Ishi, has a −.15 attitude toward Coldwell, while her attitude toward Coldwell's opponent, Bob Pawley, is −.10. If she were voting now, Ishi probably would select Pawley as the lesser of two evils. But with an attitude change of as small as .06, Coldwell could get the edge over Pawley. That .06 change could occur in several ways: Coldwell could move ahead of Pawley (from −.15 to −.09), or Pawley could move lower (from −.10 to −.16). Or they could both move in some combination that adds to .06 (such as Coldwell moving from −.15 to −.12 and Pawley moving from −.10 to −.13).

That's just one audience member's attitude shift, of course. How about the rest of the audience? Another misconception about effective persuasion is that you need to get all or most of the audience to change attitudes. Often, you can be very successful by convincing only a small portion of the audience. When selling products, for example, marketers talk about "share"; you can have a very successful business if you sell toothpaste to only a 5% share of the U.S. market. The same is true in other persuasive efforts.

Let's return to the election example. Suppose Coldwell trails her opponent by 4% (that is, 52% to 48%). She could, therefore, win by influencing a small attitude change in just over 2% of the voters from the group favoring Pawley. This highlights the need for careful audience analysis to identify the 2% most likely to change and the appropriate strategies for persuading them. We explore those issues later in the chapter.

Values

You try to change beliefs, you try to change attitudes—but values are different. You try to build your audience's motivation on the foundation of their values. Rarely would you try to change an audience member's values. Why? Values are

The May 7, 1992, issue of the *Clayton* (Georgia) *Tribune* reported on a Ku Klux Klan march in that city the previous weekend:

[The KKK] had anticipated as many as 50 members might participate in the march, but only about 13 were on hand. . . .

The Klan members started their slow march across the street from where members of the Persimmon Church of God were conducting a car wash and bake sale to raise money for their church building fund. . . .

When one of the youngsters started singing, "Jesus Loves the Little Children," every one of them joined in to serenade the Klan members—men and women—as they walked by in single file. To the observers, it was a powerful statement, a touching moment befitting the occasion.

"It was spontaneous from the children," [Raburn] Wilson [an adult member of the church group] said. "The adults had wanted them to remain silent."

In the same issue, an editorialist added:

It set the stage for the remainder of a lousy day for the Klan. "Jesus Loves the Little Children" is a very old, very familiar religious song. It has been sung louder by much larger choirs many times before, but we doubt it has ever been more magnificent.

The article concluded:

"We washed 120 cars and sold 100 cakes," Wilson said. "I don't understand it. We usually average only about 20."

Excepts from Dick Gentry (1992; May 7), Only 13 march in Klan parade; it was a non-event, official says, *Clayton Tribune*, p. D5, and Editorial, A child shall lead them, p. A4.

Values Concepts of good or desirable that motivate behavior and serve as criteria for choice and judgments

central to an individual's concept of self. **Values** are, as previously defined, "conceptions of The Good or The Desirable that motivate human behavior and that function as criteria in our making of choices and judgments" (Johannesen, 1996, p. 1). A challenge to a value is a challenge to all the person believes she or he is, and as such will create resistance in your audience. When you recognize, accept, and appeal to individuals' values, however, you can persuade your audience to change a belief, attitude, or behavior.

It may be that a person's attitudes, beliefs, and values are in conflict, but she or he may not perceive that inconsistency. Values become most evident when people must assign priorities to decide not just what is important but what is more—or most—important to them. Here's an example: Suppose some new parents haven't much money and they always pay as little as possible for purchases, so they intend to buy the cheapest car seat available for their new baby. If you can show them that a more expensive car seat is significantly safer than others, their value for their baby's safety might outweigh their value for saving money—and they might well buy your product.

Behaviors

Behaviors External, observable actions that interact with beliefs, attitudes, and values

Behaviors are external, observable actions—things people consciously and unconsciously say and do—that interact with their beliefs, attitudes, and values. You can't always know what's behind a behavior. You might see two people give a homeless person some money and a third one walk right by. Perhaps the first one accepts biblical teaching to give to the poor, and does so because of her religious belief. Perhaps the second one has felt good about giving before, decided that's the kind of person he is, and now always gives because that's his belief about himself. And, perhaps, the third one has heard authorities say that giving to beggars only keeps them from working at an honest job, so she doesn't give because she always believes what authorities say. To get a contribution from the third, the beggar would need to convince her he is seeking a job. Indeed, you see people holding signs, "Will work for food," an appeal to just that person.

Very often, people see others' behaviors and attribute them to internal beliefs and attitudes when, in fact, they come from other sources. For example, a person may express an opinion, which is the act of *expressing* an attitude, but is that a true opinion or is it said to gain acceptance or attain some goal?

An example of the relationships among values, attitudes, beliefs, and behaviors can be seen in Luker's (1984) reports on interviews with both "pro-life" and "pro-choice" advocates. The subjects were only those highly involved on behalf of their cause. Their radically different activist behaviors were intertwined with very different beliefs, attitudes, and values. In the interviews, pro-life activists expressed the view that people should engage in sexual intercourse only for pro-creation and that parenthood is not primarily a social role, but a natural and necessary human function. Pro-choice proponents, on the other hand, expressed the view that sex is to foster intimacy and give pleasure and that wanting a child and giving it psychological, social, and financial resources are essential to parenthood. Obviously, to get members of either group to change their behaviors on this issue would demand substantial internal changes as well.

Another example of such conflict between behaviors and values is reflected in the phenomenon called "NIMBY" (Not In My Back Yard). NIMBY is a short way to say that some people oppose putting such services as recycling sites or homes for juvenile offenders in their neighborhoods. These residents often acknowledge the need for the facility, but they want it in somebody else's neighborhood because it conflicts with their values, attitudes, and beliefs about family comfort, safety, and property values.

When you want to persuade someone to change, then, you must know as much as possible about them, and consider how their attitudes, values, beliefs, and needs might compete within an individual to influence behaviors. It may be that a reasonable persuasive goal is to get people to apply a higher priority to some values than others. This shift, then, may influence their behaviors.

Think of your own responses to issues to see how it works. For example, individuals who speak out with hatred against a specific group may deeply offend your *value* for equality; you may *believe* such speakers feed a dangerous level of anger; and your *attitude* may be very negative toward them. Yet, your *value* of the right to freedom of speech may be stronger and lead you to approve of their right to speak at your college.

Audience Adaptation

Throughout this book, we have talked about the importance of understanding your listeners—their backgrounds, cultures, genders, needs, attitudes, beliefs, values, expectations, and goals. When you are speaking to influence people to change, this analysis provides a psychological foundation for every choice you make, including the goals you set, the audience motives you connect with, and the preparation for opposing arguments they may encounter later.

Setting Your Goals

Your goals in persuasion involve the nature of the change you seek and the degree of shift you expect from your audience. Depending on the change you seek, you can choose from several different speech types:

- *Speech to reinforce or stimulate.* In a speech to people who already agree with your position, you want to intensify attitudes and values, and to reinforce or strengthen behaviors consistent with those feelings. Sometimes called "preaching to the converted," a speech to reinforce requires material more to evoke feelings and responses and less to prove your ideas. A motivational speaker talking to a group of salespeople exemplifies this speech type.

- *Speech to prove.* In this speech, you focus primarily on changing beliefs— on making audience members more or less certain that something is true. The emphasis here is on developing evidence and reasoning that convinces the audience. A lawyer speaking to a jury has this goal.

- *Speech to get action.* In this speech, you want your audience not only to believe, but to *act* on the beliefs. This goal requires you to prove, stimulate, and motivate audience members to respond, physically or mentally. A political speech should get the audience to believe your candidate is best *and* to vote for that person; being stimulated by your enthusiasm is insufficient if the listeners don't go to the polls and vote based on their new beliefs.

Your plan for a persuasive message must state clearly and specifically the changes you want the audience to make. Even if you will not say these goals to your audience directly, stating them for yourself helps you to design and deliver the message. For example, suppose you want to persuade your audience to give blood at a drive next week. To reach these terminal objectives, you have to accomplish some instrumental objectives—smaller steps along the way to your larger goals: "My listeners will sign the pledge form," and, "My listeners will give blood next week."

Considering Diversity

Rarely will you try to persuade an audience that is just like you. If you're speaking to one person or a thousand, it's likely that they will represent different genders and sexual orientations, various economic strata and classes, and multiple cultures. There are two very good reasons for taking this diversity into account. First, you want them to find you credible and to hear your message receptively. Second, it's considerate, ethical, and decent to accommodate your message to the cultural expectations of your audience.

Have you noticed how many people dismiss any attempt to consider others' feelings as being "politically correct"? It implies that you are hypocritical if you use language that is sensitive to people and situations, that treats others as if they mattered. If you call the head of a committee a "chairperson," instead of a "chairman," some people say you're just being "politically correct." If you say your friend is an "African American" instead of "Black," or if you adapt your message to the customs or the language expectations of a culture different from yours, you may be labeled as just being "politically correct." Those who see this as only "politically correct" say things such as, "I am who I am, and they (their audience) can like it or leave." These people miss the fact that when you use communication that considers how people feel, you are being cooriented with them. If you fail to take these factors into account, you are neither credible nor competent in reaching your audience.

How do you know everything there is to know about other folks' cultural or gender expectations? Obviously, you cannot. What you can do is learn as much as you can and adapt as well as you can to possible differences. Samovar, Porter, and Stefani (1998) suggest preparing yourself all along for considering each audience (pp. 253–267). Preparation can include reading all you can about cultures and genders and:

- *Use feedback and observation* to get a clear understanding of your own communication culture, your attitudes, and your style of communication so you can adapt it to a variety of people.

- *Know about others' expectations and be able to adapt to situations.* This can include adapting to your audience's expectations about time, setting, and customs. Learn and use insights from the styles of communication of various groups. Consider, for example, how formal or informal your audience might want you to be; how you can use humor effectively with particular groups; and how much you can expect others to understand your own uses of idiom.

- *Observe, listen, seek to understand, and develop your empathy for others.* It's true that you cannot know perfectly what another person feels, but focusing on the others, paying attention, trying to understand what they feel, and studying various groups can help a lot. Your objective must be to create messages that consider the individuals in your audience, not only to avoid building cultural blocks to communication but to develop appeals that genuinely reach their values and needs.

Determining Ego-Involvement

Social judgment theory
Individuals' attitudes influence how much they may change to another attitude position

Your goals for a persuasive speech will depend partly on just how much change you can realistically achieve. **Social judgment theory,** also known as ego-involvement theory (Sherif, Sherif, & Nebergall, 1965), provides insight into how much an audience is capable of changing. Social judgment theory suggests that individuals' attitudes serve as anchors that hold them at that position. From that point, all statements reflecting different positions can be ordered in terms of how far from the anchoring attitude they fall. These different attitude positions, then, are divided into three categories, starting with those closest to the person's present attitude. In Figure 15.3, a scale shows how statements people hear might be judged from their personal anchoring attitude.

1   *Latitude of acceptance* is a range of statements close enough to a person's attitude anchor to make the persuader's position seem reasonable.

2   *Latitude of noncommitment* is a range of statements that are too far from the anchor position for an individual to accept easily, but she or he might change if the persuasive message appeals strongly enough.

3   *Latitude of rejection* is the range of statements too far away from the anchor for a person even to consider; listeners quickly reject proposals that fall in this range.

How ego-involved a person is in the issue determines how broad or narrow his or her attitude ranges will be. Ego-involvement with issues develops in several ways. People may be publicly identified with their attitude as spokespersons for a cause, or their life experiences may have left them personally committed, or the issue may relate to important values. If their ego-involvement is high, their latitude of acceptance becomes smaller—they find fewer alternative attitudes within their range of consideration. Also, their latitude of rejection increases, leaving a small area of noncommitment. When you're analyzing your audience and planning your goals, then, you need to recognize that your listeners' present attitudes and their ego-involvement determine how extreme they may consider your ideas to be. If your position is far outside their latitudes of acceptance, therefore, you would need to work on gradual moves from a position closer to their anchors.

Suppose, for example, you are to speak *against* stricter control of pornography to a women's group that wants stronger laws. The group has taken a public position on the issue and, therefore, seems highly ego-involved. The members' latitudes of acceptance will be very small. In this case, your goal may be only to get them to reconsider one aspect of the issue—for example, "My message will

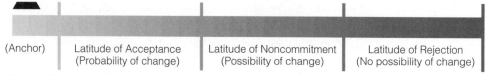

(Anchor) | Latitude of Acceptance (Probability of change) | Latitude of Noncommitment (Possibility of change) | Latitude of Rejection (No possibility of change)

Figure 15.3 *Social Judgment Theory: Latitudes of acceptance, noncommitment, and rejection with regard to persuasive messages*

get my listeners to believe that current definitions of pornography make stricter control impossible," or, "My listeners will invite me back to discuss proposals for legal redefinition of pornography."

Connecting with Motives

Understanding your audience will help you find ways to draw on their motives. In its simplest terms, persuading audiences requires getting them to believe that they will be more satisfied by following your lead or adopting your proposal than by maintaining their present position. That's motivation. As you look for ways to draw on your audience's motivations, keep in mind that people are listening to your speech because they have individual expectations and goals to which it relates. They probably have some awareness of what they want to get out of listening to you and personal objectives that relate to your message. As they listen, they may select and prioritize their plans and adapt them to what you say. As a persuader, show how your ideas can help them achieve their goals. The following insights can help in motivating your audience:

- *People may be aware of a given need only when previous, more fundamental ones have been satisfied.* Appeals to self-esteem needs are not effective if your listeners are still motivated by their needs for safety and security. You must connect your message to the level of audience needs that are not yet fulfilled and convince them that the change you want them to make will satisfy them more completely.

- *People often respond based on their evaluation of what is likely to be most rewarding and least costly* among alternative options. Your task is to make them see how changing in the way you advocate will fill their needs and offer rewards *they value*.

- *People seek consistency among their values, attitudes, beliefs, and behaviors.* When a persuasive message makes listeners aware of an inconsistency or conflict among their values, attitudes, beliefs, and/or behaviors, they experience cognitive dissonance and are motivated to change one or the other to end the dissonance (Festinger, 1957; Bem, 1967). The persuader's job is to get them to see the inconsistency and then to show them how and why the advocated change is the best way to relieve their internal dissonance.

Here is an example that incorporates all three principles. You're speaking to a community service club; you want the group to volunteer in a phonathon to raise money for a new hospital. In your speech, you get them to feel that someone who volunteers for this drive is a good person. You point out that this behavior would be consistent with their value of community service. You show how making telephone contacts for the cause helps them become known to others in the community who will appreciate their efforts and remember them for future business relationships. The listeners may have come for no more than a free lunch, but, you appeal to their need for belonging, help them to achieve balance between their values and their behavior, and show them rewards for participating in this drive. As a result, some of them decide to volunteer for your phonathon.

Anticipating Opposing Positions

You don't want someone's opposing arguments to weaken the effect of your persuasion. You need to anticipate opposition and help your audience to resist it. Should you acknowledge points of view that differ from your own or anticipate and refute what advocates on the other side might say? These questions are tough to answer, especially when you consider the time constraints of all speeches.

Research indicates that you should include (and refute) opposing viewpoints if your audience members are better educated, are initially opposed, or are familiar with or probably will encounter the other sides (Hovland, Lumsdaine, & Sheffield, 1949; Lumsdaine & Janis, 1953). In the inoculation theory, McGuire (1964) proposes that acknowledging opposing views and giving your audience reasons to reject them makes listeners less likely to be influenced when they hear those positions advocated later. McGuire compares it to the way a vaccination with a weakened form of a disease creates antibodies to protect against getting the illness. Sometimes you need to narrow your goals to allow yourself time to refute opposing arguments.

Organizational Strategies

We talk a lot about organization in this book. That's because the order in which you present ideas determines the audience's perceptions of the relative importance and relationships of all other elements of the message. A persuasive speech is built to achieve three goals: (1) present the message clearly so the audience understands it; (2) move the audience strategically (so it doesn't reject your ideas prematurely); and (3) motivate the audience to accept and act on your proposal.

Persuasive speeches can use any organizational pattern we've discussed (chronological, spatial, parts-to-whole) to communicate your ideas in clear "chunks," but any of these formats must be developed carefully within broader strategies that consider the audience traits and your persuasive goals. This section will give you several choices with examples to illustrate organizational strategy decisions.

Deductive

Deductive speech pattern Structure that begins with general conclusion and is supported by specific statements

If your proposal is not controversial and it falls at least within the audience's latitude of acceptance or slightly into the latitude of noncommitment, you might present the recommendations in the first part of your speech. You could even state the idea in the thesis statement in the introduction, and follow with your supporting arguments and evidence. This is called a **deductive speech pattern** because, as with deductive reasoning, you start with your general conclusion and develop it with specific statements.

Deductive structure follows a parts-to-whole pattern in which each main point is a reason to support the response you want from the audience. For example, if you were asking an audience that has already contributed to the Red Cross for additional funds, you might organize the body of your speech this way:

Thesis: We all should give whatever we can to the Red Cross to help the people struck by Hurricane Yolanda.

I. The Red Cross needs your help to help others in this terrible disaster.

II. The Red Cross is the best organization to help people get back on their feet.

III. The Red Cross is already mobilizing to help, but they can only go so far on what they have.

In this case, both your introduction and your conclusion would zero in on your goal, and your speech would develop the reasons your listeners should make a special donation.

Inductive

Inductive speech pattern Structure that moves from specific points to a general conclusion

When your listeners are strongly opposed, stating your goal in the beginning would cause them to reject it. That's when an **inductive speech pattern** works well. This pattern is subtle and may allow your listeners to change their previously held positions and still "save face." That's an important consideration for most audiences, but especially for those for whom saving face is a significant cultural norm.

Like inductive reasoning, this pattern moves from specific points to the conclusion you want your audience to accept. When you organize inductively, you don't reveal your position early in the speech but develop each subdivision, progressively leading to the inference you want the audience to make. You might, for example, move from the audience's values to ways these values are being violated, to reasons it's important to correct the violation of those values, to your proposal for ending the violation. When you proceed slowly and get listeners' agreement at each point, asking them to accept your ideas one part at a time, they are less likely to resist.

Suppose you are speaking to persuade state legislators who are opposed to tax increases to vote for a special tax. If you organized this deductively, they would turn you off the moment they heard the word *tax*. However, you might move them toward accepting your proposal if you organized the body of the speech inductively:

I. Our state offers tourists a wealth of entertainment possibilities.

II. Our state offers our children a poorer education than those provided in the tourists' home states.

III. Our state could offer our children a quality education if tourists provided more funding for education.

IV. Our state could fund educational improvements with a 3% tax on tourists' entertainment park admissions.

This inductive development would start with an introduction that called attention to the quality and importance of the state's tourist business. You might use a statement such as, "*American Traveler* magazine lists our state among the top tourist attractions in the United States. Last year, millions visited our entertainment parks alone. . . ." From that opening, the body leads the listeners, step by step, to see a contrast between what the state gives tourists and what tourists give the state that could support children's education. As an inductive pattern, the speech would conclude with a "therefore" statement—in this case, an appeal to support a new tax. The summary and conclusion might go something like this: "We give a world of entertainment opportunity to tourists, but a world of failure to our kids. Our tourists can afford to pay for their fun, but we can't pay for our kids' future. Let's get behind a small tax that will cost so little and yield so much."

Problem-Solution

Problem-solution speech pattern Structure that begins with need to respond to a problem and offers possible solutions

The **problem-solution speech pattern** is a popular approach to persuasive messages. The first main point develops the need to respond to an alarming situation, and the next main point provides ways to eliminate the difficulty. The problem section develops dissonance to motivate the audience by showing a conflict between the way things are and the way they should be. The solution section shows how the dissonance can be reduced. Let's use college financial aid as an example:

I. Many of our citizens do not have equality of opportunity because they do not have access to higher education. [problem]

A. College education is essential to competing on an equal footing in this society.

Can you visualize the audience that this speaker is trying to persuade? In what ways could he adapt to this setting to maximize his effectiveness? What do you suppose is going through the woman's mind as she waits her turn to speak?

Mary Kate Denny/PhotoEdit

    B. College education has become far too expensive for a large proportion of our young people.

    C. College education cannot be supported by current financial programs.

  II. Many of our citizens could have equality of opportunity if we provided them access to higher education. [solution]

    A. Equitable financial aid would guarantee all qualified students enough support to complete a bachelor's degree.

    B. Equitable financial aid would include grant packages and interest-free loans.

    C. Equitable financial aid would consider students' ability to pay and academic qualifications.

     With this development, the introduction would underscore the inequity between the American cultural values of equality of opportunity and the lack of a national economic commitment to education. The summary and conclusion, then, would drive home the point that only by increasing financial aid can this country fulfill its value of equal opportunity for all.

Motivated Sequence

Motivated-sequence speech pattern Need-satisfaction pattern that follows a psychological sequence to move the audience to speaker's desired conclusion

The problem-solution approach becomes much more powerful when it is developed along motivational lines such as those in the **motivated-sequence speech pattern** (Gronbeck, McKerrow, Ehninger, & Monroe, 1994). This approach uses a problem-solution pattern as an internal structure, but implements a psychological strategy to move the audience through five steps:

1   *Attention.* This is the introduction; as with every speech, you must immediately get the audience's attention and commitment to listening.

2   *Need.* This step lays out the issues and makes the audience understand—cognitively and emotionally—why something needs to be done. This requires explanation and proof of what the problem is and why it's serious.

3   *Satisfaction.* After making the audience feel the need, you explain the solution and ways it would meet the need that has already been established.

4   *Visualization.* In this critical step, you create an image of the solution in action. You want the audience to see and feel how things will be when the need is satisfied by the proposal.

5   *Action.* Here, you give the audience a clear call to fulfill the goal of the speech. The more concrete and definitive this step is, the better. Even if the goal is not to get the audience to take specific action, but only to get them to think about an issue, the action step should ask them to do that in such a way that it both concludes the speech and motivates the listeners to act.

Television commercials often follow this sequence. The first shot shows a couple in bed, turning away and covering their mouths rather than kissing each other. Then the voice-over says something about disgusting "morning breath." That gets your *attention* and shows you the *need* for fresh breath if you want a morning kiss. Then, you see the couple brushing their teeth or gargling with the product, the *satisfaction* step. Next, you see them happily smooching, obviously no longer afflicted with the revolting aroma of morning breath—that's *visualization.* Finally comes the *action* step, in which a spokesperson tells you how great the product is and suggests you buy it immediately.

The outline at the end of this chapter is an example of a speech asking listeners to petition for a new water purification system.

Residues

Residues speech pattern Parts-to-whole structure that considers alternatives one at a time, providing reasons to reject each, until only desired alternative remains

When your audience is likely to be thinking of ideas opposing yours, it's a good idea to use the **residues speech pattern.** A residue strategy is a parts-to-whole structure that considers alternatives one at a time, providing reasons to reject each, until only one choice remains—like boiling away the liquid in a beaker to examine the residue. The pattern is useful for several objectives:

- *To compare options.* The process of reviewing alternatives provides the advantages of considering multiple options and may help to "inoculate" listeners to reject other options when they are considered later.

- *To persuade resistant audiences.* The residues approach may be appropriate when audiences are not initially inclined toward your proposal, as the pattern explores the shortcomings of alternative approaches.

- *To combine with other patterns.* The residues pattern can be used with other structures. For example, the solution section of a problem-solution approach or the satisfaction step in a motivated sequence could follow a residues pattern.

One of our students used a residues pattern to show the class why they should invest in a specific computer system. Presenting excellent PowerPoint slides, he started by establishing the audience's high value for owning a user-friendly, convenient system. Next he previewed the criteria that would make a computer system desirable, to all of which his listeners could agree. He then went through the competing three systems, one by one, showing how they met some criteria but not others. This brought him to the system he was proposing, for which he used good evidence to demonstrate that it, in fact, met all of the criteria for the best system to buy. It was an effective way to sell a computer system, but you'll notice that this is also a very effective way for politicians to sell their proposals.

Persuasive Appeals

Years ago, Wallace (1963) summarized the substance of effective persuasive messages in two words: *good reasons.* "Reasons" indicates that your ideas are well thought out and developed logically; "good" means the reasons are consistent with your audience's values.

Wallace's advice echoes that provided centuries before. Aristotle identified three approaches to getting audiences to accept persuasive messages: *logos*, appeals to logic; *pathos*, appeals to emotions; and *ethos*, appeals to the speaker's credibility. Let's examine each.

Appeals Based on Logic

Chapter 4 develops the role of critical thinking in communication and provides guidelines for ensuring that messages are logical. Here, we'll expand on that discussion to look at specific ways to apply logical principles to your persuasive speeches, first by exploring the need to prove your ideas and then by presenting ways to use supporting material as evidence to gain credibility.

Requirements for Proof As noted previously in this chapter, there are few things about which people can be 100% certain. That might suggest that you do not need to prove every idea in your speech to be an undeniable fact. In general, however, when you make a statement, you have the obligation to prove that it is *probably* true.

Establishing probable truth so that your audience will accept your point requires you to develop evidence and logical reasoning. You need to show that the preponderance of evidence—the largest proportion of convincing supporting material—favors your position. The criteria of preponderance of evidence differs from the degree of proof required for a criminal case, in which the prosecution must prove the defendant's guilt "beyond a reasonable doubt"—or beyond any question for which there is a logical reason.

Supporting Material for Proof A list of assertions is neither persuasive nor interesting to people. It is the supporting material that clarifies, proves, and vivifies ideas, that catches people's imaginations and convinces them of what you say. Here, we'll focus on proof, because the other purposes of support are emphasized in Chapters 13 and 14. Proof usually relies on the following materials:

Examples. Real examples can help to prove inductively when you draw a general conclusion from them. (Hypothetical examples, while they may clarify and enliven your speech, do not prove because they are not true cases.) One true example, however, still is not enough. Remember that inductive reasoning requires sufficient instances to draw general conclusions. A speech about financial aid might use one real example of a brilliant person who had to drop out of school because of financial difficulty. That would clarify and vivify your point. For proof, however, you would also need statistics showing that a significant number of students had the same problem.

Statistics. Often, multiple examples are collected and reported as statistics. One example of an automobile death attributed to driving under the influence (DUI) doesn't establish a convincing link. Statistics connecting DUI with over half of all automobile deaths establishes greater credibility for concluding that drinking and driving is a serious problem. Statistics must be carefully evaluated to ensure that they actually support your particular point and that they come from reliable sources and research methods.

Testimony. As personal testimony, a layperson's report can establish what he or she saw, heard, smelled, tasted, or felt, but only an expert can provide testimony to help you prove interpretations or conclusions about events. For example, you may describe an event that you think violated someone's right to speak and you may quote the First Amendment of the Constitution, but you'll need expert testimony, such as a Supreme Court justice's opinion, to prove your interpretations are reasonable.

Appeals Based on Emotion

Emotional appeals and logical appeals have been treated separately in speech textbooks since Aristotle's time, but that is largely a matter of convenience and cultural bias. The convenience is simply to make discussion easier; the bias is something else. Western societies tend to prize rationality highly, whereas some societies value emotions tied to cultural myths, taboos, and aesthetics (Johannesen, 1996, pp. 39–40).

Databases like Info-Trac College Edition are an excellent source of supporting materials you can use to bolster your persuasive appeals. For example, some of these articles about the importance of art could be used to help you persuade a community to fund a local art museum.

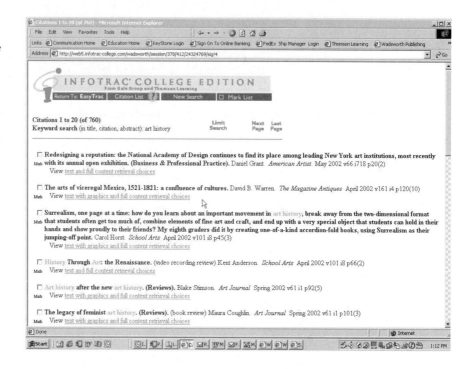

The emphasis on rationality in Western societies tends to lead individuals in those cultures to be leery of emotion, to feel that emotional responses are somehow illegitimate. To pretend that people are not emotional, however, is akin to asserting that birds are not aerodynamic. Emotions propel ideas and give them wings. To appeal effectively and ethically to audience emotions, consider how emotions develop your arguments and impact on audience responses.

Premises for Arguments Though an argument may be rational, emotional appeals often provide the premises and/or the warrant for the evidence and reasoning, connecting individual motivations, feelings, and values to build an argument and make a judgment.

Here's an example of how emotion and logic fit together in an argument: Suppose your objective is to get your audience to donate money to feed starving children. Your analysis of the audience suggests that they value life and humanity and generosity. You might decide to use pictures depicting starvation as part of your appeal. Clearly, pictures of emaciated, sick children can have a powerful emotional impact. Look at how this might appear as an argument in your speech:

> *If children are starving [supported by pictures], you should help by donating money.*

Children are starving. [*supported by statistical evidence and expert testimony*]

Therefore, you should help by donating money.

The first line is a major premise in a deductive logical pattern. The second is a minor premise, supported by evidence. The last is the conclusion that, drawing from the first two premises, meets all the rules for logical reasoning. Yet, it has an emotional impact because it uses premises that tap into the audience's values.

Now, consider another setting for which you have the same objective of getting donations. Your audience analysis tells you that this group values money higher than the welfare of children. Your appeals to these values and emotions might look like this:

If giving to help starving children provides an income tax deduction, you should donate money.

Giving to help starving children will provide an income tax deduction. [*supported by quotations from the tax code*]

Therefore, you should donate money.

This structure, too, meets all the rules for a logical argument, but the premises from which the conclusion is drawn reflect different values. In each case, you can achieve your objective: getting the donations.

Impact on Listener   People respond emotionally when issues touch their values and their sense of self. The effectiveness of emotional appeals relates to how the audience may feel about the topic or about life in general at the moment.

Fear appeals.   Often, speeches (on AIDS, crime, and drug addiction, for example) try to make people fear the effects of serious problems. Needless to say, fear appeals must be valid and substantiated to be ethical or relevant to the topic. With little validity, political commercials often exploit voters' fears about the same kinds of issues by promising that the candidate will somehow make the problems go away. Although some research has raised questions about what level of fear appeal works effectively, Eagly and Chaiken (1993) conclude that, overall, "research findings are fairly clear: The vast majority of experiments have found that higher levels of threat lead to greater persuasion than lower levels, [although] the persuasive impact of fear tends to be stronger on attitudes (toward behavior) and intentions than on behavior itself" (p. 443).

Moods.   Listeners who are in a good mood are more easily persuaded, and they make quicker decisions based more on the source's expertise and intuitive appeals than on the merits of the logical arguments. People in neutral moods are more critical and less persuasible (Isen, 1987; Worth & Mackie, 1987). A persuader who pays attention to the mood-inducing effects of the environment and context of the speech, therefore, may be able to build a more positive emotional state in the audience, which will promote openness to emotional or intuitive appeals.

Appeals Based on Source Credibility

A major thrust of this book is that your credibility as a speaker is a key to your success. In fact, in specific contexts, the source's credibility has been shown to multiply a message's impact (Birnbaum, Wong, & Wong, 1976; Lumsden, 1977). In their review of research, Eagly and Chaiken (1993) conclude that audiences "typically exhibited greater agreement with the belief and attitudes recommended in persuasive messages when the sources of these messages were portrayed as higher in expertise, trustworthiness, status, likability, or attractiveness" (pp. 429–430).

Two factors bear on your credibility when you speak: your previous reputation—the audience's view of you *prior to* a specific speech—and your actual words and actions during the speech as they affect the audience's perception of your competence, trustworthiness, objectivity, dynamism, and coorientation.

Your credibility based on your reputation *is* within your control—you influence these perceptions with everything you do. You make impressions on your listeners in their day-to-day experiences with you, their responses to previous speeches you have given, and the things they hear about you. You may recall that one of the communication principles covered in the first chapter of this book is that communication is irreversible. That fact builds future credibility positively when your actions earn it—but reduces your future impact as a persuader when negative behaviors tarnish your credibility.

What can you do to enhance your credibility during your speech presentation? Specific behaviors include finding common ground, demonstrating competence and objectivity, and speaking with appropriate dynamism.

Finding Common Ground   Much of this book focuses on coorientation and finding ways to identify with audience members and to enable them to identify with you. Coorientation requires these three components:

1   *Work for coorientational accuracy.* You'll remember that being cooriented with your listeners requires you to perceive correctly their needs, wants, beliefs—their emotional and intellectual states (Wackman, 1973). The basic key is to focus on your audience—think about *them.* Study, watch, listen, and process feedback to find how best to relate to your audience's feelings, values, and beliefs.

2   *Use self-monitoring.* As you relate to your audience, also watch your own behavior (Anderson, 1990). Monitor your verbal and nonverbal communication in relation to your audience's responses to you.

3   *Adapt your communication.* As you observe your listeners' responses, make appropriate changes in your approach to help them receive your ideas more positively (Duran, 1992).

Demonstrating Competence and Objectivity   To trust the quality of what you say, your audience needs to know that you are qualified and that you handle information responsibly. These approaches will help you show your listeners that it's worth their time to listen to you:

1   *Explain your research and experiences.* Be descriptive and honest; don't be falsely modest about your qualifications, but also do not be pompous or inflate what you know. If you have had personal experience with the topic, or conducted several interviews, or consulted scholarly sources, or have a degree in the subject, let your audience know these qualifications.

2   *Use credible sources.* You appear more objective and competent when you use sources known for objectivity and competence than when you use questionable sources. Such sources as popular magazines may give you colorful quotations or examples—but they rarely give you credible expert testimony or statistics to prove an argument.

3   *Use a variety of types of support.* Lee and Lee (1989) point out that as an advocate speaking to a heterogeneous audience, you need "to look for a variety of supporting materials that will appeal to the different predispositions various segments of the audience bring" (p. 122).

4   *Document your material.* Letting your audience know the sources of your information adds to the credibility of both your information and yourself. In fact, without documentation, you may be guilty of plagiarism. In a paper, you document by citing your sources in notes and bibliography. In a speech, you must give the audience this information orally. Artistically build the information into your language so it becomes part of your message. For example, say, "As communication philosopher Richard Johannesen points out in his 1996 book, *Ethics of Communication*, 'Plagiarism stems from the Latin word for kidnapper. It involves a communicator who steals another person's words and ideas without properly acknowledging their source and who presents these words or ideas as his or her own'" (p. 308).

5   *Acknowledge other positions.* As discussed previously, talking about other views and providing reasons to reject them may inoculate your listeners against opposing positions they hear later. In addition, acknowledging opposing positions demonstrates to the audience that you have done your homework and are aware of more than one limited perspective. Audiences tend to attribute less bias, more objectivity, and more credibility to speakers who acknowledge there are other sides to an issue (Eagly & Chaiken, 1993, pp. 355–363). For example, celebrities appear more credible and likable when their messages acknowledge some negative feature about products they endorse (Kamins, Brand, Hoeke & Moe, 1989).

Kochman (1951) describes cultural differences between African Americans and whites in what is considered persuasive communication. At a public meeting of white academics and black community activists in Chicago, communication was problematic precisely because style of arguing difference. The whites thought that they couldn't discuss the differences that the meeting was called to resolve because the blacks were "too emotional": they suggested waiting to discuss the differences later, when the others had "calmed down." The black activists, in contrast, considered it quite appropriate to argue with emotion and vehemence: to them, such behavior reflected commitment and honesty. When the whites at the meeting argued dispassionately, according to their own norms of "effective" speaking, they were considered hypocritical by the blacks who judged them, as everyone does, by their own communicative norms.

In my own study of communicative norms in the Mexican-origin community in Chicago, Mexican immigrants display a very different rhetoric in public speaking than do members of other groups, including Mexican Americans. People enculturated in Mexico weave an elaborate, and poetic, "tapestry" with their words, and when they use this style to argue in public meetings, they are sometimes, depending on the context (and, crucially, their audience), interrupted impatiently by those who prefer concise statements of particular "points," values associated with a U.S. "mainstream" style of communication.

From Marcia Farr (1994). Response to Daly and Witte papers. In A. Greenwood (Ed.), *The national assessment of college student learning: Identification of the skills to be taught, learned, and assessed* (NCES 94-286, pp. 220–226). Washington, DC: National Center for Education Statistics, pp 222–223.

Communicating with Appropriate Dynamism   Your nonverbal communication—your voice, speech patterns and articulation, body movement, facial expressions, gestures—carries your verbal message. Although people in different cultures and different contexts respond variously to different styles, the intensity and commitment you convey will affect perceptions of your credibility. The dynamism with which you present your ideas should be appropriate to you, to the audience, and to the occasion. Our best advice is to practice your speech so it has energy, vitality, variety, and sincerity. Appropriate dynamism starts with your passion for the topic and concern for your audience. As you speak, watch the feedback. Use self-monitoring, adapting the vigor of your speaking to your audience's responses. If they seem bowled over, moderate your approach. If they seem uninvigorated, step up your intensity. Your delivery should engage your listeners with you and with your message and should keep them with you until the last word of your conclusion.

Being Ethical   Your ethical choices certainly are part of your credibility, but they are much more. They are who you are. Samovar, Porter, and Stefani (1998) put it this way: "Because of the potential power of messages, you must continue to do two things: first, always be aware of this power; and second, always ask yourself what the effect of your message is on other people. This focus on your actions and the results of those actions is called, in the Buddhist tradition, being mindful" (p. 267). This means being mindful of your audience, mindful of how what you say will affect them, and mindful of the truth.

One writer says, " 'The truth shall make you free' is a phrase I have heard all my life but only recently have I understood how fundamental it is. I find that at every level—body, individual, couple, group, organization, nation—the more truth, the more success. . . . Not telling the truth is the source of most problems" (Schutz, 1984, p. 9). Scores of articles and books have been written about the American crisis in confidence, about how people simply don't believe anyone. It's amazing how much people want a little truth—and how refreshing it can be.

Being mindful of your ethics also implies careful minding of your emotional appeals to an audience. To help you keep an ethical perspective, pay attention to:

Choice.   To be ethically acceptable in this society, emotional appeals should expose, not obscure, individuals' decision-making choices. Their emotions should be respected as an important element in their rational decision making.

Relevance.   Emotional appeals should relate directly to the argument and to the audience's values. Unethical uses exploit or manipulate an audience's emotional responses. For instance, the appeal causes listeners to transfer emotions from one object to another or to generalize illegitimately or to stereotype from limited examples. Or the appeal is inconsistent with known evidence or has no evidence to support the point. In other words, the appeal to emotion is unethical if it "clearly flies in the face of what the receivers, given time, would find in their own investigations" (Ross, 1990, p. 28).

Language Choices

Your choice of words, and the way you use them, can win or lose your audience. You remember that connotative meanings, the personal reactions individuals have to specific words, include the attitudes people have about the concept (Osgood, Suci, & Tannenbaum, 1957). You would likely see a significant difference in the number of orders if a menu read "charbroiled prime filet of beef" than if it read "cooked piece of dead steer."

Excerpts from Dr. Martin Luther King, Jr's. speech, "I Have A Dream," provide examples for some language techniques that can have psychological and emotional effects on your listeners:

Metaphor. A metaphor, you'll remember, is a figure of speech that replaces one word or phrase with another to imply a comparison. King uses metaphor to respond to critics' complaints that the civil rights movement should slow down and wait for gradual change: "This is no time to engage in the luxury of cooling off or to take the tranquilizing drug of gradualism."

Imagery. King's words evoke strong sensory images. He gets the audience to see and feel vividly, often by combining imagery with his metaphors. Note the ways he evokes the senses when he says, "seared in the flames of withering injustice," and, "from the quicksand of segregation to the solid rock of brotherhood."

Sounds. Sounds can have an aesthetic appeal to the ear, and language that incorporates pleasing sounds helps give life and artistry to a speech. One method is by alliteration, using words with the same initial sound: "not by the color of their skins but by the content of their character." Another method is assonance, using words with similar vowel sounds. King achieves both alliteration and assonance when he states, "America has defaulted on that promissory note insofar as her citizens of color are concerned."

Repetition. King develops power in his words by repeating key phrases for emphasis. His repetition of the phrase, "I have a dream," gives strength to the phrase that became the title of the speech. Another powerful phrase used repeatedly comes near the end: "Let freedom ring."

Allusion. Allusion uses language that makes indirect references or suggestions without identifying directly the object or idea. For example, King (standing in front of the Lincoln Memorial) begins his speech with, "Five score years ago, a great American in whose symbolic shadow we stand, signed the Emancipation Proclamation." His references to Abraham Lincoln are clear, but are not stated overtly. (And he also worked in another alliteration.) Similarly, King frequently uses allusions that evoke the religious heritage of many of his audience members. Some examples: "solid rock," "dark and desolate valley," and the emotional words of an old spiritual, "Free at last. Free at last. Thank God Almighty, I'm free at last."

Few speakers have ever achieved a comparable level of effectiveness in terms of their strategic language choices, and King's model can help you develop your own powerful persuasive style.

Summary

Persuasion, as the process of moving your audience to change willingly their beliefs, attitudes, values, and/or behaviors, involves analyzing members' motivations and understanding their existing positions on issues. Beliefs are the degree to which listeners believe something to be a fact; attitudes are their negative or positive feelings; values are their concepts of good and bad that influence their judgments; and behaviors are the observable actions they take. Often, successful persuasion involves causing audience members to shift a few degrees on either side of neutral on an attitude scale or to move from a position of disbelief to some degree of belief that an assertion is true. Values are difficult to change because they are central to a person's self-concept, so the persuader often must get listeners to reorder important values or reinterpret the way a given attitude or behavior relates to particular values.

Persuasion requires analyzing your listeners and defining goals that are reasonable for the audience and the context. To design a speech, start by selecting an organizational pattern that considers the extent to which you will ask the audience to change and the strength of audience values pertaining to the issue. The strategy may be deductive when the change is relatively slight or inductive when audience members must be led slowly to a change. A common organizational pattern is to present a problem and then provide the solution. Often, this problem-solution pattern is embedded in a motivated sequence in which listeners are led through psychological steps of attention, need, satisfaction, visualization, and action. The solution step may take listeners through a "residues" development by rebutting alternative options until the speaker reaches the advocated solution.

Persuasive speeches develop logical and emotional appeals as well as enhance the speaker's credibility. Persuasive language is important in influencing change, because audience members bring their own connotative meanings to interpreting a persuader's symbols. Colorful, rhythmic, and expressive language such as imagery, metaphor, assonance, alliteration, and repetition all contribute to successful persuasion.

Exercises

1 For each of the following, estimate where your belief, attitude, or value might fall on the scales provided.

    a   *Beliefs*: On a scale of 0 to 100%, estimate your degree of certainty for the following:

I can develop my speaking skills.	_____ %
Higher taxes cause recessions.	_____ %
I will get a satisfying job after college.	_____ %
Everyone should have a college education.	_____ %
Cattle farming is very profitable.	_____ %

    b   *Attitudes*: On a scale of −1.00 to +1.00, estimate your attitude about each of the following:

Federal funding for abortions   _____

Voting in congressional elections   _____

The United Nations   _____

Parking on your campus   _____

Making public speeches   _____

Protecting the environment   _____

c   *Values*: On a scale from L (low importance) to M (moderate) to H (high), estimate the degree to which you value each of the following:

Financial security   _____

Ethnic heritage   _____

Your credibility as a speaker   _____

Your competence as a speaker   _____

Education   _____

Equality among people   _____

Go back and think about your ratings. On which item in each category (beliefs, attitudes, values) would you be most susceptible to change because of a persuasive message? Which would you be less likely to change? What generalizations can you draw about how people's positions relate to their persuadability on issues?

2   Working with a partner, select a topic that clearly has more than one possible side related to it. Together, identify a position you could propose in a persuasive speech and write a purpose statement for getting an audience to accept that position. Separately, each of you do one of the following:

a   Assume you would be presenting this speech to an audience that would not be too strongly opposed to your position. Identify possible main points and subpoints for a persuasive speech that reflect a *deductive* approach.

b   Assume you would be presenting this speech to an audience that would be strongly opposed to your position. Identify possible main points and subpoints for a persuasive speech that reflect an *inductive* approach.

Compare the outlines each of you has prepared. Do they both seek to achieve the same objective? In what ways do the approaches differ? Would it be realistic, assuming that each speech would have the same time limitations, to expect both speeches to achieve the same goal?

3   In a group, select one of the attitude statements from Exercise 1. Then brainstorm a list of motive appeals that *might* apply to an audience for which a speech on that topic could be prepared. Make the list as long as you can.

Then, identify a specific audience for the speech and create a plan for finding out which motive appeals would have the greatest likelihood of succeeding with that specific group.

4 Using the motivated sequence, prepare and present a five-minute speech on a topic of your choice to persuade your classmates. Be sure you accomplish each of the following steps:

a Get the audience's attention.

b Develop a need with careful use of logical and emotional appeals. Seek to create dissonance in your audience's minds as you develop this section.

c Develop a proposal for satisfying the need. Include ways in which the solution reduces the dissonance developed.

d Get your audience to sense and feel what things will be like as they visualize their lives after adopting your proposal.

e Call your audience to specific action. Consider what they should do as well as how and when they should do it.

Cyberpoints

CCC

WEB SITE

1 Want some more help with outlining a persuasive speech or to see some persuasive speech samples? Try http://phil.winona.msus.edu/lori/Assign/Effective Persuasion.htm.

2 Look at historical speeches for models of effective persuasion at http:www.ngsw.org.

3 Interested in communication careers? Take a look at workinpr.com, a Web site for the Public Relations and Communications industry. Another possibility is http://www.PR-education.org.

4 For researching your speech, you could try the *National Data Book of the Census Bureau* at http://www.census.gov/prod/www/statistical-abstract-us.html/. Another source for headline stories from newspapers, broadcast, and online sources is http://www.1stHeadlines.com.

SAMPLE PERSUASIVE SPEECH USING MOTIVATED SEQUENCE STRATEGY

Commentary

Topic: The problem of community water pollution and a desirable solution to the problem

Purpose: To motivate the audience to support a new system of water purification for the community

Thesis: Potential poisoning of our water supply through pollutants and chemicals can be prevented by adopting one of three new technologies already shown to be effective.

Organizational Pattern: This speech uses a motivational sequence to involve and move the audience through recognizing a threat and considering a response to it. Within the motivational steps, points are ordered in logical arguments to show a problem and solution.

Attention Step
The speaker uses a series of rhetorical questions, a shocking statement and statistic, and further quotations, concluding with a strong quotation to which the audience can relate as a community. These methods serve to make the topic important to the audience, develop the speaker's credibility, and motivate the audience to hear more.

Need Step
It is essential that the audience personally feel the need for a new water supply. The speech provides two main reasons, with subpoints, for the belief that this community's water could be poisoned. Each main point, is worded parallel to the other one, with wording that emphasizes the connection of the community to the potential disaster.

Outline

Attention
Pour a clear glass of water from a pitcher. Hold it out, and ask, Would you drink this water? Would you bathe in it? Wash your dishes in it? How safe do you think it is? Maybe you'd better rethink your confidence in our community's great water. People in a lot of other communities have. *The New York Times* reports that last year in Milwaukee, 43 people died from drinking the water, and many, many more became ill, one of them from drinking just enough water to take an aspirin. Seagulls polluted their water with a disease called cryptosporidiosis. Jim Elder, the head of the Environmental Protection Agency's Office of Ground Water and Drinking Water, says that "professional leaders in the water supply industry have admitted to me privately that they were scared to death by what happened in Milwaukee. They didn't think their source-water situation was that much different."

Need
  I. Our community could be poisoned by our water supply at any time because of increased pollutants.
      A. Sources of pollutants from people and animals are increasing rapidly.
      B. Current water purification methods can't keep up with the increased sources of pollutants.
  II. Our community could be poisoned by our water supply at any time because of dangerous chemical purification methods.
      A. Current water purification methods rely on chlorine.
      B. Chlorine is now suspected to be carcinogenic.

Commentary

Each subpoint would be developed with strong, credible evidence to prove the probability of water poisoning and to develop the audience's concern that their community water supply could be threatened.

Satisfaction Step

To meet this need the audience now feels, the speaker lays out two main points, showing that technologies to fix the problem exist and that these technoloogies are already working in other communities. The subpoints for each main point give specific examples with evidence to show that both are valid points.

Visualization Step

Here is when the audience must begin to see the solution working. The speaker creates for the audience an image of what it would be like to know they have healthy water. It is vivid and satisfying as a visualization.

Action Step

In referring to the water board, the speaker provides a way to achieve the image the audience has just examined. Mentioning a petition introduces a way to take action; restating the need in strong images reinforces the dreadful possibilities if action is not taken; and, finally, calling for action by signing a petition is coupled with a reaffirmation of the visualized success of new technologies for water purification.

Outline

Satisfaction

I. New technologies are available for purifying water.
   A. Ozone treatment methods kill more microorganisms than chlorine does.
   B. Granular-activated carbon systems clean out pollutants and other contaminates.
II. New technologies are working in other communities.
   A. Milwaukee has turned its situation around in a year's time at reasonable costs.
   B. Cincinnati has succeeded with granular-activated carbon systems that clean out other contaminants and eliminate chlorine at reasonable costs.
   C. One hundred communities already are using ozone treatment at reasonable costs.

Visualization

Imagine a child drinking a tall, cool glass of crystal-clear, pure water, playing in a pool, eating off of dishes without danger of becoming ill or poisoned from chlorine. Imagine a community in which we can truly say, "We've got good water."

Action

Our public water board can select and implement a new system if we have the will to motivate them. Let's all sign this petition and get our water board moving on this problem. We can't wait until our children are sick and old people are dying from a drink of water—or until we suddenly find our cancer rate has risen in town and we don't know why. We have to do it now. Please sign the petition, and take the first steps toward a community with truly clean water for its citizens.

Glossary

Acronym Word created by combining the first letters of each word in a phrase.

Active listening The mental and physical process of listening to, focusing on, and silently questioning a speaker's ideas.

Adaptability Being able to change roles in a given situation; being flexible in responding to other persons.

Advantages In evaluating proposed solutions, the positive consequences of each proposal in addition to its ability to solve the problem.

Affinity seeking Using conversation and communication strategies to get another person to like you; looking for ways to feel similar and close to another.

Affirmation A personal, positive, present-tense statement about how you feel and act in a situation that bridges your visualizations with your behaviors by redefining your abilities to yourself.

Agenda A written plan to guide the order of discussion for a meeting.

Aggressive communication Reflects a "me first" position that disregards how others might feel or what they might want; verbal or nonverbal messages that attack an individual's self-concept in order to make the person feel less favorably about him- or herself, or to inflict psychological pain.

Alliteration A series of words that have the same initial sound.

Applicability In evaluating proposed solutions, how well each meets the criteria for solving the problem.

Argument A conclusion based on data or evidence and reasoning that may or may not reflect truth or validity.

Artifacts Things that people wear, carry, leave behind, or spread around that symbolize who they are or what they value.

Assertive communication Involves openly communicating, with awareness of yourself and concern for others, what you need or want other people to know.

Associate idea To link a new idea to an old one, or a symbol to an idea to be learned, so that listeners can make connections that will help them to understand and remember information.

Assonance A series of words that contain similar vowel sounds.

Attitudes A person's stable and enduring dispositions to evaluate objects or entities (persons, places, or things) in a particular way; preset responses to something or someone.

Attribution Inferring another's beliefs, motivations, and values, and the predicting of how that person will act; blaming or crediting another on the basis of attributed characteristics.

Attribution theory "The process by which a person infers another person's motives and intentions by observing the other's behavior" (Lefton & Valvatne, 1988, p. 382).

Audience analysis Examination of listeners' characteristics, including their previous knowledge of your subject, their attitudes, and their values that relate to your speech.

Audience motives Listeners' reasons for wanting to know what a speaker can teach them.

Authoritarian leadership Rigid style in which the leader keeps tight control, makes all decisions, runs things by the book, sets schedules, and may use coercive or reward power.

Behavioral question Interview question that asks interviewees to recount ways they have acted in previous situations that relate to their future behavior on the job.

Behaviors External, observable actions that interact with beliefs, attitudes, and values.

Belief What people have learned or have come to know through experience; idea that is either true or represents what we think is true (Baum, Fisher, & Singer, 1985, p. 54).

Brainstorming Process of generating solutions by thinking without constraint of as many ideas as possible.

Bypassing A situation in which a sender and a receiver believe they have the same understanding of a communication but do not.

Cause-and-effect reasoning Reasoning that connects two sequential occurrences. Because one event occurred, the reasoner concludes that it caused another event.

Channel The medium by which a message is carried through the environment—by air waves in the case of sounds and light waves for visual cues—from the sender to the receiver.

Charge The purpose, task description, or assignment given to a group.

Chronological pattern An organizational pattern that presents ideas or events in time sequence, such as from past to present to future, or that traces a step-by-step process.

Chunking Organizing information into a few sets of logically related categories (Miller, 1956).

Closed question Either/or, yes/no, or multiple choice question that limits the options of the respondent.

Codependency Behavior by members of a family that enables other members to engage in destructive behavior. Codependent behavior is motivated by some mutual reward even in a negative situation.

Cognates Words that sound similar and carry similar definitions to words in other languages because they derive from a common root.

Cognitive dissonance theory Festinger's theory that people need to feel consistency among their attitudes, beliefs, values, and/or behaviors, and that inconsistency or dissonance motivates change.

Cohesiveness The degree to which members of a group are attracted toward each other and the group; often described as "ésprit de corps," "groupness," or "team pride." It involves loyalty, commitment, and willingness to sacrifice for the group.

Collaborative listening and questioning Process in which the speaker and the listener work as a team to develop a shared understanding through dialogue.

Communication The process of using verbal and nonverbal cues to transact mutually understood meanings between two or more people within a particular context and environment.

Communication accommodation Methods used by people to adapt to others' communication behaviors.

Communication apprehension "An individual's level of fear or anxiety associated with either real or anticipated communication with another person or persons" (Richmond & McCroskey, 1995, p. 41).

Communication climate A set of conditions, ranging from supportive to defensive, that affect how people communicate and what kinds of relationships they develop.

Communication dilemma A conflict between wanting to communicate and not wanting to be subjected to communication risks.

Competence The degree of expertise, authoritativeness, and skill a person demonstrates and the qualifications she or he possesses.

Confirming In dialogue, one person listens and asks questions that value the speaker and the message.

Confirming response Message that makes you feel recognized as a worthwhile human being with worthwhile ideas and feelings.

Conflict The tension people feel between them when they perceive that they have mutually exclusive goals or feelings.

Consistency needs Striving to maintain balance among attitudes, beliefs, values, behaviors that motivates people to choose among conflicting information.

Connotative meanings Meanings of words that depend on an individual's experience, background, values, and needs and that exist only for that person.

Consensus Decisions that represent the agreement of every member of a group; usually achieved through intensive discussion and negotiation.

Coorientation Others' sense that a person shares their interests, values, objectives, and needs and is concerned for their well-being.

Coorientational accuracy The ability to "read" others' feelings correctly.

Credibility An individual's perceptual judgment and willingness to believe in a communicator's character and message.

Critical thinking Logically analyzing the rationality of ideas and arguments to determine their validity, reliability, and value.

Culture A system of shared, beliefs, values, customs, behaviors, and artifacts that the members of a society use to cope with their world and with one another and that structures how they see things.

Decision-making group A group usually charged to go through the full range of information-gathering and problem-analysis processes to arrive at specific decisions that will be implemented.

Decision matrix A large grid, with each column labeled with one criterion from a list of ideal solutions and each row labeled with a designation for one possible solution. By filling in the cells with notes as to how each plan meets each criterion, you generate a concise set of comparisons for the proposals.

Decode To translate and interpret symbolic verbal or nonverbal cues in terms of a receiver's personal experiences.

Deductive reasoning Process of drawing conclusions about specific cases based on generalizations.

Deductive speech pattern Organizational pattern that moves from a direct, general statement of the thesis to the specific statements that develop it; appropriate to listeners who are not initially opposed.

Defensive climate Environment in which people practice self-protective behavior in response to perceived or anticipated threats, which feeds into a circular, progressively more defensive set of interactions.

DEL A derogatory ethnic label; a name that attributes to a person and his or her group a set of negative characteristics.

Democratic leadership Open style in which the leader makes sure everyone's heard, guides and facilitates discussion and decision making, and shares decision-making power.

Demographics Characteristics of people based on external attributes: age, sex, ethnicity, income, educational level, and so on.

Demonstration speech A presentation that uses a chronological approach to take an audience step by step through a process to allow them both to hear and see the material.

Denotative meanings Meanings of words as defined in a dictionary that are generally shared by speakers of a language.

Depenetration The process by which partners find less reward in their relationship and start closing off to each other.

Desirability In evaluating proposed solutions, the character of each proposal and the value systems of the members; involves the relative worth of probable outcomes and the values and ethical choices that impinge on the decision.

Detractors Sounds and words interjected when speaking, usually instead of pausing, and frequently when speakers are nervous or not concentrating fully on what they are saying.

Dialogical ethic An approach to communication that creates a climate in which people are able to be authentic about who they are; to include and confirm the worth of others; to be "present" (accessible and attentive); and to share a spirit of mutual equality (Johannesen, 1990, pp. 60–62).

Disadvantages In evaluating proposed solutions, the negative consequences that may occur even though the proposal may solve the problem.

Disconfirming response Message that makes a person feel invisible or undesirable by ignoring or giving impersonal or incongruous replies to him or her.

Dyadic communication Communication between two people, a dyad.

Dynamism The energy, vigor, intensity, and conviction with which an individual gets and maintains the interest of others.

Dysfunctional relationships Interactions in which participants play games and manipulate one another, which breaks down the optimal relationship.

Effective communication A transaction that achieves its objectives, enriches the people involved, and provides a foundation for future communication; characterized by responsibility, ethicality, and credibility.

Emblems Gestures that have well-defined meanings within a culture.

Emergent leader Individual who, although neither appointed nor elected, provides information and leadership that help groups develop effective task and group-building processes.

Emotional appeals The portions of argument that connect individual motivations, feelings, and values to the evidence and reasons for changing these beliefs, attitudes, or behaviors.

Empathic listening An approach to listening and questioning that seeks to understand the ideas and feelings of others by helping and supporting them to express their thoughts and emotions.

Empathy Understanding another's values, meanings, symbols, intentions; sharing another's joy or sorrow.

Encode To put an idea in a symbolic form for another person to interpret.

Ethics Codes or beliefs that your upbringing, religion, culture, and experience have given you as a basis for moral judgments and acceptable acts.

Ethos Aristotle's concept of the way an audience perceives a speaker's character, involving *good character, good sense, and goodwill* (Roberts, 1954, p. 91).

Euphemisms Words or phrases that deliberately gloss over the hard or potentially offensive aspects of a message.

Exploratory strategy interview An interview approach in which the interviewer may start with one or two questions, allow the interviewee to take the discussion in any direction, and then follow up by probing more deeply into the interviewee's ideas.

Extemporaneous speaking Well-prepared, well-organized, and well-rehearsed presentation of a speech that has been developed through repeated oral practice rather than through writing it out, and that is delivered with only a few notes and visuals.

Family An interdependent couple or group of people whose communication organizes its existence and who depend on one another to meet both physiological and psychological needs.

Feedback A response from the receiver that provides the original sender with information about the effects of the message.

Fishbone diagram An approach to identifying, tracking, analyzing, and visualizing cause-effect relationships in problem analysis. Diagonal lines like the ribs of a fish identify problem areas (Ishikawa, 1982).

Forum An open meeting where the entire audience may participate in the discussion by making comments or asking questions.

Game-playing A competitive, win-lose approach to manipulating communication so that one partner can achieve some personal goal.

Gender A "social, symbolic creation" one acquires through experience, time, and cultural development that influences the way you see yourself and others in relation to society, sex, and roles.

Goal conflicts Situations that arise when your personal and career goals differ from each other or from your management's objectives.

Group "Two or more persons who are interacting with one another in such a manner that each person influences and is influenced by each other person" (Shaw, 1981, p. 8).

Group and team communication Socializing and/or working with a group.

Group-building roles Communication that makes it possible for task processes to move ahead by creating a sense of groupness, an open climate, and a mutually supportive and cooperative attitude.

Group goals Results that a team has been assembled to achieve.

Groupthink "A mode of thinking that people engage in when they are deeply involved in a cohesive team, when members' striving for unanimity overrides their motivation to realistically appraise alternative courses of action" (Janis, 1983, p. 9).

Haptics The way people convey feelings or messages through touch.

Hidden agenda Unstated, individual goals and objectives, often based on motives that the individual would rather not talk about but that will affect a team's interaction and functioning.

Hierarchy of needs Maslow's theory that people are aware of and must satisfy each of a set of specific needs before going on to the next.

High-context society Typically an agrarian society, with close family and community groupings, in which people have the same knowledge about one another and their environment and thus have a basic context for their communication.

Humanify To treat another as a human being; recognizing a person's uniqueness, value, and rights, and opening up communication to a receptive, dialogic, supportive process.

Idea Thoughts as a system of chemical-electrical impulses in the brain.

Illustrators Gestures that reinforce a verbal message by "showing" what it means.

Images Vivid mental "pictures" drawn with words.

Impromptu speaking Presentation of ideas without formal preparation or rehearsal—the kind of short speech one might give to support a position or give information at a meeting.

Individual-interest/blocking roles Messages that serve a person's individual wants or needs at the expense of the team. They distract from the group-building and task processes to focus exclusively on individual wants and needs.

Inductive reasoning Process of drawing general conclusions from specific cases.

Inductive speech pattern Organizational pattern that moves through specific points progressively, leading to the conclusion; appropriate for opposed listeners who might reject a proposal if it's stated up front.

Information-gathering group A group with the charge to investigate a specific problem or issue and, usually, to prepare a report on its findings.

Information overload State in which listener has received more data than can be processed and remembered.

Instrumental objectives Series of smaller tasks a group must complete to reach its overall goal.

Interactive listening and questioning Process of developing dialogue, cooperatively analyzing ideas, and asking and answering questions.

Interpersonal bonding "The process of forming individualized relationships, affinities that are close, deep, personal, and intimate" (Bochner, 1984, p. 544).

Interpersonal communication A dynamic process that touches people emotionally and psychologically, so that their transactions influence changes in the individuals and in their relationship over time (Miller & Steinberg, 1975).

Interview A communication transaction in which participants follow a planned process of questioning and answering in order to achieve some specific purpose.

Intimate relationships Mutually supportive, trusting, enduring relationships in which partners know and care about each other and talk about things they would not share with other people; may include a sexual component.

Intrapersonal communication Communication with yourself, as you respond to stimuli from the environment, from others, and from yourself.

Jargon Language that comes out of a specialized interest or profession.

Job qualification question Interview question about specific criteria for a job or knowledge and skills necessary to fulfill them.

Kinesic Movement of the eyes, face, and body that is interpreted as a meaningful message.

Laissez-faire leadership Neutral, uninvolved style in which the leader kicks back and simply lets the group do what it wants.

Leader A person holding a designated position. An individual may be elected or appointed as president, chairperson, or department head.

Leadership Verbal and nonverbal communication behavior that influences a team's processes to achieve the members' and the team's needs and goals.

Leading question Interview question designed to solicit a response in a particular—sometimes misleading, manipulative, or unethical—way.

Learning objectives Specific, measurable, reasonable behaviors to accomplish in the acquisition of knowledge, enhancement of feelings, and/or development of specific skills.

Learning styles Individuals' preferred ways of processing new material that may use one or both sides of the brain.

Low-context society Typically a diverse, industrialized society with scattered family, community, and socioeconomic groupings, in which people cannot have the same knowledge about one another and their environment and thus have less context in common for communication.

Manuscript speaking Presentation of a speech that has been carefully written and prepared as a manuscript, often marked for emphasis and gestures, carefully and extensively rehearsed, and perhaps memorized.

Mediated communication Communication channeled through a written or electronic medium such as newspapers, magazines, radio, and television (Cathcart & Gumpert, 1983).

Memorized speaking Manuscript speaking in which the manuscript has been memorized to make it appear extemporaneous, with extensive rehearsing and revising to polish the presentation.

Mentor Someone in a position to help who encourages you, who guides you, who serves as a model for you, who finds you credible and takes an interest in your future.

Metaphor An analogy that states a comparison as if two things were really the same.

Midpoint crisis The point in a team's work when members suddenly realize that the time is half-gone but the work isn't half-finished. Members may panic but then settle down to more focused work to achieve their goal (Gersick, 1988).

Mnemonic device Memory aid that helps people tie ideas to other ideas, so the association triggers a memory.

Monochronic cultures Cultures in which people generally attend to one thing at a time; characteristic of most of North America.

Motivated-sequence speech pattern Organizational pattern that implements a psychological strategy to move the audience through the steps of attention, need, satisfaction, visualization, and action (Gronbeck, McKerrow, Ehninger, & Monroe, 1994).

Muted group A powerless group in society that does not share the metaphors and symbols of the power group and therefore is not heard in the larger arenas of power (Kramarae, 1981).

Noise Sensory disturbances in the communication channel or environment that can disrupt, distort, or totally block a message.

Nonstandard language A style or dialect that does not meet the qualities of grammar, vocabulary usage, or speech associated with "standard" language.

Nonverbal communication Communication through symbols or signals that accompanies, replaces, or carries verbal messages.

Nonverbal cues Vocal characteristics, speech patterns, body posture, facial expressions, space, time, touch, and other personal messages that communicate feelings and responses.

Objective strategy or structured interview An approach to interviewing used for selection or research interviews in which the interviewer asks a series of carefully prepared job- or goal-related questions for which there are predetermined rating scales for evaluating answers.

Objectify To treat someone as a thing rather than as a person.

Objectivity The ability to look at both sides of an issue; to suspend personal biases; to be reasonable and dispassionate; to examine evidence, reasoning, and values before taking sides.

Open-ended question Interview question that allows the respondent to answer in a variety of ways; often begins with "How," "Why," or "Where."

Organizational culture Facts, truths, realities, beliefs, and values that members of an organization perceive and create about their unit, and norms and expectations that both reflect and reinforce their ways of communicating.

Organizational pattern A description of the nature of the relationship among ideas, such as chronological, spatial, or parts-to-whole.

Panel An interactive group, often with a moderator, that exchanges information through individuals sharing ideas and asking and answering questions in a relatively informal manner.

Paralanguage Vocalic cues that affect listeners' interest in and perception and understanding of spoken messages.

Parallel structure Repeated use of the same phrasing to introduce a series of new ideas; especially useful in wording the main or subpoints of a speech, but also very effective in introducing a series of examples to support an idea.

Parts-to-whole speech pattern An organizational pattern that develops ideas that are related by being subparts of the same main topic; sometimes called "topical."

Passive-aggressive communication Involves self-protective and hostile behavior that blocks other people, halts progress, or hurts someone without being caught at it.

Passive communication Involves hiding behind silence or false agreement, which appeases others but subordinates their rights in deference to those of others or in fear of possible consequences.

Perception The process of sensing, selecting, shaping, and assigning meaning to stimuli from one's environment.

Personal space Space surrounding an individual, actively maintained to protect against threats.

Person-centered message Communication in which your message adapts to and focuses on the interests of the other person rather than focusing on yourself.

Persuasion The process of moving an audience to change willingly its beliefs, attitudes, values, and/or behaviors.

Phatic conversation Quick, brief, casual communication of little substantive content that simply reminds people they are sharing the planet with others of their kind.

Polychronic cultures Cultures in which people do many things at once; characteristic of most of Latin America.

Powerful language In a society, the language of status, position, education, and success.

Practicality In evaluating proposed solutions, the ability to implement them successfully.

Presentational communication Speaking and listening when an audience ranges in size from a few to a large crowd.

Primary question Question the interviewer has planned before the interview.

Primary source The first source in which a statement has been made through speech or publication.

Principled leadership Using ethical standards for communication and decision making, a responsibility of all members sharing leadership.

Problem-analysis group A group charged to investigate a specific problem or issue, to determine its scope and the seriousness of its impact.

Problem-solution speech pattern A popular approach to persuasive speaking that uses the first section to develop the need to respond to an alarming situation and the next section to provide ways to eliminate the difficulty.

Process An ongoing, constantly changing operation.

Professionalism An attitude, a way of approaching work, and a way of communicating that reflect involvement, competence, and pride in what you do.

Proxemics The way people use and react to space between and among themselves and/or objects.

Psychographics Characteristics of people based on internal factors: attitudes, values, needs, and so on.

Receiver The person who picks up a message through sensory organs.

Redefinition The use of language to change perceptions by changing the words used.

Regulators Nonverbal cues that control "turn-taking" in a communication transaction.

Reinforcement Process of repeatedly underscoring an idea and intensifying its importance so it stands out in the mind of the listener; providing some reward for recognizing and remembering the idea.

Rejection response Message that discards you or your ideas.

Relational rules Expectations of how couples should relate to each other, negotiated between each person's expectations of how a relationship should be.

Relational themes Patterns that emerge from what the couple talks about—the weather, work, the news—their gossip, playing, fighting.

Relaxation techniques Methods for consciously slowing breathing, lowering pulse rate and blood pressure, easing muscles, and focusing attention.

Reports Factual accounts of research or progress on a project; may be presented as work that is in progress, as an interim report, or at the conclusion of work as a final report.

Research The process of seeking answers to questions by finding information from library collections, people, and experiences.

Residues speech pattern A parts-to-whole pattern that considers alternatives one at a time, providing reasons to reject each, until only one choice remains.

Risk In evaluating proposed solutions, the potential gains achieved in solving the problem versus possible adverse consequences.

Secondary question Question that probes or follows up on answers a respondent has given.

Secondary source A source of information in which a writer or speaker has summarized, paraphrased, or quoted the original statement.

Selective attention Process of focusing on a few stimuli and not noticing others.

Self-concept The attitudes and beliefs you've developed about yourself over your lifetime.

Self-disclosure Sharing information about yourself with another person.

Self-fulfilling prophecy Situation in which a person foresees a situation or a result and then, consciously or not, makes it happen.

Self-monitoring Awareness of your own communication and its impact on others.

Self-persuasion Process by which an audience develops an internal rationale for changing in some way on the basis of material that appeals to their needs, values, beliefs, attitudes, and goals.

Self-talk Messages to yourself to improve your approach or performance.

Semantics The way people mean the words they use.

Sender The originator of a message transmitted to another person.

Sensory fatigue State in which senses become tired while processing stimuli.

Shaping In perception, the process of changing incoming stimuli to conform to expectations.

Shared leadership A trait of superteams; when *all* members take responsibility for fulfilling leadership roles.

Signs Clear, concrete, unambiguous representations of one idea that mean the same thing to everyone who shares the language.

Simulation Interview format in which the interviewee role-plays a situation so the interviewer can observe.

Situational leadership Refers to leaders who adapt their styles to accommodate differences in situations, tasks, purposes, and members.

Situational question Interview question that hypothesizes a situation and asks the interviewee to describe how she or he would handle it.

Slang Nonstandard, informal, lively, innovative language that reflects and defines the character of a group and the individuals within it.

Social exchange theory Kelley and Thibaut's theory that people weigh their prediction of the rewards or costs in an action against their minimum desired reward and against alternatives to choose what best meets their needs.

Social judgment theory Idea that an individual's attitude functions as an anchor holding that person at that position; from that point, all positions are ordered in terms of how far from the anchor they fall within three categories: a latitude of acceptance, of noncommitment, and of rejection; also known as *ego-involvement theory*.

Social penetration The gradual widening and deepening of a relationship as two people reciprocally trade self-disclosures and develop mutual trust and empathy (Altman & Taylor, 1973).

Spatial speech pattern An organization pattern that relates ideas in terms of space; sometimes called *geographic*.

Speech body Substance of a speech, structured with main points and subpoints.

Speech conclusion A speech's closing section that summarizes the ideas, guides the audience's reactions, and gives the speech impact and aesthetic balance.

Speech introduction The opening section of a speech that seeks to gain the audience's attention and prepares them for the content.

Speech to inform A presentation that provides listeners with new information or shows them new relationships among known material, such as teaching a process, a skill, or ideas.

Speech to persuade A presentation that seeks to get listeners to alter their attitudes, values, beliefs, and/or behaviors—to influence new thinking and actions.

Standard language The style "most often associated with high socioeconomic status, power and media usage in a particular community" (Giles & Coupland, 1991, p. 38).

Stereotypes Screens of expectations and judgments based on limited experiences through which people filter their perceptions.

Strategic ambiguity The deliberate use of words that may have more than one possible interpretation.

Style The way an individual uses language; the semantics, word order, grammar, and personal or group idiosyncrasies that make up his or her speech.

Superteam A team that weaves competencies, experience, attitudes, and values into processes that highly committed members use to develop their own clear visions and goals, cultures, and norms.

Supporting material Information that develops the ideas of a speech, giving it shape, substance, and energy and achieving three objectives: to clarify, to prove, and to vivify.

Supportive climate Environment in which people feel safe and are able to concentrate on the structure, the content, and the cognitive and emotional meanings of messages.

Symbols Abstractions of ideas that have as many meanings as there are people to interpret them.

Symposium A public group format in which each participant gives a speech without direct interaction among the members of the group.

Synchronous messages Hand, body, and head movements that coordinate with spoken words.

Synergy To a group what energy is to an individual; a combination of the energy, drives, needs, motives, and vitality of the members that keeps the group working toward its task.

Syntactics The order and direction of language in phrases and sentences.

Syntality To a group what personality is to an individual; group syntality reflects what the group is to itself and others. It is built through team culture, ethics, images, ways of communicating, and members' personalities.

T-chart A large sheet of paper or blackboard divided into a T for comparing the pros and cons of an idea.

Task roles Communication processes that move a group toward its goal by agreeing on the team's structure, developing flexibility and adaptability, setting goals, researching and sharing information, cooperating in open and creative critical analysis, solving problems, making decisions, completing tasks, and promoting self-improvement through feedback.

Team More than a group, a team is "a diverse group of people who share leadership responsibilities for creating a group identity to achieve a mutually defined goal" (Lumsden & Lumsden, 2000, pp. 13–14). It starts as a group but achieves higher quality, special feelings, critical processes, and shared leadership.

Team inquiry A plan for gathering and sharing information.

Territory A specific place that you feel is your space.

Thesis statement A clear, concise declarative sentence stating the central idea for a speech. It should be specific enough to identify the precise ideas, yet general enough to serve as a summary statement of the speech's content.

Thought speed Time between the rate of human speech and the rate of a listener's ability to process information.

Transactional process The nature of communication when each person participates in giving and taking bits of meaning to and from the other, to achieve a mutual understanding (Barnlund, 1968).

Transactional leadership Style in which the leader uses rewards in return for effective performance. Rewards may be actions that fulfill members' needs for interpersonal communication, satisfaction, quality of work life, or personal wants and values, including promotions and pay raises.

Transformational leadership Style in which the leader elevates, motivates, inspires, and develops members to meet their individual goals and needs and to fulfill the vision and goals of the group and the organization as well.

Transition Statement that serves both as a bridge between ideas and as a "road sign" telling the audience when the speaker is going in a different direction.

Transmit To speak or act to make verbal and nonverbal cues available to others through light, sound, or electronic channels.

Trustworthiness How consistent and honest a person's behavior is understood to be.

Turning point Specific event or occurrence that partners can identify as having contributed to incremental change in their relationship.

Values "Concepts of The Good or The Desirable that motivate human behavior and that function as criteria in our making of choices and judgments" (Johannesen, 1996, p. 1).

Verbal communication Communication using language as its symbolic code for meaning.

Verbal cues Words and structure used as symbols to convey and interpret ideas.

Visionary leadership Style in which the leader shapes and gains acceptance for a long-range team vision; a leader who is a direction setter, change agent, spokesperson, and coach; a person who leads superteams to success by setting clear and uplifting goals.

Visualization The process of forming a mental image and, through self-talk, seeing and feeling one's ideal performance in a situation.

Visual message Graphic image that helps listeners understand the content of a speech.

Vocalics All nonverbal aspects of voice and speech, including the pitch, tone, volume, range, and quality of voice, as well as detractors such as "um" and "you know."

Willingness to communicate The degree to which a person wants to participate in a range of communication situations.

Worldview "A fundamental set of perceptual assumptions that . . . includes how a culture explains forces in the universe, the nature of mankind, the kind of impersonal spirit that can do harm or good . . . luck, fate, the power of significant others, the role of time, and the nature of our physical and natural resources" (Dodd, 1991).

References

Aaron, M. C. (1999, September). The right frame: Managing meaning and making proposals. *Harvard Management Communication Letter, 2* (9), 1–4.

Abbey, A. (1991). Misperception as an antecedent of acquaintance rape: A consequence of ambiguity in communication between men and women. In A. Parrot & L. Bechhofer (Eds.), *Acquaintance rape: The hidden crime* (pp. 96–111). New York: Wiley.

Alicke, M. D., Smith, R. H., & Klotz, M. L. (1987). Judgments of physical attractiveness: The role of faces and bodies. *Personality and Social Psychology Bulletin, 12,* 381–389.

Allen, I. L. (1983). *The language of ethnic conflict.* New York: Columbia University Press.

Allen, K. L. (2000, January). Getting it across. *Across the Board, 37* (1), 78.

Altman, I., & Taylor, D. A. (1973). *Social penetration: The development of interpersonal relationships.* New York: Holt, Rinehart & Winston.

Andersen, P. A. (1999). *Nonverbal communication: Forms and functions.* Mountain View, CA: Mayfield.

Anderson, A. (1997, January). Learning strategies in physical education: Self-talk, imagery, and goal setting. *JOPERD—The Journal of Physical Education, Recreation & Dance, 68,* 30–36.

Anderson, L. R. (1990). Toward a two-track model of leadership training: Suggestions from self-monitoring theory. *Small Group Research, 21,* 147–167.

Anderson, R. C., & Nagy, W. E. (1992, Winter). The vocabulary conundrum. *American Educator, 14–18,* 44–47.

Argyle, M. (1986). *Bodily communication* (2nd ed.). London: Methuen.

Argyle, M., Alkema, F., & Gilmour, R. (1971). The communication of friendly and hostile attitudes by verbal and nonverbal signals. *European Journal of Social Psychology, 1,* 385–402.

Aristotle. (1954). *Rhetoric* (W. R. Roberts, Trans.). In F. Solmsen (Ed.), *Rhetoric and poetics of Aristotle* (pp. 1–218). New York: Random House.

Asker, B. (1998). Student reticence and oral testing: A Hong Kong study of willingness to communicate. *Communication Research Reports, 15,* 162–169.

Austin, N. K., & Peters, T. J. (1985). *A passion for excellence: The leadership difference.* New York: Random House.

Ayres, J., & Heuett, B. L. (1997). The relationship between visual imagery and public speaking apprehension. *Communication Reports, 10,* 87–94.

Ayres, J., Heuett, B., & Sonandre, D. A. (1998). Testing a refinement in an intervention for communication apprehension. *Communication Reports, 11,* 73–85.

Ayres, J., & Hopf, T. S. (1987). Visualization, systematic desensitization, and rational-emotive therapy: A comparative evaluation. *Communication Education, 36,* 236–240.

Ayres, J., & Hopf, T. S. (1991). The long-term effect of visualization in the classroom: A brief research report. *Communication Education, 39,* 75–78.

Ayres, J., & Hopf, T. S. (1993). *Coping with speech anxiety.* Norwood, NJ: Ablex.

Ayres, J., Schleisman, T., & Sonandre, D. A. (1998). Practice makes perfect but does it help reduce communication apprehension? *Communication Research Reports, 15,* 171–179.

Ballard, P. D. (1999, February). Dress for success. *The Black Collegian, 19,* 68–70.

Barber, B. R. (1984). *Strong democracy: Participatory politics for a new age.* Berkeley: University of California Press.

Barge, J. K. (1991, November). *Task skills and competence in group leadership.* Paper presented at the meeting of the Speech Communicaton Association, Atlanta, GA.

Barnlund, D. C. (1968). *Interpersonal communication: Survey and studies.* Boston: Houghton Mifflin.

Bass, B. M. (1990, Winter). From transactional to transformational leadership: Learning to share the vision. *Organizational Dynamics, 19–31.*

Basso, K. H. (1990). *Western Apache language and culture: Essays in linguistic anthropology.* Tucson: University of Arizona Press.

Baum, A., Fisher, J. D., & Singer, J. E. (1985). *Social psychology.* New York: Random House.

Baxter, L., & Bullis, C. (1986). Turning points in developing romantic relationships. *Human Communication Research, 12*, 469–493.

Beatty, M. J. (1981). Receiver apprehension as a function of cognitive backlog. *Western Journal of Speech Communication, 45*, 277–281.

Bedard, P., Borger, G., Kaplan, D. E., & Parker, S. (2000, August 14). Blinded. *U.S. News & World Report, 129* (6), p. 4.

Beebe, S. A. (1980). Effects of eye contact, posture and vocal inflection upon credibility and comprehension. *Australian SCAN: Journal of Human Communication, 7–8*, 57–70.

Behnke, R. R., & Sawyer, C. R. (2000). Anticipatory anxiety patterns for male and female public speakers. *Communication Education, 49*, 187–195.

Bell, R. A., & Daly, J. A. (1984). The affinity-seeking function of communication. *Communication Monographs, 50*, 96–97.

Bellman, G. M. (1992). *Getting things done when you are not in charge*. San Francisco: Berrett-Koehler.

Bem, D. J. (1967). Self-perception: An alternative interpretation of cognitive dissonance phenomena. *Psychological Review, 74*, 707–710.

Bem, D. J. (1970). *Beliefs, attitudes, and human affairs*. Belmont, CA: Brooks/Cole.

Benjamin, J., & McKerrow, R. E. (1994). *Business and professional communication: Concepts and practices*. New York: HarperCollins.

Benne, K. D., & Sheats, P. (1948). Functional roles of group members. *Journal of Social Issues, 4*, 41–49.

Benoit, P., Czerwinski, A., Dorries, B., Meyer, J., Sabelka, P., & Spaeder, N. (1992, October/November). From "jet screaming hootie queen" to "talking to Ralph": An undergraduate slang dictionary. Paper presented at the meeting of the Speech Communication Association, Chicago, IL.

Benoit, W. L., & Benoit, P. J. (1991). Memory for conversational behavior. *Southern Communication Journal, 56*, 24–34.

Berg, J. H., & Archer, R. L. (1983). The disclosure-liking relationship. *Human Communication Research, 10*, 269–281.

Berne, E. (1966). *The structure and dynamics of organizations and groups*. New York: Grove Press.

Berry, D. S. (1990). What can a moving face tell us? *Journal of Personality and Social Psychology, 58*, 1004–1014.

Berry, D. S., & MacArthur, L. Z. (1985). Some components and consequences of a babyface. *Journal of Personality and Social Psychology, 48*, 312–323.

Bingham, S. G. (1991). Communication strategies for managing sexual harassment in organizations: Understanding message options and their effects. *Journal of Applied Communication Research, 19*, 88–115.

Birdwhistell, R. (1955). Background to kinesics. *ETC., 13*, 10–18.

Birnbaum, M. H., Wong, R., & Wong, L.K. (1976). Combining information from sources that vary in credibility. *Memory and Cognition, 4*, 330–336.

Blakeslee, S. (1991, September 10). Brain yields new clues on its organization for language. *New York Times*, p. C1.

Blakeslee, T. F. (1980). *The right brain: A new understanding of the unconscious mind and its creative powers*. New York: Anchor Press.

Bochner, A. P. (1984). The functions of human communicating in interpersonal bonding. In C. C. Arnold & J. W. Bowers (Eds.), *Handbook of rhetorical and communication theory* (pp. 544–621). Boston: Allyn & Bacon.

Bolton, R. (1979). Listening is more than merely hearing. Reprinted in J. Stewart (1990). *Bridges not walls: A book about interpersonal communication* (5th ed.) (pp. 175–191). New York: McGraw-Hill.

Booth-Butterfield, S., & Booth-Butterfield, M. (1991). Individual differences in the communication of humorous messages. *Southern Communication Journal, 56*, 205–218.

Borden, R. C. (1935). *Public speaking as listeners like it*. New York: Harper & Row.

Borisoff, D. (1993). The effect of gender on establishing and maintaining intimate relationships. In L. P. Arliss & D. J. Borisoff (Eds.), *Women and men communicating: Challenges and changes* (pp. 14–28). New York: Harcourt Brace Jovanovich.

Bowles, J. G. (1990, September 24). The human side of quality. *Fortune*.

Bradac, J., & Mulac, A. (1984). A molecular view of powerful and powerless speech styles: Attributional consequences of specific language features and communicator intentions. *Communication Monographs, 51*, 307–319.

Bradley, P. H. (1980). Sex, competence, and opinion deviation: An expectation states approach. *Communication Monographs, 47*, 101–110.

Branden, N. (1980). *The psychology of romantic love*. Los Angeles: J. P. Tarcher.

Brandt, D. S. (1998, May). Digital presentations: Make your delivery effective. *Computers in Libraries, 18* (4), 35–37.

Brandt, D. S. (1996, May). Evaluating information on the internet. *Computers in Libraries, 16* (5), 44–46.

Braybrooke, D., & Lindblom, C. E. (1963). *A strategy of decision*. New York: Free Press.

Broome, B. J. (1991). Building shared meaning: Implications of a relational approach to empathy for teaching intercultural communication. *Communication Education, 40*, 235–250.

Brown, L. (1982). *Communicating facts and ideas in business*. Englewood Cliffs, NJ: Prentice-Hall.

Brown, M. T. (1990). *Working ethics*. San Francisco: Jossey-Bass.

Brownell, J. (1990). Perceptions of effective listeners: A management study. *Journal of Business Communication, 27*, 401–415.

Bruneau, T. (1988). The time dimension in intercultural communication. In L. A. Samovar & R. E. Porter (Eds.), *Intercultural communication: A reader* (5th ed.) (pp. 282–292). Belmont, CA: Wadsworth.

Buber, M. (1957). Elements of the interhuman: The social and the interhuman. *Psychiatry, 20*, 105–113.

Buber, M. (1958). *I and thou* (2nd ed.). New York: Scribners.

Bugental, D. B. (1986). Unmasking the "polite smile": Situational and personal determinants of managed affect in adult-child interaction. *Personality and Social Psychology Bulletin, 12*, 7–16.

Bugental, D. B. (1993). Communication in abusive relationships. *American Behavioral Scientist, 36*, 288–308.

Buhrke, R. A., & Fuqua, D. R. (1987). Sex differences in same- and cross-sex supportive relationships. *Sex Roles, 17*, 339–532.

Buller, D. B., & Aune, R. K. (1988). The effects of vocalics and nonverbal sensitivity on compliance: A speech accommodation theory explanation. *Human Communication Research, 14*, 301–332.

Burgoon, J. K. (1992, November). *Applying an interpersonal communication perspective to deception: Effects of suspicion, deceit, and relational familiarity on perceived communication*. Paper presented at the meeting of the Speech Communication Association, Chicago, IL.

Burgoon, J. K., Buller, D. B., & Woodall, W. G. (1989). *Nonverbal communication: The unspoken dialogue*. New York: Harper & Row.

Burgoon, J. K., Coker, D. A., & Coker, R. A. (1986). Communication of gaze behavior: A test of two contrasting explanations. *Human Communication Research, 12*, 495–524.

Burgoon, J. K., & Hale, J. L. (1984). The fundamental topoi of relational communication. *Communication Monographs 52*, 193–214.

Burgoon, J. K., Manusov, V., Mineo, P., & Hale, J. L. (1985). Effects of gaze on hiring, credibility, attraction, and relational message interpretation. *Journal of Nonverbal Behavior, 9*, 133–146.

Burgoon, J. K., & Saine, T. J. (1978). *The unspoken dialogue: An introduction to nonverbal communication*. Boston: Houghton Mifflin.

Byers, P., & Byers, H. (1972). Nonverbal communication and the education of children. In C. B. Cazden, V. P. John, & D. Hymes (Eds.), *Functions of language in the classroom* (pp. 3–31). New York: Teachers College Press.

Byrne, J. (1993, December 20). The horizontal corporation. *Business Week*, pp. 76–81.

Byrns, J. H. (1981). *Speak for yourself: An introduction to public speaking*. New York: Random House.

Capella, J. N., & Palmer, M. T. (1990). Attitude similarity, relational history, and attraction: The mediating effects of kinesic and vocal behaviors. *Communication Monographs, 57*, 161–183.

Carlson, D. H. (1998). Computer-based graphics tools for the graphically challenged. *Information Technology and Libraries, 18*, 182.

Carlson, D. L. (1997). Electronic communications and communities. *Antiquity, 71*, 1049–1051.

Carmichael, C. W. (1991). Intercultural perspectives of aging. In L. A. Samovar & R. E. Porter (Eds.), *Intercultural communication: A reader* (6th ed.) (pp. 129–135). Belmont, CA: Wadsworth.

Carnevale, A. P., Gainer, L. J., & Meltzer, A. S. (1990). *Work-place basics: The essential skills employers want*. San Francisco: Jossey-Bass.

Carrell, L. J., & Willmington, S. C. (1998). The relationship between self-report measures of communication apprehension and trained observers' ratings of communication competence. *Communication Reports, 11,* 87–95.

Carson, C. L., & Cupoch, W. R. (2000). Facing corrections in the workplace: The influence of perceived face threat on the consequences of managerial reproaches. *Journal of Applied Communication Research, 28,* 215–234.

Cathcart, R., & Gumpert, G. (1983). Mediated interpersonal communication: Toward a new typology. *Quarterly Journal of Speech, 69,* 267–277.

Cattell, R. B. (1948). Concepts and methods in the measurement of group syntality. *Psychological Review, 55,* 48–63.

Cegala, D. J. (1981). Interaction involvement: A cognitive dimension of communication competence. *Communication Education, 30,* 109–121.

Cegala, D. J., Savage, G. T., Brunner, C. C., & Conrad, A. B. (1982). An elaboration of the meaning of interaction involvement: Toward the development of a theoretical concept. *Communication Monographs, 49,* 229–248.

Clement, S. (1987). The self-efficacy expectation and occupational preferences of females and males. *Journal of Occupational Psychology,* 257–265.

Collier, G. (1985). *Emotional experience*. Hillsdale, NJ: Lawrence Erlbaum.

Communications Daily (1996, Oct. 22). European Union (EU, concerned that Internet and other means of advanced communications could hurt region's culture), *16* (205), 10.

Conrad, C. (1991). Communication in conflict: Style-strategy relationships. *Communication Monographs, 58,* 135–155.

Cooper, P. J., & Collins, R. (1992). *Look what happened to frog: Storytelling in education*. Scottsdale, AZ: Gorsuch Scarisbrick.

Coover, G. E., & Murphy, S. T. (2000). The communicated self: Exploring the interaction between self and social context. *Human Communication Research, 26* (1), 125–147.

Copeland, L. (1988, May). Learning to manage a multicultural work force. *Training: The Magazine of Human Resources Development,* 48–56.

Cortina, J. M., Goldstein, N. B., Payne, S. C., Davison, H. K., & Gilliland, S. W. (2000). The incremental validity of interview scores over and above cognitive ability and conscientiousness scores. *Personnel Psychology, 53,* 325.

Coughlin, J. P., & Vangelisti, A. L. (1999). Desire for change in one's partner as a predictor of the demand/withdraw pattern of marital communication. *Communication Monographs, 66,* 66–89.

Crannell, K. C. (1991). *Voice and articulation* (2nd ed.). Belmont, CA: Wadsworth.

Crawford, S. (1993, March 28). A win here, a leer there: It's costly. *The New York Times,* Sunday, p. 17.

Crounse, B. (2000, July). Talking the talk: Helpful tips on giving political speeches. *Campaigns & Elections, 21* (6), 64.

Dainton, M. (1998). Everyday interaction in marital relationships: Variations in relative importance and event duration. *Communication Reports, 11,* 101–109.

Dance, F. E. X. (1967). Toward a theory of human communication. In F. E. X. Dance (Ed.), *Human communication theory: Original essays* (pp. 288–309). New York: Holt.

de Bono, E. (1970). *Lateral thinking: Creativity step by step*. New York: Harper & Row.

Derlega, V. J., Winstead, B. A., Wong, P. T. P., & Greenspan, M. (1987). Self-disclosure and relationship development: An attributional analysis. In M. E. Roloff & G. R. Miller (Eds.), *Interpersonal processes: New directions in communication research* (pp. 172–187). Newbury Park, CA: Sage.

Deutsch, C. H. (1991, December 1). Listening to women and blacks. *The New York Times,* p. F25.

Dewey, J. (1910). *How we think*. Boston: D. C. Heath.

Diehl, R. H., & Larkin, R. P. (1998). Providing resources for researchers in the World Wide Web—some perspectives. *BioScience, 48,* 323–316.

Dodd, C. H. (1991). *Dynamics of intercultural communication* (3rd ed.). Dubuque, IA: Wm. C. Brown.

Dolphin, C. Z. (1988). Variables in the use of personal space in intercultural transactions. *The Howard Journal of Communications, 1,* 23–28.

Donaghy, W. C. (1990). *The interview: Skills and applications*. Salem, WI: Sheffield.

Dovidio, J. F., & Ellyson, S. L. (1982). Decoding visual dominance: Attributions of power based on relative percentages of looking while speaking and looking while listening. *Social Psychology Quarterly, 45,* 106–115.

Drucker, D. (2000, February.). How not to mumble. *Training and Development, 54* (2), 71.

Duck, S. W. (1994a). *Meaningful relationships.* Thousand Oaks, CA: Sage.

Duck, S. W. (1994b). Steady as she goes: Relational maintenance as a shared meaning system. In D. Canary & L. Stafford (Eds), *Communication and Relational Maintenance* (pp. 45–60). New York: Academic Press.

Duck, S., Rutt, D. J., Hurst, M. H., & Strejc, H. (1991). Some evident truths about conversations in everyday relationships: All communications are not created equal. *Human Communication Research, 18,* 228–267.

Dukerich, J. M., Nichols, M. L., Elm, D. R., & Vollrath, D. A. (1990). Moral reasoning in groups: Leaders make a difference. *Human Relations, 43,* 473–493.

Duran, R. L. (1992). Communicative adaptability: A review of conceptualization and measurement. *Communication Quarterly, 4,* 253–268.

Dwyer, K. K. (2000). The multidimensional model: Teaching students to self-manage high communication apprehension by self-selecting treatments. *Communication Education, 49,* 72–81.

Eagly, A. H., & Chaiken, S. (1993). *The psychology of attitudes.* Fort Worth, TX: Harcourt Brace Jovanovich.

Edwards, B. (1979). *Drawing on the right side of the brain.* Los Angeles: J. P. Tarcher.

Egan, K. (1986). *Teaching as story telling: An alternative approach to teaching and curriculum in the elementary school.* Chicago: University of Chicago Press.

Ekman, P., Davidson, R. J., & Friesen, W. V. (1990). The Cuchenne smile: Emotional expression and brain physiology II. *Journal of Personality and Social Psychology 58,* 342–353.

Ekman, P., & Friesen, W. V. (1967). Head and body cues in the judgment of emotion: A reformulation. *Perceptual and Motor Skills, 24,* 71–72.

Ekman, P., & Friesen, W. V. (1969). The repertoire of nonverbal behavior: Categories, origins, usage and coding. *Semiotica, 1,* 49–98.

Ekman, P., Friesen, W. V., & Ellsworth, P. C. (1972). *Emotion in the human face: Guidelines for research and an integration of findings.* New York: Pergamon.

Ekman, P., Friesen, W. V., O'Sullivan, M., Chan, A., Diacoyami-Tarlatzis, I., Heider, K., Krause, R., Le Compte, W. A., Pitcairn, T., Ricci-Bitti, P. E., Scherer, K., & Tomita, M. (1987). Universals and cultural differences in the judgments of facial expressions of emotion. *Journal of Personality and Social Psychology, 53,* 712–717.

Elgin, S. H. (1989). *Success with the gentle art of verbal self-defense.* Englewood Cliffs, NJ: Prentice-Hall.

Ellis, R. K. (2000, July). I can Hot-Foot, can you HotFoot, too? *Training & Development, 54* (7), 64.

Environmental Defense Fund/McDonald's Corporation Waste Reduction Task Force (1991, April). *McDonald's Corporation/Environmental Defense Fund Waste Reduction Task Force Final Report.* New York: EDF.

Epstein, Y. M., Woolfolk, R. L., & Lehrer, P. M. (1981). Physiological, cognitive, and nonverbal responses to repeated exposure to crowding. *Journal of Applied Social Psychology, 11,* 1–13.

Epstein, N. B., Bishop, D. S., & Baldwin, L. M. (1982). The McMaster model of family functioning. *Journal of Marriage and Family Counseling, 4* (4), 19–31.

Equal Employment Opportunity Commission (1980, November 10). Guidelines on sexual harassment. *Federal Register,* CFR sec. 1604.11.

Ericson, P. M., & Gardner, J. W. (1992). Two longitudinal studies of communication apprehension and its effects on college students' success. *Communication Quarterly, 40,* 127–137.

f.y.i. mgr: (1992, Spring). A publication for Merck managers and supervisors, 1–8.

Fabun, D. (1968a). *You and creativity.* New York: Macmillan.

Fabun, D. (1968b). *Communications: The transfer of meaning.* Beverly Hills, CA: Glencoe.

Fanning, P. (1988). *Visualization for change.* Oakland, CA: New Harbinger.

Feeley, T. H. (2000). Testing a communication network model of employee turnover based on centrality. *Journal of Applied Communication Research, 28,* 262–277.

Feeley, T. H., & Young, M. J. (1998). Humans as lie detectors: Some more second thoughts. *Communication Quarterly, 46,* 109–126.

Felder, R., & Silverman, L. (1988). Learning and teaching styles in engineering education. *Engineering Education,* 674–681.

Feldman, C. M., & Walkosz, B. J. (1992, October/November). *Communicating unclearly: The adaptive role of strategic ambiguity in interpersonal relationships.* Paper presented at the meeting of the Speech Communication Association, Chicago, IL.

Festinger, L. (1957). *A theory of cognitive dissonance.* Evanston, IL: Row, Peterson.

Fisher, A. B. (1986). Leadership: When does the difference make a difference? In R. Y. Hirokawa & M. S. Poole (Eds.), *Communication and group decision-making* (pp. 197–218). Beverly Hills, CA: Sage.

Fisher, R., & Brown, S. (1992). A strategy for building better relationships as we negotiate. In W. B. Gudykunst & Y. Y. Kim (Eds.), *Readings on communicating with strangers: An approach to intercultural communication* (pp. 393–398). New York: McGraw-Hill.

Fisher, R., & Ury, W. (1981). *Getting to yes.* Boston: Houghton Mifflin.

Fiske, S. T., & Taylor, S. E. (1984). *Social cognition.* Reading, MA: Addison-Wesley.

Fitch-Hauser, M., Barker, D. A., & Hughes, A. (1990). Receiver apprehension and listening comprehension: A linear or curvilinear relationship? *Southern Communication Journal, 56,* 62–71.

Floyd, J. J. (1985). *Listening: A practical approach.* Glenview, IL: Scott, Foresman.

Folb, E. A. (1991). Who's got the room at the top? Issues of dominance and nondominance in intercultural communication. In L. A. Samovar & R. E. Porter (Eds.), *Intercultural communication: A reader* (6th ed.) (pp. 119–127). Belmont, CA: Wadsworth.

Forsyth, G. A., Kushner, R. I., & Forsyth, P. D. (1981). Human facial expression judgment in a conversational context. *Journal of Nonverbal Behavior, 6,* 115–130.

Fox, S. (1997, November). The controversy over Ebonics. *Phi Delta Kappan, 78* (3), 237–241.

Frazier, S. H. (1994). *Psychotrends: What kind of people are we becoming?* New York: Simon & Schuster.

Garfield, C. A. (1984). *Peak performance: Mental training techniques of the world's greatest athletes.* Los Angeles: J. P. Tarcher.

Garner, A. (1981). *Conversationally speaking: Tested new ways to increase your personal and social effectiveness.* New York: McGraw-Hill.

Gauss, J. W. (2000, August). Integrity is integral to career success. *Healthcare Financial Management, 54* (8), 89.

Gersick, C. J. G. (1988). Time and transition in work teams: Toward a new model of group development. *Academy of Management Journal, 31,* 9–41.

Getting past the gatekeeper (2000, August). *Black Enterprise, 31,* p. 49.

Gibb, J. R. (1961). Defensive communication. *Journal of Communication, 11,* 141–148.

Giles, H., & Coupland, N. (1991). *Language: Contexts and consequences.* Pacific Grove, CA: Brooks/Cole.

Giles, H., & Street, R. L., Jr. (1985). Communicator characteristics and behavior. In M. L. Knapp & G. R. Miller (Eds.), *Handbook of interpersonal communication* (pp. 205–261). Beverly Hills, CA: Sage.

Gilligan, C. (1982). *In a different voice: Psychological theory and women's development.* Cambridge, MA: Harvard University Press.

Goffman, E. (1967). *On face-work, interaction ritual: Essays on face-to-face behavior.* New York: Pantheon.

Goldhaber, G. M. (1990). *Organizational communication* (5th ed.). Dubuque, IA: Wm. C. Brown.

Goldsmith, D. J. (2000). Giving advice: The role of sequential placement in mitigating face threat. *Communication Monographs, 67,* 1–19.

Goleman, D. (1991, September 17). Non-verbal cues are easy to misinterpret. *New York Times,* pp. C1, C9.

Goleman, D. (1995). *Emotional intelligence: Why it can matter more than I.Q.* New York: Bantam.

Goleman, D., Kaufman, P., & Ray, M. (1992). *The creative spirit.* New York: Penguin.

Gouran, D. S. (1969). *An investigation to identify the critical variables related to consensus in group discussions of policy* (Project No. 8–F-004). Washington, DC: U.S. Department of Health, Education and Welfare, Office of Education.

Gouran, D. S. (1982). *Making decisions in groups: Choices and consequences*. Glenview, IL: Scott, Foresman.

Gouran, D. S., & Hirokawa, R. Y. (1983). The role of communication in decision-making groups: A functional perspective. In M. S. Mander (Ed.), *Communication in transition* (pp. 168–185). New York: Praeger.

Greenberg, J., Kirkland, S. L., & Pyszcynski, T. (1988). Some notions and preliminary research concerning derogatory ethnic labels. In G. Smitherman-Donaldson & T. A. van Dijk (Eds.), *Discourse and discrimination* (pp. 74–92). Detroit: Wayne State University Press.

Greenhouse, L. (1993, October 14). Ginsburg at fore in court's give-and-take. *New York Times*, p. 1.

Grice, H. P. (1989). *Studies in the way of words*. Cambridge, MA: Harvard University Press.

Griffin, E. (1994). *A first look at communication theory*. New York: McGraw-Hill.

Gronbeck, B. E., McKerrow, R. E., Ehninger, D., & Monroe, A. H. (1994). *Principles and types of speech communication* (12th ed.). New York: HarperCollins.

Gudykunst, W. B., & Kim, Y. Y. (1992). Communicating effectively with strangers. In W. B. Gudykunst & Y. Y. Kim (Eds.), *Readings on communicating with strangers: An approach to intercultural communication* (pp. 369–371). New York: McGraw-Hill.

Gudykunst, W. B., & Ting-Toomey, S. (1992). Verbal communication styles. In W. B. Gudykunst & K. Y. Kim (Eds.), *Readings on communicating with strangers: An approach to intercultural communication*. New York: McGraw-Hill. Abridged from W. B. Gudykunst & S. Ting-Toomey (1988), *Culture and interpersonal communication* (pp. 99–115). Newbury Park, CA: Sage.

Hackman, J. R., & Walton, R. E. (1986). Leading groups in organizations. In P. S. Goodman & Associates (Eds.), *Designing effective work groups* (pp. 72–119). San Francisco: Jossey-Bass.

Hall, E. T. (1969). *The hidden dimension*. Garden City, NY: Doubleday.

Hall, E. T. (1976). *Beyond culture*. Garden City, NY: Doubleday.

Hall, E. T. (1994). Monochronic and polychronic time. In L. A. Samovar & R. E. Porter (Eds.), *Intercultural communication: A reader* (7th ed.) (pp. 264–270). Belmont, CA: Wadsworth.

Hall, E. T. (2000). Monochronic and polychronic time. In L. A. Samovar & R. E. Porter, *Intercultural communication: A reader* (9th ed.) (pp. 280–286). Belmont, CA: Wadsworth.

Halpern, D. F. (1986). *Sex differences in cognitive abilities*. Hillsdale, NJ: Lawrence Erlbaum.

Halpern, D. F. (1994, August). A national assessment of critical thinking skills in adults: Taking steps toward the goal. In A. Greenwood (Ed.), *The National Assessment of College Learning: Identification of the Skills to Be Taught, Learned, and Assessed* (pp. 24–64). Washington, DC: National Center for Educational Statistics.

Hamilton, D. L., Sherman, S. J., & Ruvolo, C. M. (1992). Stereotype-based expectancies: Effects on information processing and social behavior. In W. B. Gudykunst & Y. Y. Kim (Eds.), *Readings on communicating with strangers: An approach to intercultural communication* (pp. 135–158). New York: McGraw-Hill.

Haney, W. V. (1973). *Communication and organizational behavior: Text and cases* (3rd ed.). Homewood, IL: Richard D. Irwin.

Harvey, J. H., Orbuch, T. L., & Weber, A. L. (Eds.). (1992). *Attributions, accounts, and close relationships*. New York: Springer-Verlag.

Hastings, C., Bixby, P., & Chaudhry-Lawton, R. (1986). *The superteam solution: Successful teamworking in organisations*. Aldershot, England: Gower.

Hauser, G. A. (1988). *Introduction to rhetorical theory*. New York: Harper & Row.

Hellweg, S. A., Samovar, L. A., & Skow, L. (1994). Cultural variations in negotiation styles. In L. A. Samovar & R. E. Porter (Eds.), *Intercultural communication: A reader* (7th ed.) (pp. 286–292). Belmont, CA: Wadsworth.

Herman, L., Richards, D. G., & Wolz, J. P. (1984). Comprehension of sentences by bottlenosed dolphins. *Cognition, 16,* 129–219.

Hermann, N. (1988). *The creative brain*. Lake Lure, NC: Brain Books.

Hersey, P., & Blanchard, K. H. (1977). *Management of organizational behavior: Utilizing human resources* (3rd ed.). Englewood Cliffs, NJ: Prentice-Hall.

Hersey, P., Blanchard, K. J., & Natemeyer, W. E. (1979). Situational leadership, perception, and the impact of power. *Group & Organization Studies, 4*, 418–428.

Hirokawa, R. S., & Scheerhorn, D. R. (1986). The role of communication in faulty group decision-making. In R. Y. Hirokawa & M. S. Poole (Eds.), *Communication and group decision making* (pp. 63–81). Beverly Hills, CA: Sage.

Hobe, P. (1990). *Lovebound: Recovering from an alcoholic family*. New York: Penguin Books.

Hollander, E. P. (1978). *Leadership dynamics: A practical guide to effective relationships*. New York: Free Press.

Hollwitz, J., & Wilson, C. E. (1993). Structured interviewing in volunteer selection. *Journal of Applied Communication Research, 21*, 41–52.

Honeycutt, J. M., Cantrill, J. G., Kelly, P., & Lambkin, D. (1998). How do I love thee? Let me consider my options: Cognition, verbal strategies, and the escalation of intimacy. *Human Communication Research, 25*, 39–63.

Hopf, T., & Ayres, J. (1992). Coping with public speaking anxiety: An examination of various combinations of systematic desensitization, skills training, and visualization. *Journal of Applied Communication Research, 20*, 183–198.

Hornik, J. (1987). The effect of touch and gaze upon compliance and interest of interviewees. *Journal of Social Psychology, 12*, 681–683.

House, A., Dallinger, J. M., & Kilgallen, D. (1998). *Communication Reports, 11*, 11–20.

Houston, M. (2000, Spring). Multiple perspectives: African American women conceive their talk. *Women and Language, 23* (1), 11–23.

Hovland, C. I., Lumsdaine, A. A., & Sheffield, F. D. (1949). *Experiments in mass communication: Studies in social psychology in World War II* (Vol. 3). Princeton, NJ: Princeton University Press, pp. 201–227.

How do I deal with hostile questions? (1998, April). *Public Management, 80* (4), 27–28.

Howell, W. S. (1982). *The empathic communicator*. Belmont, CA: Wadsworth.

Howes, M. B. (1990). *The psychology of human cognition: Mainstream and Genevan traditions*. New York: Pergamon.

Infante, D. A., Hartley, K. C., Martin, M. M., Higgins, M. A., Bruning, S. D., & Hur, G. (1992, October). *Initiating and reciprocating verbal aggression: Effects on credibility and credited valid arguments*. Paper presented at the meeting of the Speech Communication Association, Chicago, IL.

Infante, D. A., Rancer, A. S., & Womack, D. F. (1993). *Building communication theory* (2nd ed.). Prospect Heights, IL: Waveland.

Infante, D. A., Riddle, B. L., Horvath, C. L., & Tumlin, S. A. (1992). Verbal aggressiveness: Messages and reasons. *Communication Quarterly, 40*, 116–126.

Infante, D. A., Sabourin, T. C., Rudd, J. E., & Shannon, E. A. (1990). Verbal aggression in violent and nonviolent marital disputes. *Communication Quarterly, 38*, 361–371.

Infante, D. A., & Wigley, C. J., III. (1986). Verbal aggressiveness:

An interpersonal model and measure. *Communication Monographs, 53*, 61–69.

Ireland, R. D., Hitt, M. A., & Williams, J. C. (1992, January/February). Self-confidence and decisiveness: Prerequisites for effective management in the 1990s. *Business Horizons*, 36–43.

Isen, A. M. (1987). Positive affect, cognitive processes, and social behavior. In L. Berkowitz (Ed.), *Advances in experimental social psychology* (Vol. 20, pp. 203–253). San Diego, CA: Academic Press.

Ishikawa, K. (1982). *Guide to quality control* (2nd ed. rev.). Toyko: Asian Productivity Organization.

Jaffe, A. (2000, June). So long, stage fright. *Success, 47* (2), 70.

Jaksa, J. A., & Pritchard, M. S. (1994). *Communication ethics: Methods of analysis* (2nd ed.). Belmont, CA: Wadsworth.

Janis, I. L. (1971). *Groupthink*. Boston: Houghton Mifflin.

Janis, I. L. (1983). *Groupthink* (2nd ed. rev.). Boston: Houghton Mifflin.

Janis, I. L. (1989). *Crucial decisions: Leadership in policymaking and crisis management*. New York: Free Press.

Janz, T. (1982). Initial comparisons of patterned behavior description interview versus unstructured interviews. *Journal of Applied Psychology, 67*, 577–580.

Janz, T. (1986). *Behavior description interviewing: New, accurate, cost-effective*. Boston: Allyn & Bacon.

Jensen, J. V. (1981). *Argumentation: Reasoning in communication*. New York: Van Nostrand.

Johannesen, R. L. (1996). *Ethics in human communication* (4th ed.). Prospect Heights, IL: Waveland.

Kaiser, S. (1990). *The social psychology of clothing: Symbolic appearances in context* (2nd ed.). New York: Macmillan.

Kamins, M. A., Brand, M. J., Hoeke, S. A., & Moe, J. C. (1989). Two-sided versus one-sided celebrity endorsements: The impact on advertising effectiveness and credibility. *Journal of Advertising, 18,* 4–10.

Katzenbach, J. R., & Smith, D. K. (1993). *The wisdom of teams: Creating the high-performance organization.* Boston: Harvard Business School Press.

Keaten, J. A., & Kelly, L. (2000). Reticence: An affirmation and revision. *Communication Education, 49,* 165–177.

Kellerman, J. L., Lewis, J., & Laird, J. D. (1989). Looking and loving: The effects of mutual gaze on feelings of romantic love. *Journal of Research in Personality, 23,* 145–161.

Kelley, H. H., & Thibaut, J. W. (1978). *Interpersonal relationships.* New York: John Wiley.

Keltner, J. W. (1994). *The management of struggle: Elements of dispute resolution through negotiation, mediation and arbitration.* Cresskill, NJ: Hampton Press.

Kendon, A. (1984). Did gesture have the happiness to escape the curse of the confusion of Babel? In A. Wolfgang (Ed.), *Nonverbal behavior* (pp. 75–114). Lewiston, NY: D. J. Hogrefe.

Kenton, S. B. (1989). Speaker credibility in persuasive business communication: A model

which explains gender differences. *Journal of Business Communication, 26,* 143–157.

Kim, Y. Y. (1992). Intercultural communication competence: A systems-theoretic view. In W. B. Gudykunst & Y. Y. Kim (Eds.), *Readings on communicating with strangers: An approach to intercultural communication* (pp. 371–381). New York: McGraw-Hill.

King, M. L., Jr. (1964). *Why we can't wait.* New York: Signet.

Kinlaw, D. C. (1991). *Developing superior work teams: Building quality and the competitive edge.* Lexington, MA: Lexington Books.

Kleinke, C. L. (1986). Gaze and eye contact: A research review. *Psychological Bulletin, 100,* 78–100.

Knapp, M. L. (1978). *Nonverbal communication in human interaction* (2nd ed.). New York: Holt, Rinehart & Winston.

Knapp, M. L. (1984). *Interpersonal communication and human relationships.* Boston: Allyn & Bacon.

Koenenn, C. (1989, February 3). The future is now. *Washington Post,* p. B5.

Kolata, G. (1991, October). Mental gymnastics. *The Good Health Magazine,* Part 2 of *The New York Times Magazine,* pp. 14–17, 42, & 44.

Kolb, J. A. (1991, November). *Leader behaviors related to team performance in research and non-research teams.* Unpublished paper presented at the meeting of the Speech Communication Association, Atlanta, GA.

Korzybski, A. (1933). *Science and sanity.* Lakeville, CT: The Non-Aristotelian Library.

Kramarae, C. (1981). *Women and men speaking.* Rowley, MA: Newbury House.

Krebs, D., & Adinolf, A. A. (1975). Physical attractiveness, social relations, and personality style. *Journal of Personality and Social Psychology, 31.*

Kunkel, A. W., & Burleson, B. R. (1999). Assessing explanations for sex differences in emotional support: A test of the different cultures and skill specialization accounts. *Human Communication Research, 25,* 307–340.

Kurzweil, R. (2000). *The age of spiritual machines: When computers exceed human intelligence.* New York: Penguin.

LaFrance, M., & Ickes, W. (1981). Postural mirroring and interactional involvement: Sex and sex-typing effects. *Journal of Nonverbal Behavior, 5,* 139–154.

Lakoff, R. (1976). *Language and woman's place.* New York: Octagon Books.

Larson, C. E., & LaFasto, F. M. J. (1989). *TeamWork: What must go right/what can go wrong.* Newbury Park, CA: Sage.

Lazowski, L. E., & Andersen, S. M. (1990). Self-disclosure and social perception: The impact of private, negative, and extreme communications. In M. Booth-Butterfield (Ed.), *Communication, cognition, and anxiety* (pp. 131–154). Newbury Park, CA: Sage.

Le Poire, B. A., & Yoshimura, S. M. (1999). The effects of expectancies and actual communication on nonverbal adaptation and communication outcomes: A test of interaction adaptation theory. *Communication Monographs, 66,* 1–30.

Leathers, D. G. (1976). *Nonverbal communication systems*. Boston: Allyn & Bacon.

Leathers, D. G. (1992). *Successful nonverbal communication: Principles and applications* (2nd ed.). New York: Macmillan.

Lee, R. E., & Lee, K. K. (1989). *Arguing persuasively*. New York: Longman.

Lefton, L. A., & Valvatne, L. (1988). *Mastering psychology* (3rd ed.). Boston: Allyn & Bacon.

Legge, W. B. (1971). Listening, intelligence, and school achievement. In S. Duker (Ed.), *Listening: Readings* (pp. 121–133). Metuchen, NJ: Scarecrow.

Levine, T. R., & Wheeless, L. R. (1990). Cross-situational consistency and use/nonuse tendencies in compliance-gaining tactic selection. *Southern Communication Journal, 56*, 1–11.

Lieberman, D. A. (1994). Ethnocognitivism, problem-solving, and hemisphericity. In L. A. Samovar & R. E. Porter (Eds.), *Intercultural communication: A reader* (7th ed.) (pp. 178–193). Belmont, CA: Wadsworth.

Ling, W., Chia, R. C., & Fang, L. (2000). Chinese implicit leadership theory. *Journal of Social Psychology, 140*, 729.

Lucia, A. (1997, April). Leaders know how to listen. *HR Focus, 74* (4), 25.

Luft, J. (1969). *Of human interaction*. Palo Alto, CA: Mayfield.

Luker, K. (1984). *Abortion and the politics of motherhood*. Berkeley: University of California Press.

Lumsdaine, A., & Janis, I. (1953). Resistance to "counterpropaganda" produced by one-sided and two-sided propaganda presentations. *Public Opinion Quarterly, 17*, 311–318.

Lumsden, D. L. (1977). An experimental study of source-message interaction in a personality impression task. *Communication Monographs, 44*, 121–129.

Lumsden, G. (1972). *An experimental study of the effect of verbal agreement on leadership maintenance in problem-solving discussions*. Unpublished doctoral dissertation, Indiana University, Bloomington, IN.

Lumsden, G., & Lumsden, D. (2000). *Communicating in groups and teams: Sharing leadership* (3rd ed.). Belmont, CA: Wadsworth.

Lynch, J. J. (1985). *The language of the heart: The body's response to human dialogue*. New York: Basic Books.

Lynch, J. J. (1990). The language of the heart. In J. Stewart (Ed.), *Bridges not walls: A book about interpersonal communication* (5th ed.) (pp. 32–37). New York: McGraw-Hill.

Major, B. (1980). Gender patterns in touching behavior. In C. Mayo & N. M. Henley (Eds.), *Gender and nonverbal behavior* (pp. 15–37). New York: Springer-Verlag.

Major, B., Schmidlin, A. M., & Williams, L. (1990). Gesture patterns in social touch: The impact of setting and age. *Journal of Personality and Social Psychology, 58*, 634–635.

Make it snappy. (1999, June). *PC/Computing, 12* (6), 178.

Malandro, L. A., Barker, L., & Barker, D. A. (1989). *Nonverbal communication* (2nd ed.). New York: McGraw-Hill.

Manusov, V. (1990). An application of attribution principles to nonverbal behavior in romantic dyads. *Communication Monographs, 57*, 104–118.

Manz, C. C., & Sims, H. P. (1991, Spring). Superleadership: Beyond the myth of heroic leadership. *Organizational Dynamics*, 18–35.

Martel, M. (1989). *Mastering the art of Q & A: A survival guide for tough, trick, and hostile questions*. Homewood, IL: Dow Jones-Irwin.

Marx, M. S., Werner, P., & Cohen-Mansfield, J. (1989). Agitation and touch in the nursing home. *Psychological Reports, 64*, 1019–1026.

Maslow, A. (1970). *Motivation and personality* (2nd ed.). New York: Harper & Row.

Matthes, K. (1991). Managing diversity: A matter of survival. *Personnel, 68*, 9.

McCarthy, B. (1990). Using the 4MAT system to bring learning styles to schools. *Educational Leadership*, 31–37.

McCornack, S. A., & Levine, T. R. (1990). When lies are uncovered: Emotional and relational outcomes of discovered deception. *Communication Monographs, 57*, 119–138.

McCornack, S. A., & Levine, T. R., Solowczuk, K. A., Torres, H. I., & Campbell, D. M. (1992). When the alteration of information is viewed as deception: An empirical test of information manipulation theory. *Communication Monographs, 59*, 17–29.

McCroskey, J. C., & Richmond, V. P. (2000). Applying reciprocity and accomocation theories to supervisor/subordinate communication. *Journal of Applied Communication Research, 28*, 278–289.

McCrum, R., Cran, W., & Mac-Neil, R. (1986). *The story of English*. New York: Elisabeth Sifton Books/Viking.

McDowell, E. E., & McDowell, C. E. (1991, November). *An exploratory study of gender, gender orientation, self-disclosure and loneliness for senior high school students*. Paper presented at the meeting of the Speech Communication Association, Atlanta, GA.

McGuire, W. J. (1964). Inducing resistance to persuasion: Some contemporary approaches. In L. Berkowitz (Ed.), *Advances in experimental social psychology* (Vol. 1, pp. 191–229). San Diego, CA: Academic Press.

Meeks, B., Hendrick, S., & Hendrick, C. (1998). Communication, love, and satisfaction. *Journal of Social and Personal Relationships, 15,* 755–773.

Mehrabian, A. (1981). *Silent messages* (2nd ed.). Belmont, CA: Wadsworth.

Metcalf, C. W., & Felible, R. (1992). *Lighten up: Survival skills for people under pressure*. Reading, MA: Addison-Wesley.

Metts, S. (1997). Face and facework: Implications for the study of personal relationships. In S. Duck (Ed.), *Handbook of personal relationships* (2nd ed.) (pp. 373–390). Chichester, NY: Wiley.

Michaelson, L. K., Watson, W. E., & Black, R. H. (1989). A realistic test of individual versus group consensus decision making. *Journal of Applied Psychology, 74,* 834–839.

Miller, G. A. (1956). The magic number seven, plus or minus two: Some limits on our capacity for processing information. *Psychological Review, 63,* 81–97.

Miller, G. R., & Steinberg, M. (1975). *Between people: A new analysis of interpersonal communication*. Palo Alto, CA: Science Research Associates.

Mills, G. E., & Pace, R. W. (1989). What effects do practice and video feedback have on the development of interpersonal communication skills? *Journal of Business Communication, 26,* 159–177.

Mongeau, P. A., & Yeazell, M. (1992, November). *Relational communication in male- and female-initiated first dates*. Paper presented at the meeting of the Speech Communication Association, Chicago, IL.

Montagu, A. (1978). *Touching: The human significance of the skin* (2nd ed.). New York: Harper & Row.

Moore, M. P. (1992, October/November). *Mystery, metaphor, and the construction of social order: Jesse Jackson's socially symbolic act*. Paper presented at meeting of the Speech Communication Association, Chicago, IL.

Morreale, S. (2000, February). Morreale's Mailbag. *Spectra, 36* (2), 13.

Morreale, S. (2000, October). Morreale's Mailbag. *Spectra, 36* (10), 11.

Morris, N. (1992, October/November). *Communicating identity: The politics of language in twentieth-century Puerto Rico*. Paper presented at meeting of the Speech Communication Association, Chicago, IL.

Muhammad, T. K. (1997, March). The scoop on newsgroup: The internet is more than the World Wide Web. *Black Enterprise, 27* (8), 37.

Nanus, B. (1992). *Visionary leadership: Creating a compelling sense of direction for your organization*. San Francisco: Jossey-Bass.

National Education Goals Panel. (1991). *The national education goals report*. Washington, DC: U.S. Government Printing Office.

NCA/Roger Starch Poll (2000, February). Gender differences in comfort with communication situations is evident in poll results. *Spectra, 5.*

Neale, M. A., & Bazerman, M. H. (1991). *Cognition and rationality in negotiation*. New York: Free Press.

Neck, C. P., & Barnard, A. W. H. (1996, March). Managing your mind: What are you telling yourself? *Educational Leadership, 53* (6), 24–28.

Nemeth, C. J., & Kwan, J. L. (1987). Minority influence, divergent thinking and detection of correct solutions. *Journal of Applied Social Psychology, 17,* 788–799.

New Testament, New International Version (1974). *Eight translation New Testament*. New York: The Iversen-Norman Associates.

New York Times (1993, January 22). p. A10 L.

Nichols, R. G., & Stevens, L. A. (1957). *Are you listening?* New York: McGraw-Hill.

Nunberg, G. (1999, December 20). The trouble with PowerPoint. *Fortune, 14* (12), p. 330.

N.Y. Department of Labor (1996). The workplace of the future. Retrieved October 7, 2000, from the World Wide Web: http://www.nyatep.org/nyskills.html.

Nye, J. L., & Forsyth, D. R. (1991). The effects of prototype-based biases on leadership appraisals, a test of leadership categorization theory. *Small Group Research, 22,* 360–379.

Oetzel, J. G. (1998). The effects of self-construals and ethnicity on self-reported conflict styles. *Communication Reports, 11,* 133–144.

Osgood, C. E., Suci, G. J., & Tannenbaum, P. H. (1957). *The measurement of meaning.* Urbana: University of Illinois Press.

Ott, J. S. (1989). *The organizational culture perspective.* Pacific Grove, CA: Brooks/Cole.

O'Sullivan, M., Ekman, P., Friesen, W., & Scherer, K. (1985). What you say and how you say it: The contribution of speech content and voice quality to judgments of others. *Journal of Personality and Social Psychology, 48,* 54–62.

Pace, R. W., & Faules, D. F. (1994). *Organizational communication* (3rd ed.). Englewood Cliffs, NJ: Prentice-Hall.

Party banter (1992, June/July). *Worth,* p. 21.

Patterson, F., & Linden, E. (1981). *The education of Koko.* New York: Holt, Rinehart, & Winston.

Pavitt, C., & Sackaroff, P. (1990). Implicit theories of leadership and judgments of leadership among group members. *Small Group Research, 21,* 374–392.

Pearson, J. C. (1989). *Communication in the family: Seeking satisfaction in changing times.* New York: Harper & Row.

Pearson, J. C., Turner, L. H., & Todd-Mancillas, W. (1991). *Gender and communication* (2nd ed.). Dubuque, IA: Wm. C. Brown.

Perkins, D., Jay, E., & Tishman, S. (1992, November). *Assessing thinking: A framework for measuring critical thinking and problem solving skills at the college level.* Paper commissioned by the U.S. Department of Education Office of Education Research and Improvement, Washington, DC.

Perkins, D., Jay, E., & Tishman, S. (1994). Assessing thinking: A framework for measuring critical thinking and problem solving skills at the college level. In A. Greenwood (Ed.), *The National Assessment of College Learning: Identification of the Skills to Be Taught, Learned, and Assessed* (pp. 65–112). Washington, DC: National Center for Educational Statistics.

Perras, M. T., & Weitzel, A. R. (1981). Measuring daily communication activities. *Florida State Speech Communication Journal, 9,* 19–23.

Philipsen, G. (1989). Speech and the communal function in four cultures. Abridged from S. Ting-Toomey & F. Korzenny (Eds.), *Language, communication, and culture* (pp. 79–92). Newbury Park, CA: Sage. In W. B. Gudykunst & Y. Y. Kim (Eds.) (1992). *Readings on communicating with strangers: An approach to intercultural communication.* New York: McGraw-Hill.

Phillips, G. M. (1991). *Communication incompetencies.* Carbondale: Southern Illinois University Press.

Pillai, R., Scandura, T. A., & Williams, E. A. (1999). Leadership and organizational justice: Similarities and differences across cultures. *Journal of International Business Studies, 30,* 763.

Pittman, F., III. (1993, May/June). Beyond betrayal: Life after infidelity. *Psychology Today,* pp. 32–38, 78–82.

Planalp, S. (1993). Communication, cognition, and emotion. *Communication Monographs, 60,* 3–9.

Plotnik, R. (1999). *Introduction to psychology* (5th ed.). Belmont, CA: Wadsworth.

Policoff, S. P. (1987, Winter). Children of chaos. *Campus Voice,* 12–14.

Porter, R. E., & Samovar, L. A. (1997). An introduction to intercultural communication. In L. A. Samovar & R. E. Porter (Eds.), *Intercultural communication: A reader* (8th ed.) (pp. 5–26). Belmont, CA: Wadsworth.

Powell, R. B., & Andersen, J. (1994). Culture and classroom communication. In L. A. Samovar & R. E. Porter (Eds.), *Intercultural communication: A reader* (7th ed.) (pp. 322–330). Belmont, CA: Wadsworth.

Pratkanis, A., & Aronson, E. (1992). *Age of propaganda: The everyday use and abuse of persuasion.* New York: W. H. Freeman.

Preiss, R. W., & Wheeless, L. R. (1989). Affective responses in listening: A meta-analysis of receiver apprehension outcomes. *Journal of the International Listening Association, 3,* 71–102.

Preiss, R. W., Wheeless, L. R., & Allen, M. (1990). Potential cognitive processes and consequences of receiver apprehension: A meta-analytic review. Reprinted in M. Booth-Butterfield (Ed.) (1991), *Communication, cognition, and anxiety.* Newbury Park, CA: Sage.

Rafenstein, M. (1999, December). How to compromise. *Current Health 2, 26* (4), 30.

Rawlins, W. K. (1993). Communication in cross-sex friendships. In L. P. Arliss & D. J. Borisoff (Eds.), *Women and men communicating: Challenges and changes* (pp. 51–70). Ft. Worth, TX: Harcourt Brace Jovanovich.

Ray, G. B. (1986). Vocally cued personality prototypes: An implicit personality theory. *Communication Monographs, 53,* 266–276.

Redding, W. C. (1984). *The corporate manager's guide to better communication.* Glenview, IL: Scott, Foresman.

Reis, H. T., Wheeler, L., Nezlek, J., Kernis, M. J., & Spiegel, N. (1985). On specificity in the impact of social participation on physical and psychological health. *Journal of Personality and Social Psychology, 48,* 456–471.

Reisner, R. (1993, May/June). How different cultures learn. *Meeting News, 17*(6), 30–31.

Remland, M. S., Jones, T. S., & Brinkman, H. (1992, October). *Interpersonal distance, body orientation, and touch in the dyadic interactions of northern and southern Europeans.* Paper presented at the meeting of the Speech Communication Association, Chicago, IL.

Revah, S. (1998, April). The language of the digitally hip. *American Journalism Review, 20* (3), 12–14.

Richmond, V. P., & McCroskey, J. C. (1995). *Communication: Apprehension, avoidance, and effectiveness* (4th ed.). Scottsdale, AZ: Gorsuch Scarisbrick.

Richmond, V. P., & McCroskey, J. C. (2000). The impact of supervisor and subordinate immediacy on relational and organizational outcomes. *Communication Monographs, 67,* 85–95.

Richmond, V. P., & Roach, K. D. (1992). Willingness to communicate and employee success in U.S. organizations. *Journal of Applied Communication Research, 20,* 95–115.

Riecken, H. (1975). The effects of talkativeness on ability to influence group solutions of problems. In P. V. Crosbie (Ed.), *Interaction in small groups* (pp. 238–249). New York: Macmillan.

Roach, K. D. (1998). Teaching assistant communication apprehension, willingness to communicate, and state communication anxiety in the classroom. *Communication Research Reports, 15,* 130–140.

Robert, H. M., III, & Evans, W. J. (Eds.). (1990). *Robert's rules of order newly revised.* Glenview, IL: Scott, Foresman.

Roberts, W. R. (Trans.). (1954). Aristotle, *Rhetoric.* New York: The Modern Library.

Rogers, Carl. (1980). *A way of being.* Reprinted in J. Stewart (Ed.) (1990). *Bridges not walls: A book about interpersonal communication* (5th ed.). New York: McGraw Hill.

Rokeach, M. (1973). *The nature of human values.* New York: The Free Press.

Roloff, M. E. (1981). *Interpersonal communication: The social exchange approach.* Beverly Hills, CA: Sage.

Ross, R. S. (1990). *Understanding persuasion* (3rd ed.). Englewood Cliffs, NJ: Prentice-Hall.

Russo, N. (1967). Connotation of seating arrangement. *Cornell Journal of Social Relations, 2,* 37–44.

Salopek, J. J. (1999, September). Is anyone listening? *Training and Development, i9,* 58–59.

Samovar, L. A., & Porter, R. E. (1994). An introduction to intercultural communication. In L. A. Samovar & R. E. Porter (Eds.), *Intercultural communication: A reader* (7th ed.) (pp. 4–26). Belmont, CA: Wadsworth.

Samovar, L. A., & Porter, R. E. (Eds.) (2000). *Intercultural communication: A reader* (9th ed.). Belmont, CA: Wadsworth.

Samovar, L. A., Porter, R. E., & Stefani, L. A. (1998). *Communication between cultures* (3rd ed.). Belmont, CA: Wadsworth.

Satir, V. (1990). Paying attention to words. In J. Stewart (Ed.), *Bridges not walls: A book about interpersonal communication* (5th ed.) (pp. 63–68). New York: McGraw-Hill.

Scheff, T. J., & Retzinger, S. M. (1991). *Emotions and violence: Shame and rage in destructive conflicts.* Lexington, MA: Lexington Books.

Schramm, W. (1973). *Men, messages, and media.* New York: Harper & Row.

Schultz, B. (1986). Communication correlates of perceived leaders in the small group. *Small Group Behavior, 17,* 51–65.

Schutz, W. C. (1967). *The phenomenology of the social world.* Chicago: Northwestern University Press.

Schutz, W. (1984). *The truth option: A practical technology for human affairs.* Berkeley, CA: Ten Speed Press.

Scroggs, G. F. (1980). *Sex, status, and solidarity: Attributions for nonmutual touch*. Paper presented at the meeting of the Eastern Psychological Association, Hartford, CT.

Seiter, J. S., Larsen, J., & Skinner, J. (1998). "Handicapped" or "handi-capable"?: The effects of language about persons with disabilities on perceptions of source credibility and persuasiveness. *Communication Reports, 11*, 2.

Serant, C. (1992, February). Enhancing your visibility. *Black Enterprise*, 39.

Shannon, C. E., & Weaver, W. (1949). *The mathematical theory of communication*. Urbana: University of Illinois Press.

Shaw, M. E. (1981). *Group dynamics: The study of small group behavior*. New York: McGraw-Hill.

Sherif, C. W., Sherif, M., & Nebergall, R. W. (1965). *Attitude and attitude change: The social judgment-involvement approach*. Philadelphia: Saunders.

Simon, H. A. (1977). *The new science of management decision* (rev. ed.). Englewood Cliffs, NJ: Prentice-Hall.

Skow, L., & Samovar, L. A. (2000). Cultural patterns of the maasai. In L. A. Samovar & R. E. Porter, *Intercultural communication: A reader* (9th ed.) (pp. 90–98). Belmont, CA: Wadsworth.

Smith, D. E., Willis, F. N., & Gier, J. A. (1980). Success and interpersonal touch in a competitive setting. *Journal of Nonverbal Behavior, 5*, 26–34.

Smith, L. K., & Fowler, S. A. (1984). Positive peer pressure: The effects of peer monitoring on children's disruptive behavior. *Journal of Applied Behavior Analysis, 17*, 213–227.

Smith-Heffner, N. J. (1988). Women and politeness: The Javanese example. *Language in Society, 17*, 535–554.

Smitherman-Donaldson, G., & van Dijk, T. A. (Eds.). (1988). *Discourse and discrimination*. Detroit: Wayne State University.

Solomon, C. M. (1990). What an idea: Creative training. *Personnel Journal, 69*(5), 64–71.

Stacks, D. (1992, November). *Toward a theory of persuasion: Impact of neurophysiological processing on persuasive message reception*. Paper presented at the meeting of the Speech Communication Association, Chicago, IL.

Stamp, G. H., Vangelisti, A. L., & Daly, J. A. (1992). *Communication Quarterly, 40*, 177–190.

Steil, L. K. (1981). On listening . . . and not listening. *Executive Health, 18*, 1–6.

Stephan, W. G., & Stephan, C. W. (1992). Intergroup anxiety. In W. B. Gudykunst & Y. Y. Kim (Eds.), *Readings on communicating with strangers: An approach to intercultural communication* (pp. 16–29). New York: McGraw-Hill.

Stephen, A. (1999, June 14). Fondle a woman: Pay $250,000. *New Statesman, 128*, p. 20.

Stewart, C. J., & Cash, W. B., Jr. (1991). *Interviewing principles and practices* (6th ed.). Dubuque, IA: Wm. C. Brown.

Stewart, J. (1990). Interpersonal communication: Contact between persons. In J. Stewart (Ed.), *Bridges not walls: A book about interpersonal communication* (5th ed.) (pp. 13–31). New York: McGraw-Hill.

Stewart, J. (1999). Introduction to the editor and to this book. In J. Stewart (Ed.), *Bridges not walls: A book about interpersonal communication* (7th ed.). Boston: McGraw-Hill.

Stewart, J., & Thomas, M. (1990). Dialogic listening: Sculpting mutual meanings. In J. Stewart, *Bridges not walls; A book about interpersonal communication* (5th ed.) (pp. 192–210). New York: McGraw Hill.

Stewart, J., & Zediker, K. (2000). Dialogue as tensional, ethical practice. *Southern Communication Journal, 65*, 224–242.

Stewart, L. P., Stewart, A. D., Friedley, S. A., & Cooper, P. J. (1990). *Communication between the sexes: Sex differences and sex-role stereotypes* (2nd ed.). Scottsdale, AZ: Gorsuch Scarisbrick.

Street, R. L., Jr., Brady, R. M., & Putnam, W. B. (1983). The influence of speech rate stereotypes and rate similarity on listeners' evaluations of speakers. *Journal of Language and Social Psychology, 2*, 37–56.

Strodtbeck, F., & Hook, L. (1961). The social dimensions of a twelve man jury table. *Sociometry, 24*, 297–215.

Sullivan, J. J., Albrecht, T. L., & Taylor, S. (1990). Process, organizational, relational, and personal determinants of managerial compliance-gaining strategies. *Journal of Business Communication, 27*, 332–355.

Sunnafrank, M. (1992). On debunking the attitude similarity myth. *Communication Monographs, 59*, 164–179.

Sussman, N. M., & Rosenfeld, H. M. (1982). Influence of culture, language, and sex on conversational distance. *Journal of Personality and Social Psychology, 42,* 66–74.

Sweeney, J. B. (1994). Unpublished and untitled student paper.

Swenson, J., & Casmir, F. L. (1998). The impact of culture-sameness, gender, foreign travel, and academic background on the ability to interpret facial expression of emotion in others. *Communication Monographs, 66,* 214–230.

Tannen, D. (1990). *You just don't understand: Women and men in conversation.* New York: Morrow.

Thornton, J. S. (1990, August). Leadership traits that work worldwide. *Association Management,* 22–23.

Tice, L. (1983). *Investment in excellence.* Seattle: The Pacific Institute.

Ting-Toomey, S. (1987, May). *A comparative analysis of the communicative dimensions of love, self-disclosure maintenance, ambivalence, and conflict in three cultures: France, Japan, and the United States.* Paper presented at the meeting of the International Communication Association, Montreal, Canada.

Ting-Toomey, S. (1988). Intercultural conflict style: A face-negotiation theory. In Y. Y. Kim & W. B. Gudykunst (Eds.), *Theories in intercultural communication* (pp. 213–235). Newbury Park, CA: Sage.

Toffler, B. L. (1986). *Tough choices: Managers talk ethics.* New York: John Wiley.

Toulmin, S. (1958). *The uses of argument.* Cambridge, England: Cambridge University Press.

Toupin, L. (1999, December 20). Putting the 'power' back into a PowerPoint presentation. *Design News, 54,* 39.

Trenholm, S., & Jensen, A. (1988). *Interpersonal communication.* Belmont, CA: Wadsworth.

Trost, J. (1990). What do we mean the same by the concept of family? *Communication Research, 17,* 431–443.

Tuckman, B., & Jensen, M. (1977). Stages of small-group development. *Group and Organizational Studies,* 419–427.

Tuppen, C. (1974). Dimensions of communicator credibility: An oblique solution. *Speech Monographs, 41,* 253–266.

Tusing, K. J., & Dillard, J. P. (2000). The sounds of dominance: Vocal precursors of perceived dominance during interpersonal influence. *Human Communication Research, 26* 148–171.

Tyler, T. R., Rasinski, K. A., & Spodick, N. (1985). Influence of voice on satisfaction with leaders: Exploring the meaning of process control. *Journal of Personality and Social Psychology, 48,* 72–81.

Ungerleider, S. (1992, July/August). Visions of victory. *Psychology Today,* pp. 46–52 and 83.

Ury, W. (1991). *Getting past no: Negotiating with difficult people.* New York: Bantam Books.

USA Today Magazine (2000, August). How much time do kids spend with dad?, 129, 2663, p. 4.

U.S. Department of Labor (1999). *Futurework: Trends and challenges for work in the 21st century.* Washington, DC: Government Printing Office.

Vangelisti, A. L. (1993). Communication in the family: The influence of time, relational prototypes, and irrationality. *Communication Monographs, 60,* 42–54.

von Oech, R. (1983). *A whack on the side of the head: How to unlock your mind for innovation.* New York: Warner Books.

Wackman, D. B. (1973). Interpersonal communication and coorientation. *American Behavioral Scientist, 16,* 537–550.

Waldron, V., & Applegate, J. L. (1998). Similarity in the use of person-centered tactics: Effects on social attraction and persuasiveness in dyadic verbal disagreements. *Communication Reports, 11,* 155–165.

Wallace, K. R. (1955). An ethical basis of communication. *The Speech Teacher, 4,* 1–9.

Wallace, K. R. (1963). The substance of rhetoric: Good reasons. *Quarterly Journal of Speech, 49,* 239–249.

Wallas, G. (1926). *The art of thought.* New York: Harcourt, Brace.

Walters, L. (1993). *Secrets of successful speakers: How you can motivate, captivate and persuade.* New York: McGraw-Hill.

Watzlawick, P., Beavin, J. H., & Jackson, D. D. (1967). *Pragmatics of human communication: A study of interaction patterns, pathologies, and paradoxes.* New York: Norton.

Weatherall, A. (1998). Women and men in language: An analysis of seminaturalistic person descriptions. *Human Communication Research, 25,* 275–292.

Weekley, J. A., & Gier, J. A. (1987). Reliability and validity of the situational interview for a sales position. *Journal of Applied Psychology, 72,* 484–487.

Weick, K. (1979). *The social psychology of organizing* (2nd ed.). Reading, MA: Addison-Wesley.

Weisner, W. H., & Cronshaw, S. F. (1988). A meta-analytic investigation of the impact of interview format and degree of structure on the validity of the employment interview. *Journal of Occupational Psychology, 61,* 275–290.

Wellins, R. S., Byham, W. C., & Wilson, J. M. (1991). *Empowered teams: Creating self-directed work groups that improve quality, productivity, and participation.* San Francisco: Jossey-Bass.

Wells, B., & Spinks, N. (1991, Spring). Conflict management: A communication skills approach. *The Bulletin of Organizational Communication, 3* (1), 6.

Westley, B., & MacLean, M. (1957). A conceptual model for communication research. *Journalism Quarterly, 34,* 31–38.

Wexley, K. N., & Latham, G. P. (1981). *Developing and training human resources in organizations.* Glenview, IL: Scott, Foresman.

Wharton Applied Research Center. (1981, September 14). *A study of the effects of the use of overhead transparencies on business meetings: Final report.* Philadelphia: University of Pennsylvania.

Wheeless, L. R., Frymier, A. B., & Thompson, C. A. (1992). A comparison of verbal output and receptivity in relation to attraction and communication satisfaction in interpersonal relationships. *Communication Quarterly, 40,* 102–115.

Where to drop a lisp or pick up an accent: Speech therapist tells how it's done. (1993, August 11). *New York Times,* p. B4 L.

White, R. K., & Lippett, R. O. (1960). *Autocracy and democracy.* New York: Harper & Row.

Whitehead, J., Jr. (1969). Factors of source credibility. *Quarterly Journal of Speech, 54,* 59–63.

Whorf, B. L. (1964). *Language, thought, and reality.* Cambridge, MA: MIT Press.

Williams, F. (1987). *Technology and communication behavior.* Belmont, CA: Wadsworth.

Wilmot, W. W. (1979). *Dyadic communication* (2nd ed.). Reading, MA: Addison-Wesley.

Wilmot, W. W. (1987). *Dyadic communication* (3rd ed.). New York: McGraw-Hill.

Wolf, S. E. (1991, February). Editorial opinion, *Vis à Vis,* 12.

Wolvin, A. D., Berko, R. M., & Wolvin, D. R. (1993). *The public speaker/The public listener.* Boston: Houghton Mifflin.

Wolvin, A. D., & Coakley, C. G. (1991). A survey of the status of listening training in some Fortune 500 corporations. *Communication Education, 40,* 152–164.

Wood, J. T. (1994). *Gendered lives: Communication, gender, and culture.* Belmont, CA: Wadsworth.

Wood, J. T. (2001). *Gendered lives: Communication, gender, and culture* (4th ed.). Belmont, CA: Wadsworth.

Wood, W. (1987). Meta-analytic review of sex differences in group performance. *Psychological Bulletin, 102,* 53–71.

Woodall, W. G., & Burgoon, J. K. (1981). The effects of nonverbal synchrony on message comprehension and persuasiveness. *Journal of Nonverbal Behavior, 5,* 207–223.

Woodall, W. G., & Burgoon, J. K. (1983). Talking fast and changing attitudes: A critique and clarification. *Journal of Nonverbal Behavior, 8,* 126–142.

Woolfolk, R. L., & Woolfolk, A. E. (1974). Effects of teacher verbal and nonverbal behaviors on student perceptions and attitudes. *American Educational Research Journal, 11,* 297–303.

Worth, L. T., & Mackie, D. M. (1987). Cognitive mediation of positive affect in persuasion. *Social Cognition, 5,* 76–94.

Yerby, J., Buerkel-Rothfuss, N., & Bochner, A. P. (1990). *Understanding family communication.* Scottsdale, AZ: Gorsuch Scarisbrick.

Zakahi, W. R., & Duran, R. L. (1985). Loneliness, communication competence, and communication apprehension: Extension and replication. *Communication Quarterly, 33,* 50–60.

Zietlow, P. H., & Sillars, A. L. (1988). Life stage differences in communication during marital conflicts. *Journal of Social and Personal Relationships, 5,* 223–245.

Zorn, T. E. (1991). Construct system development, transformational leadership and leadership messages. *Southern Communication Journal, 56,* 178–193.

Name Index

Subject Index

Photo Credits

This page constitutes an extension of the copyright page. We have made every effort to trace the ownership of all copyrighted material and to secure permission from copyright holders. In the event of any question arising as to the use of any material, we will be pleased to make the necessary corrections in future printings. Thanks are due to the following authors, publishers, and agents for permission to use the material indicated.

Chapter 1. 1: Pennie Tweedie / Getty Images

Chapter 2. 25: Lisa Quinones / Stockphoto.com **28:** Seth Resnick / Stock, Boston

Chapter 3. 51: Tony Freeman / PhotoEdit

Chapter 4. 77: © Paul Barton / corbisstockmarket.com **84:** Elizabeth Crews / The Image Works

Chapter 5. 99: Gay Lumsden **107:** left, Empics / Neal Simpson / Woodfin Camp & Associates **107:** right, Niedringhaus / AFP

Chapter 6. 121: Aneal Vohra / Index Stock Imagery **130:** J. Sohm / The Image Works

Chapter 7. 145: © Joseph Nettis / Stock, Boston Inc. / PictureQuest **156:** R. Lord / The Image Works

Chapter 8. 167: Lawrence Migdale / Photo Researchers, Inc. **173:** Skjold / The Image Works

Chapter 9. 192: Bob Daemmrich / The Image Works **203:** Bob Daemmrich / The Image Works

Chapter 10. 214: Bob Nelson / Stockphoto.com **220:** © Paul Barton / corbisstockmarket.com

Chapter 11. 239: Bill Bachmann / The Image Works **244:** © Jon Feingarsh / corbisstockmarket.com

Chapter 12. 264: Michael Doolittle / The ImageWorks **273:** top, Spencer Grant / Photo Researchers, Inc. **273:** bottom, Bob Daemmrich / The Image Works

Chapter 13. 293: Anne Dowie **309:** Al Campanie / Syracuse Newspapers / The Image Works

Chapter 14. 318: Michael Siluk / The Image Works **334:** Chip Henderson / Getty Images

Chapter 15. 341: Bob Adelman / Magnum **356:** Mary Kate Denny / PhotoEdit